Not-Forgetting

Not-Forgetting

Contemporary Art and the
Interrogation of Mastery

ROSALYN DEUTSCHE

The University of Chicago Press   CHICAGO AND LONDON

The University of Chicago Press, Chicago 60637
The University of Chicago Press, Ltd., London
© 2022 by The University of Chicago
All rights reserved. No part of this book may be used or reproduced in any manner whatsoever without written permission, except in the case of brief quotations in critical articles and reviews. For more information, contact the University of Chicago Press, 1427 E. 60th St., Chicago, IL 60637.
Published 2022
Printed in the United States of America

31 30 29 28 27 26 25 24 23 22   1 2 3 4 5

ISBN-13: 978-0-226-81960-0 (cloth)
ISBN-13: 978-0-226-81959-4 (paper)
ISBN-13: 978-0-226-81961-7 (e-book)
DOI: https://doi.org/10.7208/chicago/9780226819617.001.0001

Library of Congress Cataloging-in-Publication Data

Names: Deutsche, Rosalyn, author.
Title: Not-forgetting : contemporary art and the interrogation of mastery / Rosalyn Deutsche.
Other titles: Contemporary art and the interrogation of mastery
Description: Chicago ; London : The University of Chicago Press, 2022. | Includes bibliographical references and index.
Identifiers: LCCN 2022022550 | ISBN 9780226819600 (cloth) | ISBN 9780226819594 (paperback) | ISBN 9780226819617 (ebook)
Subjects: LCSH: Art, Modern—20th century. | Art, Modern—21st century. | Feminism and art. | Psychoanalysis and art. | Art and war. | BISAC: ART / Criticism & Theory | ART / History / General | LCGFT: Essays.
Classification: LCC N7445.2 .D48 2022 | DDC 709.04—dc23/eng/20220714
LC record available at https://lccn.loc.gov/2022022550

♾ This paper meets the requirements of ANSI/NISO Z39.48-1992 (Permanence of Paper).

Contents

Introduction   1

Part One: Psychoanalytic Feminism

1   Not-Forgetting: Mary Kelly's *Love Songs* (2006)   13
2   Inadequacy: Silvia Kolbowski's History of Conceptual Art (2004)   24
3   Darkness: The Emergence of James Welling (2002)   39
4   Breaking Ground: Barbara Kruger's Spatial Practice (1999)   56
5   Louise Lawler's Rude Museum (2006)   69

Part Two: Radical Democracy

6   Christopher D'Arcangelo's Elliptical Interruptions (2020)   89
7   The Art of Not Being Governed Quite So Much:
    Hans Haacke's Polls (2007)   108
8   Art from Guantánamo Bay (2020)   123
9   Reasonable Urbanism (1999)   131

Part Three: War Resistance

10 Un-War: An Aesthetic Sketch (2014)   161
11 Museum of Innocence (2014)   177
12 "We don't need another hero": War and Public Memory (2017)   184
13 Louise Lawler's Play Technique (2017)   203
14 Mary Kelly's Attunement (2017/2020)   218
15 Martha Rosler's Unrest (2018)   232

Acknowledgments 239   *Notes* 243   *Index* 283

Introduction

We live in a time of emboldened cruelty and perpetual war. The essays collected here explore the intersection of contemporary art with three practices that counter the prevailing destructiveness: psychoanalytic feminism, radical democracy, and war resistance. Although *Not-Forgetting* is divided into thematic parts, it advances a single project. For the counter-practices it engages with—and the artworks it discusses—are linked as critiques of the human subject's quest to master the world.[1]

While I was preparing this volume for publication, having already chosen its title, I came across the term "not-forgetting" used to describe the mission of the Hague Tribunal, the court established by the United Nations to prosecute atrocities, including mass rape, committed during the Yugoslav Wars of 1991 to 2001.[2] My book's title, then, can serve as a synonym for bearing witness and for exercising critical memory, which I advocate in several of these essays. Critical memory, or what the French philosopher Paul Ricoeur calls "the duty of memory,"[3] is the ethical antidote to the repressive, narcissistic, and instrumental memory embodied in official monuments, such as the war memorials I discuss in "We don't need another hero" and "Un-War: An Aesthetic Sketch," and in institutions like the National September 11 Memorial Museum in Lower Manhattan, the topic of "Museum of Innocence." In this last essay, I adopt Sigmund Freud's ideas about the pathogenic effects of repression in individuals as a model for the dangers of collective repression, which, like that of individuals, modifies reality, alienating the collective—say, a nation—from truth and from the outside world.[4] Seeking to ward off danger, such repression is itself dangerous, not only to the group that employs it but to those the group turns away from. Viewed as an analogue for the act of critical remembrance, not-forgetting is newly relevant in the current moment, when, as I write, White supremacists in the United States and elsewhere defend racist and colonialist statues and seek to censor knowledge of slavery and its legacy.

Originally, however, when I conceived of *Not-Forgetting*, its title had a different source, the French philosopher Alain Badiou's theory of "the event." As I explain in greater detail in the opening essay, "Not-Forgetting: Mary Kelly's *Love Songs*," Badiou defines an event as something—a happening—that interrupts existing conditions, calling into question the political, personal, or artistic system within which it takes place. Examples are the French Revolution, an amorous passion, and Schoenberg's invention of the twelve-tone scale.[5] The event vanishes, but it initiates a "truth-process" in which hitherto unknown possibilities appear, opposing consensus and dominant opinion. The event also produces a subject that, caught up in the event's alterity and unpredictable course, is compelled to "decide a new way of being." That subject does not return to continuity but perseveres in the interruption, always approaching present circumstances from the perspective of the event.[6] Badiou uses the term not-forgetting to name such faithfulness to the event, a fidelity that for him is the foundation of an ethico-politics of refusing conservatism.

Feminism was my event (although Badiou does not seem to consider it one), and the origin of this book.[7] It seized me around 1970, when I was helping to organize protests against the American War in Vietnam. Like others in the women's liberation movement, I campaigned for reproductive rights and against legally mandated gender inequalities as well as those that are common practice but unofficial, embedded, for example, in marriage and childcare arrangements. Galvanized by the slogan "the personal is political" and profoundly influenced by the writings of Simone de Beauvoir—*The Second Sex*, of course, but particularly her multivolume autobiography—I questioned the kinship relations prescribed by bourgeois and patriarchal society, trying to free myself from what Beauvoir calls the hierarchy of "the well-regulated human heart," in which friends occupy a level below that of biological family and husbands.[8] Needless to say, my goal was not to achieve equality in the existing social world but, rather, to make a better, less violent world, to enter the public realm otherwise, as Virginia Woolf thought women must do if they want to prevent war, an argument I apply to art practice in "Louise Lawler's Rude Museum."[9]

Later in the 1970s and early 1980s, something different made an appearance among feminists: critiques of patriarchy encountered emerging postmodern critiques of the way power and violence are exerted not just legally or forcefully but in the act of representing and, in so doing, producing meanings and subjects for those meanings. The articulation of the two critiques changed feminist ideas about the long-recognized connection between visual representation and the oppression of women. While by no means abandoning problems of inequality and of improving the situation of women through legislation, feminists in the disciplines of film and art theorized a "politics of vision," which analyzed the role played by looking at images in the establishment and maintenance of a patriarchal order of sexual difference, a development I describe in "Breaking Ground: Barbara Kruger's Spatial Politics." "Images of women" gave way to "woman as image" or "woman as sign" as the object of postmodern feminist visual analysis. Each formulation stands for a different conception of the location of meaning in visual representation: the former conceives of images as entities containing stable thematic content that can be extracted by equally stable viewers and judged to be positive or negative, true or false, in relation to meanings and identities that exist outside representation altogether; the latter, adopting a linguistic model, places the image in a viewing situation, examining how the relationship among image, spectator, and spatiotemporal context construct meaning and identity. The woman-as-image discourse interpreted the figure of the female body as an iconic sign of patriarchal desire, thereby exposing and troubling constructions of femininity in the field of vision.[10] This discourse remains valid, but it is crucial to acknowledge that in its inaugural years it generalized the female body, which it treated as race-neutral. This universalization of the White female body meant turning a blind eye to the specificity of the violence exerted against the Black female body in White supremacist imagery. Describing the context in which she created her *Kitchen Table Series* (1990), a landmark photo-and-text work about vision and Black female subjectivity, Carrie Mae Weems recalls that "everybody was . . . talking about" the film theorist Laura Mulvey's 1975 essay "Visual Pleasure and Narrative Cinema."[11] Mulvey had theorized woman-as-image as a signifier of what she famously called "to-be-looked-at-ness." Mulvey's essay was important to Weems, but the conversation around it, says the artist, "excluded the black female body. It was just not a part of the discussion."[12]

The encounter between feminism and postmodernism also changed the discourse about postmodernism in the visual arts, which in its early years had been indifferent to feminism, an indifference that the art historian Craig Owens apologized for in 1983.[13] There were, of course, multiple critical postmodernisms that varied according to discipline—art, architecture, literature, sociology, philosophy, and so on—and political viewpoint. For me, the postmodern critique of representation mattered because it was integral to the challenge leveled by such anticolonialist and poststructuralist philosophers as Aimé Césaire, Frantz Fanon, Jean-Françoise Lyotard, Michel Foucault, and Jacques Derrida to the authority of Western culture and knowledge and to the grandiose conception of the human being that has been produced by the West, a conception inextricably linked to modernity, colonialism, racism, and coloniality.[14] I did not, however, embrace the widely proclaimed end of metanarratives (itself a metanarrative) but, rather, as Ernesto Laclau puts it, the "weakening" of their authoritarian claims to rest on absolute, extrasocial foundations.[15] By then, I was a doctoral student in an art history department that was largely immersed in two related projects: theorizing the meaning of postmodernism in the visual arts and mobilizing critical theory and structuralist and poststructuralist philosophy to question the idealist myths of aesthetic autonomy and quasi-divine, sovereign artists that had long dominated the discipline.[16] Both projects sought to "call art down from the heavens"—to borrow from Cicero—and set it in "the cities of men," the earthly realm of social relations.[17]

At the same time, mostly in women's study groups, I was reading psychoanalytically informed texts by contemporary French and British feminists who stressed the socially and psychically constructed, and therefore unstable, nature of masculinity and femininity. The constructionist thesis converged with the poststructuralist contestation of the Western metaphysical notion that a fundamental order of meaning exists in itself, in things themselves, as what Derrida calls "presence."[18] Psychoanalysis provided the key to understanding the role played by unconscious desire in the sexual politics of vision. The introduction into feminism of poststructuralism and psychoanalysis and the intense controversy it provoked among feminists (not to mention those eager to exploit divisions among feminists) are often categorized under the rubric of "the eighties." But this designation has interpretive value only if it is used to refer not to a literal decade but to a configuration of ideas, texts, and practices. Less restrictive than periodization by decade is British psychoanalyst Christopher Bollas's concept of "generational consciousness," which, says Bollas, "reflects a generation's interpretation of its place in historic time." Generational consciousness designates a collective identification with persons, events, places, ideas, and things—"generational objects"—that may be reacquired and transformed by later generations, becoming "metagenerational."[19] Suggesting that the meaning of past events and actions is not fixed, Bollas's theory is in keeping with other concepts of temporality that have long informed my work: Mikhail Bakhtin's account of the nonlinear time of the novel, which I describe in "Reasonable Urbanism," and Jacques Lacan's assertion that personal history—and the time of psychoanalytic experience—unfolds in the tense of the future anterior. "What is realized in my history," writes Lacan, "is not the past definite of what was, since it is no more, or even the present perfect of what has been in what I am, but the future anterior of what I shall have been for what I am in the process of becoming."[20] The first two essays in *Not-Forgetting*, which discuss, respectively, Mary Kelly's multigenerational history of feminism and Silvia Kolbowski's feminist approach to (art) history, argue that the same is true of collective, political history. It, too, takes place in the future anterior tense. In this light, the historical configuration called "the eighties" is incomplete; it has not yet fully occurred but mutates over time, bearing on the ethico-politics of the current moment in unexpected ways. Simultaneously, the pivotal artists and theorists of that configuration carry it into the present, reimagining both past and future and becoming newly significant metagenerational figures.[21]

Among my host of generational objects, two phrases, both from 1984, stand out for the concision with which they formulate the effects of relinquishing the epistemological grandiosity embodied in universalizing systems of knowledge that render other knowledges and their subjects inferior: Gayatri Chakravorty Spivak, responding to an interlocutor who has implied that poststructuralism is violent, defines it instead as "a radical acceptance of vulnerability," and Lyotard writes that postmodern knowledge "refines our sensitivity to differences."[22] Lyotard and Spivak summarize what is most profoundly at stake in postmodernism/poststructuralism: calling us out of our narcissism, asking us to question ourselves, and encouraging humility, it obliges us to respond to rather than react against the rights and distress of others, a response-ability that for the ethical philosopher Emmanuel Levinas, is "the essence of the reasonable being in man."[23] I elaborate on Levinas's assertion in "Reasonable Urbanism." Sensitivity to differences and acceptance of vulnerability remain vital watchwords now, when hopes for a less violent future lie in acknowledging interdependency and common vulnerability, as I suggest in "Christopher D'Arcangelo's Elliptical Interruptions," *Not-Forgetting*'s most recent essay.

Postmodernism, poststructuralism, postcolonialism: these internally diverse intellectual currents, whose recognition of the limits of knowledge has been productive and, in some cases, foundational for generations to come, transformed my feminism into a critique of a certain way of being human that I ultimately encapsulated in the term "masculinism." As I use it, masculinism refers to a drive toward ideals of wholeness, mastery, and dominion that, disavowing vulnerability and claiming autonomy, meets differences and otherness in relations of subordination, erasure, incorporation, or other modes of conquest. In "Mary Kelly's Attunement," I define the masculinist subject as one that universalizes itself, claiming to comprehend and represent the social totality and to speak on behalf of an abstract humanity. In this sense, masculinism is not a quality possessed by male persons but, rather, as postcolonial theorist Homi Bhabha writes, "a *position* of social authority."[24] "In fact," Bhabha explains,

> it would be perfectly possible for a woman to occupy the role of a representative man, in the sense I am giving to that term. For "masculinism" as a position of social authority is not simply about the power invested in the recognizable "persons" of men. It is about the subsumption or sublation of social antagonism; it is about the repression of social division; it is about the power to authorize an "impersonal" holistic or universal discourse on the representation of the social.[25]

Both men and women identify with the masculinist position (even if men have historically occupied it) when they are stricken by what Trinh T. Minh-ha names the "victory disease."[26]

Non-gender-exclusive feminism, which challenges masculinism and informs all the essays in *Not-Forgetting*, is the natural ally of other anti-authoritarian discourses that seek to dethrone the subject of mastery: in particular, radical democracy and war resistance, which I touched on in two earlier books, *Evictions: Art and Spatial Politics* (1996) and *Hiroshima after Iraq: Three Studies in Art and War* (2010). In the present volume, I delve more deeply into both discourses. With regard to radical democracy, I constantly return to the French political philosopher Claude Lefort, whose ideas I detail in three of this book's esssays: "Reasonable Urbanism," "The Art of Not Being Governed Quite So Much," and "Christopher D'Arcangelo's Elliptical Interruptions." Suffice it to recall here that Lefort defines democracy not only as a form of government but as a mutation in the form of society and that he places uncertainty at the heart of the new form. With the destruction of monarchical regimes in the late eighteenth century, references to absolute foundations of social unity disappear, and this disappearance of extrasocial guarantees opens the meaning of the social order to democratic debate.[27]

In order to contend with the masculinist drive, the shared project of feminism, war resistance, and radical democracy requires a psychoanalytic approach to human subjectivity, an approach I take throughout this book. For one thing, like democracy, the key object of psychoanalytic thought—the unconscious mind—undermines certainty. In 1935, Sigmund Freud told a lay audience that humanity has suffered two "outrages upon its naïve self-love": the Copernican and Darwinian revolutions, which established that the earth is not the center of the universe and that, descended from the animal world, human beings possess "an ineradicable animal nature."[28] But, Freud concluded, "man's craving for grandiosity is now suffering the third and most bitter blow," this time from the psychoanalytic revolution, "which is endeavouring to prove to the 'ego' of each one of us that he is not even *master* in his own house, but that he must remain content with the veriest scraps of information about what is going on unconsciously in his own mind."[29] We are, that is, inhabited by psychic realities that motivate our emotions, attitudes, and behavior but are largely illegible to us. Given that moral and political conviction both causes war and endows it with an aura of virtue, Freud's challenge to the delusion of self-mastery is vital to antiwar discourse. Not only does psychoanalysis call such conviction into question. It also investigates the psychic resources that are mobilized to wage war, especially the human capacity for regression to earlier stages of mental development and the unconscious destructiveness, aggression, and cruelty inherent in being human.[30] In addition, as I contend in "Un-War: An Aesthetic Sketch," following the Italian psychoanalyst Franco Fornari, psychoanalysis exhorts us to take responsibility for the unconscious. Responsibility is urgent because the alternative is the disavowal of internal cruelty, a psychic operation that entails projecting violence into the external world, outside the individual or social subject. Disavowal thus initiates a search for enemies that, because they are designated as bad objects, can be hated, even annihilated, without guilt—whether they are nations, races, cultures, ethnicities, genders, sexualities, or religions.

Psychoanalysis is also indispensable for anyone who, in the words of the political philosopher Judith Shklar, "puts cruelty first" among the "ordinary" human vices.[31] Referring to what he calls "the worst cruelty"—making oneself and others suffer just *"for the pleasure of it"*—Derrida proposes that psychoanalysis, by virtue of Freud's concept of the death drive, is the only discourse of knowledge that can open itself to the possibility that cruelty is irreducible in the psyche.[32] Psychoanalysis is, then, also the only discourse capable of interrogating the relationship between this cruelty of the psyche and social destructiveness, which is to say, war and warlike actions. The necessity of such an interrogation is a major theme of *Not-Forgetting*.

Most of the essays in *Not-Forgetting* focus on close readings of works by individual artists—Christopher D'Arcangelo, Hans Haacke, Mary Kelly, Silvia Kolbowski, Barbara Kruger, Louise Lawler, Martha Rosler, James Welling, and Krzysztof Wodiczko—or, in the case of one text, a small group of artists—Lawler, Sanja Iveković, and Robert Filliou. With a few exceptions, my work developed alongside that of these politically and ethically conscious artists, who share more than a few of my generational objects. One essay examines a highly visual gay novel. The book also contains two short texts commissioned by *Artforum* and aimed at a less academic readership; one of these criticizes a museum, the other, an exhibition. Collectively, the essays argue that art has something significant to contribute to the project of making a less warlike, more humane world. At least a certain kind of art. All the artworks I discuss make clear that they are not self-contained entities but, rather, social relationships with viewers, whom they approach as subjects that construct rather than passively consume the meaning of art objects. In the words of the artist and writer Judith Barry, these works "make a space"—for dialogue, for the appearance of "hitherto *unthought* configurations of reality," for the "self to account for itself." In short, they make a space that is hospitable to the alterity of the event.[33] Deploying aesthetic tactics invented by Minimalism, Conceptual Art, video installation, institutional critique, and feminist critiques of vision—tactics such as site-specificity, debate-specificity, use of text, direct address, appropriation—the art in *Not-Forgetting* turns toward the viewing subject, disrupting the fantasies that construct and maintain the masculinist position of social authority: fantasies of visual neutrality, autonomy, disembodied and total viewpoints, monological voices, and stable, universal identities. This art intervenes in the phantasmatic visual scenes that stage masculinist desire, failing to deliver plenitude and thereby preventing the subject of mastery from developing in front of them. Even when politics is not their explicit thematic content, such works are deeply political, a point exemplified by James Welling's abstract photographs, the topic of "Darkness: The Emergence of James Welling." I argue that Welling abstracts his depicted but largely unrecognizable objects in the sense of drawing them away from the grasp of the spectator, whose (self-)satisfaction in knowledge gives way to unknowing and to the ability to be surprised. Evoking the shadow of the unconscious, these images belong within the postmodern feminist critique of subjectivity in representation, whose challenge to the fantasy of mastery is urgently political because, as Claudia Rankine writes about the universalizing pretensions of whiteness, "fantasies cost lives."[34]

Postscript: On organization and chronology

Readers may notice that the boundaries enclosing *Not-Forgetting*'s thematic sections are permeable. Some texts that appear in one category could well be placed in another. An anonymous reviewer of the book's manuscript remarked that this ambiguity testifies to the essays' interdependence, and, to be sure, feminist, antiwar, and radical democratic discourses collaborate closely in the texts written after 2006, when, with "Louise Lawler's Rude Museum," I started to write about war.[35] In these later texts, *Not-Forgetting*'s categorical ambiguity reflects the claim, which I have made elsewhere and affirm in "Not-Forgetting: Mary Kelly's *Love Songs*" and "Un-War: An Aesthetic Sketch," that, while some leftist critics use the urgency of the current war situation to devalue feminism as a political project, the feminism I am in solidarity with is indispensable to war resistance; the two cannot be separated.[36]

"Reasonable Urbanism" (1999) and "Breaking and Entering: Barbara Kruger's Spatial Practice" (1999), the two earliest essays in *Not-Forgetting*, form a bridge from my 1996 book *Evictions: Art and Spatial Politics*,[37] which, as the subtitle indicates, deals with contemporary art's relationship to the conflicts that organize, are hidden by, and trouble urban space. But *Evictions* also documents a rupture in my own work, one that arose because when I wrote the essays in that book's first section, "The Social Production of Space," I had not fully brought the feminist critique of representation to bear on my critique of space. I had struggled for some time with how to bring the two together. By 1989, however, I no longer had a choice, for that year two prominent Marxist geographers, whose ideas about space I had previously relied upon, published books that echoed the cultural theorist Frederic Jameson's earlier claim that postmodernism was simply "the cultural logic of late capitalism." Like Jameson, these geographers blamed postmodernism—and the feminist voice within it—for fragmenting a leftist political project that, they assumed, was previously unified by a pregiven economic foundation.[38] Compelled to respond, I argued that such foundationalist theories of the capitalist production of space serve to shore up these geographers' own production of a masculinist space of the political against recent challenges by postmodern feminism. The second and third sections of *Evictions*, "Men in Space" and "Public Space and Democracy," pursue this argument. In "Agoraphobia," the book's final chapter, which brings the concept of the democratic public sphere into discourse about public art, I enlisted the aid of a group of artworks informed by feminism—among them, the early photomontages of Barbara Kruger—to question the ideals of impartiality, unity, abstract reason, and universality embodied in certain critical theories of the public sphere. It was liberating to integrate my critique of space with the feminist critique of representation, and when, a couple of years later, Ann Goldstein, curator of a Kruger exhibition at the Museum of Contemporary Art in Los Angeles, invited me to contribute to the show's catalogue, I took the opportunity to expand my interpretation of Kruger's work as a feminist engagement in spatial politics. The result was "Breaking and Entering: Barbara Kruger's Spatial Practice." The other essays about the work of feminist artists that are gathered in Part One of *Not-Forgetting* quickly followed. Likewise, "Reasonable Urbanism" deepened my criticism of neo-Marxist spatial theory but in a different way, elaborating on the discourse of radical democracy, which I had introduced in "Agoraphobia." I further explore radical democracy in the other essays that make up Part Two of *Not-Forgetting*, two written before and two after I delivered the 2008 Wellek Library Lectures at the University of California, Irvine. The Wellek lectures, which were published in 2010 as *Hiroshima after Iraq: Three Studies in Art and War*, were a turning point in my work, since they explicitly asked, within a psychoanalytic perspective, what art has to offer to the discourse of war resistance, a question implicit in "Louise Lawler's Rude Museum." Inaugurating my exploration of art's relation to war as a social institution, the Wellek lectures gave rise to the essays that form Part Three of *Not-Forgetting*.

PART ONE

Psychoanalytic Feminism

1

Not-Forgetting:
Mary Kelly's *Love Songs*

The age of protected democracy in which we live—when, as Giorgio Agamben writes, security is the normal technique of Western democratic governments—has had a serious impact on art that wants to play a role in deepening and extending the public sphere.[1] Among the most urgent consequences are state censorship: for example, New York Governor George Pataki's recent cancellation of plans to make the Drawing Center part of the World Trade Center memorial complex; and criminal prosecution: the federal government's ongoing indictment of Steven Kurtz, a member of the Critical Art Ensemble. A consequence of another kind, one that has captured less attention but that also limits art's participation in a richly agonistic public life, is a worsening of the left melancholy that surfaced in cultural discourse, including art discourse, in the 1970s.

"Left melancholia" was Walter Benjamin's derogatory term for a mood afflicting leftists who remain more attached to past political ideals—even, according to philosopher Wendy Brown, to the *failure* of a political ideal—than to possibilities of political change in the present.[2] Brown says that the left melancholic renders his political analysis thing-like and frozen, unamenable to transformation. Applying Benjamin's analysis to contemporary times, she argues that today's left melancholic adheres to a traditional leftist representation of the political, a representation that includes "notions of unified movements, social totalities, and class-based politics."[3] The melancholic therefore laments the challenges that have been posed over the last few decades to such unitary models of social change, scornfully calling them, among other names, "postmodern." The most basic challenge was the calling into question of the idea that society is totalized by a single, economic antagonism, which is the absolute foundation of all other social antagonisms and therefore governs all emancipatory struggle. Against this questioning, the left melancholic tries to reground the political in the authority of an ontologically privileged foundation, insisting, as Stuart Hall observed in 1988, on the determinism of capital and dismissing the political importance of postmodernism's concern with the subject and subjectivity.[4] A current example is the introduction to *Afflicted Powers: Capital and Spectacle in a New Age of War*, a book about the Iraq War that has attracted the interest of certain sectors of the art world. After wrongly claiming that academic leftists of the recent past dismissed the political significance of capitalism, the authors write, "It is 'the end of Grand Narratives' and 'the trap of totalization' and 'the radical irreducibility of the political' which now seem like period items."[5] The phrases they place in scare quotes and mock as outdated stand of course for various postmodern, poststructuralist, and feminist critiques of traditional leftist political analysis.

Brown suggests that left melancholy has a narcissistic dimension because the frozen analysis to which it clings once formed the basis of leftist self-love, giving "its adherents a clear and certain path toward the good, the right, the true."[6] Insofar as left melancholy rests on an image of society and of social change that is centered on the presence of an element that guarantees wholeness, the analysis is also masculinist. Hardly surprising, then, is the left melancholic's rejection not only of postmodernism but also of the feminist voice associated with postmodernism. For it was postmodern feminists and, in particular, feminist artists, who explored the role played by totalizing images in producing and maintaining masculinist subjects. This exploration implied that subjective, psychic transformation, like material transformation, is an essential component, rather than mere epiphenomenon, of social change. Also predictable, then, is that critics and historians afflicted by left melancholy (including some who once theorized the meaning of postmodernism but now regard it as nothing more than "the cultural logic of late capitalism") would refuse to register the full impact of the feminist critique of the meaning of the political. Leftists may use the pressing nature of the current political situation to legitimate this refusal, but in the age of protected democracy, when the pursuit of mastery has become a self-evident virtue, the feminist critique seems more rather than less urgent.

The left melancholic's insistence on a pregiven ground of society and of political struggle restricts the growth of democratic public spheres. For one thing, as Claude Lefort argues, the public sphere emerged precisely when the democratic revolutions withdrew the ground, making the meaning of society uncertain and, as a consequence, open to debate. For another, being in public means responding to the presence of others and therefore calls us

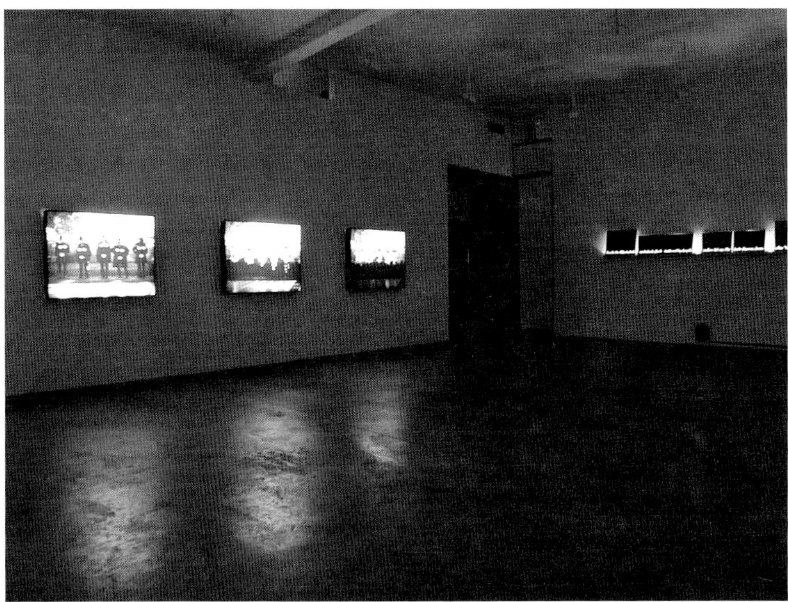

1.1 Mary Kelly, *Love Songs*, 2005. Installation view, *Flashing Nipple Remix* and *Sisterhood is POW . . .*, front gallery, Postmasters Gallery, New York. Courtesy the artist and Mitchell-Innes & Nash, New York. © Mary Kelly.

out of our narcissism. Artists who want their work to be part of democratic public life are faced with the task not only of challenging protected democracy but of resisting left melancholy. One way of doing so—suggested to me by Mary Kelly's exhibition *Love Songs*, held last fall at Postmasters Gallery in New York City—is through fidelity to the event of feminism (fig. 1.1).

"Fidelity to the event" is a concept formulated by the philosopher Alain Badiou. Like left melancholy, the phrase implies a relationship to the past, a type of history and memory of earlier radicalism. To distinguish fidelity from nostalgic memory, Badiou describes the relationship as one of "not-forgetting." Fidelity to the event is also Badiou's name for a new conception of ethics, which he defines as a refusal of conservatism.[7] The event for Badiou is something that happens in a situation, something that supplements, but does not complement, the order within which the event takes place, whether it is the political, personal, or artistic order. Examples are the political event of the French Revolution, the personal event of an amorous passion, and the artistic event of Schoenberg's invention of the twelve-tone scale. The event cannot be understood within the framework of already-constituted knowledges. It "punches a hole" in such knowledge, releasing what Badiou calls a "truth-process." The event is revolutionary, though not in the sense of something absolute that, as Julia Kristeva puts it in her criticism of revolution, will solve all problems.[8] Rather, the event presents hitherto unknown possibilities that put an end to consensus or dominant opinion in the order it disrupts; its course is uncertain, and, importantly, it compels the subject to "decide a new way of being." The subject becomes the bearer of a fidelity to the event when she decides henceforth to relate to the situation from the perspective of the event. "To be really faithful to the event," Badiou writes, "I must completely rework my ordinary way of living my situation."[9] After Schoenberg, for instance, I do not go back to writing romantic music. I persevere in the interruption. I do not break with the break and return to continuity. But neither do I make the event absolute, giving it total power and turning it into a new dogmatism. For the event, cautions Badiou, does not reveal the substance of the situation in which it occurs. Rather, it names the void of the situation. For example, the void of the political order is the meaning of the political community. If, as Lefort argues, the democratic revolutions constituted an event that did away with references to absolute sources of the meaning of the people and opened the political community to question, then to endow the people with a substantial identity, to name the unnamable, is to betray the democratic event and, of course, destroy the public sphere it invents.

For Badiou, the subject of a fidelity does not preexist the event. Rather, the subject is someone caught up in the event, "simultaneously himself and in excess of himself." The event and the unpredictable course of the process it unleashes "pass through" this someone, who thereby becomes engaged in the invention of a new subject, a subject she has chosen to be and that extends beyond herself. The question faced by the subject of a fidelity is "how will I, as some-one, *continue* to exceed my own being . . . via the effects of being seized by the not-known?"[10]

Kelly's *Love Songs* demonstrated fidelity to an event that Badiou does not mention: feminism, which, questioning masculinist conceptions of both the subject and the political, attempted to construct more democratic forms of each.[11] As its title indicates, Kelly's exhibition treated the political event of feminism as also a personal one, an amorous passion, giving new meaning to the slogan of the Women's Liberation Movement "the personal is political." This slogan challenged both mainstream and traditional critical conceptions of the public sphere, which draw a rigid divide between public/political and private/nonpolitical space. Whereas the public-private division once forced women's issues into privacy, today the division is shored up by left melancholics, who exclude feminist explorations of subjectiv-

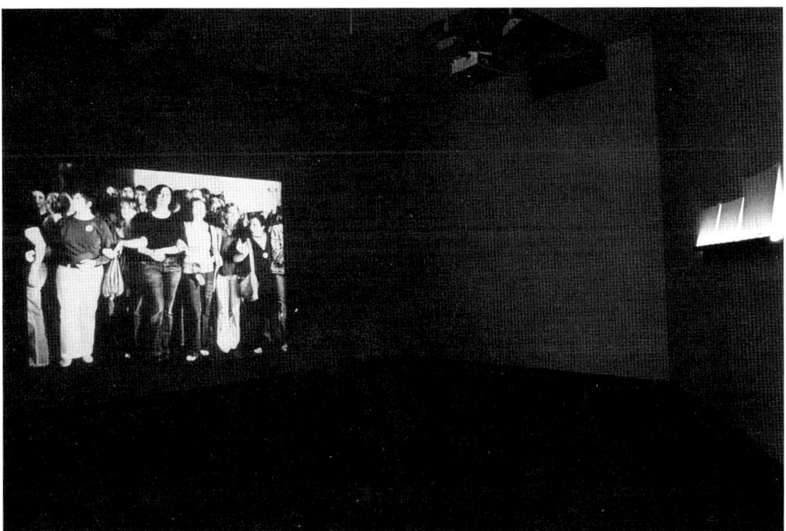

1.2　Mary Kelly, *Love Songs*, 2005. Installation view, *WLM Remix* and *Seemed Right*, back gallery, Postmasters Gallery, New York. Courtesy the artist and Mitchell-Innes & Nash, New York. © Mary Kelly.

ity from the public sphere. Against this exclusion, Kelly created a space— a kind of theater—dedicated to the history, memory, and post-memory of a feminism that mixes the personal and the political, a space in which the boundaries between the two could not be pinned down.

In her theater of not-forgetting, Kelly used a material that serves the philosopher as a metaphor for the event: light. The event, says Badiou, is "a kind of flashing supplement that happens to the situation"; it bursts forth as if into flame and gives off light, which disappears, leaving a "trace" in the situation, a kind of after-image that refers back to the vanished event and guides the subject's fidelity.[12] *Love Songs* contains such traces: it took place in a darkened gallery; the only light emanated from the works in the show (fig. 1.2).

Running like a frieze around three walls of the gallery's front room was a work called *Sisterhood Is POW . . .*, a title that transforms the early feminist slogan "Sisterhood is powerful" into a phrase that registers the powerful impact—the POW—of feminism as an event. *Sisterhood Is POW . . .* consisted of thirty-six black, cast-acrylic panels incised with laser-cut script. Supported on wooden shelves, the panels were lit from behind by strip lighting, which illuminated the words and turned them into literal "words of light," Walter Benjamin's term for photography, a name that links photographs to language. Divided like lines of poetry, Kelly's text expresses her subjective not-forgetting of her participation in an episode of the British Women's Liberation Movement, a demonstration against the Miss World Contest held at the Albert Hall in London in 1971. Undertaking a type of historical work that Drucilla Cornell calls "the recollective imagination,"[13] Kelly recalls what was taking place inside and outside the Hall: inside, the Miss World contest, where "contestants flash / teeth and leg-length" as "judges tot up the / facts: figures, faces"; outside, a protest against this spectacle of patriarchal femininity in which "demonstrators, / arms locked, hands firm, fingers longer, / more lucid, flash / luminous nipples and / crotches at fans." The group of panels bearing short phrases and placed at slightly varying heights resembled a cluster of picket signs contesting oppressive constructions of the feminine.

On the room's fourth wall hung another, related work, *Flashing Nipple Remix*, consisting of three light boxes containing large black-and-white photographic transparencies. The activities pictured in the photographs are based on a snapshot in Kelly's archive. The archival photo documents the street theater protest described in *Sisterhood Is POW . . .* and could be considered a trace of feminism as an event. Over their clothing, in the area of their breasts and genitals, protestors had placed bright lights, ironically mimicking the performance going on inside the Albert Hall. The first photo in *Flashing Nipple Remix* depicts a contemporary restaging of the protest by five young women. Representatives of a new generation of feminists, the women wore the same lights as the original protestors and set them in motion by shaking their bodies with increasing vigor. The women became radiant as their bodies dissolved into luminous streaks and patterns of light. A student of mine observed that the moving lights served as "a vehicle to problematize the definition of a woman by way of anatomical form. . . . Through their actions, the women become complex, ineffable figures of their own definition, defying the notion of a woman as an object presented for the enjoyment of the viewer."[14] The photos can also be read as somewhat humorous images of Badiou's subject of a fidelity, of, that is, women caught up in the flashing event of feminism, using a trace to guide them (fig. 1.3).

Love Songs continued in Postmasters' back room, which contained two works that echoed those in the front. *Seemed Right*, placed on the right-hand wall, repeated the form of *Sisterhood Is POW . . .*, only its acrylic panels were white, not black. As in *Sisterhood Is POW . . .*, the panels contain the recollections of older feminists, whom Kelly had asked to describe their initial responses to the Women's Liberation Movement. The most common answers, once again written in light, a form that matched their thematic con-

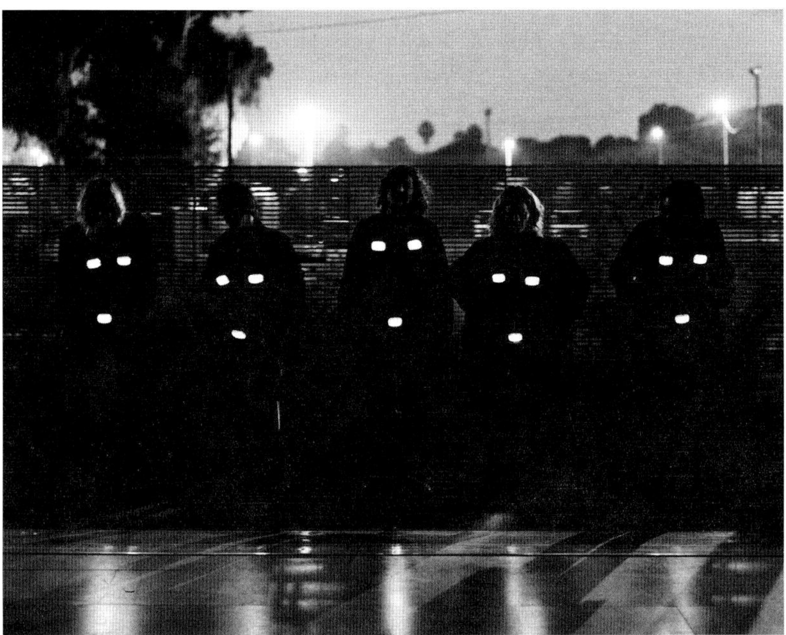

1.3 Mary Kelly, *Flashing Nipple Remix*, 2005. Detail, one of three black-and-white transparencies in light boxes. Courtesy the artist and Mitchell-Innes & Nash, New York.
© Mary Kelly.

tent, characterized feminism as an event: "seemed right," "just made sense," "like a lightning bolt!"

Across from *Seemed Right*, on the room's left-hand wall, Kelly projected a ninety-second film loop titled *WLM Demo Remix*. Like *Flashing Nipple Remix*, the film depicts both an early Women's Liberation Movement demonstration and its contemporary restaging. This work, however, uses an actual archival photo, a trace of the event, to represent the original demonstration, which took place in New York City in 1970, one of several demonstrations held across the United States to mark the fiftieth anniversary of the Nineteenth Amendment, which gave American women the right to vote. Like *Flashing Nipple Remix*, *WLM Demo Remix* portrays a transgenerational haunting. An image that carries the legacy of an earlier generation of feminists appears to the new generation. Likewise, the women in the later image inhabit those in the earlier one. Using a slow dissolve to combine past and present images, a technique that imitates the scene of the unconscious mind, the loop begins with the later image—the photo of the restaging—which gradually fades and disappears as the earlier image emerges and grows clearer.

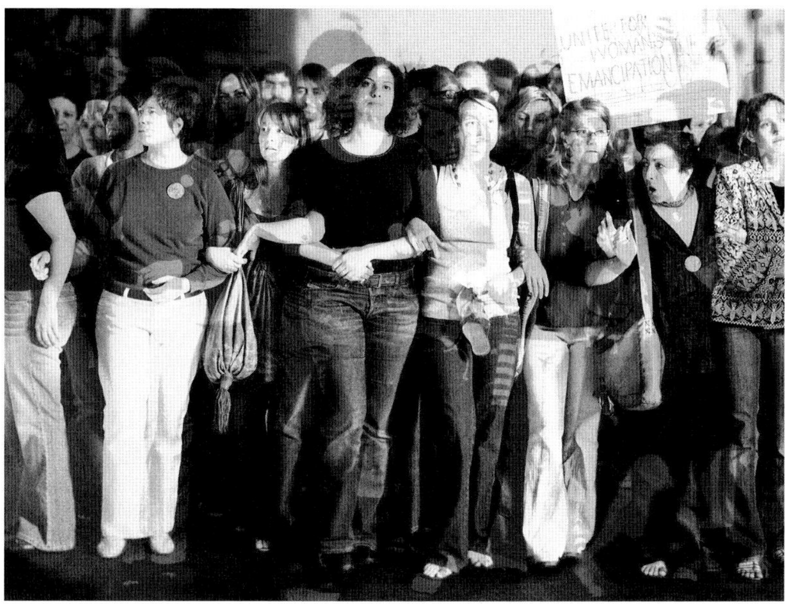

1.4 Mary Kelly, *WLM Remix*, 2005. Still, 1:30 min. black-and-white film loop. Courtesy the artist and Mitchell-Innes & Nash, New York. © Mary Kelly.

The image of the restaging never fades out completely, however, but always remains visible behind the earlier one, which, it should be noted, itself does not picture an originary event because the 1970 demonstration, mounted by a second wave of feminists, was haunted by earlier street performances— late nineteenth- and early twentieth-century suffragist parades. The archival photo, then, also depicts a restaging. Literally and figuratively, Kelly's work is a visual remix: a recording produced by bringing together ingredients in a new formation that modifies their identities (fig. 1.4).

The phrase on the demonstrators' sign oscillates between "Unite for Women's Emancipation," which appears in the archival photograph, and, in the restaged image, "From Stone to Cloud." A clear political exhortation to bring about emancipatory change, an exhortation recalling those of the suffragists, alternates with a far more cryptic word-image that describes a particular kind of change: a transformation from a thing-like thing, an entity—a stone—into something capable of remixing—a cloud. In the context of Kelly's exhibition, "from stone to cloud" can be read as a metaphor for at least two interrelated changes: mutations in the identity of feminism as a political movement and mutations in the identity of the subject seized by feminism. Each moves away from a fixed state and grows into something defined by its ability to change, to be reborn, liberated. Feminism as an event and the subject of a fidelity to it leave behind a conception of politics grounded in solid foundations and ascend to a more democratic one that exists in multiple incarnations and changes shape as it articulates with other political aims and objects, for example, human rights. Politics as a remix.

"From stone to cloud" is taken from a poem by Sylvia Plath titled *Love Letter*. Kelly's choice of *Love Songs* as the title of her exhibition bespeaks a debt: The show may be influenced by Badiou, but it operates, quite literally, under the sign of Plath, whose life and poetry have long haunted feminists, and whose poem begins:

> Not easy to describe the change you made
> If I'm alive now, then I was dead,
> Though, like a stone, unbothered by it,
> Staying put according to habit.

Plath wrote the poem six months after giving birth to its addressee, a baby girl, who, as the poet describes it, also gave birth to her. Since the 1970s, when she made *Post-Partum Document*, Kelly has been interested in the mother-child relationship. Following Badiou, she suggests that it might be considered a form of fidelity to the event of love.[15] More important, she compares the relationship to the intersubjectivity of a political project; in particular, to the kind of love that existed among feminists in the early women's movement. This love, she claims, characterized a feminist community that recognized difference and, as a result, attempted to forge nonhierarchical forms of political organization.[16] The implied "you" to whom Kelly writes her love songs is, I think, both new and older feminists, with their own irreconcilable difference, as well as feminism itself, which gave birth to a new subject and whose own birth the women quoted in *Seemed Right* also address, saying, as Plath does, "I knew you at once."

Jacqueline Rose, in her superb book *The Haunting of Sylvia Plath*, observes that in Plath the boundary between personal, psychic history and political history is uncertain.[17] For this reason, Plath has been severely chastised by critics who want to separate the two. But she has also served as a site of contestation about the meaning of the feminist formulation that the personal is political. Rose points out that some feminists claim that Plath's late work reveals the emergence of the poet's authentic self.[18] Plath, they say, was emancipated into a resolute identity. Those who interpret Plath in this manner often render her personal journey political by turning it into an allegory of feminism understood as a movement whose goal is to enable the emergence of a transcendent female selfhood. *Love Letter* suggests otherwise. In this and other poems, the stone stands for separateness from other things. And it is precisely this hard separateness that characterizes the phallocentric self, the self understood as constituted outside of relationships, a private rather than a public being. Because Plath describes her liberating transformation as a move *away* from a stonelike state, the transformation cannot accurately serve as an image of a feminism that wants to move *toward* self-constituted female subjectivity—especially if we consider *Love Letter* in relation to *Magi*, a poem penned by Plath one day later. There, the narrator, fantasizing a group of transcendent beings hovering over a baby's crib, shrinks from their "loveless" abstractions and asks, "What girl ever flourished in such company?"[19] Kelly, like Rose, claims Plath for a different feminism, one grounded in the continual opening and remixing of feminist politics and the feminine rather than in conclusive identities that foreclose mutation. In *Love Songs* "from stone to cloud" counters—protests against— the danger that feminism and the subject of feminism might, as Rose cautions, "find itself reproducing the form of phallocentrism at the very moment it claims to have detached itself most fully from patriarchal power."[20]

Both fidelity to the event and left melancholy remember the past and write history. But unlike triumphalist historical narratives, in which emancipation leads to resolution, Kelly's history is written in the tense of the future anterior, an order of time in which, as Cornell observes, reimagining never ends.[21] Theorizing the future anterior as the time of personal history, Jacques Lacan wrote, "What is realized in my history is not the past definite of what was, since it is no more, or even the present perfect of what has been in what I am, but the future anterior of what I shall have been for what I am in the process of becoming."[22] Lacan's description of personal history recalls Walter Benjamin's philosophy of political history. The historian, as Benjamin famously wrote, does not reconstruct the past "as it really was" but, bringing past and present into a constellation, "seize[s] hold of a memory as it flashes up at a moment of danger."[23] Kelly mixes Badiou and Benjamin— two philosophers of the flash and of revolutionary not-forgetting. For in *Love Songs* the Women's Liberation Movement cannot be distinguished from the transformations it undergoes in the hands of a new generation and, perhaps most important, in both generations' fantasies. *WLM Demo Remix*, for example, literalizes the future anterior, never allowing the image of the 1970s demonstration to appear in isolation. And while the image of the restaged demonstration does *technically* resolve, it, too, cannot be separated from its counterpart by virtue of its status as a theatrical reenactment, a repetition with difference, in which a group of women literally assume an image and, in this way, claim a relationship to an event in which they did not participate. Kelly's performers enact a mimetic identification that for Cornell forms the basis of feminist politics.[24] As a psychic narrative of repetitive time mixes with and reimagines a historical narrative of progressive time, Kelly writes feminism and herself as what they will have been for what they are in the process of becoming.

The principal way in which Kelly's fidelity to the event differs from left melancholy is in its refusal to "break with the break," to go back to prefeminist ideas of politics and history. In keeping with this fidelity, Kelly neither absolutizes the event nor takes up an authoritarian position in relation to a younger generation. Rejecting the paternal role, which would demand identification with a supposedly authentic feminism, Kelly foregrounds the category of fantasy, exploring her own and her young performers' imaginary investments in feminist history and politics. In this way, too, the subject of a fidelity diverges from the left melancholic, who must disavow his participation in fantasy, precisely in order to defend his fantasy of mastery.

2

Inadequacy: Silvia Kolbowski's History of Conceptual Art

In 1989, Michael Asher participated in *L'art conceptuel, une perspective,* an exhibition that represents one of the first institutional attempts to define Conceptual Art.[1] Asher's contribution, which took the form of a proposal, was the only new work in the exhibition—all others dated from the 1960s and 1970s—and therefore the only one able to call attention to the specific circumstances of its display. Reviving the historical conceptualist practice of placing advertisements in art publications, Asher proposed that announcements of *L'art conceptuel* be taken out in various scholarly art journals, with the aim of notifying art historians "that a new historical perspective is being mapped on to conceptual practice." Asher did not oppose the historicization of Conceptual Art. On the contrary, he wrote that "historical objectification ought to be accelerated while there is still a collective experience and memory which can assist in the clarity of an analysis."[2] But, as his statement makes clear, he assumed that history bears the imprint of memory, and, what is more, he urged historians to proceed self-reflexively, "simultaneously opening up a space to ask fundamental questions regarding history making."[3] Silvia Kolbowski did not know about Asher's proposal, but nearly ten years later, in a project titled *an inadequate history of conceptual art* (1998–99), she responded to its call, producing just such a metahistorical space, though one opened up in a work of art rather than an art-historical text.

Unaware of Conceptual Art during its heyday, and her student years, in the late1960s and 1970s, Kolbowski approached it later, by way of psychoanalysis and feminism. By the early 1980s, she belonged to an interdisciplinary group of feminists who were developing a psychoanalytically informed critique of subjectivity in representation, and she was exhibiting with a group of artists who likewise turned toward the subject, challenging myths of visual purity and disinterested vision by exploring the image as a site of unconscious investments and investigating the role played by vision—looking at images—in establishing and maintaining hierarchies of sexual difference.[4] Of course, the feminist critique of vision was interwoven with conceptualist strategies, so much so that one critic, reviewing *Difference: On Sexuality and Representation*,[5] an early exhibition of art informed by psychoanalytic feminist ideas about vision and sexuality, and one in which Kolbowski took part, wrote that "there hasn't been such a purely Conceptual art exhibition in New York museums since the summer of 1970." In fact, she continued, "in feminism, Conceptualism may have found its greatest and most urgent subject."[6] Yet Kolbowski's direct encounter with historical Conceptual Art was belated: "What was decisive for me in moving away from abstract, by then monochromatic, painting around 1976 was my growing engagement with feminism," she recalls.

> This shift, together with my growing interest in psychoanalytic theory, and my engagement with some of the strategies referred to as appropriationist in the 1980s, resulted in photographic work like the *Model Pleasure* series, which I produced starting in 1982.But toward the late eighties, I began to question the way in which this work was displayed; in other words, I was not satisfied with its matter-of-fact placement on the walls of galleries and museums. . . . So in the mid-to-late 1980s, I read whatever texts I could find on historical Conceptualism. I was interested in earlier attempts to deal with the spatial aspects of institutions, of natural and urban settings, and of display conventions.[7]

Kolbowski's path to Conceptual Art is manifest in *an inadequate history of conceptual art*, for, I want to argue, the work views Conceptual Art—or, more precisely, contemporary histories of Conceptual Art—within the perspective of subsequent artistic developments and, in particular, through a feminist lens. Not just because it includes female voices; not just because it defines Conceptual Art in terms intended, as Kolbowski puts it, "to allow for an inscription of women artists" into the movement's history,[8] but also, and most significantly, because, in keeping with the wish of a certain kind of feminism, it pleads for what Jacqueline Rose calls an "ethics of failure"—a wish announced by the word "inadequate" in the work's title.[9] "Inadequate" does not function here as a derogatory adjective, one that indicates the presence of deficiencies that can and must be corrected if Kolbowski's account of the artistic past is going to measure up to an ideal of complete, which is to say, adequate historical knowledge. Rather, inadequate describes the condition of all cultural histories, since history is a representation of—a narrative about—the past and therefore unequal to reality. It does not correspond to things as they were. And narrativity is inadequate for another reason: it arises from desire, a desire, as Hayden White says, introducing the problem of subjectivity into the writing of history, "to have real events display the coherence, integrity, fullness, and closure of an image of life that is and can only be imaginary."[10]

"Inadequate" functions interrogatively as well as descriptively in Kolbowski's title, questioning from a feminist standpoint not only the possibility but the very ideal of historical adequacy or completeness. For if, as Joan Wallach Scott wrote in the 1980s, women's history has offered "a critique of history that characterized it not simply as an incomplete record of the past but as a participant in the production of knowledge that legitimized the exclusion or subordination of women,"[11] feminists have since argued that historical knowledge performs this legitimizing role most effectively precisely when it claims completeness, when, that is, it disavows failure. In the absence of an a priori, unifying ground of history, one deriving from a source outside the social world, completeness can only be achieved through a gesture of exclusion, an elimination of otherness that affirms and at the same time prevents history's cohesiveness. When, however, historians refer to a substantive foundation that totalizes history and generates the limits of their narratives, they justify and conceal their exclusions, rendering them invisible and withdrawing them from the terrain of contestation. Kolbowski's history, by contrast, insists on its own inadequacy and, in doing so, stresses the importance of acknowledging rather than overcoming the failure of representational adequacy, insofar as history fails when, opening itself to the voices of others, it questions the rhetorical certainties of its reception of the past. Hence, inadequacy's ethico-political dimension.

Kolbowski made *an inadequate history* as a contribution to, and commentary on, a rediscovery of Conceptual Art that began more than a decade ago. An early sign of the rediscovery was the appearance of the term "neo-conceptualism," which has since settled into the vocabulary of art discourse, where it is used loosely to categorize diverse, even ideologically opposing, art practices—those of Kolbowski included—that mobilize the movement's principal signifiers—amateur photographs, texts, diagrams, appropriation, pastiche—and thus have a conceptualist look. In addition, major exhibitions of Conceptual Art, accompanied by scholarly catalogues, spanned the 1990s, inaugurated in Paris by *L'art conceptuel, une perspective*, whose purpose was to build "something like a history of Conceptual Art."[12] In 1996, the Los Angeles Museum of Contemporary Art mounted *Reconsidering the Object of Art: 1965–1975*, which was followed in 1999 by *Global Concep-*

tualism: Points of Origin, 1950s–1980s at the Queens Museum in New York.[13] Anthologies, monographs, and collections of documents appeared.[14] Lucy Lippard's classic record of the movement, first published in 1973, was reprinted.[15] And art historians undertook the task of historicizing Conceptual Art. Two of the most important histories are Benjamin Buchloh's highly influential "Conceptual Art 1962–1969: From the Aesthetic of Administration to the Critique of Institutions," written for the Paris exhibition catalogue, and Alexander Alberro's *Conceptual Art and the Politics of Publicity*, which, published in 2003, postdates *an inadequate history* and thus demonstrates the ongoing relevance of Kolbowski's work.[16]

The return to Conceptual Art contains diverse tendencies. One, exemplified by the term "neo-conceptualism," treats the movement largely in terms of style and therefore detaches it from its radical history. "It seemed like this return was just too smooth and fast,"[17] says Kolbowski, who, against the superficiality of this aspect of the return, emphasizes the historicity of Conceptual Art while still remaining open to the possibility of its contemporary relevance as an aesthetically and politically radical practice. She hopes, as Simon Leung does, that Conceptual Art might be "returned to criticality, and continued beyond a reproduction of spectacles and effects."[18]

The return to Conceptual Art has, of course, produced less superficial histories, among which at least two orientations can be distinguished.[19] *Global Conceptualism*, for one, exemplified the tendency to expand the movement to embrace broad chronological periods—the 1950s–1980s—as well as a wide range of international artists working in a conceptualist manner. It produced a cultural history that, while significant for its openness to non-canonical artists and otherwise marginalized groups, offers illusions of plenitude and thus runs the risk of fostering a type of pluralism that neutralizes differences, in the sense of antagonisms, within the field of Conceptual Art, thereby doing away with the dimension of the political. A second approach is taken in recent accounts of Conceptual Art written by art historians whose desire to historicize Conceptual practices goes hand in hand with the mobilization of historical-materialist modes of cultural analysis that use the discourse of political economy to draw the line between the political and nonpolitical. Like Kolbowski, these writers stress Conceptual Art's historical and political character but, unlike Kolbowski, they drastically restrict the movement's scope, tightening its temporal and geographical borders in what can seem like an attempt to assuage any uncertainty of definition. One might say that they go too far in the opposite direction from global conceptualism, for some of the most theoretically rigorous materialist histories, while extremely valuable in their complexity and difference from neutralizing accounts, prompt serious reservations, since they are uncompromisingly androcentric, building canons of Conceptual Art that eliminate women. Of equal, if not greater concern is the fact that they ignore contemporary feminist challenges to totalizing visions of art, politics, and history and, against these challenges, eliminate otherness from all three, pushing sexuality to the back of the aesthetic, political, and historical mind. To be sure, art historians sometimes acknowledge the absence of women and, more rarely, of feminism from their histories. In fact, such caveats have become quite common in introductions to books about contemporary art in general, where they tend to minimize, even while admitting to omissions, which, since the absence of a topic can be the first clue to its presence, actually structure these art histories.

Consider as examples the two texts I cited earlier: Alberro's *Conceptual Art and the Politics of Publicity* and Buchloh's "Conceptual Art 1962–1969." In the introduction to his book, Alberro, who, it should be noted, has elsewhere written an insightful review of *an inadequate history*,[20] explains that he has limited his investigation to the emergence of Conceptual Art in relation to Seth Siegelaub, the freelance curator who promoted conceptual artists in New York in the 1960s. This limitation, Alberro says, produced several exclusions, including the elimination of female artists from the history of early Conceptual Art. Nonetheless, he concludes, it sharpened his focus, permitting him to "glimpse" the relationship of Conceptual Art to a new moment of multinational capitalism characterized by the growth and manipulation of information.[21] In the end, then, the limitation emerges as a positive feature, one that offers a more adequate picture of Conceptual Art, a claim that ignores the way limitations construct rather than reveal their objects of study. Uncharacteristically for Alberro, this statement disavows the discursive character of his book's object, treating Conceptual Art as the ground rather than the effect of art-historical knowledge. By contrast, acknowledging the productive nature of discourse, while it does not erase Conceptual Art's connection to the information society, allows us to see that, instead of clarifying the politics of early Conceptual Art, Alberro's limitation is itself political: it permits a return to an art-historical method that uses political economy as the ontologically privileged ground of aesthetic politics. The most serious problem raised by such a limitation is not the women it hides but the masculinist bias, the drive toward ideals of unity and completion, of the history it authorizes.

Buchloh's politicized history of Conceptual Art poses similar problems for feminism, telling as it does a story of conflict between competing groups of male artists, whose work represents opposing stances in relationship to advanced capitalist society: on the one hand, those like Joseph Kosuth, who developed what Buchloh calls an "aesthetic of administration" and thus submitted art to the logic of advanced capitalism, and, on the other hand, Daniel Buren, Marcel Broodthaers, and Hans Haacke, who, following in the footsteps of Robert Morris and Lawrence Weiner, turned this aesthetic into a critique of institutions that exposes the social institutions "from which . . . the logic of administration emanate[s] in the first place."[22] Buchloh establishes a relationship between the economic and the cultural that is mediated by the specific, relatively autonomous, genealogy of modern and contemporary art. Still, he ultimately grounds Conceptual Art's relation to the political in the way it reflects the post-war, managerial phase of capitalism or restates as artistic problems social problems that are governed by economic antagonism. Not surprisingly, as Griselda Pollock once wrote in a similar context—a critique of art history—this account produces "peculiar closures on the issue of sexuality."[23] Consequently, Buchloh's politicized history of Conceptual Art remains blind to feminism, which is to say, to otherness in the realm of the political. This is regrettable since Buchloh's definition of Conceptual Art could just as easily have opened onto feminism, for he rightly describes Conceptual Art as "the most rigorous elimination of visuality and traditional definitions of representation" in contemporary art.[24] Yet he makes not even a token mention of feminist critiques of vision, concluding his narrative with the institution-critical work of Buren, Haacke, and Broodthaers, who, he argues, again rightly, assaulted "the false neutrality of vision that provides the underlying rationale for those institutions."[25] Buchloh's exclusion of feminism is legitimated by his determination of 1969—the closing date of his title—as the year Conceptual Art died. In his text, however, he dates the movement's disappearance to 1975,[26] a contradiction that may point to an underlying anxiety over chronological and political boundaries. Even within his own chronology, then, Buchloh could have located the end of Conceptual Art's radical legacy not in the institutional criticism of Buren, Haacke, and Broodthaers, important as it was, but in the art informed by feminism that, beginning in the 1970s, enlarged institutional critique to embrace questions of subjectivity, desire, and sexuality and thus rendered *even more rigorous* Conceptual Art's challenge to the falseness of visual neutrality. Instead of cleansing Conceptual Art of feminism and sexuality, he could, for instance, have concluded his history with a work such as Mary Kelly's *Post-Partum Document* (1973–79), which, like Haacke's work of the same period, both built on and deviated from Conceptual Art. Using the conceptualist practice of documentation, Kelly combined it with both institution-critical and psychoanalytic feminist strategies. Begun in

1973, *Post-Partum Document* falls within the period Buchloh designates as that of the emergence and operation of Conceptual Art.[27] Including Kelly's work would have meant being mindful not only of women but of feminism, and this in turn would have required Buchloh to modify, indeed weaken, the foundation of his history and to open up the boundaries of his concept of the political, articulating economic with other social antagonisms.

An inadequate history responds to current accounts of Conceptual Art by introducing memory—and with it, the unconscious mind—into the writing of history.

In 1998, adopting a conceptualist practice, Kolbowski asked sixty artists to follow a set of directions:

> Briefly describe a conceptual art work, not your own, of the period between 1965 and 1975, which you personally witnessed/experienced at the time. For the sake of this project, the definition of conceptual art should be broad enough to encompass such phenomena of that period as actions documented through drawings, photographs, film, and video; concepts executed in the form of drawings or photographs; objects where the end product is primarily a record of the precipitant concept, and performative activities which sought to question the conventions of dance and theater.

She requested that they speak solely from memory, conduct no research, and reveal neither their own identities nor those of the artists and works they recalled. Forty artists agreed to produce such inadequate accounts, and in the end Kolbowski tape-recorded twenty-two stories. As the artists spoke, she also videotaped their hands, focusing attention on the very element of art-making that Conceptual Art wanted to do away with: the hand of the artist.

The result, a record of the artist's own precipitant concept, was a kind of performance first staged by Kolbowski in 1999 at American Fine Arts Co., a New York gallery with two adjacent exhibition spaces (fig. 2.1). On a wall in the gallery's front room, Kolbowski projected a nine-by-twelve-foot silent video loop showing enlarged close-ups of the artists' moving, gesturing hands. On the same wall in the back room, she played the acoustic loop of the artists' stories, which she had arranged chronologically according to the dates of the conceptual artworks that the artists described, or, rather, the dates as the artists remembered them, which in some cases are wrong, as a printed sheet distributed in the gallery informed viewers. The handout also listed the participants, but individual voices and hands remained anonymous. The two components of the installation—sound and image—were de-synchronized so that any individual artist's voice was heard in con-

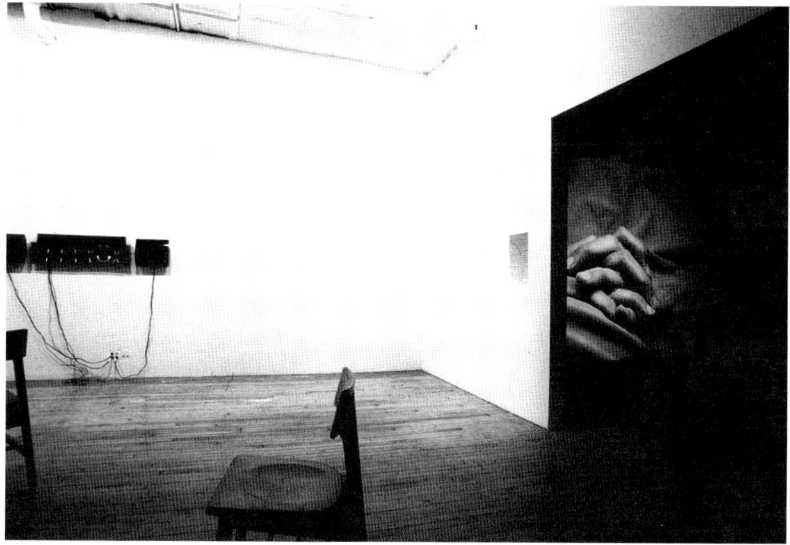

2.1 Silvia Kolbowski, *an inadequate history of conceptual art*, 1998–99. Video and audio installation, looped. Installation view, American Fine Arts, New York, 1999. Courtesy the artist.

junction with an image of the hands of a different artist. Because of this disjunction and because, for technical reasons, Kolbowski used only half of the video footage, thereby making the audiotape twice as long as the video, hands frequently changed in the middle of a spoken testimony; or viceversa: a new testimony began but the hands remained the same. Coupled with the physical division of the gallery, the inability to connect sound and image, to locate them in a single person, placed the viewer in an ungrounded space, depriving her of the centered, distanced position of full knowledge from which to receive the work, the artists' "testimonies," or, for that matter, the past, which was never available as a totality.

The acoustic recording unfolded on a sleek Bang & Olufsen Beosound 9000 CD player, whose advertising slogan, Kolbowski later revealed, asserts that the player is "Created. Not made,"[28] a claim echoing what may be the most common description of Conceptual Art: An art of ideas. Not handmade objects. However, the CD player did not stand for Conceptual Art itself but for the superficial, mechanical aspect of its current rediscovery. For, as Alberro astutely observes, the "slickly designed, state-of-the-art Bang & Olufsen" actually differs from Conceptual Art, contrasting sharply with an "artmaking practice that dreamed of democratizing the realm of the aesthetic by employing low-tech materials." And this difference corresponds to another: that between historical Conceptual Art and its current rediscovery, between, that is, "a previously iconoclastic artistic movement and its return in a new historical context," where it has become "a catchall that has little to do with the rigorous definitions of the original movement."[29]

The soundtrack of *an inadequate history*, on which the artists tell their stories about Conceptual Art, highlights the difficulties that beset memory: falsifications, gaps, repressions, displacements, and denials. What is remembered has also fallen into oblivion. Mnemonic uncertainties surface on the level of thematic content as speakers acknowledge the inadequacies of their accounts. Almost no one claims accuracy. One speaker inquires into the motivations of memory and forgetting, wondering why a *particular* work has stuck in her mind. Another is simply "stuck," bereft of anything more to say. Several voices equivocate about what they saw or where they were when they saw it. Exact dates or locations cannot be recalled or are misremembered. One speaker brings to the fore the question of memory by recalling a work *about* memory, while another alludes to an accidental head injury that occurred just before she viewed the work, making her memory "*still* a little peculiar," a statement that casts doubt on the ordinariness of any memory. A few stories seem rehearsed—maybe as a protest against what is perceived as the control of the questioner or as a defense against material that might unwittingly erupt in memory. One artist, describing a work by Michael Asher, doubts whether it took place. "I heard about this piece," she says, "but you know, it maybe even wasn't done." Perhaps disingenuous, her professed uncertainty nonetheless illuminates memory's tricks.

Uncertainty is not confined to content, however. Slips of the tongue, laughter, stuttering, stumbling repetitions, and throat-clearing and other afflictions of the voice also disrupt the coherence of the artists' stories, functioning like metonyms of *an inadequate history*'s broader attempt to disrupt or, as Kolbowski puts it, "slow down" the historicization of Conceptualism. Various kinds of otherness eliminated from dominant histories reappear— multiplicity, voices of women, the voice of feminism, and the unconscious or otherness within.

Orchestrating this reappearance, Kolbowski extends a feminist project she began in the late 1980s, in, for example, "Interview: A Conversation Between" of 1988, a work that, like *an inadequate history*, questions the writing of cultural history. Commissioned by Maryanne Staniszewski for a special section of *Flash Art* devoted to Conceptual Art, "Interview" was a one-page, site-specific artist's project that mimicked the format of standard *Flash Art* interviews.[30] Later, when Kolbowski documented "Interview" in a book of her projects, she reconstructed the context in which the work had originally

INTERVIEW

A

CONVERSATION

BETWEEN

SILVIA KOLBOWSKI

Artist,Writer: I'll begin by asking you to **Writer,Artist**: talk about your recent work . . . **A,W**: or to describe your professional **W,A**: development, or to locate the **A,W**: central theme of . . . or to **W,A**: explain why your work exhibits **A,W**: such consistency or consistent **W,A**: inconsistency . . . your approach to . . . **A,W**: you like to . . . would you **W,A**: agree . . . would you say that . . . **A,W**: influences . . . but couldn't one also say . . . **W,A and A,W**: questions we may not return to later.

W,A: Finding a "voice," in Art, and its institutional modes of academic or journalistic representation, Art History and Criticism . . . **A,W**: (modes which are also parts of everyday "speaking" . . .) **W,A**: the difficulty of writing or imaging a voice which is more than a "register of situations in the world," or a "transitory label of natural events." **A,W**: Voices that attempt more than to indicate with resignation, or underline with emphasis . . . **W,A**: A voice(s) that attempt(s) more than a "revelation" of **A,W**: (petrified?) **W,A**: conditions, more than empty gestures waiting to be contextualized. But while this projected voice would risk "fullness" **A,W**: of a kind, it would not be the fullness of a nostalgic presentation of stable "truths" or "facts" about a culture **W,A**: (for who determines their singularity?). **A,W**: Instead, this voice would articulate the limited truths of contingent histories and realities **W,A**: (without falling back on fantasies of generalized overdetermination). **A,W**: The objects or formulations we send out into the world are of incontrovertibly hybrid parentage: as producers we never achieve sovereign authorship. We may subscribe to a fantasy of free-will in determining whether or not we will be politically engaged. But (regardless of any desire not to be) we are each of us, everyday, engaged by the political, determining and determined by the social.

W,A: (A writer sets out to develop a the-

ory of Renaissance, literary, male "self-fashioning," to identify a period of a "new stress on the executive power of the will", "the role of human autonomy in the construction of identity." As the work progresses he finds his project altered through the discovery of "no moments of pure 'unfettered' subjectivity.") **W,A**: How does the contemporary persona of creativity fit into this schema? As a reassuring model of self-determination?

A,W: The presentation of "impartial" facts: once a viewer or reader absorbs them, is s/he an expert? All expertise has its object, a marriage analogous to a binarism through which lines of power are drawn. The desire for the order of expertise is given impetus by a fantasy of binarism. **W,A**: One way to think about the formation of subjectivity: to see it as being contingent on which of three processes one has access to—the policing, adherence to, or trespassing of lines of power. **A,W**: (Which is not to say that the assumption of these positions—inscribed within fields demarcating codes of sexuality, class, race, among others—is marked by serial logic, rather than by intersecting trajectories or overlapping edges.) **W,A**: A voice that tells a story of irregularities, rather than unified visions, versions—*or* unified objections. A story of overlapping stories, **A,W**: that attempts to recognize and enlarge upon something that is usually unstated in a monolithic "cultural reality," the stakes for women and marginalized groups, in accepting or undoing the pulled-together, monological voice. **W,A**: Someone writes: "She has been warned of the risk she incurs by letting words run off the rails, time and again tempted by the desire to gear herself to the accepted norms . . . **A,W**: Instead of the pulled-together voice, a voice that would risk the fullness of specificity and elaboration, without assuming a pedagogical role, tone, cadence, or expectation, all of which would infan-

talize the reader, viewer by creating two fundamental positions—that of knowledge and its other, **W,A**: To undermine the "Voice of Culture" someone proposes a voice that is "Not too closed (omnipresent, all-knowing, unitary), nor too opened (illusory counter-absence, absolute pluralism)." **A,W**: Is there a potential for putting this kind of voice into play in Art, an institutional set of practices and relations that for the most part pays homage to the self-contained, singular object which stands as a testament to an integrated oeuvre? (Or to seemingly disjointed oeuvres that are pulled together though their institutionalized claim to the quirky individualism of creative genius.) **W,A**: Criticism or art historical texts categorize cultural practices in order to make "sense" of them, "establishing an itinerary or an evolutionary logic," without "placing their own reality in jeopardy." **A,W**: What roles do such practices perform? How are they made to appear "natural"? To disappear? Whose logic is made to stand for an image of social coherency?

A,W: In a tone of approbation or "neutrality," a curator/critic writes of a "direction" in contemporary art: "There is no apparent will to intervene in the social context . . . but rather to step aside from it and celebrate/commemorate the absence of the real." **W,A**: There are conceptions of the real that lie somewhere other than that of a purely relativist or non-existent category (the stuff of most fantasies that afford absolute distance) or that of a concretely definable (positivist) totality that leaves unquestioned the stakes in its particular articulations. (Who "speaks" and to whom, as well as what is left "unspoken"?) History with a capital **A,W**: H, Art with a capital A do not question their "own status as interpretation." If they did, might they have to take symptomological account of themselves, and thus see themselves as part of a larger picture? **W,A**: (Might have to listen for the methodological voices that are embedded within. Acknowledge the politics of methodology in relation to the formation of identity)? **A,W and W,A**: Questions we may return to later . . .

FlashArt 103

2.2 Silvia Kolbowski, "Interview: A Conversation Between," *Flash Art*, November/December 1988. Magazine project. Courtesy the artist.

intervened by placing a photograph of her interview next to a photograph of a *Flash Art* interview with the Marxist cultural critic Fredric Jameson, positioning Jameson's interview, published one year before Kolbowski's work, as one of the absent objects of her site-specific critique.[31] Wearing the camouflage of the magazine's interview layout, she subverted the unitary voice of some of the cultural critics who speak through it (fig. 2.2).

Kolbowski's interview was a self-interview, a conversation "between" Silvia Kolbowski, who is represented by two interlocutors who go by the names of "Artist, Writer"(A, W) and "Writer, Artist" (W, A). The two discuss what W, A calls the difficulty of finding "a voice in Art, and its institutional modes of academic or journalistic representation, Art History and Criticism." Fracturing her own identity, Kolbowski took a step toward forging a voice that might break up what A, W calls the "pulled-together, monological voice" and its unitary versions of cultural reality. "What," ask both A, W and W, A, "are the stakes for women and marginalized groups, in accepting or undoing the pulled-together, monological voice" of "History with a capital H, Art with a capital A?"[32] W, A, hopes that the new voice might tell "a story of irregularities, rather than unified visions, versions—*or* unified objections."[33]

W, A's mention of "unified objections" suggests that the monological cultural histories she protests against include not only traditional but certain critical ones, such as Jameson's famous "Postmodernism, or the Cultural Logic of Late Capitalism," first published a few years earlier, in 1984. In this essay and earlier texts leading up to it, Jameson countered mainstream cultural history by calling for a return, following challenges raised by feminists and others, to a leftist representation of society as a complete totality unified by a substantive foundation of economic antagonism. Asserting that "only Marxism can give us an *adequate* account of . . . the cultural past,"[34] he argued that while "black and ethnic cultures, women's or gay literature, 'naïve' or marginalized folk art and the like" should, like peasant cultures, be reaffirmed, this "affirmation of . . . non-hegemonic cultural voices remains ineffective" if they are not restored "to their proper place in the dialogical system of the social classes."[35] Jameson thus urged a return to a conception of politics governed in advance by class struggle, by, that is, the unified objection to oppression. As a result, he accused feminists and so-called "special-interest" groups of fostering "micropolitics," which, he insisted, fragments and endangers emancipatory politics. In his *Flash Art* interview, Jameson explained that he has attempted to evaluate postmodern culture in relation to the "infrastructural reality of late capitalism" and to create a unitary model of culture and society.[36] Four years earlier, the art historian Craig Owens had defended feminist challenges to Jameson's unified objection as itself oppressive, saying that what concerns feminists "is the distance [totalizing theory] maintains between itself and its objects— a distance which objectifies and masters."[37]

The same year that W, A and A, W raised feminist objections to the unified objection, Kolbowski made a second work about history titled *Enlarged from the Catalogue: The United States of America* (1988). Installed at New York's Postmasters Gallery, *Enlarged from the Catalogue* encouraged a critical reading of the homogenizing version of history told in the catalogue of the American Wing at the Metropolitan Museum of Art. As one element of her exhibition, Kolbowski created her own catalogue, one composed of translucent pages of text interspersed with pages of color photographs. The texts included excerpts from the Metropolitan's catalogue, which, in its words, "offers a unified and coherent view of the periods and cultures represented by the Museum's collections." For example, the Metropolitan catalogue describes eighteenth-century America as a "refined urban society" and recounts the way American Abstract Expressionists expressed the "needs, desires, and impulses shared by all mankind." Along with these excerpts, Kolbowski included four other texts. One is an original story written by Kolbowski in the first-person voice of a fictional museumgoer as she follows and questions the museum's guide. The other texts consist of portions of a slave narrative, of an account of a legal case brought by a Native American woman, and of a 1946 course in English for Chinese students that explains the correct use of gendered pronouns. Kolbowski inserted pages containing the added texts between pages with the excerpts from the Metropolitan catalogue, whose unified history the new texts—the voices of others—at once render visible and interrupt. Kolbowski's rearrangement of the Metropolitan's catalogue puts the museum's unified history out of order, and consequently has something in common with the discontinuity between voices and hands in *an inadequate history*, a discontinuity that, intensified by the focus on memory, also interferes with the coherence of history. Both works, and the *Flash Art* interview, share the goals of feminist history, which, according to Marianne Hirsch and Valerie Smith, "has done more than restore to cultural memory the stories that have been forgotten or erased from the historical record. It has defamiliarized and thus reenvisioned traditional modes of knowing the past," questioning "cultural recall and forgetting."[38]

In comparing Kolbowski's earlier interventions in history to *an inadequate history* I am suggesting that the latter's object of analysis is not the individual artists who speak in the work and who are willingly inadequate. The speakers' anonymity, reinforced by the asynchrony of sound and image, militates against psychobiographical readings. The work is less about the memories of individual selves than it is about *the* self, the subject of memory. Although *an inadequate history* focuses on individual stories, which serve as forceful vehicles of cultural memory, it is the accumulation of stories, the chorus of voices, that holds in check the generalizing, homogenizing tendency of history. The artists' singular voices construct a collective,

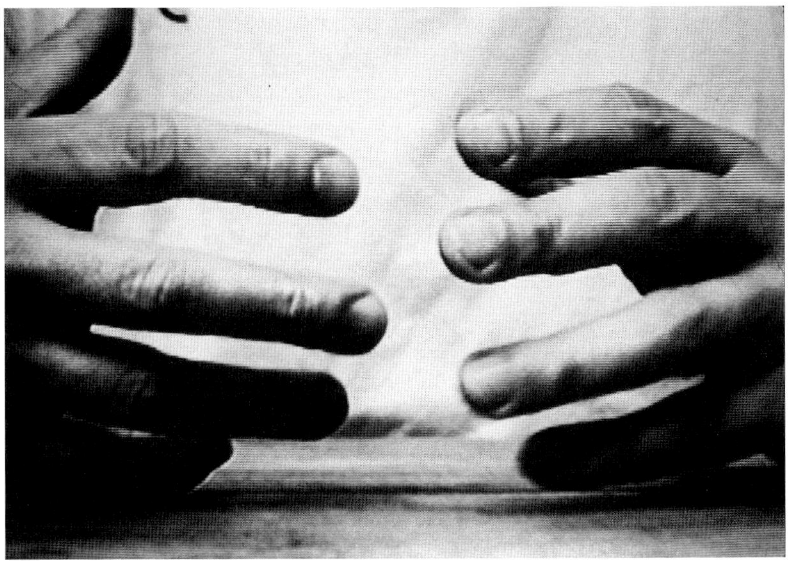

2.3 Silvia Kolbowski, *an inadequate history of conceptual art*, 1998–99. Still, video and audio installation. Courtesy the artist.

though heterogeneous, countermemory, which, given its obvious vicissitudes, cannot be seen as constituting an authentic alternative history, but which instead slows down and tests the work's real object of analysis: the contemporary recall and forgetting of the artistic past. Like *Flash Art*'s interviews with cultural critics in "Interview," contemporary cultural histories are the absent object of Kolbowski's debate-specific project.

But it is not conscious memory alone that interrupts the coherent voice of history in *an inadequate history*, for Kolbowski couples the remembering voices with bodily gestures, and these constitute a second form of memory and of expression, one that supplements the verbal discourse. The artists' hands tap, trace, count fingers, point, indicate, lie perfectly still, or hold and play with objects—cigarette holders, lighters, coffee cups, spoons, glasses, paper clips, and pencils (fig. 2.3, plate 1). One set of hands, which seems to be staging its own performance, incessantly picks at its nails. Such gestures, mingled with the failings of the speaking voice, make up a type of speech that calls into question the idealist notion that language—in the present case, the language of history—directly reflects thought, since gestures represent the bodily discourse of the unconscious, which can only speak indirectly. In putting together gestural and spoken accounts of the past, then, Kolbowski also forges a link between history and psychoanalysis. For one thing, she highlights the presence of a decentered language of the body, but, more importantly, she stages what Juliet Flower MacCannell characterizes as Freud's discovery of "a new *hybrid* form of expression" that *combines* bodily and verbal speech.[39] In a passage that reads like an unwitting description of *an inadequate history*, MacCannell writes that for Freud "words had to be seen against the backdrop of a body that was also saying something, in another mode, about itself and its needs and desire."[40] In the psychoanalytic setting, hybrid discourse often expresses a patient's desire not to know something. If, in a kind of anatomical joke on Conceptual Art, *an inadequate history* focuses on, literally enlarges, the hands of the artist, it does not do so in order to recover traditional procedures of artmaking. After all, the work uses only conceptualist methods. Rather, the prominence of the hands, vehicles of unconscious and bodily memory, restores doubts about traditional procedures of history-making, whose repressions, as we have seen, produce histories of Conceptual Art that, among other things, don't want to know about feminism.

What does memory—and its relation to the unconscious—do to history? The philosopher of history Dominick LaCapra says that memory, despite its lapses and tricks, because of its lapses and tricks, is informative. Precisely because it represents its past object inaccurately, it tells us about the anxiety-ridden nature of the reception of that object,[41] foregrounding the mechanism of repression that produces stories about the past. Consequently, memory poses questions to history: What historical problems are still alive or invested with emotion? Why? When are contradictions and gaps in historical texts symptoms of underlying problems? How is the historian implicated in the historical problems she treats? What is the historian's transferential relation to the past?[42] How, that is, do his fantasies, conflicts, and desire not to know bear on the story he writes? Saul Friedlander regards such questions as especially pertinent when the historian is representing "a recent past or a past considered to be of cardinal relevance for the identity of a given group," as in histories of Conceptual Art. In these instances, says Friedlander, the writer of history cannot avoid the transferential relation.[43] Against historians who position memory as the other of history, either denigrating or elevating it, LaCapra and Friedlander agree that, while history and memory are not the same, there can be no clear-cut opposition between the two. After all, Friedlander reminds us, "historicization itself is part of the construction (or reconstruction) of memory."[44] History and memory test each other, and "while historiography is in principle the critical eye scanning the constructs of memory, when it deals with a past that is present the historian may be unaware of presuppositions and a priori positions."[45] In such a case, Friedlander implies, memory can function as the critical partner, as it does in *an inadequate history*, where it scans the current historicization of Conceptual Art.

I began this essay by suggesting that *an inadequate history* helps produce the metahistorical space that Michael Asher called for in 1989, a space that, instead of offering a history of Conceptual Art per se, meditates on how that history is written. Kolbowski creates this space by bringing the frailties of memory to bear on, and undo, the rigidities of history. Precisely in undoing history, however, her work *makes* history, at least as that activity has been defined by Michel de Certeau. "What we initially call history is nothing more than a narrative," says Certeau,

> When we receive this text, an operation has already been performed; it has eliminated otherness and its dangers in order to retain only those fragments of the past which are locked into the puzzle of a present time, integrated into the stories that an entire society tells during evenings at fireside. These signs that are arranged into a legend can be analyzed, however, in another way. Here another history begins. It tends to establish heteronomy ("That's what happened") within the homogeneity of language ("That's what they say," or "That's what we read.") It produces the historical dimension within the element of a test. More strictly speaking, it is tantamount to *making* history.[46]

For Certeau the term "making history" does not merely foreground the constructed or written nature of historical narratives. To make history for him is to make history inadequate, which is to say, to test and unmake those narratives by exposing them to the presence of others and otherness, a project I earlier equated with an "ethics of failure." The term, as I said, belongs to Jacqueline Rose, though the concept it signifies is shared by many. In a remarkable essay about war and psychoanalysis, Rose recalls Freud's speculation that one cause of war is the conviction of total, adequate knowledge.[47] Following D. W. Winnicott and Virginia Woolf, she emphasizes the importance of being willing to fail and of challenging, even ridiculing, professional searches for adequate knowledge. In 1983, Craig Owens challenged the way the profession of art history had organized itself by neglecting the feminist voice in postmodern culture, the voice that, he argued, questioned the totalizing ambitions of cultural histories and listened to "the discourse of others."[48] Twenty years later, the feminist voice is once again in danger of suppression by art history, but it emerges in Kolbowski's inadequate history, insisting that histories fail, and are therefore made, in the ethico-political moment, when, instead of reacting triumphally against alterity, they respond to it by calling into question and perhaps letting go of their own foundations.

3

Darkness: The Emergence of James Welling

The photographic art of James Welling came to critical attention in the early 1980s at Metro Pictures, a gallery in New York City.[1] Welling appeared in the gallery's inaugural exhibition in 1980 and in a second group show called "Photograph," which was held the following year. He had two solo exhibitions there in 1981 and 1982 of, respectively, his aluminum foil and drapery photographs and also presented *Diary of Elizabeth and James Dixon (1840–41)/ Connecticut Landscapes*, a work he had begun in 1977.

At the time, Metro Pictures was frequented by a group of critics who had embarked on the task of theorizing the meaning of postmodernism in the visual arts. For them, the gallery's founding had the quality of a manifesto; it announced the arrival and set forth the principles of a new body of work destined to unsettle established aesthetic paradigms and alter our understanding of art. In addition to Welling, the artists included Troy Brauntuch, Jack Goldstein, Louise Lawler, Sherrie Levine, Robert Longo, Richard Prince, Cindy Sherman, and Laurie Simmons. Metro Pictures gathered these artists into a constellation and made it possible to see coherence in their work. All took photographs. All questioned the myth of photographic transparency that inspired traditional documentary photography, the myth that a photograph or, for that matter, any visual image reveals meanings that are located in the object it is a picture of. At the same time, all rejected the idea that informed the alternative to documentary, art photography, that a work of art is a self-contained totality transcending the circumstances of its existence. I think it is safe to say that no one worried about elevating photography to the status of art since it was precisely the elevated status of art they were challenging as they made their work against an entire aesthetic tradition organized around a belief in the autonomy of the aesthetic image. This tradition shut its eyes to the meaning of vision and, especially, its relation to desire.

Using diverse strategies, these artists took part in what Roland Barthes called "the structuralist activity," whose aim was to reveal the social functions, rather than fixed truths, of cultural objects such as photographs and works of art.[2] This activity was hardly confined to artists who showed at Metro Pictures, which was only one gallery that nurtured the growth of critical postmodernism. A recent catalogue lists the following artists who, along with Welling, were "part of a larger critical re-evaluation of photography in contemporary art": Vikky Alexander, Richard Baim, Ellen Brooks, Ellen Carey, James Casebere, Sarah Charlesworth, Barbara Ess, Louise Lawler, Sherrie Levine, Barbara Kruger, Allan McCollum, Richard Prince, Cindy Sherman, and Laurie Simmons.[3] Others were Victor Burgin, Silvia Kolbowski, and Alan Sekula. By exploring how meaning is produced by cultural structures, not God or nature, artists like these rendered visible the conventions that construct seemingly natural meanings in visual images and thus destroyed the illusion that the significance of an image derives from a source outside the social world. In a deconstructive spirit they challenged the belief that an order of meaning exists in itself, in the image itself, as presence. Consequently, they turned attention away from the internal relationship among the elements that composed the image—in this they were indebted to Minimalism—and toward the relationship between the image and what lies outside its frame, an exterior that includes the viewer, the human subject, who was the real object of structuralist inquiry. As Barthes explained, the structuralist, unlike the humanist subject is not "man endowed with meanings but man fabricating meanings": *homo significans*.[4] In the absence of a substantive identity, *homo significans* creates himself in a process of identification with images, which means that autonomy is simply the effect of a disavowed dependency.

To suggest that visual images produce rather than reveal or, what amounts to the same thing, conceal meanings, which are located not only outside any individual image but outside representation altogether, is not, as critics of postmodernism often fear, to question the existence of reality in the sense of a world external to thought. Artists engaged in a critique of visual representation raised an entirely different question: withdrawing the ground of the image, they treated it as a position determined by a relationship with a subject. The withdrawal of the ground has two, interrelated effects: it casts doubt on the claim often made by *homo significans* that its images *are* the world and thwarts our ability to construe the world as an object for the self. An oft-quoted remark expresses Welling's general agreement with the postmodern gesture of making visible the uncertainty that is the condition of representation: "I'm not interested in reproducing the world so much as creating a discourse on the world. . . . I'm asking questions which I think post-modern photography can address."[5] For Welling, photography is a way of seeing the world.

Homo significans is the "you" that was greeted and interrogated in Barbara Kruger's now classic photomontages of the early 1980s, which used the technique of direct address to acknowledge the viewer's presence and reveal the image's relational nature.[6] *Homo significans* is also the arranger of pictures referred to by Louise Lawler in the photographic works that she calls collectively *Arrangements of Pictures*. Lawler's early exhibitions at Metro Pictures were installations that grouped works by other artists against colored rectangles painted on the gallery's walls. Lawler also took photographs of art objects in contexts of display: museums, galleries, homes, corporations, and urban spaces.[7] Her rearrangements of these existing arrangements of pictures demonstrated that the meaning of works of art depends on institutional circumstances and also called attention to the desires that underlie seemingly objective, disinterested modes of aesthetic presentation. Likewise, Cindy Sherman addressed *homo significans*, simultaneously eliciting and thwarting his quest for the identity of the woman in her photographic series *Untitled Film Stills* of 1977–82. And Sherrie Levine invited him to observe himself searching for an original image—and hoping to find a stable meaning—in her framed photographs of photographic reproductions of masterpieces of art history, some of which were photographs from the start: *Untitled (After Walker Evans)* (1981), *Untitled (After Egon Schiele)* (1982), *Untitled (After Ernst Ludwig Kirchner)* (1982), and *Untitled (After Alexander Rodchenko)* (1984). All of these artists' works refused to take shape as images in whose presence the controlling subject can develop, invisibly. Instead, they turned toward the subject, not to solicit participation but to raise critical questions about desire in visual representation: Why do we look? What are we looking for? The closer these works advanced toward the viewer, the less they seemed to contain a hidden, stable truth to which the viewer might penetrate and around which the meaning of the image might reach closure, and the more vertiginous the subject's fall into uncertainty.

To illustrate the turn toward the subject in the art of the early 1980s, I have referred to four women artists whose work influenced feminist theories of subjectivity in visual representation. In part I have done so to recall the connection between feminism and the critique of modernism by artists like those who showed alongside Welling. Whereas the dominant version of modernism that was codified in the writings of Clement Greenberg adhered to an ideal of the artwork as a complete spatial totality, which, grasped in the moment of aesthetic contemplation, places the viewing subject in a position of mastery, feminists explored this position and the image on which it depends as fantasies that are constructed and maintained through the subordination, appropriation, and repression of others. Against the pursuit of mastery, they issued an ethical plea for what Gayatri Spivak, in another context, called "a radical acceptance of vulnerability."[8]

But there is another, more specific, reason that I chose four artists whose work was informed by feminist ideas about visual representation: On the present occasion—a Welling retrospective—I feel obligated to respond to the way in which such work has been devalued in recent literature about Welling, a devaluation that, as I shall argue, also reduces the significance of Welling's art. Michael Fried and Walter Benn Michaels extract Welling's photography from its early context and set up a hierarchical opposition between Welling and other postmodern photographers, describing his work not simply as different from but at odds with and elevated above theirs. To begin with, Fried says that Welling repudiates Minimalism's treatment of the work of art as a subject-object relationship—which Fried terms "'bad' objecthood"—in favor of a notion of the transcendent artwork, whose state of completeness both depends upon and triumphs over the partiality of the things pictured in the photograph. In this aesthetic model, the viewing subject, too, achieves perfection—a state of being without flaw that Fried once famously called "grace"—as he exercises a vision capable of grasping the aesthetic totality.[9] Perfection, of course, is a condition from which it is possible only to fall, so it is unsurprising when Fried concludes that Welling's "deepest and most constant concerns"—especially his concern with overcoming partiality—implies "a rejection of an entire set of [postmodern] attitudes that would grant to artistic activity *only* the roles of performance, appropriation, demystification, critique."[10]

Michaels, too, creates a Greenbergian Welling, accomplishing this in two steps: like Fried, he defines the work of art as a complete totality, and he reduces photography to the empirical fact of reproduction. Both avoid subjectivity. In a talk on "Photography and Art" delivered in 1992 Michaels said that a Welling photograph can "assert its own shape against the shape of the [partial] objects it's a photograph of" and therefore, unlike "the postmodernist practice of photographers like Sherman," resolve "the problem posed for photography as art."[11] An earlier text claims that Welling's work differs from postmodern photography because it "insists on" rather than "mistrusts" photographic representation: "Welling's photographs are essentially photographs of some object" because, says Michaels, they make clear the difference between the surface of the photograph and the surfaces of the objects photographed. For example, in Welling's early suites of aluminum foil, drapery, and diary photographs, "the foil is crumpled in a way that the photograph isn't; the cloth is folded and the paper is bent or curved."[12] For Michaels, the difference between the photograph's literal and depicted shapes proves that Welling refuses to give in to what Michaels mistakenly regards as postmodernism's denial of the independent existence of the objects that photographs are of, their referents. It also proves that Welling holds firmly to the view that photography's essence lies in its status as the product of a mechanical recording device, a camera. A photograph, says Michaels, is a representing thing, repeating the positivist dream of early photographers in which photography presents an object as it exists outside the deformations of human language without, as Alan Sekula puts it, "the mediation of hand or tongue."[13] Michaels concludes that in calling attention to the referent—what Fried calls "good objecthood"—Welling's photographs "eliminate the position of the human subject" and instead "insist upon the position of the camera." He then opposes Welling's "insistence on" against postmodernism's "problematization of" the referent.

It is, of course, true that postmodernism raised questions about the status of the referent in representation, refusing, as I have already argued, to close the gap between image and reality and protesting against the subject's claim that its images are the world. Michaels, however, misconstrues the nature of the protest, characterizing it as a denial of the referent, in the sense of the world taken as an object of discourse, which he in turn confuses with reality, in the sense of the world external to discourse. Evading the basic premise of postmodernism in the visual arts—that representation produces an object as something to be *comprehended*—Michaels arrives at the conclusion that postmodernists are merely contemporary incarnations of late nineteenth-century opponents of paper money. "The hard money mistrust of representation," he says, is "now called postmodernism."[14] Absurd as it seems to say so, however, postmodernists believe paper money is real—that it has value—precisely because they don't believe that "real money" is real, in the sense of possessing intrinsic rather than socially produced value.

Michaels suggests that because Cindy Sherman and Sherrie Levine ignore photography's essence as a mechanical recording device they resemble Walter Benjamin, who also failed to appreciate fully that photography is constituted by the mechanical. Michaels is correct in a sense, for, as Eduardo Cadava points out in an essay on Benjamin and photography, Benjamin approached photography in terms not of the mechanical but rather of the technical, though translations of his writings have suggested otherwise.[15] The difference is that technology, as Benjamin said, "is obviously not a purely scientific phenomenon. It is also an historical one."[16] Similarly, artists involved in a critique of representation did not circumscribe photography by the machinery of science. For them, a photograph was neither a likeness nor a mechanical reproduction of the world but something far more mysterious: an image, something that needs a subject to function at all. Michaels's criticism is marked by inversion: Reducing photography to the empirical fact of mechanical reproduction, he claims that it was postmodernists like Sherman and Levine who reduced photography's possibility as art and who, by contrast with Welling, must "content themselves with commentary on the impossibility of originality, inevitability of appropriation, etc."[17]

To place Welling over and against other artists who critically reevaluated photography in the 1980s is to diminish the complexity and difficulty of his difference from them. For Welling's photographs *were* different, and the difference could be disquieting, in a poetic sort of way. For one thing, the aluminum foil and drapery series consist of single-frame still photographs in contrast to the photomontages or combinations of images that comprised the work of many, though certainly not all, other artists involved in a critique of visual representation. For another, the photographs in these series seemed at first sight to lack any resemblance to objects in the external world or to bear only the most obscure likeness to natural appearances. Though not technically abstract, they could be regarded as abstractions, where abstraction is a state in which something is drawn or taken away—in Welling's case, the photographed object. As Rosalind Krauss puts it, the issue in Welling's early photographs was one of "holding the referent at bay, creating as much delay as possible between seeing the image and understanding what it was of."[18]

In 1984, Welling had made it clear that this was precisely the visual process he hoped to set in motion with the draperies and aluminum foils. Looking at these works involves the viewer in an ambiguous alternation between abstract and documentary readings: "From a distance, the photograph reads as a dark rectangle on a white field. Closer, its manifest subject is visible and the viewer is forced to ask, what is it?"[19] The subject matter of the second series is draped velvet fabric, whose darkness overspreads the visual field, and on which lie scattered flakes of white phyllo dough, like patches of light. The photographed object, however, is only the manifest subject. As the caption of one drapery photograph—*In search of . . .*—indicates, the latent, postmodern subject is the viewer's quest for meaning in the image. For Welling, the materials he photographed were important because they

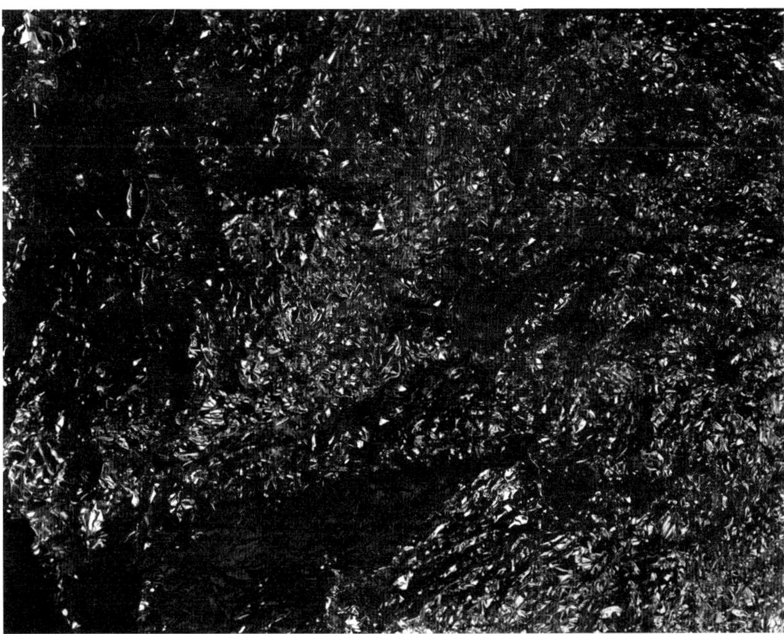

3.1 James Welling, *The Wayfarer*, 1980. Gelatin silver contact print. Courtesy the artist.

generate images and thus are capable of fulfilling, or of promising to fulfill, the viewer's desire: "The subject is not the materials, but the procedures (tearing, folding, scattering) from which the image is constructed." Welling named other photographs in the series after images the material generated, at least in his imagination: *Island*, *The Waterfall*, and *Wreckage*. In these, the phyllo dough flakes no longer read as patches of light against dark fields but as pools of foam from rushing water or the debris of a shipwreck. Of course, it was precisely in the act of making the material visible as a material that generates images that the artist withdrew the image and, more to the point, destroyed its illusion of substantive meaning. Welling framed the work's real subject matter—the conditions of photographic representation—in such a way that, as he put it, "it always gives way to uncertainty" (figs. 3.1 and 3.2).

Still, it is not entirely accurate to say that Welling chose his materials solely because they lend themselves to formal operations of image making, for they also have iconographic significance. More than once, for example, Welling has enumerated the symbolic connotations of draped fabric. In 1984 he wrote, "With the photographs of drapes I'm involved in the numerous things draped fabric evokes: flags, drapes, curtains, bunting, sails, interiors, etc."[20] He enlarged the inventory in 1988 in a short text dis-

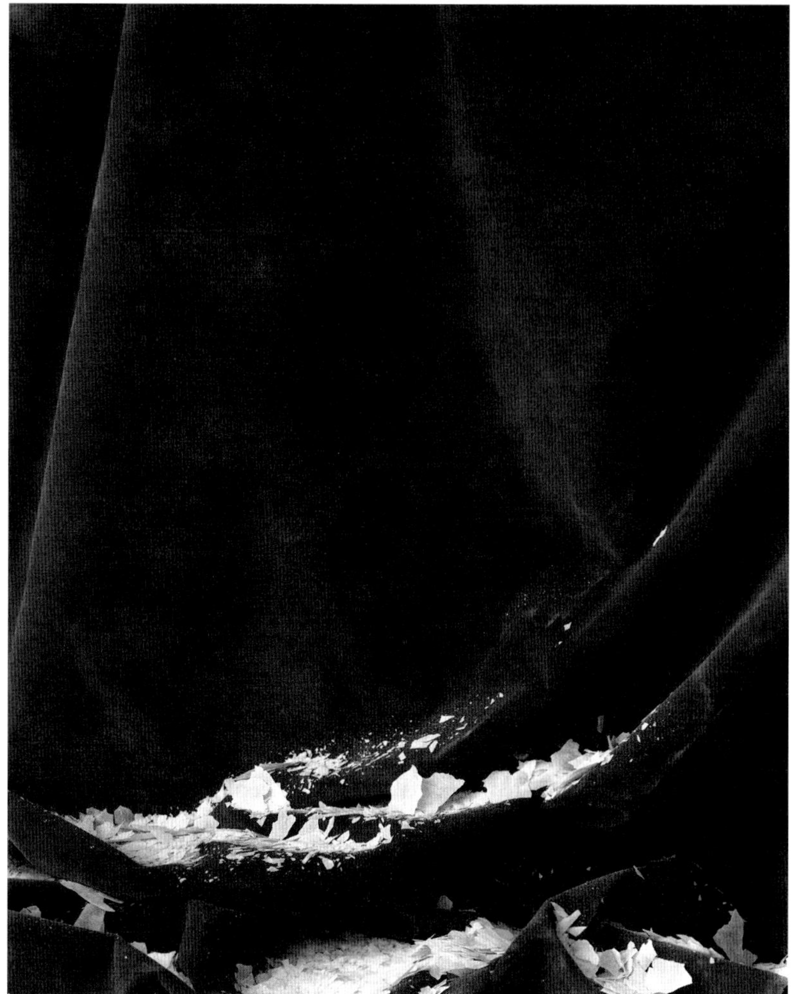

3.2 James Welling, *The Waterfall*, 1981. Gelatin silver contact print. Courtesy the artist.

tributed at an exhibition at New York's Christine Burgin Gallery, where he showed photographs that revisited the theme of draped fabric, this time without the flakes of dough. The text reads like a Baudelairean roll call of the associations—what the poet called "correspondences"—awakened in viewers when they see objects that send "echoes from afar":

> Photographs titled with roman numerals of brown fabric, of rust color, of wind billowing folds, of all the things drapery connotes, a feeling of mortality, of elegy and also of sails, flags, bunting, of things which in them-

selves are worth considering, not waiting to reveal or of something missing, of things although distant still with us, of Brown Decade interiors, of other interiors and exteriors, and also of fields, of brick factories, or railroads, of other things . . .

Drapery, the object that awakens associations, also evokes photography itself, which, however much it promises to deliver the presence of its object, only hands over "something missing."

The difference between Welling's early photographs and the work of other postmodern artists, then, was hardly of the order of a disagreement and, in an important respect, was more apparent than real. For while it is true that Welling did not examine how images signify in specific social institutions such as, say, cinema, television, advertising, and museums, as other artists did, his exploration of abstraction consisted in drawing away the photographed object, clouding the visual field, and troubling vision understood as simple recognition, and therefore served only to stress the definition of the image that informed all postmodern photography, no matter how figurative its content: an image is a representation of an absent object. David Joselit is right, then, to argue that Welling's early work erodes the security of any presumed boundary between abstract and figurative representation. He is also right to stress the commonality between Welling's aluminum foil photographs and the strategy of appropriation used by such artists as Levine, Prince, and Kruger. According to Joselit, appropriation, or the act of rephotographing and reframing fine art and commercial images, "functioned as a form of abstraction by demonstrating that meaning is fundamentally arbitrary and contingent upon the conditions of display."[21] Nonetheless, Joselit does draw a distinction—correctly, I think—between the concept of abstraction that can be applied to appropriated images, on the one hand, and the kind of abstraction that informs Welling's aluminum foil photographs, on the other. In the latter, he says, "the photographic field is hunted back to its constituent elements . . . light and shadow are unmoored from the contours of any recognizable object."[22] For Joselit, "Welling's significance as an artist hinges on his multifaceted meditations on the possibility of abstraction in photography."[23]

"James Welling: Abstract" affirms Joselit's claim but also poses a question, one to which I shall return: Why is Welling's ongoing interest in photographic abstraction significant? The exhibition includes completely abstract series of photographs that span the artist's career: *Tile Photographs* (1985), *New Abstractions* (1998), *Mystery Photographs* (2000), *Degradés* (1991–98), and *Tricolor Photographs* (2000–2001). It includes photographs like the early *Aluminum Foils* and the *New Drapes* (2000), which, while not totally abstract, "hold the referent at bay." It contains the *Light Sources* (1992–98), a suite of photographs in which the object can sometimes be recognized and sometimes not. True, there are documentary series, which seem to counteract the tendency toward abstraction—*Los Angeles Architecture* (1976) and *New Landscapes* (1999), for example. But their presence reproduces at the level of the exhibition an ambiguity that haunts Welling's individual photographs and series of photographs—between recognizability and unrecognizability of the photographed object and between resolution and irresolution of the photographic image. It thus highlights the threat of abstraction that pervades Welling's entire photographic project.

I use the term *threat* instead of Joselit's *possibility* because it suggests a certain vulnerability to abstraction that underlies representation and subjectivity, a vulnerability that Welling's photographs register and even dramatize. In proposing that Welling's abstractions dramatize vulnerability and, what is more, that this accounts for their significance and their aching beauty, I diverge from Joselit who, like Michaels and Fried, ultimately assimilates Welling's abstractions to modernism and therefore to the ideals of unity, presence, and completeness—in short, invulnerability—that formed the foundations of modernism. For example, Joselit claims that in *Los Angeles Architecture* and *Light Sources* the artist's treatment of light "does for photography what modernism did for painting: it captures volume as a play of surface."[24] Later, he analyzes the *New Abstractions*, a series of black-and-white abstract images that were generated by a three-step process in which Welling first placed strips of Bristol board on photosensitive sheets and exposed them to light, digitally scanned the resulting photograms or cameraless photographs to make negatives, and, finally, produced photographs from the negatives. Joselit ties the *New Abstractions* to modernism by means of the notion of medium specificity: because they are photographs generated from other photographs, they "achieve a form of nonobjectivity specific to the medium." What's more, he interprets the resemblance between the *New Abstractions* and the Abstract Expressionist canvases of Franz Kline as an explicit statement of the artist's solidarity with the ethos of gestural modernism.

Sending Welling back into a modernism based on an assumption of the plenitude of the aesthetic image, Joselit steps back from the implications of his earlier, important insight that there can be no bright line between abstraction and figuration since the meaning of a photograph is fundamentally arbitrary. For to acknowledge the arbitrary nature, the groundlessness, of the photographic image is to place photography in the realm of language, the paradigm of all representational systems, and this necessitates the further recognition that photography is structured like a language; it has no positive or final terms, only differences between elements, a condition that makes plenitude impossible. In language, meaning continuously appears and continuously fades or resolves and dissolves—to use photographic terminology, one based on the differentiation not of linguistic elements but of light and darkness. Photography and therefore knowledge and vision, for which photography serves as a figure, are vulnerable to endlessly repeated abstraction, where abstraction is a state in which both the photographed object and the clarity of the image are drawn or taken away. Vulnerable, too, is the viewing and knowing subject, who depends on the image. What distinguishes Welling's description of his work as a discourse—a use of language to talk about the world—from modernist interpretations of his art is that whereas for the latter photography, whether it is seen as arbitrary or motivated in relation to its referent, is canceled by the unity and stability of the aesthetic image, the basic premise of Welling's approach is that there can be no stability of image or subject. Both are objects in crisis. Nor does Welling's work treat instability as a "failure" to be overcome in moments of visual mastery. Instead of inviting triumphalist reactions, instability should be acknowledged to avoid transforming the world into our possession; we should, as Jacqueline Rose has urged, "hang on to failure."[25] Many critics remark that light is a recurrent theme of Welling's photographs, and this is accurate insofar as light is understood as the condition of the emergence of—at once—image and subject. More important, however, is that the persistent tendency of Welling's photography toward abstraction awakens us to the fact that, as Cadava writes, in homage to Benjamin, "the light of photography never arrives alone. It is always attended by darkness."[26]

As far back as 1974, in a black-and-white videotape of ashes in a fireplace, Welling set the stage for his approach to photography as a language that focuses on the relations between light and darkness, past and present, life and death (fig. 3.3). Sarah J. Rogers notes the self-reflexiveness of *Ashes:* observing light in the shallow space of a fireplace, Welling wanted to create a similar space in his art.[27] The analogy is not simply formal, however, since the still, dry ashes that remain after the light of the fire call to mind that other motionless product of the action of light, a photograph. The stills from *Ashes,* like the later draperies and aluminum foils they resemble, illustrate the aesthetic strategy that Craig Owens, borrowing from the vocabulary of literary criticism, which in turn borrowed from André Gide, called photography *en abyme:* "It tells us in a photograph what a photograph is."[28] Photography *en abyme* pictures its own activity and in doing so challenges the seeming

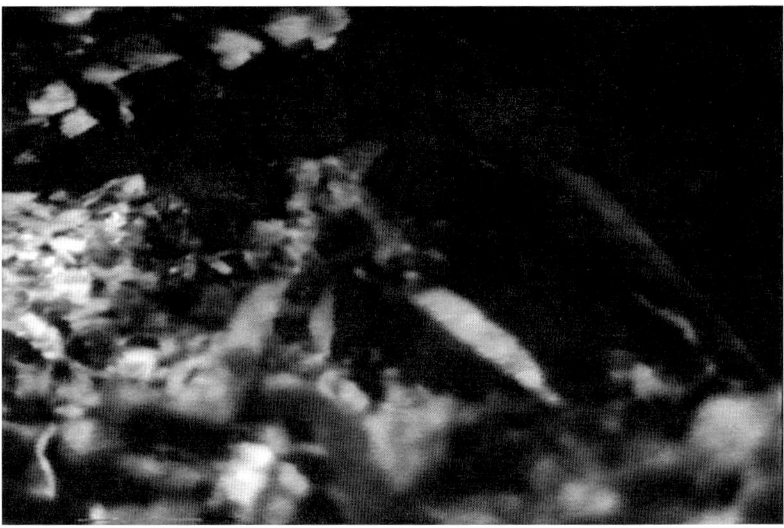

3.3 James Welling, *Ashes*, 1974. Still, helical-scan videotape. Courtesy the artist.

naturalness of the photographic image, raising "serious doubts about [photographs'] capacity to convey anything but a sense of loss, of absence."[29] *Ashes* goes even further, connecting photography not only to the absence but also to the destruction of its object and likening the light that fixes a photographic image to that of a consuming flame which reduces the photographed to ashes.

As a figure of photography, *Ashes* brings to mind a sentence that Louis Daguerre sent to Nicéphore Niepce around the time of the birth or, better, what Gregory Batchen calls the conception, of photography: "I am burning with desire to see your experiments from nature."[30] Like Daguerre's words, *Ashes* discloses the longing embedded in presumably detached acts of scientific observation, in, that is, the dream of knowing and seeing with which photography has long been intimately involved. Yet even as the metaphor of ashes links photography to an irresistible drive to control by looking, it works in opposition to that control, raising the specter of the fragility of the photographer's look. For just as the light of photography can devour the photographed object, so can it deprive the viewing subject of the image. As Welling once explained to me, photography is not the production of an image by light so much as the control of light to produce an image—itself a form of control—against the danger of darkness, which haunts photography in the form of both too much and too little light.

A few years after *Ashes*, in *Diary of Elizabeth and James Dixon (1840–41)/*

Connecticut Landscapes, which he began in 1977 and worked on for nearly ten years, Welling again focused on the ambiguities inherent in photography's opening to light. This work makes explicit photography's essential connection to memory, which, because what is remembered has fallen into oblivion, also recalls us to darkness. *Diary/Landscapes* is composed of two sets of images placed side-by-side. One set consists of photographs of a diary kept by Welling's great-great-grandparents during a journey abroad. Discovered by the artist in 1976, the diary dates from 1840, the year after the announcement of the discovery of photography. Welling's photographs are close-up shots that show portions of the diary's handwritten pages. The diary is so close that we can see the texture of the paper and in some images ink that has seeped through from the other side of a page. Areas of the pages are illuminated; others are cast into shadow. Some pages are pierced by stems of dried flowers and miniature evergreen branches that were obviously gathered and pressed by the diary's authors as souvenirs of their trip. Visual aids to a text, the mementos articulate the relation between vision and language, as does Welling's transformation of the viewer of the images into a reader of texts. Like ashes, the mementos also serve as figures of photography: for one thing, they are remains and, for another, they flatten into a surface the things of the world that the diary's authors passionately collected as they struggled to preserve the experience of their trip. Welling paired each image of the diary with an image from a second series of photographs that documents other journeys, repeated trips taken by the artist through contemporary, snow-covered landscapes in Connecticut, which had been not only the home of the diary's authors but also the artist's own home. Wintry light from overcast skies, occasionally broken by the sun, defines these exquisitely detailed scenes. The play of light and shadow echoes that in the diary photographs. Both echo the act of memory, which comes with forgetfulness (fig. 3.4).

Rosalind Krauss reads *Diary/Landscapes* as an allegory of the violation inherent in the advent of light and of the vision it makes possible:

> What is the wound inflicted by the parting pages of a diary written in 1840 and now, for the first time, opened in 1977? A private document that had stowed away in darkness not only the thoughts of its writer but as well the tiny physical mementos she had preserved there against the impact of time—leaves, fern-fronds, petals—this was the diary of a young woman's voyage to Europe. For the first time in over a century light floods those pages, triumphing over them, ravishing them.[31]

Yet while it is true that Welling exposes the diary to light and to the photographer's and viewer's ravishing look, at the same time he protects or shades

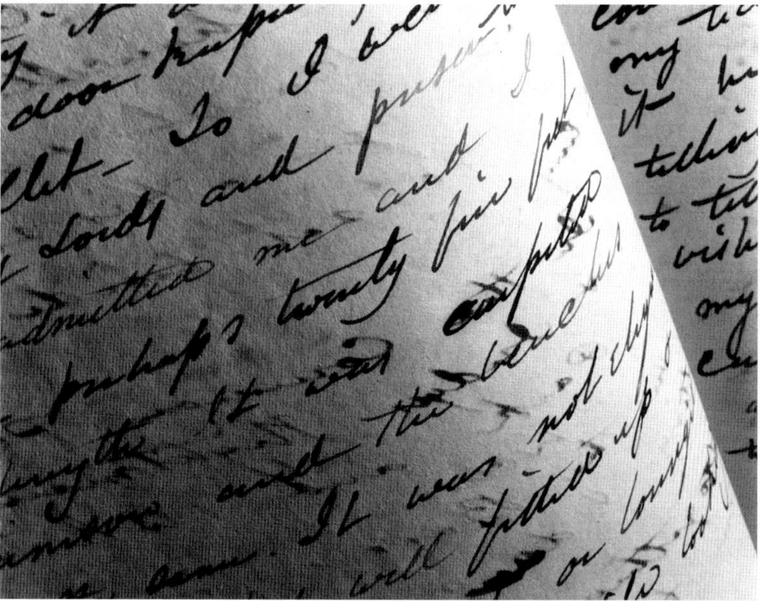

3.4 (*above and facing page*) James Welling, *Diary of Elizabeth and James Dixon (1840–41)/ Connecticut Landscapes*, 1977–86. Gelatin silver contact print. Courtesy the artist.

it. The extreme close-up position from which the pages are seen, the very emblem of the photographer's burning desire, renders the text illegible, as do the shadows that eclipse sections of the pages, though, to be sure, we receive tantalizing glimpses. In addition, as Krauss says, the diary itself "delivers a kind of counterblow to the light" because it brings with it an uncanny sense of something past recurring, a sense that disrupts the security of the present, as well as the self-presence of photographer and viewer.[32] The experience of uncanniness does not come only with photographs of certain objects such as diaries; it is built into the very structure of photography, which possesses the strange combination of spatial immediacy and temporal anteriority that Barthes called its "having-been-there" quality.[33] Photographic space is disorienting because, never free of the impact of time, it exposes the past to the present in a way that at once illuminates and darkens each.

Diary/Landscapes stages this mutual de-constitution. Pictures of a diary kept by the artist's departed relatives appear next to pictures of the artist's former home. The work does not just picture a memoir but is itself explicitly memoirist and thus brings the artist into what Mikhail Bakhtin, in a study of the novel, called "a zone of contact" with the world he depicts.[34]

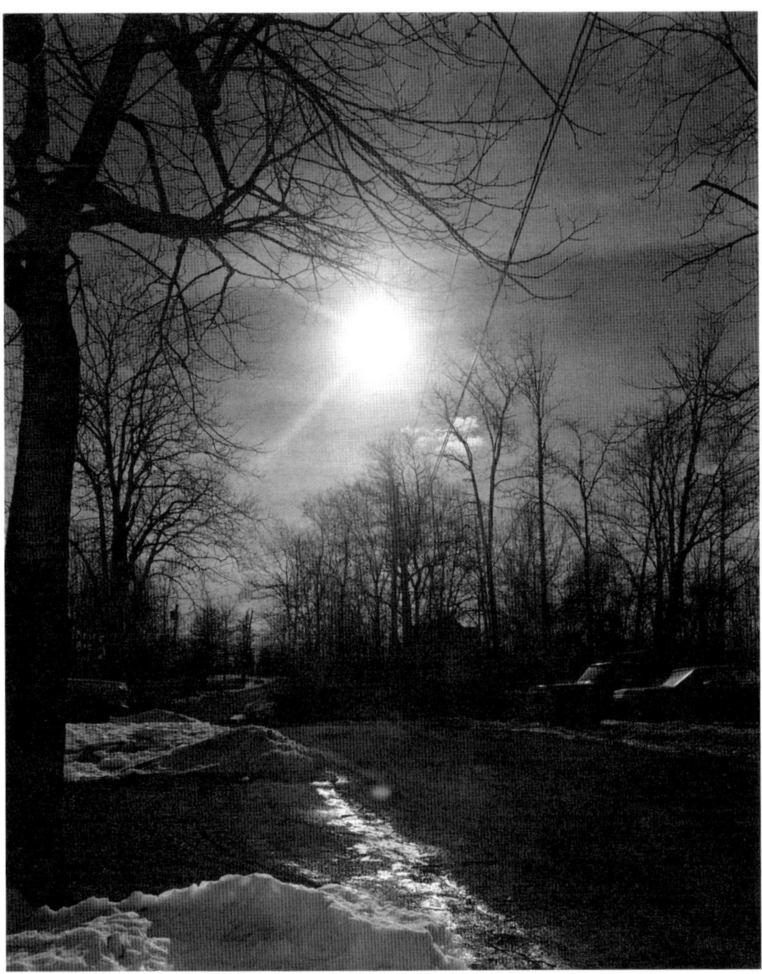

At the same time, the photographic memoir brings the distant past it portrays into contact with an unfinished present. Photographed and photographic object are seen in relation not to a mechanical recording device but to a human subject that both keeps alive and, as Krauss suggests, ravishes a past, whose surfacing simultaneously interrupts the present. Cadava writes beautifully about this aspect of the photographic experience, noting that Walter Benjamin's ideas about the process of reading novels apply equally to the process of looking at photographs. A certain question, says Cadava, "keeps the reader's interest burning: how to learn that death awaits us?"[35] Benjamin, in his essay "The Storyteller," which inspired Cadava's comments, writes that the reader of a novel looks for characters "from whom he derives the meaning of life," and therefore "must, no matter what, know in advance that he will share their experience of death."[36] Welling creates such characters in *Diary/Landscapes*, a work whose meaning depends upon yet exceeds its autobiographical specificity for, like *Ashes*, it tells us what photography is, revealing that to look at a photograph is to take a winter's journey: a photograph fails to deliver the security of a presence because, putting the viewer in touch with the mortality of the photographed object, it recalls him to his own mortality.

Michael Fried draws attention to the dark tonality of Welling's early photographs, rightly observing that it is "one of the formal leitmotifs of his art"[37] Fried explains that the darkness of these works is the effect of various technical operations, which include the "carefully controlled underexposure" of some of Welling's earliest photographs and, in later works, innovative printing processes that, as Fried points out, actually entail an excess of light and make darkening seem to be "a function of a special sensitivity in the recording surface rather than being inherent in the photographed scene."[38] According to Fried, viewers may be unaware of exactly how Welling produces the effect of darkness, but they nonetheless receive an "impression of technical and artistic command." For Fried, the darkness of Welling's photographs attests to the artist's control of his medium and ultimately to the work's aestheticism.[39] No one can doubt Welling's technical skill. Metaphorically, however, which is to say, in terms of its significance, literal darkness in his early work performs a different, even opposing function: inseparable from abstraction, which draws away both object and image, it testifies not to the mastery but to the vulnerability of photography's subject.

Welling continued to stress vulnerability in later works, such as the *Degradés* of 1991–98, which are not always dark but sometimes light, even colorful. Like all photographs, however, the *Degradés* were made in darkness. Welling held sheets of photographic paper under an enlarger, which shone light onto them. During each exposure, he slowly moved the paper to mark it with the minute, imperceptible transitions of light that produce the gradual range of painted or photographed colors that the French call a *dégradé*. He then placed the paper in a lightproof box and processed it in a color processor. The result was a series of abstract photograms that do not record an object but, rather, time, movement, and, especially, the artist's difficulty in controlling the exposure to light, a difficulty manifested in effects such as bands of bright color that emerge abruptly in some images or, in others, a shading not into a slightly different color but into tones of gray and black.

The title of the work encapsulates themes that have always been central to Welling's art. In addition to its specialized meaning for the arts, the noun *dégradé* is phonetically indistinguishable from the verb *dégrader*, which means both to shade off and, like the English *degrade*, to lower. *Se dégrader* means to lower oneself or fall into disrepair. In the abstract *Degradés*, as in the nearly abstract aluminum foil and drapery photographs, Welling invented a system, or, as he once called it, a machine, for generating the differences—in this case, gradations of color—that make an image and therefore meaning possible. Shading creates variations not only in light and color but also in meaning. However, the same system makes an image impossible since, emerging from a play of differences between elements rather than from a ground, the closed space of an image cannot be detached from a sense of what endangers the security of that space. An excess of light indeed produces darkness, for it threatens the image and interferes with vision, bringing the subject down in the world. The *Degradés* dramatize the threat.

Light interrupting vision is a figure of the darkness that befalls the subject when it is exposed to the alterity of something that is both outside and inside itself, something that touches it from afar and disrupts its seeming self-possession, like an old travel diary or the unconscious mind. Insisting on the interruption, on the darkness that comes with light, Welling's work reminds us that the world cannot be made wholly manifest and is therefore not the possession of a subject. It does not belong to me. Like the work of the artists he exhibited with twenty years ago, though differently, Welling's investigation of abstraction questions mastery and opens up the possibility of transforming the forms of subjectivity that have been celebrated in our culture and of constructing more reasonable ways for *homo significans* to be, with others, in the world.

4

Breaking Ground: Barbara Kruger's Spatial Practice

Barbara Kruger enters social spaces and undoes them. Museums, galleries, parks, train stations, bus stops, billboards, newspapers, and magazines. Indoor spaces and outdoor spaces. So-called public spaces and so-called private spaces.[1] She reveals the presence of power in apparently neutral spaces, ostensibly beautiful spaces, and spaces that purport to be merely functional. She uncovers the social conflicts internal to spaces that seem harmonious and insinuates tensions and differences into spaces that repress them beneath the appearance of homogeneity—whether the space in question is an art institution, work of art, city, self, category, discipline, social group, nation, or any other would-be unity. She explores the relationship between space and violence—not just the violent events that take place in space but, more important, those that produce space and that, as the architecture theorist Mark Wigley writes, are perpetuated when we focus only on the violence that disrupts space: "What binds violence and space together is not the discrete events which appear to disturb the spaces we occupy but the more subterranean rhythms that already organize those very spaces. . . . The most decisive aspect of space is the one that is never discussed."[2]

Kruger breaks this silence. Calling attention to the acts of exclusion required to produce space—to enclose something within a boundary—she challenges the conception that space is a closed interior, whose limits are fixed by a pregiven ground. Rather, limits are marked off and space constructed as a coherent inside by a gesture of refusal, that is, by setting something aside. The operation of dividing an inside and an outside—an operation of power—makes space possible. Taking account of exclusions, Kruger treats space not as an entity but as a relationship. At stake is democracy itself, if by this we mean a form of society where it is possible to question power. For while references to a substantive ground that unifies a particular social space, or totalizes the space of society as a whole, naturalize and conceal the exclusions that constitute space, the withdrawal of the ground has the opposite effect: Bringing exclusions to the fore, it allows them to enter the terrain of contestation. Some critics mistake Kruger's exploration of violence for violence itself. But she remains firmly committed to an art practice that is akin to what Michel de Certeau calls "spatial practice": the skillful use of established spaces in a way that activates, transforms, and troubles them by opening them to their outside.[3]

Another name for the withdrawal of the ground of social space is "openness to the other." As Jacques Derrida writes, the question of space cannot be detached from the question of alterity since, in the absence of a totalizing ground, the identity of space comes into being only through a relationship with an "other" and as a consequence cannot be internally complete.[4] The sense of a coherent space is inseparable from a sense of what threatens the security of its boundaries, and the appeal to a ground disavows the threat by banishing or degrading otherness. By the same token, the collapse of the ground gives otherness a voice, a voice that tells us of the presence of something that is not an object for the self and so reintroduces plurality into social space.

All that seemed beneath you

Kruger's work welcomes this voice, which reached its crescendo in a group of installations she mounted between 1989 and 1991 in galleries in Chicago, Los Angeles, and New York City.[5] Earlier, in her photomontages of the 1980s, Kruger had superimposed written texts on preexisting, often mass-media photographs, using words to interrupt what Roland Barthes famously called the "rhetoric of the image"—the strategies whereby the visual image imposes its message on viewers.[6] By extension, Kruger's texts also interrupted the rhetoric of the institutional spaces in which visual images are displayed, particularly spaces devoted to aesthetic vision, such as museums and galleries. Actually, she had placed words over images even earlier, in a series of photocollages she made in 1979 and 1980, but it was in the following decade that pronouns appeared in her work and that she adopted the tactic she terms "direct address." Now her texts, and therefore her images, talked to a recipient—a "you"—and postulated a speaker—an "I" or "we," who is aligned with the work and who might, like "you," be real or fictive. Or vice versa: sometimes her texts contained the word *I* or *we* and only implied "your" presence. Some texts included both "I" and "you." One effect of staging conversations between image and recipient was to make it clear that an image, like any space, is not a self-contained object with an inherent meaning but rather a social relationship or, more accurately, an object whose meaning arises in social relationships, including the relationship with the viewing subject. The thematic content of Kruger's images and texts frequently suggests that this relationship involves violence. There are, for instance, images of a detonated bomb, exploding house, skull, skeleton, broken mirror, autopsy, or knife blade. There are texts that read, "We have received orders not to move," "You delight in the loss of others," "Your assignment is to divide or conquer," or "You kill time."

Through direct address, Kruger inscribed the image in relations and, what is more, situated these relations in time, the implied present of the "I" or "we" who speaks. Like other tactics deployed by Minimalist, site-specific, Conceptual, and institution-critical artists of the 1970s and 1980s—tactics that in diverse ways challenged the idealizing strictures of modernism— direct address transformed exhibition spaces. It called art and art institutions down from the heavens—from, that is, the abstract realm in which they had been placed by notions of aesthetic transcendence—and set them in the concrete social world. Kruger also brought the spectator down to earth, challenging the abstract subjectivity presupposed by dominant aesthetic discourses, the art viewer assumed to stand outside race, class, gender, and sexuality and to be uninflected by history or an unconscious. As Craig Owens writes in an essay on the way in which Kruger uses and interrupts stereotypes, pronouns like "I/we" and "you" are deictic terms. As such, they "might be defined as 'carnal discourse'" because, Owens argues, they "refer directly to the bodies of speaker and addressee; through them, Kruger's pronouncements acquire body, weight, gravity."[7] Deixis specifies rather than abstracts, and Kruger's use of these terms counters the symbolic violence exercised by the stereotype, a conventional representation that imposes social identities, that reduces, immobilizes, and keeps others in their place. Just as it opened up the space of the stereotype, Kruger's direct address opened up the space of museums and galleries, whose operations, at least as described by the art historian Norman Bryson, resemble those of the stereotype. Consider "the experience of extreme violence perpetrated by modernist space upon the bodies of those who enter such spaces," writes Bryson:

> Just think how hallowed and sacred such spaces are, how physicality is guaranteed to have been excluded long before the viewer enters this particular

space. Its extreme refinement is accompanied by a dephysicality, a loss of the viewer's embodiment, except by a reduction of the viewer to some kind of a very abstracted phenomenological subject. This is a relationship of violence.[8]

But while "you" indicates a concrete addressee in the sense of a specific rather than abstract being, it does not designate a preexisting spectator with a fixed identity. "You" is not solid. Quite the reverse. The personal pronoun "you" has no stable or absolute referent but denotes a position marked and transformed by relationships with others. In the very act of pointing to the presence of "you," Kruger's texts call "your" identity into question.

Kruger included photomontages in her installations of 1989–91, but she also inscribed texts directly on the galleries' surfaces, blowing her words up to architectural scale and thus heightening the viewer's bodily experience of the space. By infiltrating the gallery with language, which is the paradigm of all representational systems, she announced that architecture, no matter how quiet and immobile it seems, is also a system of representation that addresses subjects and projects messages. She destroyed its seeming naturalness. The impact was especially dramatic at New York's Mary Boone Gallery, then in Soho, where Kruger covered walls, floors, and ceilings with words, transforming the gallery itself into a kind of living, speaking body. But all three exhibitions contained a text inscribed in huge letters across the galleries' floors. The New York version, placed on the floor of Mary Boone's front room, read: "All that seemed beneath you is speaking to you now. All that seemed deaf hears you. All that seemed dumb knows what's on your mind. All that seemed blind sees right through you. All that seemed silent is putting the words right into your mouth" (plate 2).

In both form and thematic content, Kruger's message animated the space and disrupted its fixity. Through direct address, it set up differentiated positions within an apparently monolithic space. Fused with the architectural elements that structure the physical space of the gallery, the message referred to the hierarchical divisions that structure social spaces, including the one in which the viewer stood—the cultural institution. The words invoked acts of violence: blinding, silencing, injuring, and effacing. Integrated with the gallery's literal ground and thus merging linguistic and nonlinguistic systems of representation, the words pointed to the violence inherent in a discourse of grounds, a discourse through which space consolidates its identity by disavowing its status as representation, by making its exterior disappear. This space—it might be a cultural institution but also a self or a nation, to name only two identities to which Kruger alludes in the larger installation—is the addressee of the text, its "you," a you that stabilizes itself by disregarding the feelings and wishes of others, by walking all over them. Yet even while emphasizing the violence that you exercises upon others, the text displaced the you, confronting it with the very menace it fears as, under the pressure of other voices—other subjectivities—the ground breaks up beneath "your" feet. "The ear is receptive to conflicts," writes the philosopher and psychoanalyst Julia Kristeva, "only if the body loses its footing."[9] The work itself spoke from the position of these voices. They were its "we," the interlocutor implied by, but unable to be, you. Kruger's floor text is emblematic of a plea that runs through all her work, giving it its ethical and political force—a plea to respond to, rather than react triumphantly against, other voices, to meet them in relations other than those of domination and conquest.

Whose morality?

I use the adjective *ethical* in conjunction with *political* to distinguish it from *moral*, a term Kruger profoundly distrusts because of its association with the aggressive self-confidence of those who use it to neutralize differences by arranging all people under a single law. Moralists, she says, "construct a world for others"[10] or, put another way, consign otherness to oblivion. On the rear wall of her Mary Boone installation, in the gallery's back room, the words *Forget morality* appeared in small type in a mural-scale photograph, whose larger message, superimposed on an image of a naked woman in a gas mask pinned to a cross, read, "It's our pleasure to disgust you." The morality Kruger rejects is part of a discourse of certainty and grounds. It posits an unambiguous moral order, a firm universal set of values, which in turn form the basis of a unitary social order. Morality positions those who deviate from moral norms as representatives of society's "outside," evicting them from contests over the meaning of social life. It thus evades the dimension of the political. But ethical responsibility is incompatible with moral certainty. It presses us to interrogate conventional morality and, in this way, resembles sin, about which Oscar Wilde wrote, "In its rejection of the current notions about morality, it is one with the higher ethics."[11] *Untitled (It's our pleasure to disgust you)* (1991) echoes Wilde's playful defiance of the use of religion to sanction self-righteous morality. By contrast, responsibility emerges when we abandon references to a noncontingent ground of social life and in doing so acknowledge the presence of others, legitimate debate about what is socially legitimate and illegitimate, and invent democratic politics. Ethical responsibility is not prior to but coextensive with

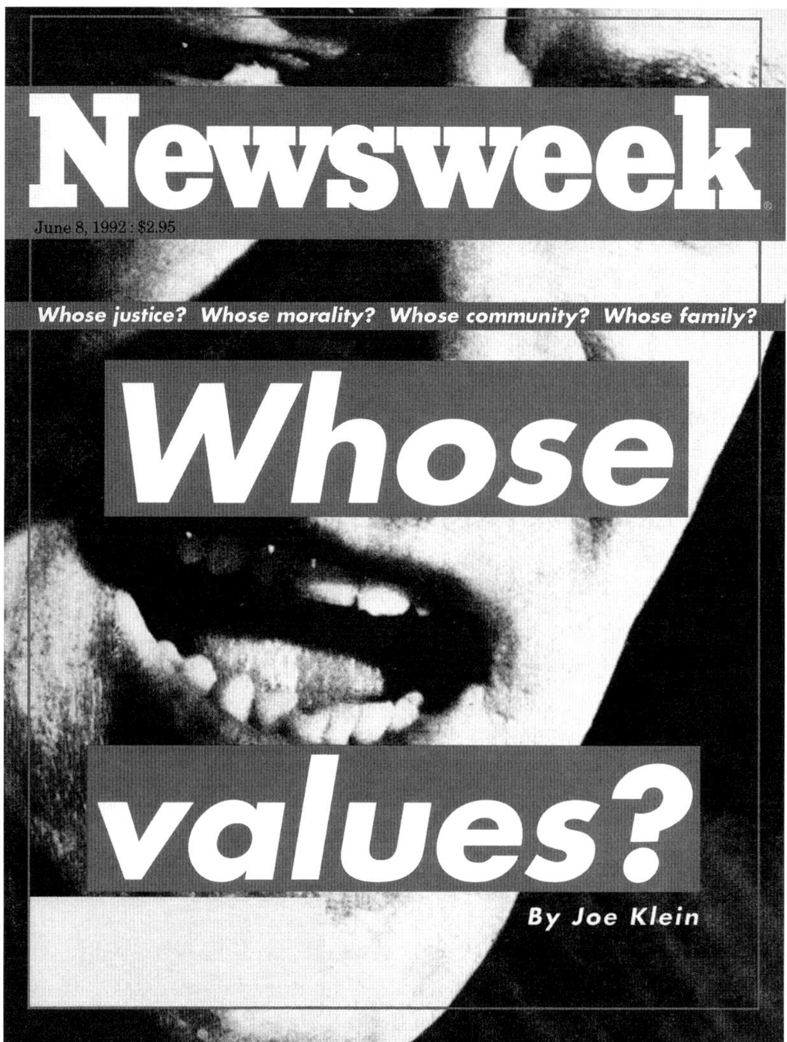

4.1 Barbara Kruger, *Whose justice? Whose morality? Whose community? Whose family? Whose values?*, cover for *Newsweek* magazine, June 8, 1992. Courtesy the artist.

politics, an inseparability that has been captured in the term *the ethico-political*.[12] Responsibility comes in when we become aware that morality is a question.

"Whose morality?" In 1992, Kruger posed this question, along with several others—Whose justice? Whose community? Whose family?—on the cover of *Newsweek*, unfurling it in red, white, and blue graphics across a close-up photograph of a man's face (fig. 4.1).[13] The photo is cropped to emphasize the man's furious expression and his scolding mouth, which is highlighted by its position sandwiched between two words that form the cover's biggest question: "Whose values?" Kruger's cover publicized the magazine's feature story, which deals with the contemporary discourse of values dominating American politics. The face belongs to a moral crusader, even a witch-hunter. *Newsweek*'s story stayed within the boundaries of current moral discourse, speaking approvingly of the emphasis on values as a remedy for "self-indulgence" and questioning it only to the extent of reporting on disagreements about how best to effect a cure. The article observed some conflicts taking place within the space of the discourse about morality.

Kruger's cover looked at the violence that constitutes this space. First, it broached the question of subjectivity—*Whose* values? Used as an interrogative, the pronoun *whose* asks what person or persons? As a genitive, it asks, belonging to or connected with whom? These questions cast doubt on the presumption of unanimity embedded in appeals to a singular morality based on some impersonal foundation. They demand specification, link morality to possessiveness and property, embody it, suggest that it has an agent, and urge us to investigate his identity. At first sight, it might seem that Kruger drops an obvious clue: the moral crusader pictured on the cover, the speaker interrupted by her questions, is a man. Yet "whose," like "you," is a pronoun with no fixed meaning except one of relation. The identity we are after cannot be determined outside of a context of use. It is not a male person but a masculinist position, one that men may have historically occupied but with which women as well as men can identify— where the masculine is understood as an orientation toward the ideals of unity, completion, and mastery. The masculinist subject claims to encompass the whole. Given that Kruger's cover has raised the issue of subjectivity in representation and has suggested further that morality belongs to the masculine subject, morality emerges not as a set of universally valid, unimpeachable truths but as a rhetorical instrument upon which this subject, whatever its pretensions to wholeness, depends. The question "whose morality?" does not only provoke us to uncover the identity of powerful persons who espouse morality—that, after all, is no mystery—but to ask which identity is produced by morality. Perhaps morality, far from an antidote to self-indulgence, is, precisely, the indulgence of a self that tries to stabilize its identity by condemning others. Perhaps morality, as Kruger has written elsewhere, is "a censorious image" of this subject's "own (im)perfection."[14]

Your image of perfection

Kruger's work has persistently warned that the greatest temptations to violence lie in images of perfect spaces. Consider the texts in some of her early photomontages: *Untitled (Perfect)* of 1980, *Untitled (Memory is your image of perfection)* of 1982, and *Untitled (You are the perfect crime)* of 1984. Consider also the title of the design project she did in 1986 in collaboration with Laurie Hawkinson, Henry Smith-Miller, and Nicholas Quennell: *Imperfect Utopia: A Park for the New World.* Or the four vinyl images she included in a 1997 installation. Each consisted of a photograph of a dead public figure overlaid and bordered with phrases uttered by a critical voice establishing its superiority by obsessively looking for flaws in others: "Not ugly enough," "Not angry enough," "Not useless enough," "Not silent enough," "Not skinny enough," "Not numb enough," "Not dead enough," and so on.[15]

Kruger's concern with the relationship between violence and the drive to perfection intensified in the early 1980s, as her work became informed by, and contributed to, feminist ideas about the politics of vision. These ideas were crucial to the deepening and extension of politicized art practice, since it was precisely the assumption that aesthetic vision is pure and disinterested that concealed the power relations embedded in the art institution and the work of art—widely regarded as preeminent spaces of perfection. Artists and critics who developed an analysis of the politics of visual representation did not only investigate the thematic content of artworks and other images. They explored the role played by vision in constituting the identity of the human subject and, moreover, the reproduction of this subject by social forms of visuality. They proposed that early processes of identity formation affect vision throughout our lives. Psychoanalysis became central to the exploration because it offered a theory of the constitution of the subject that is tied to an account of the establishment of the difference between the sexes. And, most important for feminism, psychoanalysis theorized the place assigned to the woman in sexual differentiation, an operation in which vision comes into play. Freud, for example, in his work on fetishism, had linked masculine identity to a search for visual plenitude, a search that he connected in turn to the disavowal of sexual difference inherent in the "perception" that woman, in contrast to man, is "castrated." In Freud's famous account, the boy looks at the woman, sees that she is different, thinks that she has "lost" the phallus, and fears that if she has lost it so can he. He sets up another visual object to substitute for what is "missing," an object that serves to deny difference. Feminists argued that cultural images of woman have performed the same function.[16] In Jacqueline Rose's words, "women are meant to *look* perfect, presenting a seamless image to the world so that the man, in that confrontation with difference, can avoid any apprehension of lack."[17] Woman as image is an idealized self-image, which aims to reassure viewers of their own perfection. But not only the iconography of woman serves this fantasy. Any image whose form is seen to be flawless—the self-contained, autonomous artwork, for example—also reassures the viewer that he is whole, that nothing is missing in the field of vision, and thus upholds a visual economy that cannot be separated from a hierarchical sexual economy.

But, as Slavoj Žižek writes, the fact that woman does not have the phallus can only be translated into the "perception" that she has "lost" the phallus if it is presupposed that she should have it—if, that is, it is believed that there is a prior state of wholeness, signified by the possession of the phallus, from which it is possible to fall.[18] The transformation of difference into castration disavows the fact that the lost state does not exist. For in the absence of a unifying essence, the subject is formed through psychical relations with external objects and images in a process initiated by loss—the loss of the illusory experience of oneness with the mother's body. The "complete" self is not one with itself but, rather, depends on the very images from which it claims detachment, a dependency it disavows. The fixed nature of masculine identity is, then, an effect of disavowal, a delusion, and not a harmless one. It necessitates the subordination or repudiation of difference, the transformation of difference into opposition or sameness, and demands that the feminine be fixed—repaired, made stationary, captured—by masculine force.

In the 1980s, art informed by feminist ideas about vision—work by such diverse artists as Kruger, Sherrie Levine, Silvia Kolbowski, Victor Burgin, Mary Kelly, Laurie Simmons, and Cindy Sherman, among others—staged and disrupted a visual economy in which woman as image and, beyond iconography, coherent visual form shore up masculine fantasies of completion. This work built on and enlarged earlier critiques of art institutions. It moved beyond questions related to the content of images and beyond context—at least insofar as context was understood as a social world external to images—to take in the question of looking. It explored not only what we see—what appears inside the boundaries of the image—but also how we see—the invisible operations that produce the seemingly natural spaces of image and viewer and, in so doing, challenged notions of visual purity at their core. For if official modernist doctrine treated the aesthetic image as the very emblem of a perfect space—a self-contained totality—

and if this image of art formed the foundation of the claim that art institutions are politically neutral, the feminist critique of vision withdrew the support. It exposed the perfect space as a relationship of violence.

Kruger's *Untitled (Memory is your image of perfection)* (1982) brings this relationship to light. The written text "Memory is your image of perfection" is superimposed on a photograph of an x-ray photograph of a woman's body. Kruger's photo is, then, a picture of vision—vision of a particular kind: x-rays impinge on material bodies, penetrate to the body's interior, and search for something there. The x-ray can therefore be read as a figure of a certain model of vision as transparency, which presupposes a detached observer, on the one hand, and an order of meaning that exists in the image itself—as presence—on the other. In this model, the viewer reaches beyond the "merely" contingent realm of surface incident, or superficial circumstances, to find an essential truth around which the meaning of the image might reach closure. The skeleton in Kruger's photo belongs to a female body. We know this because high heels and jewelry show up on the x-ray, rendering it at once grisly and comical. The "you" to whom the image is counterposed thus acquires a gender. It designates a masculine viewer, who can construct himself as whole—a space without flaw—only by seeking and finding a particular fixed meaning, a truth of the feminine that precedes representation. Kruger's iconography of the skeleton gives literal form to the petrifying, deathlike effect that masculine vision exerts on its objects (fig. 4.2).

But Kruger also brings the skeleton to life, giving the feminized image a feminist voice that thwarts "your" grasping vision. Her work resists taking shape as an object in whose presence the masculine subject can develop. It ruptures the visual field. For one thing, Kruger's image sees the viewer—it addresses him—and in collapsing the distance between the two, sees through "your" pretensions to detachment and disinterest. For another, the skeleton does not meet "your" expectations. It fails to deliver the prized property: the essential truth of the feminine. There is, as Kruger seriously joked in a later work about vision and knowledge as violation, a work picturing a doctor standing over a woman's corpse and studying her heart, which he has just cut out and holds in his hands, "No Radio."[19] Femininity is not a closed interior, a space whose boundaries are marked off by a unifying presence that belongs to it as a property (fig. 4.3). Indeed, the femininity of the skeleton in *Untitled (Memory is your image of perfection)* is produced by external objects—bracelets, rings, necklaces, shoes—emblems of the social effects that mark the surface of the female body and construct it as a feminine interior. In Kruger's x-ray, which I have read as a figure of a type

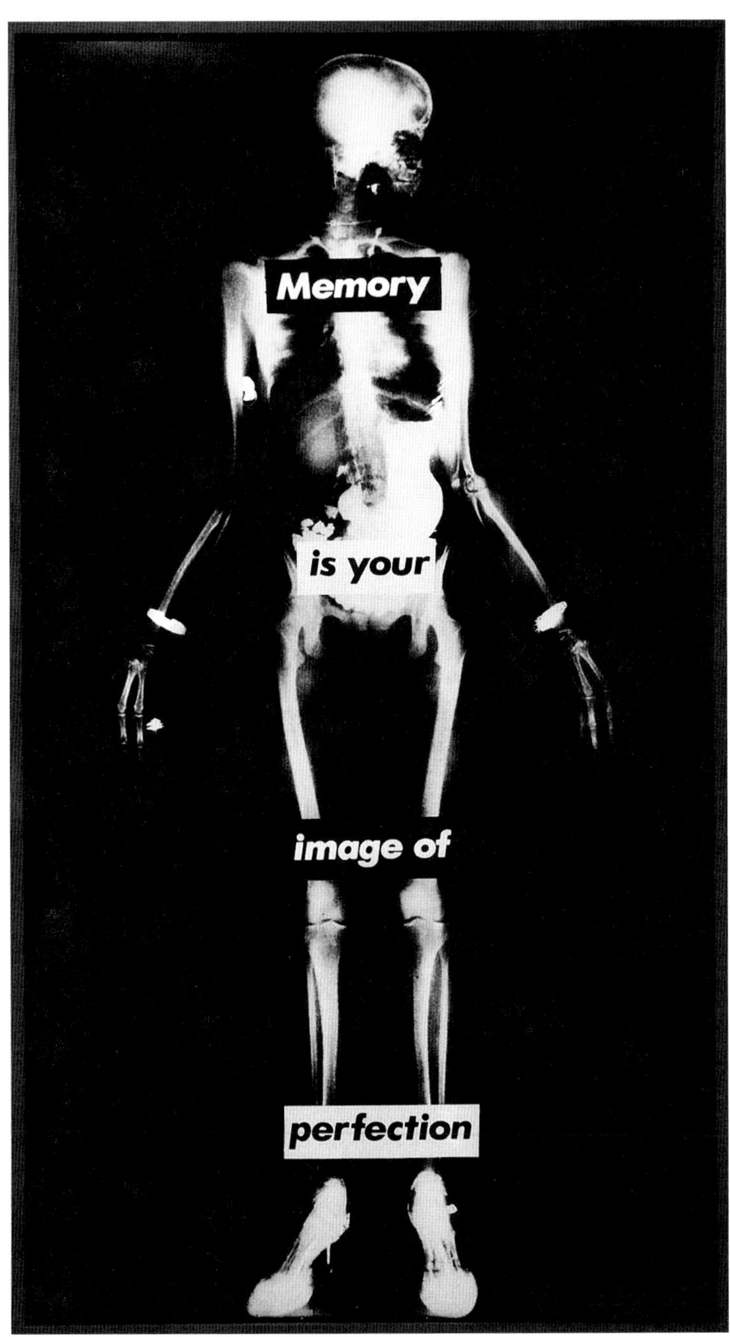

4.2 Barbara Kruger, *Untitled (Memory is your image of perfection)*, 1982. Gelatin silver print. Courtesy the artist and Museum of Contemporary Art San Diego. Museum purchase with funds from the Museum of Contemporary Art San Diego Benefit Art Auction 2002, International and Contemporary Collectors, and Nancy B. Tieken. © Barbara Kruger.

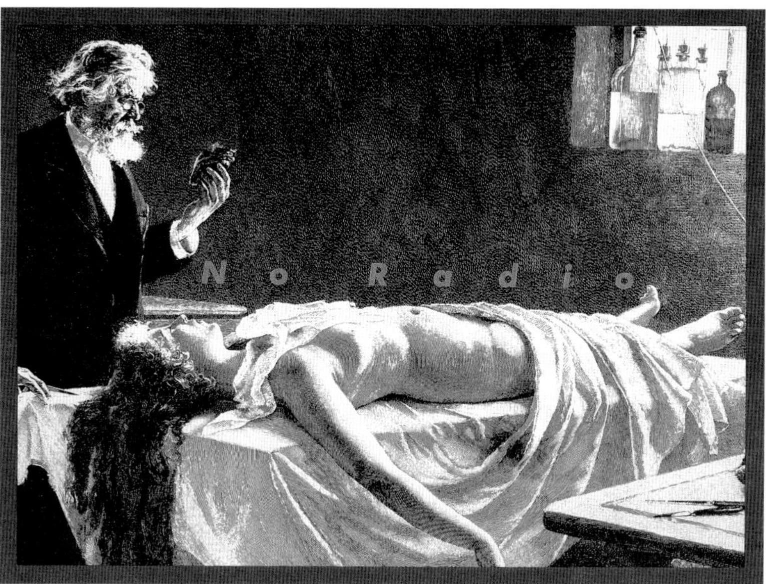

4.3 Barbara Kruger, *Untitled (No Radio)*, 1988. Photograph and screenprint in painted wood artist's frame. Doris and Donald Fisher Collection at the San Francisco Museum of Modern Art. Photo: San Francisco Museum of Modern Art. © Barbara Kruger.

of vision that tries to avoid the apprehension of lack, the masculine subject encounters what it fears, a fear activated by the knowledge that there is difference in the world and against which it constructs a memory that erases difference.

"Memory" as "your image of perfection" is an image of "your" perfection, a process not of recalling but, rather, of trying to forget what has been learned. Yet because memory, the evocation of things past, includes unconscious as well as conscious processes, it involves the pressure of things hidden but *not* forgotten—skeletons in the closet. Constructions of perfect spaces contain their own moments of unease. They are, in Kruger's words, "images of (im)perfection." If, as I have argued, the boundaries of space are not the stable effect of a ground but the unstable effect of a relationship, space has inscribed within its very being something that is not itself. Closure fails. In itself, this offers no hope for a less violent way of living with others. For is it not precisely to deny failure—to be without flaw—that space tries to cleanse itself of otherness, free itself of conflict, expunge its "outside"? In light of this question, Kruger's skeleton summons a counter-memory: the remembrance of a human history filled with masses of skeletons produced by attempts to shore up images of perfection, attempts that arise when a body larger than that of the individual subject—a body-politic, like a nation or race, with which the subject may identify—sets out to protect its boundaries against perceived dangers to its phantasmatic integrity. And in response to this question, Kruger's work of two decades, which has created what might be called ethico-political spaces—spaces that challenge our certainties by opening themselves to the presence of others—issues an appeal similar to that with which Jacqueline Rose concludes some psychoanalytic reflections on violence: "Hang on to failure if you want to avoid going to war."[20]

: 5 :

Louise Lawler's Rude Museum

On the brink of World War II, Virginia Woolf advised women to remember, learn from, and use derision, of which they had long been objects.[1] *Three Guineas*, Woolf's classic essay of ethico-political thought, counts derision among the great "un-paid teachers" of women, educating them about the behavior and motives of human beings, about, that is, psychology, a field that Woolf, unlike many leftist critics today, did not separate from that of the political.[2] Before writing the essay, Woolf had received requests for contributions from three organizations, each promoting a different cause: women's education, the advancement of women in the professions, and the prevention of war. At least that is the book's conceit. She responded by linking the three movements, making clear that for her the goal of feminism was not just equality for women but a better, less warlike society. Since, she argued, the professions as currently practiced encourage qualities that lead to war—grandiosity, vanity, egoism, patriotism, possessiveness, combativeness—women must not simply become educated professionals but do so differently: "How can we enter the professions and yet remain civilized human beings; human beings, that is, who wish to prevent war?"[3] Women can help, she suggested, by refusing to be deferential to the esteemed professions and instead considering it their duty to express the opinion that professional customs and rituals are contemptible. And what better way to accomplish this task than through humor, which, as Mignon Nixon notes, following Freud, discharges psychic energy, has pleasurable effects, and "promotes the defiance of deference"?[4] Woolf's humor was of the type that Freud called "tendentious." It served the purpose of criticizing authority and, like hostile jokes, exploited "something ridiculous in our enemy."[5] Here is a sample from her observations on professional dress:

How many, how splendid, how extremely ornate they are—the clothes worn by the educated man in his public capacity! Now you dress in violet; a jeweled crucifix swings on your breast; now your shoulders are covered with lace; now furred with ermine; now slung with many linked chains set with precious stones. Now you wear wigs on your heads; rows of graduated curls descend to your necks. Now your hats are boat-shaped, or cocked; now they mount in cones of black fur.[6]

Woolf derided men's professional trappings because of the hierarchical distinctions of rank and the will to power they signified: "Every button, rosette and stripe seems to have some symbolical meaning. Some have the right to wear plain buttons only; others rosettes; some may wear a single stripe; others three, four or five. And each curl or stripe is sewn on at precisely the right distance apart—it may be one inch for one man, one inch and a quarter for another."[7] Distinctions of dress, like adding titles before or letters after names, were designed to show superiority and to arouse competition and jealousy. Therefore, the professional fashion system encouraged "a disposition towards war."[8]

Today, some critics find Woolf's hope that women, by virtue of their earlier exclusion, might change the professions outdated, irrelevant to a historical period in which women have to a considerable extent entered public life. Yet latent in Woolf's plea—what necessitates it—is, I think, the thoroughly timely recognition that the opposite is just as likely to occur: women can identify with the masculinist position. "It would be perfectly possible for a woman to occupy the role of a representative man," as Homi Bhabha puts it, explaining why he uses the term *masculinism* not to designate the power of actual male persons but to denote a position of power authorized by the claim that one comprehends and represents the social totality.[9] Masculinism understood in this sense is a relationship that can be sustained only by declaring war on otherness, by subjugating that which cannot be fully known. Woolf believed that cultural institutions cultivate the triumphalist relationship. Alert, like her antifascist contemporary Walter Benjamin, to the barbarism underlying every "document of civilization,"[10] she approached such documents warily. No venerated institution was safe from her derision. She even listed the British Royal Academy of Art, the institution that safeguarded standards of professional competence in art, among the great "battlegrounds," whose members, she said, "seem to be as bloodthirsty as the profession of arms itself."[11]

Woolf was referring to combative behavior between the male academicians, but the Academy inflicted another kind of violence, one that can be discerned in Johann Zoffany's portrait of the academicians, *Life Class at the Royal Academy* (1772), a painting that has been an icon of feminist art history since Linda Nochlin used it to illustrate her landmark essay of 1971, "Why Have There Been No Great Women Artists?"[12] Nochlin treats Zoffany's conversation piece as a document of sexism, a work that shows an aspect of historical discrimination against women in the arts. Zoffany presents the academicians gathered around a nude male model at a time when women were excluded from access to the male nude and therefore from history painting, the most prestigious genre in the Academy's hierarchy. He solves the problem of including the Academy's two female founding members, Angelica Kauffmann and Mary Moser, by portraying them as painted portraits hanging on the wall. Directly facing the nude model, lit by a chandelier, stands Sir Joshua Reynolds, president of the Academy and author of the *Discourses on Art*, which he addressed as lectures to the "Gentlemen" of the Royal Academy between 1769 and 1790. But, according to the critic Naomi Schor, "Reynolds" does not just name a historical person; it is also "the proper name for the idealist aesthetics he promotes."[13] The classical busts and figures strewn around Zoffany's life class allude to this aesthetic. Schor concludes that Reynolds's classical discourse, in which genius consists of the ability to comprehend a unity—what Reynolds enthusiastically called "A WHOLE"—and in which the feminine is associated with the detail, which endangers masculine wholeness, cannot be separated from the discourse of misogyny (fig. 5.1).[14]

Idealist approaches to art are hardly limited to eighteenth-century classicism; they have remained alive for centuries in the widespread notion that the work of art is a complete, autonomous entity that elevates viewers above the contingencies of material life. Zoffany's *Life Class*, then, is not just a period piece that documents women's historical exclusion from art education. It also records the transformation of the female figure from artist to image, from viewing subject to visual object, to what feminists two hundred years later theorized as a signifier of "to-be-looked-at-ness."[15] It documents, that is, the representational economy that Freud called fetishism, a perversion that originates in the phallocentric attempt to triumph over the female body. Zoffany unwittingly shows us that the aesthetic institution is a masculinist battleground—an authoritarian rather than democratically agonistic realm—in a somewhat different sense than Woolf had in mind.

So far I have argued that Woolf's feminist challenge to cultural institutions is not gender-exclusive. Just as women can identify with masculine positions, men, who historically have occupied actual positions of power, can dis-identify with them. There can, that is, be a nonphallic masculinity. Still,

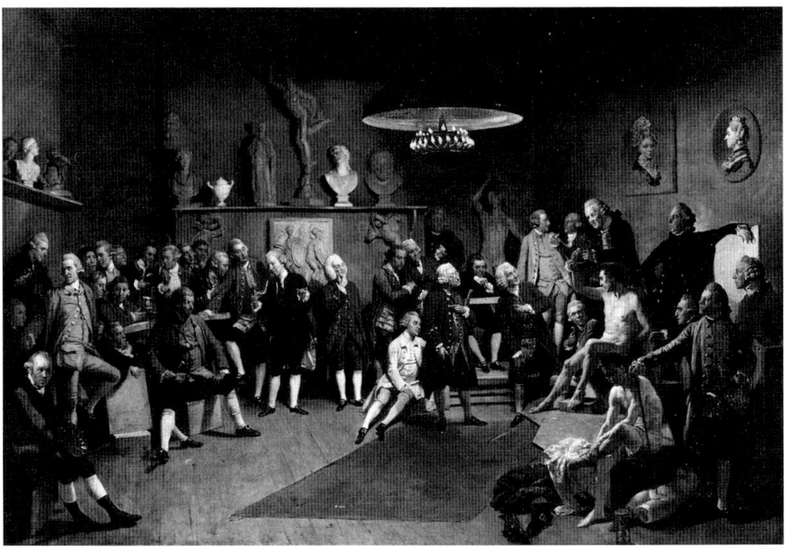

5.1 Johann Zoffany, *The Academicians of the Royal Academy*, 1771–72. Oil on canvas. Courtesy the Royal Collection Trust. © 2021 Her Majesty Queen Elizabeth II.

it is interesting to note that when, in the 1970s and 1980s, a group of mostly female artists, including Louise Lawler, entered art institutions in order to explore them as, precisely, battlegrounds, they did so differently than the first wave of institution-critical artists.[16] For whereas Marcel Broodthaers, Hans Haacke, Daniel Buren, and Michael Asher had drawn attention to the presence of economic and political power in the seemingly pure and neutral space of the museum and to the way the museum embodies dominant ideology and so exercises discursive power, and whereas works like Broodthaer's *Décor: A Conquest* (1975) and Haacke's *MoMA Poll* (1970) had, in different ways, specifically connected museums to war, the second wave—such diverse and mostly female artists as Lawler, Victor Burgin, Andrea Fraser, Judith Barry, Silvia Kolbowski, Barbara Kruger, Adrian Piper, Sherrie Levine, Fred Wilson, and Mary Kelly, among others—at once extended and questioned the critique.[17] Art historians have proposed a number of ways to distinguish between the work of the so-called first "generation" of institutional critics and the second, postmodern generation, Lawler in particular: the second questions the authority of its own voice rather than simply challenging the authoritarian voice of museums, corporations, and governments;[18] Lawler locates institutional power in a "systematized set of presentational procedures, whereas Asher, Buren, Haacke, and Broodthaers situated power in a centralized building or elite";[19] Lawler explores not only the contextual production of meaning but, in deconstructive fashion, the boundlessness of context.[20] Still another difference is that, unlike the first generation, feminist postmodernists were influenced by psychoanalysis and recognized to varying degrees the political importance of articulating relationships between psychical and social realms. Following in Woolf's footsteps, they approached institutions of aesthetic display not only as producers of bourgeois ideology but as spaces where dangerous, masculinist fantasies are solidified.

Lawler may not have been an exponent of psychoanalytic feminism, but many of her photographs lead us into the heart of such "solid wishes." And they do so with what Birgit Pelzer aptly calls a "dose of derision."[21] Literary theorist Kenneth Gross uses the term *solid wishes* in *The Dream of the Moving Statue*, a book about relationships between figural statues and fantasy, about statues *as* fantasies. "Works of sculpture," writes Gross, are "solid wishes, or vehicles of a wish for things that *are* solid."[22] It seems fitting, then, that some of the works in which Lawler most astutely exposes the art institution's fantasy life are a group of photographs, taken in the late 1970s and early 1980s, that depict figural sculpture, and, in particular, classical and neoclassical statues, in museum settings. *Statue before Painting, Perseus with the Head of Medusa, Canova* (1982) is exemplary. It served as the introductory image in Lawler's first published portfolio of the photographs she calls "arrangements of pictures." The black-and-white portfolio, itself an arrangement of pictures, appeared in the Fall 1983 issue of the journal *October*. Lawler's "arrangements" depict art objects in their contexts of display, calling attention to the presentational apparatus of specific arts institutions and, at the same time, to "art as institution," a phrase coined by the German sociologist Peter Bürger to refer to a more dispersed aesthetic apparatus: "The concept 'art as an institution' . . . refers to the productive and distributive apparatus and also to ideas about art that prevail at a given time and that determine the reception of works."[23] In such works as *Statue before Painting*, Lawler puts existing museological arrangements of artworks on display and makes visible the elements of the presentational apparatus, which, though authoritative, generally lie on the margins of the museumgoer's visual and cognitive field—architecture, labels, vitrines, pedestals, guards, installation shots, catalogues, security systems, and so on. Lawler appropriates the museum's arrangements and rearranges them in a manner that recalls Freud's approach to dream interpretation, an approach that rearranges the space of the dream, bringing its peripheral elements, its details, into focus (and vice versa) in order to analyze the dream-work that distorts the wish at the dream's core. While it is tempting to see Lawl-

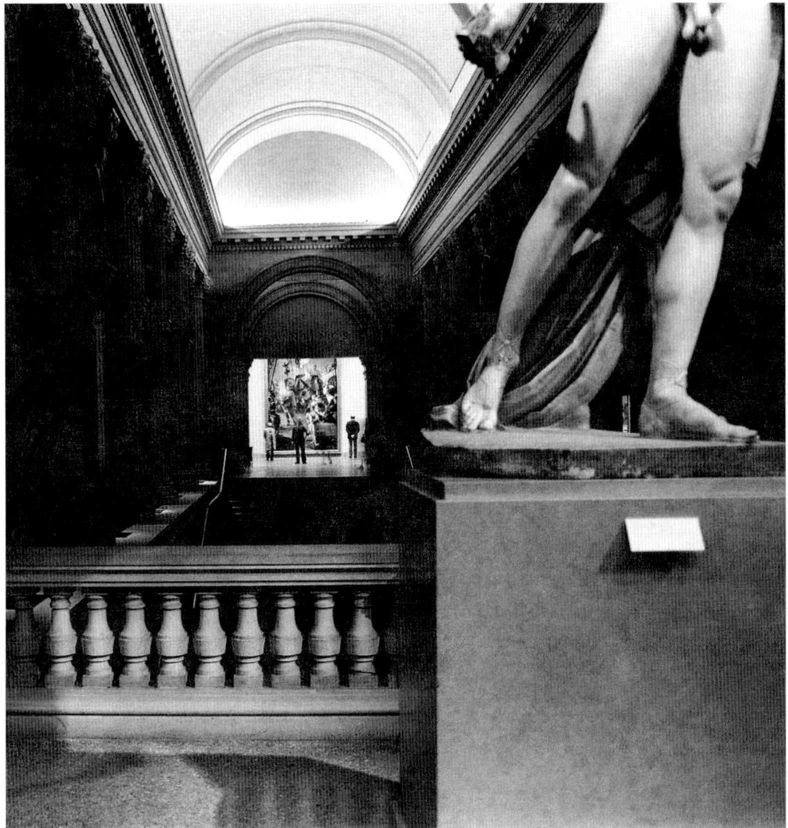

5.2 Louise Lawler, *Statue before Painting, Perseus with the Head of Medusa, Canova*, 1983. Gelatin silver print with text on mat: "STATUE BEFORE PAINTING, Perseus with the Head of Medusa, CANOVA." Courtesy of the artist and Metro Pictures, New York.

er's arrangements, with their fragmented objects, exaggerated details, and enigmatic juxtapositions, as dream scenarios, they might more accurately be regarded as analyses of the museum's "dreams," of the desire embodied in its arrangements (fig. 5.2).

Lawler shot *Statue before Painting, Perseus with the Head of Medusa, Canova* in New York's Metropolitan Museum of Art, from the vantage point of the museum's Great Hall Balcony, where Antonio Canova's marble statue was then located. The statue occupied a position on the neoclassical museum building's processional axis, which begins at the steps leading to the main entrance, continues through the Great Hall and central staircase—both are overlooked by the balcony—and culminates at the arched entrance to the galleries of European paintings. *Perseus* stood across from the entrance, be-

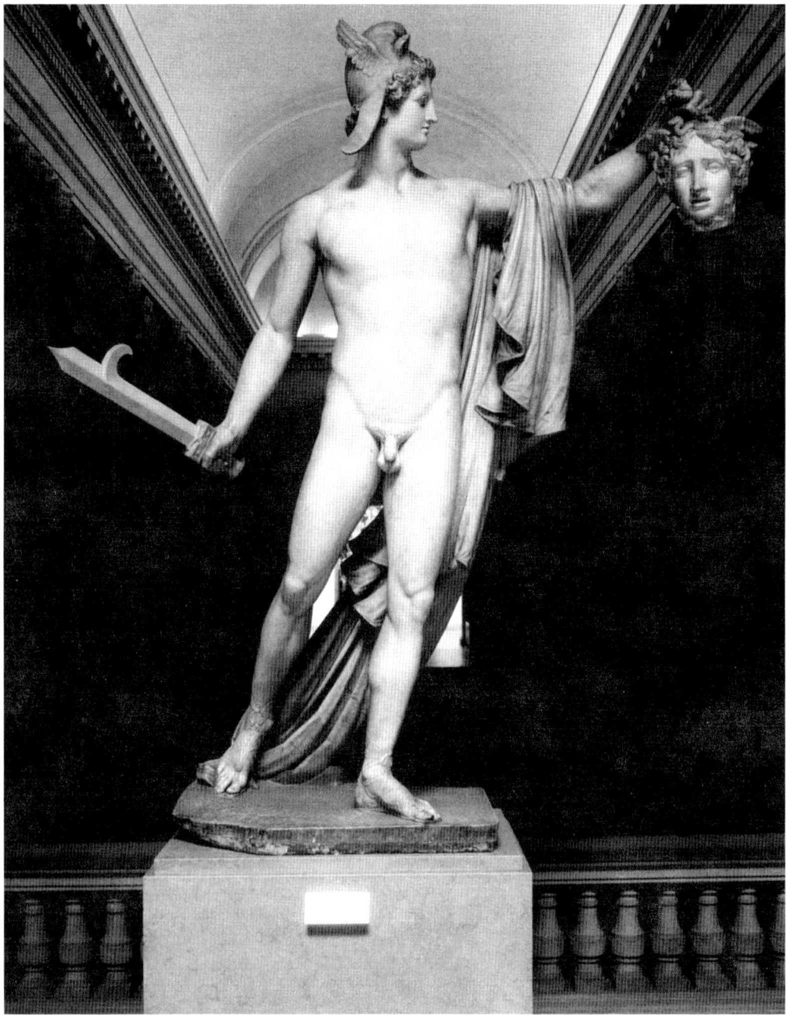

5.3 Antonio Canova, *Perseus with the Head of Medusa*, 1804–6. Marble. Installation view, Metropolitan Museum of Art, New York. Image: Art Resource, NY. © The Metropolitan Museum of Art.

neath an echoing arch on the balcony (fig. 5.3). The museum's official guidebook describes it as a second, more refined version of a sculpture that, when first executed and exhibited in Canova's studio between 1770 and 1800, "was acclaimed as the last word in the continuing purification of the Neoclassical style."[24] Like "Reynolds," "Canova" is a proper name for idealist aesthetics, whose patriarchal relations of sexual difference, observed in Zoffany's *Life Class*, are concretized in the roughly contemporaneous *Perseus*. Seen in Lawler's photograph from a low, oblique angle and radically cropped so that it is cut by the upper edge of the photograph, Canova's statue, its phallus, and its pedestal—architectural equivalent of the phallus—occupy the forefront of the viewer's vision. At the same time, pushed to the right edge of the image, the statue is dislodged from its central position, disrupting the museum's symmetrical arrangement.

Behind Perseus, beyond the balcony's balustrade, the staircase, flanked by colonnades of Corinthian columns, rises from the Great Hall below and leads to the double arches through which visitors, after ascending the stairs, enter the collection of paintings. Framed by the arches hangs Giovanni Battista Tiepolo's *The Triumph of Marius* (1729), the opening exhibit in the anteroom to the museum's history of Western painting (fig. 5.4). Its upper portion is sliced by the lower edge of the sign inscribed with the word *Paintings*, a mutilation that corresponds to that of the Perseus statue, which Lawler brings into visual alignment with the Tiepolo. In a second correspondence, the colossal painting dwarfs its spectators, who look up at it in an attitude that rhymes with our own angle of vision of statue and phallus in Lawler's photograph. Lawler accentuates this point of view, placing her viewers in a position that mimics not only that of the depicted viewers of Tiepolo but that of a small child catching sight of its parents' genitals. She thus suggests, perhaps unwittingly, that the psychic life of the museum bears a relation to infantile fantasies. The juxtaposition of the spectators' stance in front of the Tiepolo and Lawler's upward glance at Perseus literalizes both the deference with which art as institution treats works of art and the veneration with which classical antiquity regarded the phallus, defined as the figurative representation of the male organ. Drawing attention to the way the museum's arrangement includes a prescribed position for viewers, one that enforces a certain mode of spectatorship, Lawler simultaneously, as we shall see, makes Perseus the butt of derision and consequently repositions her audience, inviting them to defy deference.

First, however, note one more similarity between the Tiepolo and the Canova, this one on the level of thematic content: each depicts a violent conquest in which a male protagonist establishes his authority by mastering difference—racial and sexual, respectively. Each glorifies war. In the museum's words, *The Triumph of Marius* "shows the Roman general Gaius Marius in the victor's chariot while the conquered African king Jugurtha walks before him, bound in chains. . . . The Latin inscription on the cartouche at the top translates, 'The Roman people behold Jugurtha laden with chains.'"[25] For his part, Canova portrays the classical hero Perseus holding aloft the head of Medusa, which he has just severed. Medusa, of course, is the female

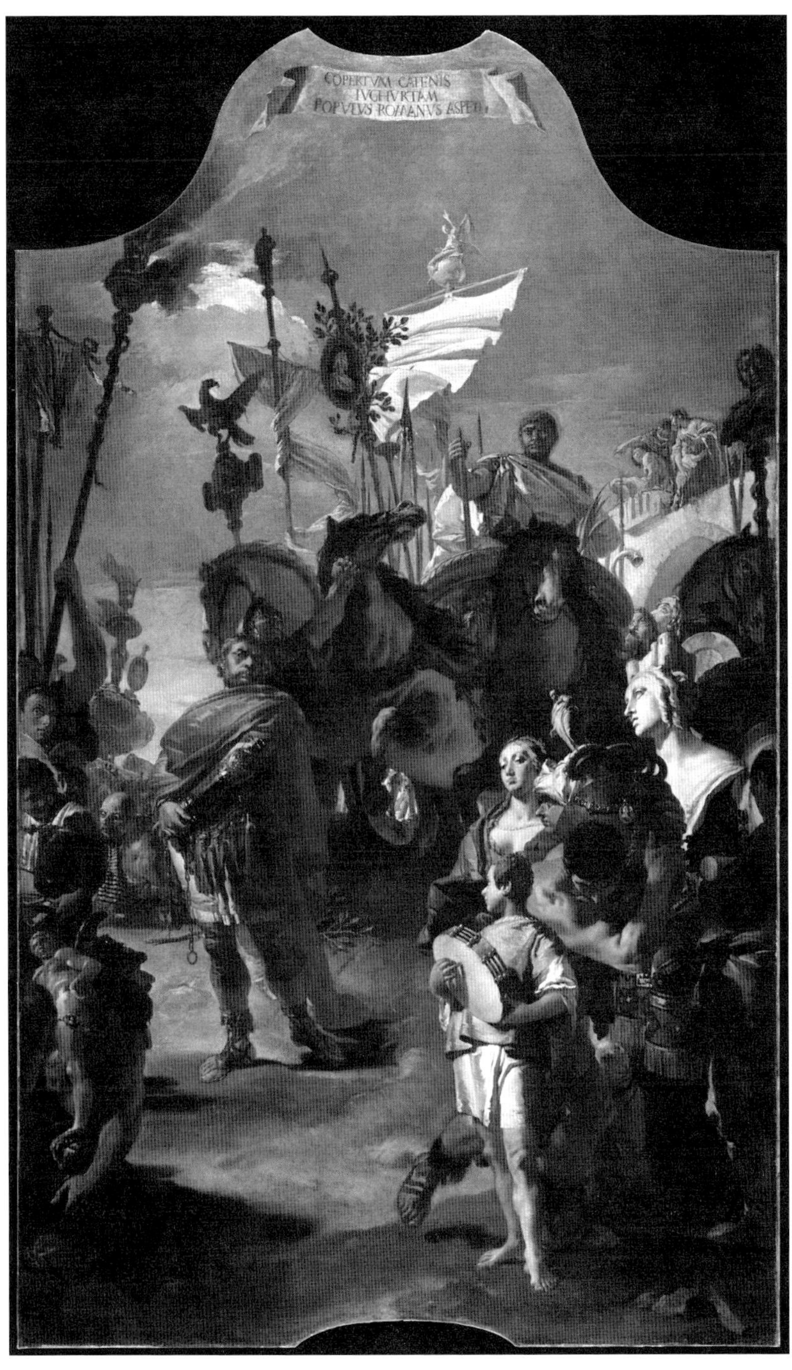

5.4 Giovanni Battista Tiepolo, *The Triumph of Marius*, 1729. Oil on canvas. Courtesy the Metropolitan Museum of Art.

monster of classical mythology, who had snakes instead of hair and whose look turned men to stone.

At the time, Medusa's head had considerable currency among psychoanalytic feminists working in the visual arts, largely because in 1922 Freud had written a short essay about it and because in 1973, in an equally short text, "You Don't Know What Is Happening, Do You Mr. Jones?," precursor to her famous "Visual Pleasure and Narrative Cinema," Laura Mulvey had used Freud's interpretation as the basis of a theory of phallocentric investments in looking at images.[26] Additionally, Medusa had become a symbol of feminist subversion of phallocentric mastery in such writing as Hélène Cixous's "The Laugh of the Medusa" of 1975.[27] Freud, as is well known, analyzed Medusa's head as a fetish: an object—visual, in this case—of masculine fixation that originates in fear of the female body, which is (mis)perceived as castrated, as missing the penis and, more importantly, the phallus, signifier of the presence that makes the subject whole. For Freud, Medusa's horrifying, decapitated head, surrounded by hair, symbolizes the female genitals and therefore the horror of castration. At the same time, it serves as a "token of triumph" over castration anxiety, an object that disavows and conquers the threat of sexual difference. Visually, it contains multiple penis replacements in the form of Medusa's snake-hair, and on the narrative level, it turns men to stone, thus stiffening them and reassuring them of the presence of the penis. Mulvey argued that just as Medusa's head is an image not of a woman but, rather, of the threatened masculine subject restored to wholeness, so in a culture ordered by phallocentric categorizations of human beings, in which the feminine is equated with absence and loss, images of women have served, in various ways, as self-images of men, or, more importantly, of the narcissistic masculine ego. The feminist discourse about fetishism was concerned with the nature of masculine subjectivity, especially as it is reinforced by vision.

When *October* published Lawler's "Arrangements of Pictures" it miscaptioned *Statue before Painting*, calling it *Statue before a Painting*. The editorial "correction"—the insertion of the indefinite article *a*—stemmed from a failure to get the title's joke, to understand that it is a joke. For the real title mimics the phrase *ladies before gentlemen*, which is part of and here stands for an idealizing patriarchal discourse that supposedly places women on pedestals. In conjunction with the photograph, the title links patriarchal ideals and idealist aesthetics, which the neoclassical statue represents, suggesting that there is an alignment of sexual and aesthetic hierarchies in the museum. The image reverses the order of genders in the original phrase, for here it is a male statue—a phallic figure—that stands before a painting and occupies a pedestal. But the reversal only reveals the true gender relations behind idealizing arrangements, showing that in the patriarchal visual field "the true exhibit is always the phallus," as Mulvey puts it.[28] To an extent, Lawler retrieves the artistic practice, prevalent among certain sculptors in the mid-1950s to late 1960s, of what Mignon Nixon, in her superb study of Louise Bourgeois, calls "posing the phallus." This practice, Nixon argues, targeted the phallus with humor, which has the political effect of under-mining it as a patriarchal symbol and inverts the seriousness of fetishism.[29] Yet Lawler's work differs from that of the earlier artists since, instead of sculpting a phallus, she uses her customary techniques of appropriation and montage—of "making meaning by juxtaposition and alignment"[30]—to pose a found phallus, one of the many "readymade" phalluses that prolifer-ate in art museums, like snakes on Medusa's head. Posing the phallus in the context of an institution-critical work, in which Perseus takes up a position as guardian of the museum's painting collection, *Statue before Painting* ex-hibits the role played by art as institution in reproducing sexual norms and maintaining the patriarchal overvaluation of the phallus.[31] For one thing, the photograph comments on the historical exclusion of female artists from the museum and, for another, it alludes to the male-dominated revival of traditional painting that was being legitimated by art institutions in the 1970s and 1980s. But Lawler's photograph plays a bigger joke on the Met-ropolitan. It hints that what underlies, what precedes or comes before the museum's aesthetic arrangements is the desire solidified in both the form and subject matter of Canova's statue of Perseus. The idealized, neoclassical sculpture, substitute for an ideal body, materializes the phallocentric fan-tasy of the self, a self that in its dream of autonomy disavows its constitutive exclusion of and relation to others. In fact, Jacques Lacan, writing about the mirror stage as the matrix of narcissistic ego-formation, described the mir-ror image—external reflection of an idealized self—as "the *statue* in which man projects himself."[32] And the iconography of Perseus and Medusa fore-grounds, as does the story told in Tiepolo's painting, the subordination and conquest of otherness—the warlike disposition—necessary to maintain the narcissistic fiction. The phallic statue metonymically alludes to the tri-umphalist subject positioned by the museum's idealist aesthetic.

Statue before Painting deprives Perseus of his token of triumph; Medu-sa's head is pushed outside the frame, Perseus is decapitated, and it would seem that Medusa, herself a kind of sculptor, has turned him to stone. Of course, this also fulfills his wish, soothing as well as testifying to his cas-tration anxiety. Still, the most striking feature of the photograph is its at-tack on the integrity of the male body. The photographic cut challenges the sculpture's closure, exposing it to its outside. According to Christian Metz, the photographic cut, which produces "the off-frame effect in photography," is a figure of castration because "it marks the place of an irreversible absence, a place from which the look has been diverted forever."[33] Lawler's cut directs the diverted look to three objects that remain in the frame and that, as fetishes, represent attempts to establish integrity and disavow vulnerability—pedestal, phallus, and museum label, an element that visually echoes the phallus and no doubt bears the artist's proper name, the "Name-of-the-Father," Lacan's name for the patriarchal order of sexual difference.[34] Precisely by giving prominence to these elements, Lawler takes away their authority,[35] as she does that of the grand staircase, itself an elevating structure that symbolically lifts visitors, just as the pedestal lifts the work of art, above the contingencies of everyday social life, encouraging them to take up the self-regarding position that Georges Bataille described in his definition of the museum as, precisely, a mirror:

> It is not just that the museums of the world as a whole today represent a colossal accumulation of riches but, more important, that all those who visit these museums represent without a doubt the most grandiose spectacle of a humanity liberated from material concerns and devoted to contemplation. We need to recognize that the galleries and the objects of art form only the container, the content of which is constituted by the visitors. . . . The museum is the colossal mirror in which man finally contemplates himself in every respect, finds himself literally admirable, and abandons himself to the ecstasy expressed in all the art magazines.[36]

Statue before Painting reveals and refuses the museum's positioning of the spectator, and it does so with supreme economy. Like a really good tendentious joke that, according to Freud, allows the teller and the recipient or, in our case, artist and viewer, to enjoy the pleasure of being impolite to "the great, the dignified and the mighty."[37] Indeed, Lawler calls one of her later arrangements of pictures, really an arrangement of statues, *The Rude Museum* (1985; fig. 5.5).

"Rude" refers to the photograph's subject matter—a museum devoted to the work of nineteenth-century French sculptor François Rude—but it can also be read as a pun that alludes to the barbaric fantasies fostered in art institutions and, more, to the acts of impropriety with which Lawler herself, in this and other photographs, rearranges museums and, as I have argued, exposes their fantasies. It alludes, that is, to Lawler's own rude museums. The actual Rude Museum, located in the transept of St. Etienne church in Dijon, consists of casts of works by Rude, a great patriot and admirer of the

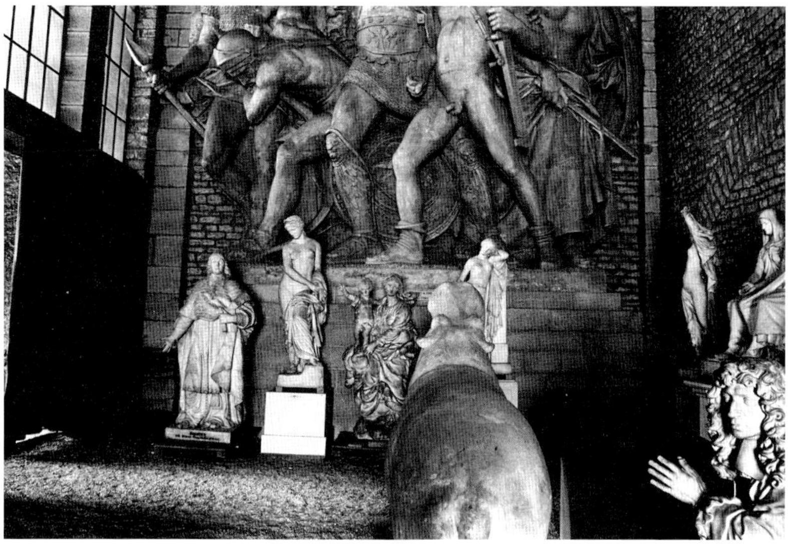

5.5 Louise Lawler, *The Rude Museum*, 1985. Courtesy of the artist and Metro Pictures, New York.

antique, though given in his sculpture to romantic gestures. Dominating the upper portion of Lawler's photograph is a plaster cast of Rude's most famous work, the high stone relief on the Arc de Triomphe in Paris, *Departure of the Volunteers in 1792*, popularly known as *La Marseillaise* (1833–36). Near the center of the relief, which is severed by the frame of Lawler's picture so that the enormous figure of an especially militaristic Liberty hovering above cannot be seen, is a classically inspired male nude marching off to war. Like Canova's *Perseus*, Rude's soldier is beheaded by Lawler's cropping of the photograph, a cut that foreshadows the fate of later victims of the French Revolution. In the foreground, its foreshortened backside turned to the viewer, crouches a large hippopotamus sculpted by François Pompon (1855–1933). Stretching up its head and opening its mouth, it gawks at the hero's exposed phallus. The hippo could be regarded as yet another target of Lawler's humor, but I prefer to think of it as her ally, a *repoussoir* element that not only pushes back the principal scene but functions, by virtue of its comical deference (and open jaws), as a formidable threat to the phallic figure—as a rude viewer in the Rude Museum, like Lawler and those willing to listen to her tendentious joke.

For derisive impropriety, also made possible with the help of wild animals, nothing surpasses *Birdcalls* (1972/1981), an audiotape on which Lawler squeals, squawks, chirps, twitters, croaks, squeaks, and occasionally warbles the names—primarily the surnames—of twenty-eight contemporary male artists, from Vito Acconci to Lawrence Weiner.[38] Recorded by Terry Wilson, the tape sounds as though different species of birds are calling out to one another in some natural setting, say, a forest or garden. In 1984, Andrea Miller-Keller, a curator at the Wadsworth Atheneum, one venue where the work has been played, nicknamed it *Patriarchal Roll Call* (fig. 5.6).[39]

When Lawler made the tape she was unaware of the precise difference between the two types of sound signals made by birds: calls and songs. For the title, she selected *calls* because she thought that *song* connoted pleasure for the bird whereas *call* seemed more strident.[40] Her choice turned out to be highly accurate, in keeping with the intention and execution of the work, since it is typically male birds that burst into songs, which are complex patterns of notes used to attract mates or establish territory. Calls, by contrast, consist of one or more short, repeated notes that convey messages about specific situations. If, for instance, a predator enters the immediate environment, birds give distress, alarm, and rally calls to signal the presence of a threat and to coordinate group activity against it.[41] Similarly, Lawler's *Birdcalls* originated in an act of self-defense. "In the early 1970s," she tells Douglas Crimp,

> my friend Martha Kite and I were helping some artists on one of the Hudson River pier projects. The women involved were doing tons of work, but the work being shown was only by male artists. Walking home at night in New York, one way to feel safe is to pretend you're crazy or at least be really loud. Martha and I called ourselves the "due chanteusies," and we'd sing off-key and make other noises. Willoughby Sharp was the impresario of the project, so we'd make a "Willoughby Willoughby" sound, trying to sound like birds. This developed into a series of bird calls based on artists' names. So, in fact, it was antagonistic.[42]

The birdcalls started out as a humorous anti-predator response to the presence of two dangers in Kite and Lawler's habitat: physical attack in the streets of the city and discrimination in the alternative art world. Drawing a perhaps inadvertent parallel with real birds, Lawler describes the first birdcalls as "instinctual."[43] Interestingly, however, bird calls, including alarm calls, are not just involuntary, impulsive emotional displays but systems of communication that can be controlled.[44] Their frequency is affected by the presence or absence of companions, a phenomenon that ornithologists call the "audience effect." Some bird sounds are learned;[45] some sentinel birds even give "false alarms." The birds' capacity for control and subversion accords with Lawler's tactics in *Birdcalls*, for while she situates herself in

VITO ACCONCI

CARL ANDRE

RICHARD ARTSCHWAGER

JOHN **BALDESSARI**

ROBERT BARRY

JOSEPH BEUYS

DANIEL BUREN

SANDRO CHIA

FRANCESCO CLEMENTE

ENZO CUCCHI

GILBERT and GEORGE

DAN GRAHAM

HANS HAACKE

NEIL JENNEY

DONALD JUDD

ANSELM KIEFER

JOSEPH KOSUTH

SOL LEWITT

RICHARD LONG

GORDON MATTA-CLARK

MARIO MERZ

SIGMAR POLKE

GERHARD RICHTER

ED RUSCHA

JULIAN SCHNABEL

CY TWOMBLY

ANDY WARHOL

LAWRENCE WEINER

5.6 Louise Lawler, *Birdcalls*, 1972/81. Audio recording and text. Courtesy of the artist and Metro Pictures, New York.

nature, which patriarchal systems of representation and sexual difference have traditionally opposed to culture and associated with the feminine, she treats it as a place not of confinement but, rather, of retreat and concealment, a refuge where she can escape Mulvey's "to-be-looked-at-ness" and what Michel Foucault called the "trap" or "cage" of visibility.[46] Occupying the place prescribed for women (and in this regard it should be noted that *bird* is slang for a young woman), but only in jest—literally *playing* nature—she appropriates it as a base from which to make forays, using sound as ammunition, into the territory of culture and to introduce tension into its hierarchical, gendered dichotomies, destroying their seeming naturalness. Heard but not seen, she challenges the proper name, the narcissistic ego, the Name-of-the-Father, and therefore the art world's relations of sexual difference, commenting on the fact that at the time she made *Birdcalls* "artists with name recognition were predominantly male."[47]

Lawler produced the first publicly presented tape of *Birdcalls* in 1981, when, as Crimp has pointed out, the upcoming *Documenta 7* (1982) was an object of much art-world discussion.[48] Rudi Fuchs, the international exhibition's director, planned to reaffirm the phallocentric, aestheticist notion of the work of art as a complete totality transcending its conditions of existence, and he therefore gave pride of place to Neoexpressionism, a male-dominated trend of the 1970s and 1980s, which to a considerable extent represented a regression to aestheticism.[49] In preparatory versions of *Birdcalls*, Lawler had included only Minimalist, Postminimalist, Conceptual, and Pop artists. Now, she added Neoexpressionist painters Sandro Chia, Francesco Clemente, Enzo Cucchi, Anselm Kiefer, and Julian Schnabel, targeting the new upsurge in masculine name-recognition with feminist name-calling.

Birdcalls is an anomaly in Lawler's production, her only sound piece, unless one counts the two versions of A MOVIE WILL BE SHOWN WITHOUT THE PICTURE (1979 and 1983). Yet its derisive tactics are quintessential Lawler. When she plays *Birdcalls* during presentations of her work, Lawler simultaneously projects an arrangement of slides. Some bear the names of the artists who are being called. These are interspersed with slides of both her own and the male artists' works. Following the title slide, the first, introductory image is always *Statue before Painting, Perseus with the Head of Medusa, Canova*, and this arrangement indicates that there is a commonality between tape and photograph. Both, for example, use mimicry. In 1982, Lawler wanted to produce a record of *Birdcalls* and planned to decorate the jacket with a photograph of a parrot—that excellent mimic—looking suspiciously over its shoulder and set against a brilliant red background.[50] The record was never made, but, subsequently, Lawler used the parrot photograph in other contexts, titling it *Portrait* (1982) (plate 3). Given its initial connection to *Birdcalls*, it might be regarded as a self-portrait, in camouflage. Except that Lawler's mimicry is far from mechanical. It is, rather, one of the skills she has honed to warn audiences away from the danger of "a position of passive agreement"[51] with the art institution's grandiose fantasies, whose warlike effects, as Virginia Woolf knew, are no laughing matter.[52]

PART TWO

Radical Democracy

Christopher D'Arcangelo's Elliptical Interruptions

In January 1975, a very young artist named Christopher D'Arcangelo chained himself to the doors of New York City's Whitney Museum of American Art, then located in the Marcel Breuer building on Madison Avenue. A statement about anarchism was stenciled on his back. Later that year, D'Arcangelo staged related guerilla performances at the city's other major art museums: the Museum of Modern Art, Solomon R. Guggenheim Museum, and Metropolitan Museum of Art. Two others followed in 1976 and 1978, at the Norton Simon Museum of Art in Pasadena, California, and the Louvre in Paris. These museum "actions," as they are widely called (although D'Arcangelo simply describes them as "works"), were important contributions to the developing art practice of institutional critique. They have also been referred to as museum "occupations," and this designation makes clear that institutional critique engages in spatial politics.[1] It disrupts the space of art institutions and does so by troubling the boundaries that establish such spaces, as they do all spaces. Recall Martin Heidegger's famous definition of space: "A space is something that has been made room for, something that is cleared and free, namely within a boundary. . . . A boundary is not that at which something stops, but as the Greeks recognized, the boundary is that from which something *begins its presencing.*"[2] A space, "something that has been made room for"—whether it is a building, city, organization, discourse, identity, category, or so on—does not preexist the boundary that marks its limits. Rather, that something comes into being—begins to be present—in the act of drawing the boundary, which divides what the space is and what it is not, inside and outside, identity and nonidentity, same and other. Space is relational—it divides and connects—and there is no space without the force of exclusion.

Although institution-critical works generally target individual art institutions—say, a museum like the Whitney, MoMA, or Met—the object of the practice as a whole is the space not of single art institutions but, rather, of art *as* institution, a phrase coined by the German sociologist of literature Peter Bürger to designate a social subsystem comprised of "the productive and distributive apparatus [of art]."[3] Art as institution refers to the mechanism of artistic production, including the art school or artist's studio, and circulation—museum, gallery, auction house, journal, book, class, or talk by an art historian—all the equipment that positions an object as a work of art. Art as institution also includes the ideas about art that prevail at a given historical moment. The principal idea in bourgeois society, says Bürger, has been the idealist notion of aesthetic autonomy,[4] the doctrine that a work of art is a complete, self-governing totality, whose essential meaning inheres in itself, apart from the circumstances in which it exists. Institutional critique challenges art as institution by, as Craig Owens puts it, shifting viewers' attention from work to frame, to all the changing conditions that surround and enclose works of art and largely determine their meaning.[5]

If, as Heidegger says, a space is produced by drawing a boundary and dividing identity from nonidentity, the psychoanalytic concept of repression can help illuminate the political effects of this process. For repression is itself an exclusionary spatial operation, one that constitutes the domain of the unconscious, placing it outside consciousness and thereby dividing psychic space. "*The essence of repression,*" writes Freud, "*lies simply in turning something away, and keeping it at a distance, from the conscious.*"[6] The division does not fully succeed, however. Rather, the repressed material "exerts continuous upward pressure in the direction of consciousness,"[7] whose coherence is disturbed by what it has tried to get rid of. Repression thus creates what Freud, theorizing conflicts between individuals and society, calls "discontents."[8] Subsequent thinkers have adopted Freud's term to refer to the disquiet caused by the repressions that simultaneously found and disrupt a variety of social spaces—that of normative femininity, to give just one example.[9] Psychoanalytic insights into the permeability of boundaries and the consequent vulnerability of the spaces they institute is a key aspect of what W. H. Auden refers to as Freud's "technique of unsettlement," which, says the poet, "foresaw the fall of princes."[10] Auden's evocation of the failure of power—the fall of princes—captures the political significance of psychoanalytic thought: its threat to mastery of and dominion over self and world, a threat that Freud emphasized, asserting that with the discovery of the unconscious "man is not even master in his own house."[11] The striking

French students of May 1968 detected something similar about power's vulnerability when they adopted as their rallying cry the Situationist slogan "under the pavement, the beach." The slogan referred not only to the literal sand the students found when they tore up cobblestones to throw at police, but also to the shifting and fluid histories and the conflicts that are hidden beneath and "exert continuous upward pressure" on the apparent cohesion and unity of urban space. In 1991, Barbara Kruger announced the emergence of comparable destabilizing forces in aesthetic and cultural space. Kruger covered the floor of the front room of the Mary Boone Gallery in Soho, New York, with an enormous text that read, "All that seemed beneath you is speaking to you now. All that seemed deaf hears you. All that seemed dumb knows what's on your mind. All that seemed blind sees through you. All that seemed silent is putting the words right into your mouth."[12] Kruger's dialogic text addresses a collective "you" and therefore implies a "we" that has been blinded, silenced, effaced, and otherwise injured by the mastering subject of Western cultural discourse. Now "we" speaks, hears, and sees, shaking the illusory solidity of the ground on which "you" has stood. "Power suffers," writes the spatial philosopher Henri Lefebvre, theorizing the conflictual nature of space, "as in Shakespearean tragedy. The more it consolidates, the more afraid it is. It occupies space but space trembles beneath it."[13]

Some years before formulating his ideas about the vulnerability of spaces to their founding repressions, Freud reflected on a topic with equally important implications for institutional critique: the destructiveness of human beings. Freud stressed the intractability of unconscious aggressivity and violence. They cannot be eradicated, he insisted in an essay on the barbarism of World War I.[14] The Italian political philosopher Paolo Virno builds on the same premise, arguing that because humans are destructive animals they need the restraining force of institutions to protect them from catastrophic expressions of violence. But institutions themselves—political and nonpolitical—are dangerous insofar as their claim to protect us can take authoritarian forms that give rise to a second catastrophe: what Virno calls "the atrophy of openness to the world."[15] Along with destructiveness, openness to the world is intrinsic to being human, but it wastes away when institutions try to fortify their boundaries by imposing supposedly universal and timeless rules on a supposedly uniform society. Institutions can actually protect us, says Virno, only if they impede both catastrophes—unrestrained destructiveness and atrophy of openness to the world. And they can perform this dual apotropaic function only if they belong to the Aristotelian category of "that which can be different than what it is."[16] If, that is, they can conceive of their own transformation and dissolution. According to Virno, republican institutions, by contrast with authoritarian ones, acknowledge and turn toward their contingency, remaining perpetually open to the introduction of difference and to changes that cannot be predicted in advance.[17]

For more than fifty years, institution-critical artists have sought to democratize art as institution by exploiting its vulnerability, which is to say, by exposing it to its outside. Few have done so as viscerally as Christopher D'Arcangelo, especially in the New York museum actions with which I began this essay. Documenting his Whitney action, D'Arcangelo lists his body as one of its artistic materials.[18] Placing his physical presence at the center of his practice, he also exposed his own vulnerability to bodily and legal harm.

D'Arcangelo may always be associated with vulnerability, partly for biographical reasons: his artistic career was brief, four years; he committed suicide in 1979 at the age of twenty-four; nothing was published about him in his lifetime; and after his death, he fell into relative obscurity for three decades, known mostly by word of mouth. In 2009, however, Cathy Weiner, his partner for the five years before his death, and the D'Arcangelo Family Partnership donated his archive to New York University's Fales Library. The gift included writings by the artist, who extensively documented his work, along with photographs, recordings, letters, objects, and ephemera, among other things. In 2011, D'Arcangelo's first solo exhibitions in the United States opened, and only at this point did historicization of the artist begin.[19]

Then there is the best-known photograph of D'Arcangelo, the one in which he occupies the Whitney Museum, and in which his slender body just looks so vulnerable (fig. 6.1). It was freezing cold on January 31, 1975. As he recounts it, D'Arcangelo walked across the Breuer building's ramp, over its surrounding "moat," took off his jacket and shirt, and, with his back facing the street, chained himself to the handles of the front doors of the museum. "In so doing," he writes, "I was able to lock the door of the museum and also lock myself to the museum."[20] No one could leave or enter through the main doors. People who ventured up the ramp could read the statement stenciled on his exposed back: "When I state that I am an anarchist, I must also state that I am not an anarchist, to be in keeping with the (_ _ _ _) idea of Anarchism. Long Live Anarchism." Some people were angry; some thought D'Arcangelo was crazy; others were curious. The first people to speak to him were museum visitors. He answered their questions about the anarchist statement and about what he was doing. After about ten minutes, the museum's security force arrived. They tried to clear the ramp and to direct visitors to other entrances and exits. They asked D'Arcangelo if he had keys to the lock; he answered "no." One security man brought a large bolt cutter but was told he could not use it because the nine-foot steel chain was case-hardened. According to a witness, a conversation developed between the artist, the security force, and about five other people, and it became obvious that D'Arcangelo was not as much of a threat as he had first appeared to be. Nonetheless, the Whitney personnel set up screens around him, one on the outside and one on the inside, rendering him invisible.[21] A few minutes later, D'Arcangelo took a key from one of his boots, unlocked himself, got dressed, and, as Jeffrey Deitch observed, "took the subway home."[22]

D'Arcangelo did not emerge as unscathed from his second action, which took place in February at the Museum of Modern Art. Entering MoMA's third floor, he stapled a small museum reproduction of Pablo Picasso's *Guernica* next to the actual painting, where studies for the work were displayed, and stapled a stencil of his anarchist statement over the reproduction. Just as he was about to spray-paint the stencil so that the reproduction would be seen through the statement and, in that way, fuse anarchism with Picasso's war resistance, guards arrived and, according to an eyewitness, violently restrained him:

> One of the guards viciously grabbed him from behind pinning him against the guard, making him unable to move even after chris explained he wouldn't try to escape. many people by now were in the area watching the violence happen in front of a painting that also depicted violence. around me in this atmosphere you began to realize that this painting represented something beyond aesthetics. You were able to see museum guards do their job besides giving directions. To see that the violence this guard was using on chris was his right because chris was an intruder and could cause possible violence to a painting. The thinking behind this guard's action was obvious[ly] the thinking of all museums in their right to show you their possessions.[23]

Police were called; they handcuffed D'Arcangelo and drove him away in a patrol car. MoMA pressed charges, and the artist spent eight hours in the Tombs in lower Manhattan before being arraigned and set free. Eventually, MoMA dropped the charges after D'Arcangelo agreed that he would never again perform unauthorized activities in the museum. At some point during this incident, his father, the Pop artist Allan D'Arcangelo, recalls asking him why he was going after museums: "Chain yourself to the Chase Manhattan Bank doors," he apparently said. "Close the banks."[24] His son, however, like other institution-critical artists, understood that cultural and financial power are intimately connected.

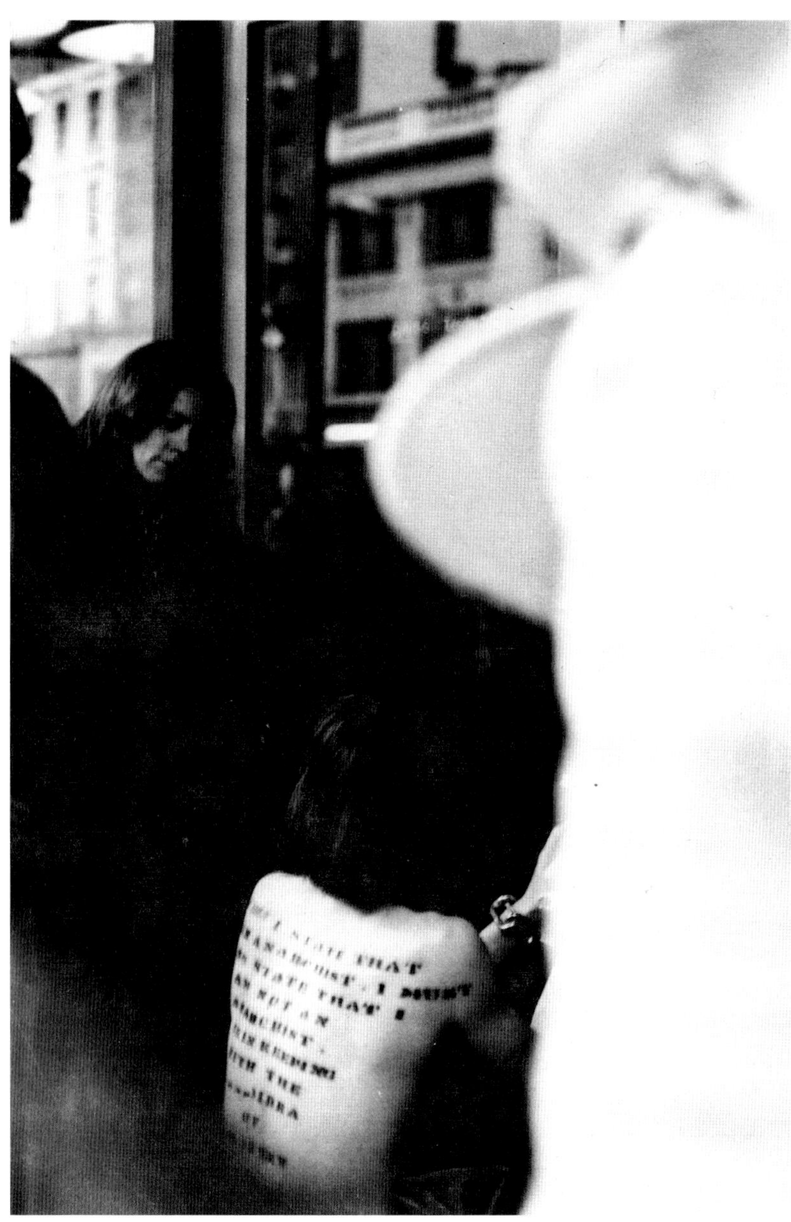

6.1 Christopher D'Arcangelo, unauthorized action at Whitney Museum of American Art, New York, 1975. Photo: Cathy Weiner. Courtesy of Cathy Weiner and Fales Library and Special Collections, New York University. © Cathy Weiner.

Three months later, D'Arcangelo again looked "horribly vulnerable" as he lay face down and handcuffed on the floor in the rotunda of the Guggenheim Museum.[25] But his Guggenheim occupation provoked a more comical, if still somewhat violent, police response than the one at MoMA. D'Arcangelo walked to the center of the museum's lobby, removed his shirt, exposing the anarchist statement on his back, took off his boots, and handcuffed his wrists and ankles. He placed the keys to the handcuffs next to him in an envelope that was stamped with the anarchist statement. Security personnel arrived, and police were called. According to one witness, a cop took out his handcuffs in order to clamp them onto D'Arcangelo's wrists, but of course the artist was already handcuffed. When someone discovered the envelope with the keys, a policeman unlocked the handcuffs, freeing D'Arcangelo, who then left escorted by the police (fig. 6.2).[26]

In these works, D'Arcangelo, like other institution-critical artists, revealed the presence of power in spaces that present themselves as pure and neutral. Using the apparatus of repressive power—chains, locks, handcuffs, as well as the security personnel and police that the museums inevitably summoned—he also dramatized the less visible kinds of violence exercised by art institutions. In form and thematic content, then, the New York museum actions were *about* vulnerability, in at least one sense of the word. They exhibited artists' and museumgoers' susceptibility to control, coercion, violence, or attack. At the Whitney, MoMA, and Guggenheim, D'Arcangelo demonstrated what Norman Bryson, analyzing the museum as a site of disciplinary power, describes as

> the experience of extreme violence perpetrated by modernist space upon the bodies of those who enter such spaces. . . . Just think how hallowed and sacred such spaces are, how physicality is guaranteed to have been excluded long before the viewer enters this particular space. Its extreme refinement is accompanied by a dephysicality, a loss of the viewer's embodiment, except by the reduction of the viewer to some kind of a very abstracted phenomenological subject. This is a relation of violence.[27]

D'Arcangelo dramatized such museological violence while, as I will argue, protesting against it with the presence of his body, which resisted abstraction and disappearance.

But "vulnerability" does not mean only susceptibility to danger. It also connotes openness, exposure to others, and interdependency—qualities that, if acknowledged, are capable of counteracting the violence Bryson describes, as well as other kinds of violence. As beings-in-the world, which is to say, as human beings, we are all vulnerable, all relational and dependent,

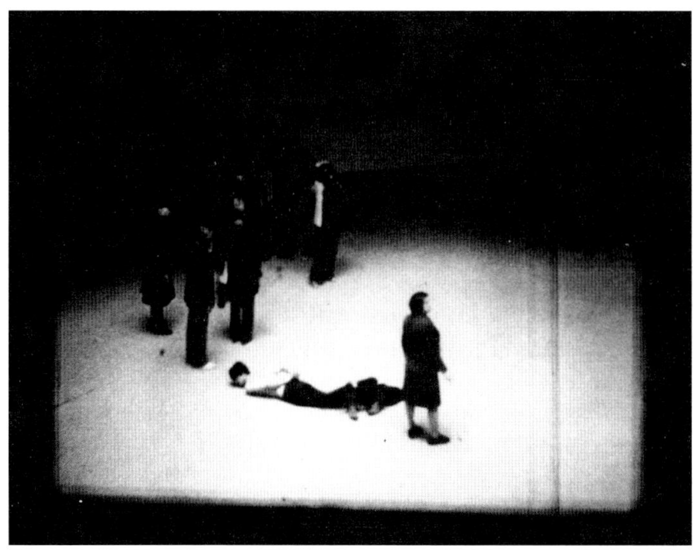

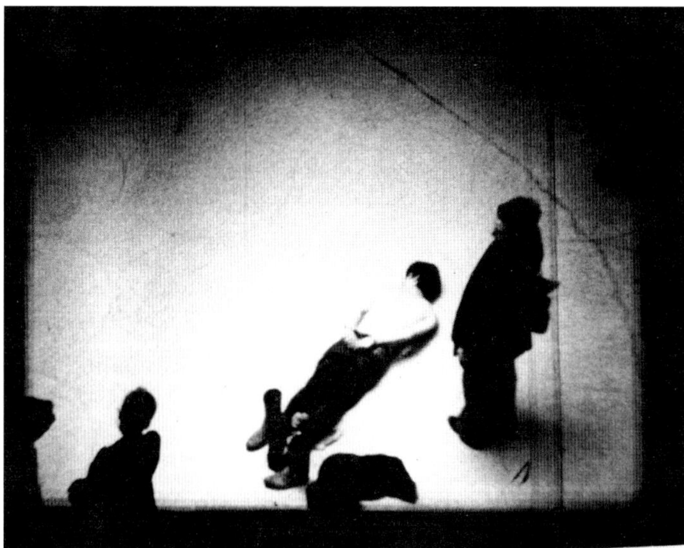

6.2 Christopher D'Arcangelo, unauthorized action at Solomon R. Guggenheim Museum, New York, 1975. Photo: Cathy Weiner. Courtesy of Cathy Weiner and Fales Library and Special Collections, New York University. © Cathy Weiner.

no matter how forcefully we disavow it in fantasies of autonomy. Vulnerability in this sense is an attribute not just of individuals but of collectivities. While D'Arcangelo's work is about vulnerability as a state of endangerment, it is also about this other type of vulnerability, which can be regarded as a state of possibility insofar as recognizing and tolerating it might lead to receptivity and, as Judith Butler suggests, nonviolence.[28]

Consider the artist's anarchist statement, which itself is vulnerable. Stenciled on his back during the Whitney and Guggenheim performances, appearing in some form in all his museum actions, the statement, in D'Arcangelo's words, was the foundation of his entire practice:

> WHEN I STATE THAT I AM AN ANARCHIST, I MUST ALSO STATE THAT I AM NOT AN ANARCHIST TO BE IN KEEPING WITH THE (_ _ _ _) IDEA OF ᗯSIHƆЯ∀N∀. LONG LIVE ᗯSIHƆЯ∀N∀.[29]

The two "anarchisms" are stenciled backward and upside down. In an equally topsy-turvy manner, D'Arcangelo begins his statement with a paradox, one that, as he writes, turns the declarative statement into a question: to be an anarchist he must not be one.[30] The sentence seems self-contradictory but expresses a possible truth. Perhaps D'Arcangelo means that insofar as anarchism rebels against rules and constraints, it cannot be pinned down; its boundaries must remain unfixed and unlimited, a proposition in accord with Paolo Virno's idea that truly protective institutions must be open to contingency and negation. D'Arcangelo then adds that the paradox conforms to "the (_ _ _ _) idea of anarchism," deploying an ellipsis, four underscore marks that indicate the suppression, omission, or disappearance of letters and words, in this case, an adjective. In other versions of the statement, D'Arcangelo toyed with variant forms of the ellipsis—four dashes, four periods, unbroken underscore lines of varying lengths, twelve short dashes, ten periods.[31]

An ellipsis is an erasure that inscribes a loss. A few years later, D'Arcangelo again inscribed a loss, this time in a work made for Artists Space, an alternative gallery then located on Hudson Street in New York's Tribeca neighborhood. Having been asked by the director, Helene Winer, to curate an exhibition, Janelle Reiring invited D'Arcangelo, along with Louise Lawler, Adrian Piper, and Cindy Sherman, to contribute to a group show. Reiring selected the four artists because, she said, "their work addresses how art is presented and, in turn, how it is seen."[32] For her contribution, Lawler designed a new logo for Artists Space, which she placed on the poster and catalogue cover for Reiring's show. It is hard to miss the logo's resemblance to today's best-known symbol of anarchy, the circle-A.[33] The capital A, first

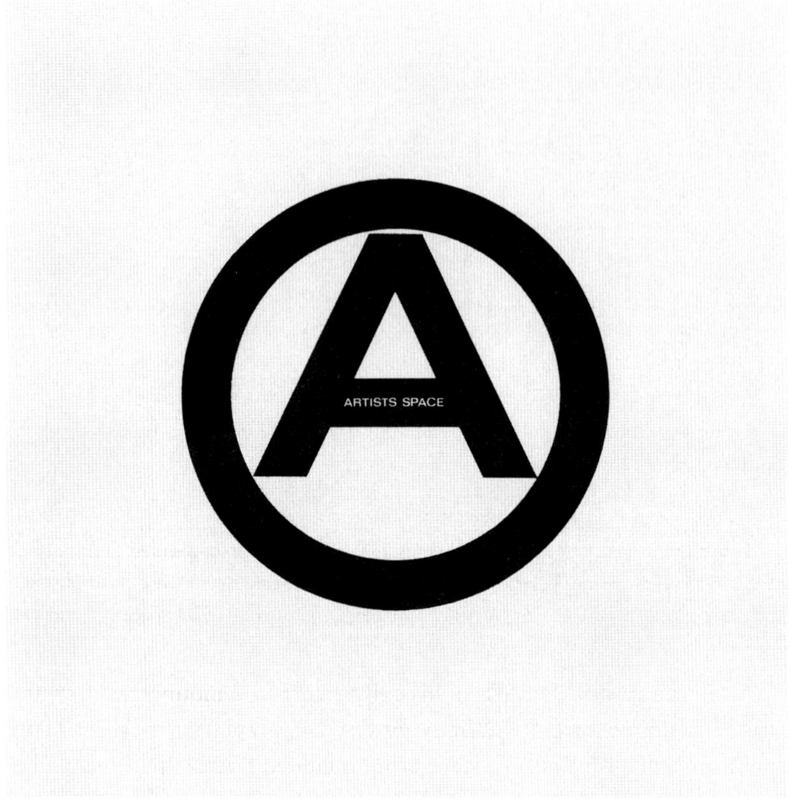

6.3 Poster designed by Louise Lawler for _ _ _ _ _ _ _ _ _ _, *Louise Lawler, Adrian Piper and Cindy Sherman, are participating in an exhibition organized by Janelle Reiring at Artists Space, New York, September 23–October 28, 1978*. Printed paper. Courtesy of the artist and Metro Pictures, New York.

letter of the word "anarchy," enclosed within a capital O, first letter of "order," refers to the anarchist Pierre-Joseph Proudhon—that "connoisseur of paradox"[34]—who claimed in his 1840 book *What Is Property?* that "society seeks order in anarchy."[35] D'Arcangelo knew the book, and in an archival note he even invented a Proudhonian syllogism: "Property is theft. Art is property. Art is theft" (fig. 6.3).[36]

D'Arcangelo's contribution to the Artists Space show was twofold. In the gallery, among the other artists' work, he hung four texts about the ideology and economic function of art spaces. The texts, the first of which is titled "Artists Space: Where are you and What's in a name?," urge viewers to look at and think about the design and function of the space in which they are standing: "Read the brochure, look around." D'Arcangelo's second

6.4 Invitation to _ _ _ _ _ _ _ _ _ _ , *Louise Lawler, Adrian Piper and Cindy Sherman are partici-pating in an exhibition organized by Janelle Reiring at Artists Space, September 23 to October 28,* 1978. Artists Space, New York, 1978. Printed paper. Courtesy of Artists Space.

contribution was the removal of his name from the announcement, installation, catalogue, and all publicity for the show, replacing it with a blank space. Only the NY *Gallery Guide* listing included D'Arcangelo's name because by the time the artist made his proposal it was too late to delete it.[37] Yet because D'Arcangelo's blank space appeared in a list of artists' names, the missing element was not totally invisible. Rather, D'Arcangelo simultaneously pointed to and erased his name (fig. 6.4).

Something similar can be said about the word that might have filled the ellipsis in the artist's anarchist statement. For we learn from his notebooks that at one point he intended to place the word "true"—upside down—between the parentheses.[38] This explains the four rather than three dashes that are customary in ellipses. "True," however, is not a lost presence D'Arcangelo wanted to recover. Not only did he turn it on its head and ultimately remove it, but what he left in the form of an ellipsis is a trace of a presence that, to quote Jacques Derrida's 1978 reflection on the ellipsis, "has never been present."[39] There has never been a true anarchism. The erasure of an adjective suggests that anarchism should not be qualified. This would be the case with any adjective but especially with *true*, which connotes certitude, fixity, inevitability, closure—qualities that Derrida calls "another name for death"[40] and that D'Arcangelo seemed to equate with the death of anarchism.

The art historian Dean Inkster astutely notes that D'Arcangelo's ellipsis invites comparison with the phrase "anarchism without adjectives." Inkster and Sebastien Pluot chose the phrase as the title of the 2011 D'Arcangelo show they curated at Artists Space.[41] In 1889, the Spanish anarchist Fernando Tarrida del Mármol, following in the footsteps of Antonio Pellicer, coined the expression *anarquismo sin adjectives* in a lecture he delivered in Barcelona. The next year, he published it in the French communist paper *La Révolte*.[42] The late nineteenth century was a period of conflict among anarchist factions in Spain; particularly bitter was the schism between collectivists and communists. The conflict concerned the best economic system for a future anarchist society. Along with his colleague Ricardo Mella, Tarrida called on anarchists to abandon such divisions and instead create alliances between groups, recognizing that *any* preconceived economic plan is itself coercive and therefore inconsistent with anarchism.[43] Those who embraced the slogan "anarchism without adjectives" opposed capitalism and private property, of course, and tended to support a coexistence of alternative economic systems. But, they argued, economic preferences are secondary to the shared anarchist goal of abolishing coercive authority. The only rule of an anarchist society would be free experimentation. Anarchism without adjectives was embraced by anarchists outside of Spain, including the American feminist author Voltairine de Cleyre. No evidence has emerged that D'Arcangelo knew this history, but his anarchist statement adopts its spirit. *Upside down words, an inverted sentence, an ellipsis, a paradox*: D'Arcangelo stages an adjective-free anarchist revolt in language. As in the later removal of his name in the Artists Space work, "something invisible is missing" and consequently, as Derrida says, with regard to the grammatical ellipsis, meaning falls out of language.[44] The ellipsis signifies lack, incompletion, and failure to achieve fullness and unity.

In 2003, more than thirty years after his first meditation on the ellipsis, Derrida linked the grammatical meaning of ellipsis to a second, mathematical meaning of the term.[45] In geometry, an ellipsis or ellipse is a curved figure with more than one focal point. The focal points of an ellipsis, unlike those of a circle, do not coincide with each other. Derrida therefore treats the circle as a figure of meaning that is closed in on itself and the ellipsis—an eccentric circle—as a trope for meaning that is "different from itself: in play; at stake." The ellipsis signifies both lack—something missing—and nonidentity—difference. "We are," says Derrida, "between the 'minus one' [lack] and the "more than one [difference]."[46] The elliptical is always lacking and at the same time always more than what it is. D'Arcangelo's use of the ellipsis, then, challenged closure at the level of the sentence, giving anarchism what Derrida calls "an elliptical essence," putting it into play.[47]

But Derrida isn't finished playing with the ellipsis, for at this point he remarks, quite unexpectedly, that "this turn or trope that we call the ellipsis" might have an essential affinity with democracy.[48] He then theorizes a concept that he names "democracy to come."[49] The words "to come," connoting something whose full presence is continually deferred, points to both the structural incompletion and endless promise of democracy. Clearly, Derrida's democracy is not simply a form of government, the form that Oscar Wilde described as "the bludgeoning of the people, by the people, for the people."[50] Derrida's democracy is, rather, a radical form of society, one in which it is possible to question power. Democracy, says Derrida, "is the only system, the only constitutional paradigm, in which, in principle, one has or assumes the right to criticize everything publicly."[51] According to the political philosopher Claude Lefort, this right to critical speech springs from the fact that the hallmark of democracy is the disappearance of certainty about the meaning of society. With the democratic revolution, says Lefort, previously irrefutable foundations of power—God, nature, reason—become "an empty place."[52] Emerging in the absence of a "true" meaning of the social order, the empty place is an elliptical interruption that opens society to ongoing contestation, heterogeneity, and unpredictability. Like the republican institution for Virno, and the future society for anarchists without adjectives, democracy is an event beyond program—a question. Fittingly, D'Arcangelo described his final museum action, performed at the Louvre in 1978, as neither an action nor an occupation but, rather, a "demonstration/question,"[53] a title that can be projected backward onto all the artist's actions insofar as all are elliptical interruptions of the would-be circularity of art institutions.

From 1973 to 1979, D'Arcangelo periodically assisted the institution-critical artist Daniel Buren, who exerted a strong influence on the younger artist's work. Buren's first important solo exhibition had taken place in 1968 at the Galleria Apollinaire in Milan, where he glued paper with his trademark industrially printed vertical stripes over the gallery's door, closing off access to the exhibition space. The size and shape of Buren's artwork were determined by its frame—in this case, the gallery's literal door frame, which stands, more broadly, for art as institution. Buren closed the door to the exhibition space in order to make the institution visible and available for critical interrogation. Facing a blocked door, visitors were also sent back into the city—a space that idealist aesthetics severs from the realm of art.

Five years later, in an installation titled *Within and Beyond the Frame*, for which D'Arcangelo served as assistant, Buren made abundantly clear that he

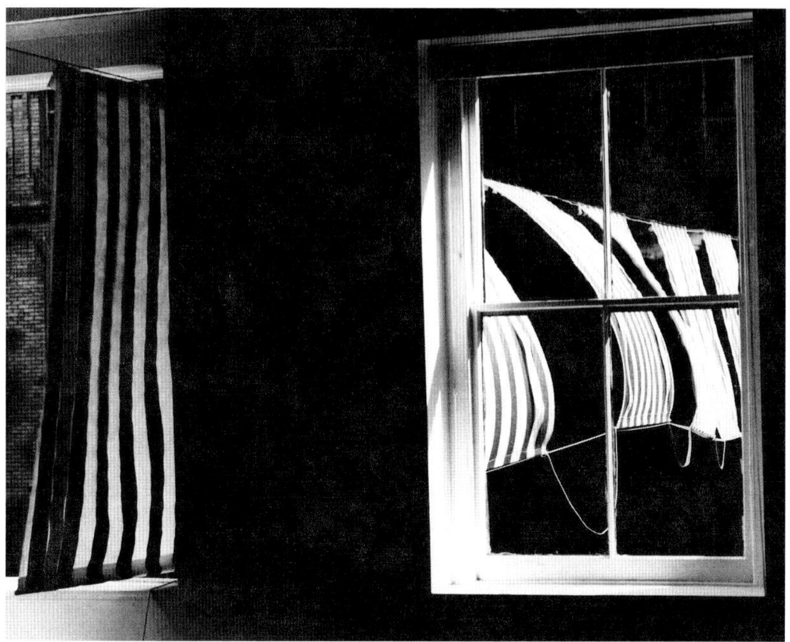

6.5 Daniel Buren, *Within and Beyond the Frame*, work in situ, *1973*. John Weber Gallery, New York. Photo-souvenir © DB-ADAGP Paris.

was concerned with the relational nature of the inside and the outside of the art institution, of the gallery and the city—of the within and the beyond. At John Weber Gallery in New York's Soho art district, Buren hung nineteen panels of commercially produced black-and-white striped fabric, each the exact height of the gallery's windows. He covered the outermost stripes with white acrylic paint, a gesture that identified the panels with paintings. Suspended from a cable that went out the window and was attached to the building across the street from the gallery, the panels hung at regular intervals, nine across the gallery's interior, nine outside, and one half in and half out (fig. 6.5). According to Buren, this last panel functioned as the "balance beam for [the] entire work."[54] Its placement dictated that the gallery window in which it hung had to be removed for the duration of the piece, thereby threatening the security of the interior. *Within and Beyond the Frame*, said Buren, simultaneously "hurls itself" out of the calm of the gallery into the turbulence of the city and reenters the protective interior space through the window, an architectural element that signifies the permeable barrier between art and life.[55] *Within and Beyond the Frame* exposed the gallery to the weather, a danger that in 1970 Buren had likened to that of critical questioning.[56]

Two years later, poised at the threshold of the Whitney Museum's glass doors, D'Arcangelo's body occupied a liminal position similar to that of Buren's balance beam. But Buren's abstract element—the striped panel—was replaced by D'Arcangelo's exposed and restrained yet dissenting body. The substitution had three effects: it dramatized the institution's regulatory power, aligned D'Arcangelo's work with direct-action protest, and, as mentioned earlier, resisted the museum's abstraction of the body. Citing Spinoza—"we do not know what the body is capable of"—Lefebvre writes that "the body, at the very heart of space and of the discourse of Power, is irreducible and subversive.... What is more vulnerable, more easy to torture than the reality of a body? And yet what is more resistant?" Separate from the space in which it exists, "the body opposes it. It will not allow itself to be dismembered without a protest, nor to be divided into fragments, deprived of its rhythms, reduced to its catalogued needs, to images and specialisations."[57] Chained, marked by anarchism, resistant—D'Arcangelo's body was an emphatically political one, which, persisting in a condition of vulnerability, pitted what Judith Butler calls the force of nonviolence against the museum's violence. "Persistence in a condition of vulnerability," writes Butler, "proves to be its own kind of strength, distinguished from one that champions strength as the achievement of invulnerability."[58] Literally closing the Whitney while his anarchist statement challenged the closure of meaning, D'Arcangelo implicitly called on the museum to open itself to its outside.

D'Arcangelo's later action at the Metropolitan Museum issued this call explicitly. D'Arcangelo walked into the museum, removed his shirt, revealing his trademark anarchist statement, and handcuffed himself to the foot of one of the lobby's large octagonal benches. He distributed a text titled "Open Museum Proposal" to museum visitors (fig. 6.6):

THE OPEN MUSEUM PROPOSAL

To The Metropolitan Museum of Art,

The museum functions as a "criteria space", it determines the value of objects and activities in our daily lives. By supporting certain objects the museum creates an unbalanced system of values in the world. In order to determine the relationship of the needs of our daily lives and the values put forth by the museum I am making the following proposal;

A. That The Metropolitan Museum of Art open it's doors for seven consecutive days to any one wishing to place any object or perform any activity in the museum.

6.6 Christopher D'Arcangelo, unauthorized action at Metropolitan Museum of Art, New York, 1975. Photo: Cathy Weiner. Courtesy of Cathy Weiner and Fales Library and Special Collections, New York University. © Cathy Weiner.

B. That the museum vanquish its power to control the nature of the above objects and activities.
C. That all works of art now installed by the museum not be removed for the seven days.
D. That the museum purchase television and radio time to invite people to take part in this seven day event.

In conjunction with this proposal I am now performing a work which is being done in the spirit of the open museum.[59]

The Open Museum Proposal forecasts a later work that originated in May 1978, when D'Arcangelo was invited to take part in an exhibition at the Rosa Esman Gallery on 57th Street in New York (fig. 6.7). In response, he submitted a text, which he proposed to display and keep on file at the gallery for the duration of the show:

I have been invited to use part of the display space in this Invitational exhibition at the Rosa Esman Gallery. The display space I will use, is all the space not used by the works of the four artists invited to exhibit in the same Invitational. . . . The way I will use this space is to invite you to display any product you wish in that space. All products displayed must be for sale. An agreement must be reached between Rosa Esman and yourself as to the cost of the product being displayed and the percentage taken by the gallery. Also if your product is not sold, you must collect your product no later than July 28th 1978.

Directly addressing viewers, D'Arcangelo turned their attention to what he elsewhere referred to as "curatorial control,"[60] asking them to reflect on the way artworks become visible as artworks, a process the institution generally conceals: "You are asked to look at the works," he writes, "and not to take into account the factors that make the works visible in this context, i.e. a ruse."[61]

Needless to say, Rosa Esman rejected D'Arcangelo's proposal and "uninvited" him to the show. However, D'Arcangelo attended the opening, at which he clandestinely sold apples and distributed a text titled "Look Out for what you Look At" (fig. 6.7). The text narrates the story of his invitation and "un-invitation," asking, "What does it mean to be uninvited? Would you like to buy an apple?"[62]

D'Arcangelo's New York occupations can be likened to slightly earlier guerrilla interventions in the city's museums. The MoMA occupation, in particular, stands firmly within a lineage of antiwar actions at that institution. In

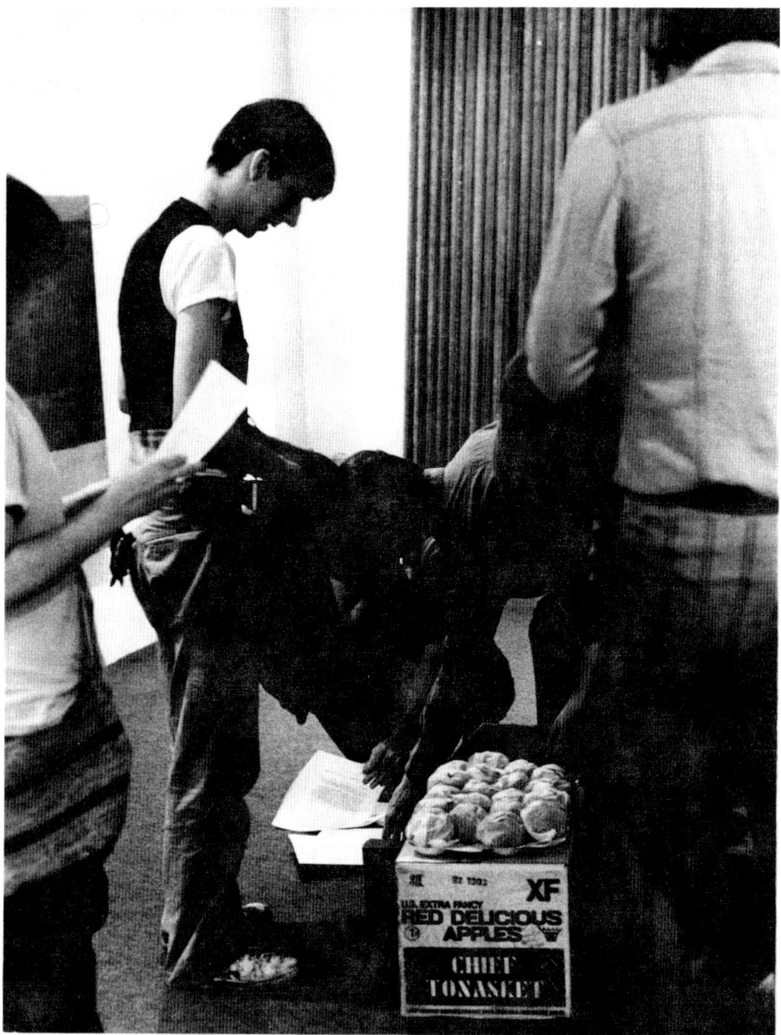

6.7 Christopher D'Arcangelo, unauthorized action at Rosa Esman Gallery, New York, 1978. Photo: Cathy Weiner. Courtesy of Cathy Weiner and Fales Library and Special Collections, New York University. © Cathy Weiner.

1969, during the American war in Vietnam, the Guerilla Art Action Group (GAAG) entered MoMA's lobby and threw a hundred leaflets on the floor. Inside their clothing, they had concealed plastic bags of beef blood, which exploded as they sank to the floor at the end of the performance, bloodying the leaflets. GAAG's leaflet lists the war-profiteering activities of corporations with which the Rockefeller family was affiliated. "Therefore," it con-

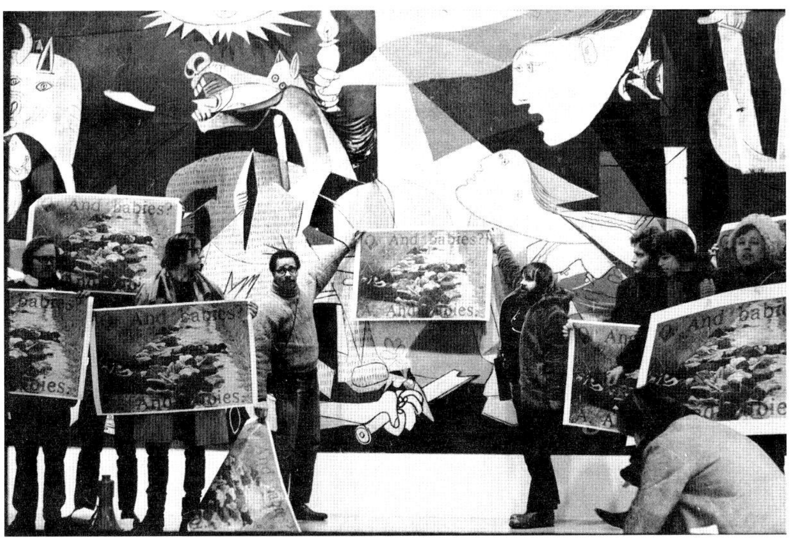

6.8 Art Workers' Coalition and Guerilla Art Action Group protest in front of Pablo Picasso's *Guernica* at the Museum of Modern Art, New York City, January 8, 1970. Photo: Jan van Raay. Courtesy Jan van Raay.

cludes, "we demand the immediate resignation of all the Rockefellers from the Board of Trustees of the Museum of Modern Art."[63] A year later, calling for an end to the war, the Art Workers Coalition (AWC) demonstrated in front of Picasso's *Guernica*, holding copies of an agitprop poster that reads *Q. And babies? A. And babies.* The words are superimposed over a news photograph depicting a scene from the massacre committed by US forces at My Lai. Paying homage to Picasso's work, which protested against the Nazi terror-bombing of the Spanish town of Guernica in 1937, the AWC drew a parallel between the atrocities perpetrated by the fascists in Spain and by the US military in Vietnam (fig. 6.8).

There is, however, at least one difference between these guerilla protests and those of D'Arcangelo. D'Arcangelo made no explicit demands. But the single exception—the Metropolitan action—brings out a demand implicit in all the others: a demand (hopefully not impossible) for an art institution that cultivates the vulnerability essential to democracy.

The Art of Not Being Governed Quite So Much: Hans Haacke's Polls

For nearly four decades, Hans Haacke has put his art at the service of extending and deepening democracy—broadly defined not only as a form of government but as a form of society in which it is possible to question power and to engage in contests over the social order. According to the political philosopher Claude Lefort, the democratic possibility emerges when, with the French and American declarations of the rights of man at the end of the eighteenth century, the power of the state is no longer attributed to a transcendent source, such as nature or divine law. Now, power is located inside the social world; it derives from "the people." But they, too, have no transcendent or substantial identity. So democracy gives rise to public space, a realm of political interaction that appears when the meaning of the people becomes uncertain—in the deep sense of lacking a proper foundation—and is therefore open to debate.[1] Less a site than a process, the public sphere, the condition of democratic politics, sets in motion what Etienne Balibar calls "a universal right to politics," the right of all to both constitute the social order and put it at risk.[2] Michel Foucault, who theorized what he saw as modern society's proliferation of techniques to govern individuals and society, techniques that exceed but also include those of the state, might have defined this democratic right as equal freedom to raise the perpetual question of "how not to be governed." Not how not to be governed at all but "how not to be governed quite so much," how, that is, to limit and transform government: "how not to be governed *like that*, by that, in the name of those principles, with such and such an objective in mind and by means of such procedures, not like that, not for that, not by them."[3] Haacke asserts the primacy of the nongovernmental aspect of democratic politics more colloquially: "One should never leave politics to the politicians"[4]

Since 1969, Haacke has persistently attempted to universalize the "art of not being governed quite so much"—the art, that is, of critique—by expanding his audience's capacity for public life and encouraging the appearance of a public sphere. Although, so far as I am aware, no critic has theorized this attempt as the unifying principle of Haacke's oeuvre, "democracy" and related terms appear frequently in texts on, and by, the artist. Conversing with his like-minded colleague, the radical sociologist Pierre Bourdieu, Haacke has said, "A democratic society must promote critical thinking, including a constant critique of itself. Without it, democracy will not survive."[5] Art historian Walter Grasskamp mentions Haacke's "democratic earnestness," which he fears "is beginning to sound old-fashioned in some circles."[6]

It would be a grave error to treat Haacke's passion for democracy as out of date, for today, democracy's survival is indeed in question and the freedom of critical speech, as Judith Butler puts it, in a "sorry" state.[7] We live in the age of protected democracy, of what the philosopher Giorgio Agamben has described as a permanent state of exception.[8] Technically, a state of exception is a state-declared suspension of democratic law, with the supposed aim of protecting democracy. The founding modern example occurred in 1933, when, on the day after the Reichstag fire, Hitler convinced President Hindenburg to sign a decree "for the Protection of the People and the State," which restricted the individual and civil liberties guaranteed by the Weimar Constitution. Agamben argues that since then, the creation of a permanent state of exception, even when it is not declared in a technical sense, has become an essential practice of democratic states, although the tendency in Western democracies is to replace an official state of exception with a prioritization of security as the technique of government.[9] Instead of declaring states of exception, governments issue exceptional laws.[10] In the United States, for instance, soon after the attack on the World Trade Center, which, needless to say, has escalated the "protection" of democracy, President Bush issued a military order that authorized "indefinite detention" and trial by "military commissions" of noncitizens suspected of terrorist activities. The order created a new category of individuals: detainees, who, like Jews in Nazi concentration camps, are neither prisoners nor persons accused but who have lost all legal status and have no rights.[11]

The erosion of rights in the current period of protected democracy poses a threat to cultural institutions that declare a right to politics. One example, closely tied to the creation of detainees, since both are legitimated by the "War on Terror," is the cancellation in 2005 of plans to relocate New York City's Drawing Center to the World Trade Center memorial complex, a position for which it had been selected in June 2004 by the Lower Manhattan Development Corporation. Under the leadership of its director Catherine de Zegher, the Drawing Center had long excelled at the democratic art of critique. A salvo of antiterrorist rhetoric set off the campaign against the Drawing Center when a *Daily News* headline announced that the presence at Ground Zero of a museum that had shown art critical of the Bush administration would "violate" the public "again."[12] The newspaper thus defined art that instantiates democracy as, in the words of Yates McKee, itself a kind of terror—"aesthetic terror."[13] The following day New York Governor George Pataki, adopting the newspaper's vocabulary of aesthetic violence and violation, proclaimed, "We will not tolerate anything on that site that denigrates America . . . or freedom."[14] In the name of protecting freedom, Pataki pronounced Ground Zero a site where the freedom of critical speech is suspended. "We would never be able to accept censorship," responded De Zegher, a defense of freedom of expression that she reiterated a month later when the Drawing Center's forthcoming exhibition, *Persistent Vestiges: Drawing from the American-Vietnam War*, became controversial, no doubt due, at least in part, to the similarities between its theme and the current war in Iraq. In March 2006, De Zegher resigned her position, ostensibly because the Drawing Center's board decided that she was not suited to fund-raising. It seems clear, however, that the board was unwilling "to play hardball," as Haacke has suggested art institutions must, to support her unequivocal defense of the critical independence of art.[15]

Haacke sometimes uses a meteorological metaphor to underscore the inseparability of art and society: art is a particular "geographical" area in a general social climate, which decides the direction a society will take.[16] Today, the art world is a micro-region in a climate of antidemocratic ideology. In 1950, adopting the same metaphor, Theodor Adorno worried that such a climate entailed "the danger of a large-scale following of antidemocratic movements if they should get under way."[17] To fight against this potential he called for "decisive changes of that cultural climate which makes for the over-all pattern."[18] The current urgency of such changes gives new relevance to Haacke's early democratic works, inviting us to reconsider their significance in light of democratic theory instead of the systems and social science theories with which they have been historically, and by no means incorrectly, associated.

Haacke began the process of forming the art audience into a democratic public, one that thinks and acts politically, in1969, not in his native Germany but in the United States (fig. 7.1). Radically shifting aesthetic direction rather than, as is often claimed, merely taking the "natural" or "inev-

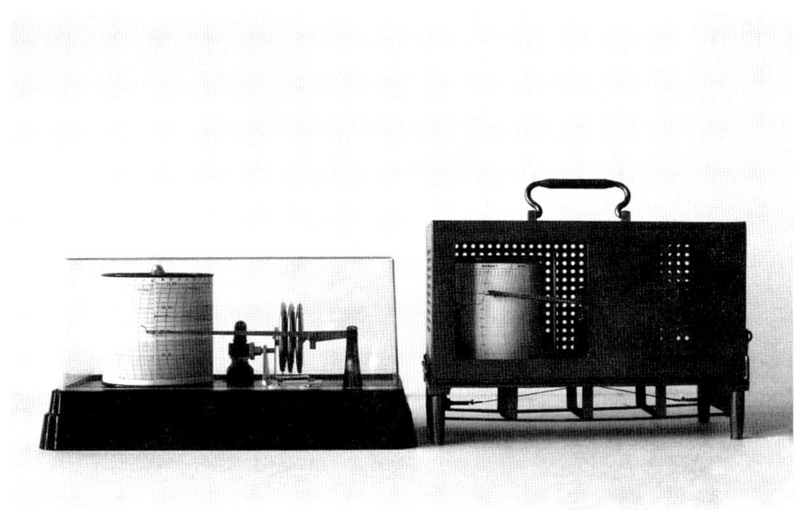

7.1 Hans Haacke, *Recording of Climate in Art Exhibition*, 1969–70/2009. Hygrothermo-graph, barograph, and chart paper. Courtesy the artist and Paula Cooper Gallery, New York. © Hans Haacke/Artists Rights Society (ARS), New York.

itable" step of extending his previous interest in biological and physical systems to social systems, he began conducting polls and surveys of visitors to museums, galleries, and other exhibition spaces.[19] A few years later, he installed polls in Krefeld, Kassel, and Hanover, but his first five took place or were proposed in the United States. However, it was Haacke's experience of German fascism—the economic and political opponent of democratic relations and freedoms—that led him to keep his ear to the ground in order to detect the presence or approach of antidemocratic tendencies within democracies. In Germany, he had circulated among various artistic groups concerned with forging a democratic culture in a post-fascist country. In the early 1960s, as Grasskamp points out, he identified with the interest of the Groupe de Recherche d'Art Visuel in making art accessible to those without art-historical training, an attempt that was understood as democratization.[20] But it was with the polls that Haacke's art (despite the fact that he has never been influenced by Adorno) began overtly to follow Adorno's "new categorical imperative . . . imposed by Hitler upon unfree mankind: to arrange their thoughts and actions so that Auschwitz will not repeat itself, so that nothing similar will happen."[21]

Haacke's first poll, and, arguably, his first work of institutional critique—*Gallery-Goers' Birthplace and Residence Profile, Part 1* (1969)—took place at the

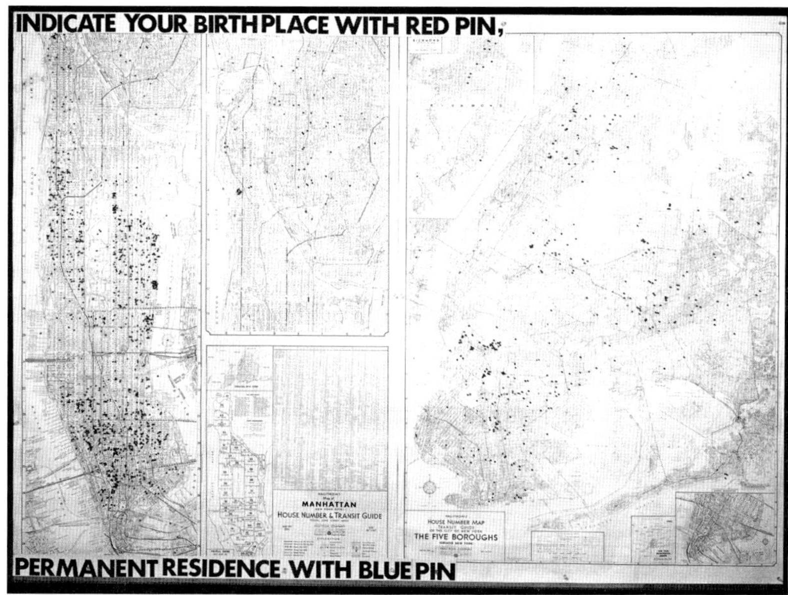

7.2 Hans Haacke, *Gallery-Goers' Birthplace and Residence Profile, Part 1*, 1969. Printed map on cork board, red and blue pins. Courtesy the artist and Paula Cooper Gallery, New York. © Hans Haacke/Artists Rights Society (ARS), New York.

Howard Wise Gallery in New York City (fig. 7.2).[22] On the gallery walls, the artist hung maps of Manhattan, the five boroughs of New York City, the New York metropolitan area, the United States, and the world, along with a text that issued instructions to visitors: "Indicate your birthplace with red pin, permanent residence with blue pin." *Gallery-Goers' Birthplace and Residence Profile* was Haacke's first work to take the social world as its explicit object of study. But the poll inaugurated an equally important change in the *form* of Haacke's art. Previously, he had experimented with a variety of methods to include the audience in his work, for example, using materials that reflected the viewer, as in *A8–61* (1961), or making objects that registered, and sometimes were altered by, the presence of viewers, as in *Photoelectric Viewer-Controlled Coordinate System* (planned 1966; executed 1968). Influenced by Minimalism, he had tried throughout the 1960s to open up his works to their exhibition contexts. The polls implemented a new tactic: direct address. Haacke's instructions spoke to the gallery-goer in a type of sentence—the direct imperative—that issues a command or, in Haacke's case, makes a request: "Indicate." A subject in the second person—"you"—is always understood as the addressee of a verb in the imperative mood.

In subsequent polls, Haacke addressed viewers both imperatively and interrogatively. The first time he asked direct questions was in a proposal for a poll to be conducted at the Jewish Museum's *Software* exhibition in 1970, when he planned to introduce a new polling method—the multiple-choice questionnaire. Visitors would have been directed to answer computer-generated demographic and, in another shift, sociopolitical questions, such as "In your opinion is the moral fabric of this country strengthened or weakened by the U.S. involvement in Indochina?" and "Is the use of the American flag for the expression of political beliefs, e.g. on hard-hats and in dissident art exhibitions, a legitimate exercise of free speech?" At the end of the exhibition, visitors would have been offered printouts of the processed answers in the form of continuously updated statistical profiles of the museum audience. Because of equipment failure, the *Software* poll never materialized and Haacke instead installed a version of *News* (fig. 7.3), but all later polls took the form of multiple-choice questions, whose content was tailored to the country and the historical moment in which they were shown and whose answers were tabulated either manually or by machine.

If, as Haacke has noted, Marcel Duchamp was the first artist to reveal "the symbolic power of the context,"[23] and if he did this by, as Rosalind Krauss writes, redefining the making of art as "the speculative act of posing questions,"[24] then Haacke literalized Duchamp's interrogative heritage. Works that asked questions include *MOMA-Poll*, installed at New York's Museum of Modern Art in 1970; the poll that Haacke proposed for a one-person exhibition at the Guggenheim Museum in 1971 and that was partially responsible for the museum director, Thomas Messer, canceling the show;[25] and polls conducted at the Milwaukee Art Center (1971), the Museum Haus Lange in Krefeld (1972), *Documenta 5* in Kassel (1972), the John Weber Gallery in New York (*John Weber Gallery Visitors' Profile 1* and *2*, 1972 and 1973), and the Kunstverein Hannover (1973). Haacke always exhibited the tabulated results in the form of either printouts or, as in the *John Weber Gallery Visitors Profiles*, bar graphs and charts.[26] All polls used the apparatus—ballots, ballot boxes, key punch cards, questionnaires—of some of the core institutions of representative democracy—voting, demographic studies, opinion surveys—in order to foster the growth of direct democracy.

In "The Constituency," an essay written in 1976 and published in 1977, Haacke analyzes the data he gleaned from the *John Weber Gallery Visitors' Profile 1* and *2*.[27] The polls, he says, showed that the audience for art comes from the college-educated middle and upper middle classes. In this way, they challenged the idealist notion of aesthetic universality, a notion promoted by art institutions—or, to use Peter Bürger's term for a more

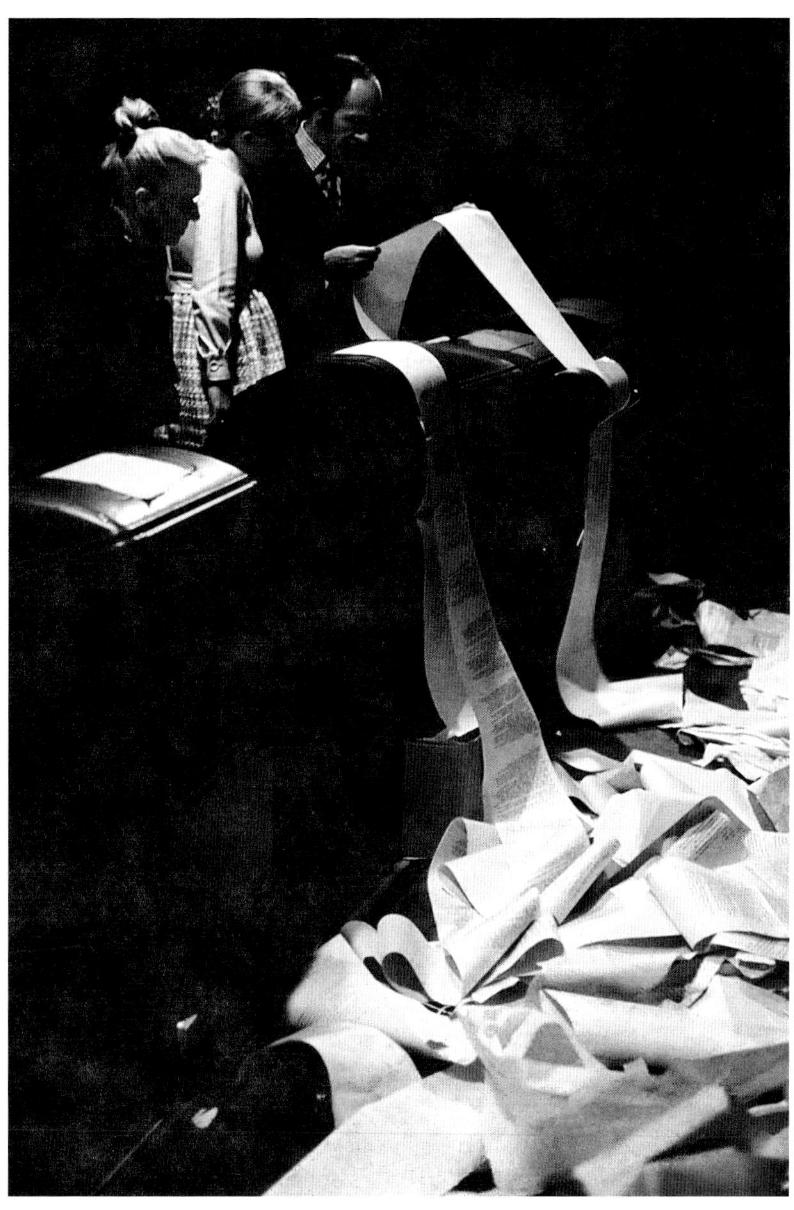

7.3 Hans Haacke, *News*, 1969/2008. Installation view, *Software*, Jewish Museum, 1970. Courtesy the artist and Paula Cooper Gallery, New York. © Hans Haacke/Artists Rights Society (ARS), New York.

dispersed aesthetic apparatus, "art as institution"[28]—which, as a consequence, withdraw art from social life. But coupled with the polls' data, the use of direct address also disrupted the discourse of the gallery and museum. Acknowledging the presence of viewers, direct address countered the then-dominant doctrine of American formalist critics like Michael Fried, who a few years earlier, in his essay "Art and Objecthood," had insisted that a work of art must turn its back on the viewing subject in order to maintain its ability to cohere as a self-contained totality, an entity whose meaning remains constant despite changing circumstances.[29] Direct address, as I have argued elsewhere, announces that a work of art is not such an entity but, rather, a social relationship with a context that includes a viewer or, more accurately, an object whose meaning arises in social relationships.[30] Direct address brings art and art institutions down from the heavens—down, that is, from the abstract realm in which they are placed by doctrines of aesthetic transcendence—and sets them in the social world. It also brings the spectator down to earth, countering the abstract subjectivity constructed by the museum. Haacke's "you" is not some universal citizen of art or phenomenological spectator standing outside class, race, gender, and history. Rather, she is a concrete subject located in time—the implied present of the "I" who speaks to "you"—and what is more, in social space, which is the explicit subject matter of *Gallery-Goers' Profile.*

Even while describing the polls as participatory, art historians have tended to neglect the manner in which Haacke spoke to the viewer, and, as a result, they sometimes characterize *Gallery-Goers' Birthplace and Residence Profile, Part 1* as simply a positivist sociological project or "mere data collection," because the activity it asked viewers to perform required no decision-making and had no explicit political content.[31] It is true that in this and other polls Haacke used sociological methods, like the politico-scientific survey, that have been subject to critique for a number of reasons: they fail to take into account their own mediating effect on the purportedly independently existing data they gather; they present us with an imaginary plenitude—"the voice of the people"—while in reality limiting what is politically thinkable; and they function as technocratic instruments, constructing a "political discourse produced by experts rather than the dominated classes, who have no control over their political 'tongue.'"[32] Bracketing concrete inequalities, including unequal access to the right to speak, polls, in Bourdieu's words, recognize only "the electoral imperative of formal equality before the questionnaire."[33]

It is also true that Haacke drew important conclusions about the art-world population from the data he collected in *Gallery-Goers' Birthplace and*

Residence Profile and the other polls.[34] Yet to restrict the works' meaning to their supposedly straightforward sociological methodology and to the face-value of their data is to play down the fact that bringing the sociological into the space of the aesthetic was an interventionist gesture that modified the identity of both fields. As far back as 1975, sociologists Howard S. Becker and John Walton noted that the resemblance between social science research and Haacke's work is superficial, though they also took him seriously as a social scientist studying power.[35] They argued that because "Haacke works in the same social spaces as those his work describes," his art "differs profoundly from social studies of the powerful" and even has greater power.[36]

Drawing attention, visually and textually, via maps and instructions, to the fact that the spectator and gallery are situated, *Gallery-Goers' Birthplace and Residence Profile* made clear that the art institution is a material rather than transcendental site, one whose identity, far from being autonomous, is constructed as pure by excluding other sites. Eroding art-as-institution's aura of isolation, it engaged in a politics of space that investigated the way in which purportedly self-contained spaces are actually produced by a gesture of exclusion, an investigation sharpened in 1971 in the artist's real-estate pieces.[37] Simply by insisting on the fact of spatial location, then, Haacke performed a democratic action that Bertolt Brecht describes in his 1933–34 essay "Writing the Truth: Five Difficulties": he withdrew support from "a great many lies."[38] Brecht's essay has inspired the artist since he read it in a high-school anthology when he was eighteen years old, and its influence pervades the polls. Truth, says Brecht, is not "a lofty and ambiguous generality." Often it is "something practical, factual, undeniable, something to the point . . . something statistical."[39] It takes away the "rotten, mystical implications" of words.[40] Haacke had sought to demystify the word "art" prior to his first poll, which confronted the lofty claims of the art institution with, precisely, something practical and dry: concrete location, a fact that poses questions about the art world's relation to the broader organization of social space. Brecht's notion of withdrawing support from lies is akin to Foucault's "politics of truth," a practice in which the subject questions the truths promulgated by powerful institutions.[41]

Perhaps most important, the use of direct address was Haacke's first maneuver in a campaign to form his audience into a public. For a public, writes Michael Warner, "exists by virtue of being addressed."[42] It is constituted in a moment of attention or "active uptake."[43] To address a public, then, is not simply to speak to an empirical referent; it is also to "make" a public. Of course, as Warner argues, "no *single* text can make a public"; it must be part of a context in which a previously existing discourse can be supposed and a responding discourse postulated.[44] Haacke's text—*Gallery Goers' Birthplace and Residence Profile, Part 1*—responded, as we have seen, to the discourse of the art institution, which addresses its public as unsituated, ahistorical, disembodied beings. The poll addressed them differently. Haacke describes his polls as an early form of institutional critique that attempted to produce a self-portrait of the art public, and thereby "create awareness among the art public about itself."[45] Which is to say that, "like other products of the consciousness industry," the polls had the potential, as Haacke wrote in another context, to shape "their consumers' view of the world and of themselves" and lead "them to act upon that understanding."[46] In making visible the fact that art audiences are always addressed as a public and in making those audiences aware of themselves as a public, Haacke's polls set down the condition for the audience to transform itself into a different kind of public, one composed of de-subjugated subjects practicing the art of critique.

Marking a departure from the census-like *Gallery Goers' Birthplace and Residence Profile, Part 1*, the famous *MOMA-Poll* mimicked a different sociological method—the public opinion survey. At *Information*, an exhibition of Conceptual Art held in 1970 at New York's Museum of Modern Art, Haacke posted a wall text that read, "Question: Would the fact that Governor Rockefeller has not denounced President Nixon's Indochina policy be a reason for you not to vote for him in November? Answer: If 'yes' please cast your ballot into the left box, if 'no' into the right box." At the entrance to MoMA, museumgoers were supposed to be given ballots that were color-coded on the basis of the visitor's status: full-paying visitor, member of the museum, holder of a courtesy pass, or visitor on Monday, when admission to the museum was free. Below the wall text stood two transparent ballot boxes equipped with photoelectric counting devices into which visitors could cast ballots. Every evening, a chart displayed a tally of responses that were organized by category of visitor. Mounted during a period of mass protests in the United States against the Vietnam War, the bombing of Cambodia, and the killing of four Kent State students who had demonstrated against the bombing, *MOMA-Poll* was the first (with the exception of the aborted *Software* proposal) to poll its viewers on a timely political question (fig. 7.4).

The question not only asked for an opinion on a seemingly extra-aesthetic political event but cunningly—to use one of Brecht's and Haacke's favorite words—asked them to question the politics of the museum. For, as a review of *Information* in the *New York Post* made clear, members of the family of Rockefellers, a name practically synonymous with big capital, had founded

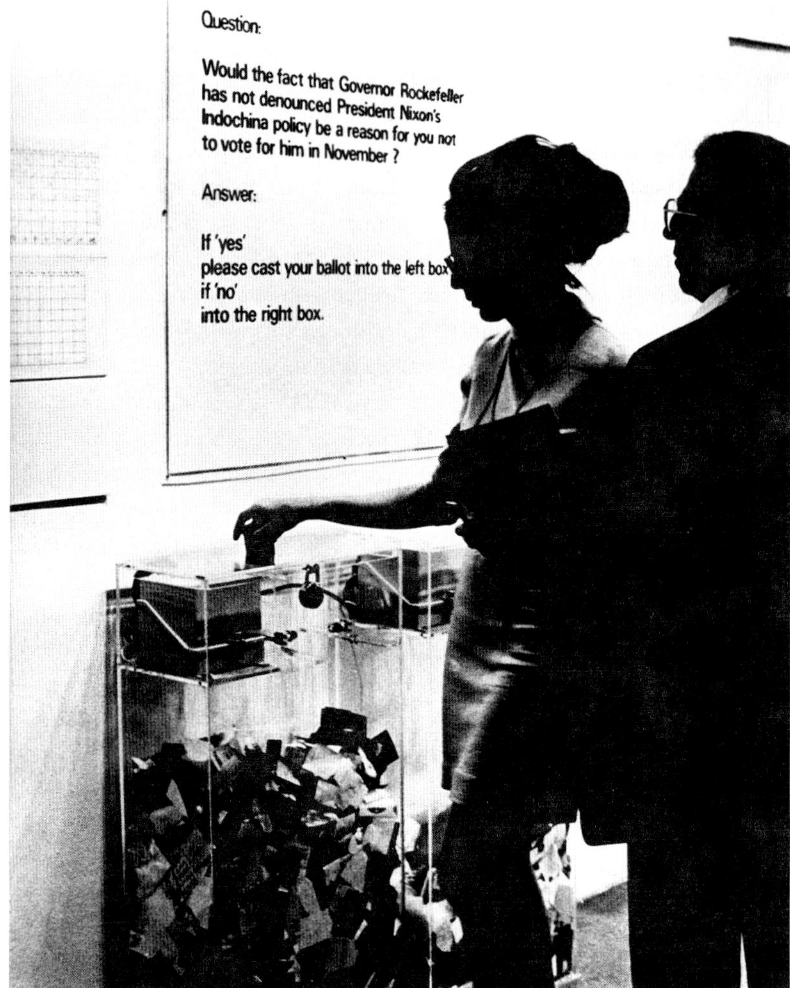

7.4 Hans Haacke, *MOMA-Poll*, 1970. Two transparent ballot boxes with automatic count-ers, color-coded ballots. Courtesy the artist and Paula Cooper Gallery, New York. © Hans Haacke/Artists Rights Society (ARS), New York.

and long governed the Museum of Modern Art.[47] In a passage that indicates the artist's interest in using mass media to further the workings and expand the reach of his art, Haacke pointed out that the reviewer "succinctly pro-vided the necessary background information for understanding the socio-political field for which this work was designed."[48] Governor Rockefeller was a member of the museum's board of trustees at the time of *MOMA-Poll*, and his brother David, chairman of Chase Manhattan Bank, was also chairman of the museum's board. David's position is especially significant in light of Haacke's democratic ambitions. For it was he and a group of other "private citizens," who, three years after *MOMA-Poll*, would bring together prominent government, business, academic, and professional figures to form the Trilateral Commission, an organization whose mandate was to foster a new world order controlled by the liberal democracies of North America, Western Europe, and Japan. Among the reports issued by various task forces of the commission was one on the "governability of democracy," which concluded that increasing demands for political participation in the 1960s had weakened governmental authority and, indeed, all authority based on hierarchy, wealth, and expertise. What the report described as an "excess of democracy" produced a crisis of democracy that must be resolved by a return to passivity on the part of the people.[49] Like other, less blatantly authoritarian writers who nonetheless advocate relegating the tasks of governing liberal democracies to elites, the authors of what became known as "the Huntington Report" (after its American member Samuel Huntington) called for eliminating the public sphere—the very public that Haacke, one of those who had taken democracy "too seriously," sought to foster by withdrawing support from authoritarian truths in Rockefeller's own museum.

In revealing the presence of power in a space where it is rendered invisible by aestheticist ideologies and revealing that the war was not external to the museum, *MOMA-Poll* challenged the closed nature of the art institution, disrupting its privacy by linking it to its supposed outside. The work was public, then, in the sense of being political and in the sense of being open. The poll addressed its audience not as private beings but as members of social groups situated in a historical context. It was public rather than individual. Exposing to scrutiny the concealed economic and ideological structure of the museum and asking viewers to question the role played by specific economic interests in defining a culture that the museum presents as serving the universal interest, it was public as opposed to secret. In the context of the *Information* exhibition, it was educational in that it provided information not for its own sake but to bring about the freedom to discover the truth. In short, *MOMA-Poll* transformed aesthetic space into one where power could be questioned, constituting its audience into a public capable of giving itself the right to politics.

Benjamin Buchloh, one of the most astute interpreters of Haacke's polls, has repeatedly asserted that Haacke's work not only reveals "the dissolution of the functions of the museum (once the spaces of commemoration and historical competence) under the impact of the museum's association with the culture industry" but also fulfills the "traditional function of the museum as an institution of the bourgeois public sphere."[50] Buchloh contends that traditionally the museum provided "visitors with historical objects that would allow them to reconstruct aspects of their (cultural) past and (fictitious) identity and to develop models and theories of how history and identity should be constructed and written in the present."[51] Buchloh believes, as I do, that Haacke's work produces a public sphere. But when he designates that sphere "the bourgeois public sphere" and when he says that "Haacke's work investigates the 'structural transformation of the public sphere' of art,"[52] he claims for Haacke a particular conception of public life, turning him into the artistic equivalent of the philosopher Jürgen Habermas, whose 1962 book *The Structural Transformation of the Public Sphere: An Inquiry into a Category of Bourgeois Society* is the archetypal account of the public sphere as a lost democratic ideal.[53] The public sphere, according to Habermas, arose in the eighteenth century with the advent of bourgeois society, which inaugurated a strict division between the private and the political realms. In the safety of the private sphere, the bourgeoisie could pursue financial gain unimpeded by society or the state. But bourgeois society also gave rise to a set of institutions through which the bourgeoisie could exercise control over the actions of the state while renouncing the claim to rule. In the public sphere, which was in principle open and accessible to all, the state was held accountable to citizens. There, supposedly autonomous individuals emerged from privacy and, casting aside private interests to commit themselves to matters of common concern, constituted themselves into a public by engaging in rational-critical debate. Habermas knows that the idea of the bourgeois sphere was never realized, but he remains committed to the ideal of a singular, unified public sphere in which impartial subjects bracket their status, transcend concrete particularities, and reach a supposedly noncoercive consensus that represents the interests of a coherent social whole. Remaining within the Frankfurt School paradigm of the culture industry, Habermas says that the public sphere declined with the rise of mass media, which, among other developments, eroded the secure border between public and private life.

Yet it is precisely the strict public-private opposition on which Habermas's ideal is based that, in the eyes of other public sphere theorists, makes the bourgeois public sphere oppressive and is responsible for what Oskar Negt and Alexander Kluge, two of Habermas's most trenchant critics, call its "inner violence."[54] This violence, say Negt and Kluge, stems from the fact that the main struggle of the bourgeois public sphere is waged against everything that resists its universalizing tendency, an annihilation of particularities that is no more democratic than the commodity form of production, which levels all differences to abstract exchange value.[55] Whereas Habermas clings to the ideal of the bourgeois public sphere and contrasts it with its supposedly disintegrated mass-media form, for Negt and Kluge the two public spheres are identical mechanisms for excluding particularities.[56]

Buchloh is right to say that Haacke's works urge the museumgoer to develop models for constructing history. They do so, however, in a way that challenges, rather than restores, the traditional relationship of Habermas's public to historical consciousness. For the history of the bourgeois public runs parallel with a tendency not toward history-making but, according to Negt and Kluge, toward "historical impoverishment."[57] To make history, by contrast, is to disrupt the homogenizing historical stories traditionally told in museums, stories that paper over the injustices and conflicts concealed by what Nietzsche called "monumental history"[58]—the history of past greatness, which is seen as universal, eternal, monolithic—or by what Negt and Kluge characterize as "the past on horseback."[59] Beginning with the polls, as we have seen, Haacke cast doubt on the universalizing discourse that circulates in spaces of aesthetic display, challenging it not with an equally depoliticizing pluralism but by withdrawing support from lies through attention to the particular. *Gallery-Goers' Birthplace and Residence Profile, Part 1* suggested that access to the art institution, like access to the bourgeois public sphere, is socially determined and differentially allocated rather than universally granted. And if in the polls the process of participation was, as Buchloh writes, "the consequence of the spectator's privileged educational and professional status," was this not, instead of a failing, precisely one of the facts the works intended to reveal?[60] I, then, want to claim virtually all of Haacke's works since the polls for a "counter" public sphere of history—counter, that is, to the bourgeois public sphere, which systematically repudiates large areas of historical experience.

After the polls, Haacke's democratic practice grew in a variety of directions. Many works—*Manet-PROJEKT '74* (1974) was the first—contested the forgetting of German fascist history, exposing and warning against the persistence of antidemocratic tendencies in the German cultural climate. Others—like *On Social Grease* (1975) and *Der Pralinenmeister* (1982)—investigated the antidemocratic dangers of increasing corporate power in the art world. *Décor* (1989), *Calligraphie* (1989), and *Helmsboro Country* (1990) explicitly directed attention to attacks on the spirit of the American Bill of Rights or the French Declaration of the Rights of Man and Citizen. Continuing Haacke's tireless examination of authoritarian trends, *State of the Union* (2005) raised questions about the United States government's actions in the aftermath of September 11th. *We believe in the power of creative imagination* (1980), *Voici Alcan* (1983), and *MetroMobiltan* (1985), to name only three, supported specific struggles for equality, such as the fight waged against the gross violation of human rights under South Africa's apartheid government, and brought to light the role played by culture in legitimating oppressive regimes.

In 2000, Haacke installed a work titled DER BEVÖLKERUNG (To the Population) at the Reichstag in Berlin (plate 4). In one of the building's interior courtyards, large neon letters spell the words DER BEVÖLKERUNG in a typeface matching that of the inscription DEM DEUTSCHEN VOLKE (To the German People), which appears on the architrave of the Reichstag's neoclassical facade. DER BEVÖLKERUNG testifies to the continuing influence of Brecht, whose essay on writing the truth states, "In our times anyone who says *population* in place of *people* or *race* . . . is by that simple act withdrawing his support from a great many lies."[61] Sixty years later, Haacke took Brecht's advice, which remains pertinent in a period of widespread anti-immigrant sentiment and violence. For just as the Nazi regime murdered millions of people in the name of "das deutsche Volk," an identity based on the nationalist myth of a unity of race and territory, so today the phrase on the Reichstag suggests that immigrants residing permanently in Germany, and their German-born children, are not part of the German people and therefore not represented by parliament. They are what the French philosopher Jacques Rancière names "the uncounted." For Rancière, democratic politics takes the form of inscribing "the uncounted in a space where they are countable as uncounted."[62] DER BEVÖLKERUNG is such an inscription, one that, setting up a dispute with DEM DEUTSCHEN VOLKE, confirms the equality of all German residents.

In a sense, then, DER BEVÖLKERUNG stages the right of immigrants to be governed by the democratic state. But the work contains another element. Haacke's letters stand in a trough of soil brought by members of parliament from various parts of Germany, including a former concentration camp, a Jewish cemetery, and a place where immigrants were murdered. Foreseeing the growth of weeds, Haacke stipulated that these not be removed. The resulting wild plant reserve, a symbolic microcosm of the country, warns against current attempts to repeat the Nazi's largely successful effort to eliminate those they considered troublesome and undesirable. And it performs another metaphorical operation. Like all of Haacke's works since the polls, it stages a right that is especially urgent in the age of protected democracy: to practice the art of not being governed.

:8:

Art from Guantánamo Bay

Soon after September 11, 2001, the George W. Bush administration issued several acts and orders authorizing indefinite detention without charge of suspected terrorists and military trials with no civilian oversight of noncitizens. Like formally declared states of exception—the founding modern instance was Germany's 1933 restriction of the individual and civil liberties guaranteed by the Weimar Constitution—such exceptional orders claim to protect democracy by suspending its laws, including, in this case, the cardinal principle of American justice: innocent until proven guilty.[1] Subsequently, in 2002, the US opened a complex of detention camps at Guantánamo Bay, Cuba, that, in the words of Amnesty International, "has become emblematic of the gross human rights abuses perpetrated by the US government" in the name of the "war on terror."[2]

President Barack Obama amplified Bush's legacy when he signed the National Defense Authorization Act for Fiscal Year 2012, affirming presidential authority to hold suspected terrorists indefinitely, including US citizens arrested on American soil, and thereby, according to the American Civil Liberties Union, making it more difficult to close Guantánamo.[3] For sixteen years, Guantánamo's detainees, of whom forty remain[4]—though President Trump once pledged to refill the prison—have been held incommunicado, so that those of us living in metropolitan centers receive little direct information from them. One exception is Mohamedou Ould Slahi's *Guantánamo Diary*, which reached us in 2015 but only after a six-year legal battle and, even then, with about twenty-five hundred black-bar redactions.[5] It was, therefore, rather astonishing when, late in 2017, thirty-two vividly colored paintings and works on paper along with a handful of intricately crafted sculptures created by eight inmates living behind the walls of this monstrous institution made a public appearance at New York's John Jay College of Criminal Justice, under the Romantic title *Ode to the Sea: Art from Guantánamo Bay*.[6]

The curators of the exhibition were Erin L. Thompson, an associate professor at John Jay; Charles Shields, a language artist; and Paige Laino, digital archivist for the Skowhegan School of Painting and Sculpture. They decided to pursue the project after discovering that lawyers who had worked with Guantánamo detainees had "file cabinets stuffed full of prisoners' art," which they had received as gifts or for safekeeping.[7] Notably, as Thompson writes, half of the artists, like hundreds of detainees before them, were released when it was found that they pose no threat to the US.[8] After *Ode to the Sea* received international press coverage, the Department of Defense decided that prisoners' art belongs not to the artists but to the US government and can no longer leave Guantánamo.[9]

The small size, modest installation, and off-the-beaten-track location of *Ode to the Sea* belied the show's political gravity. Framed or placed in vitrines, the Guantánamo artworks were displayed in the President's Gallery—little more than a hallway on the college's sixth floor—with minimal contextualization other than the show's title, printed on the wall; an eleven-page black-and-white xeroxed handout; and, serendipitously, the ubiquitous word *justice*, which visitors encountered throughout the John Jay building as they found their way, not without some difficulty, to the exhibition. There is, however, an informative, limited-edition catalogue, available online, that was not distributed at the show itself.[10] This catalogue contains interviews with some of the artists; essays by Thompson, Laino (who compares the treatment of the detainees' art with that of the paintings made by President Bush, which were reviewed by several prominent art critics), and Mansoor Adayfi, a former detainee; an excerpt from a book wherein Trevor Paglen describes insignia designed and worn by military personnel working at black sites; moving poems, including one by a former detainee (which also appears in the exhibition); and, finally, color reproductions of all the artworks, accompanied by brief explanatory texts.

It is surprising to learn that most of the works originated in art classes, where shackled prisoners received art supplies and some kind of unspecified instruction. According to the catalogue, an official art class was started in late 2008 or 2009 on the camp authorities' initiative.[11] Before that, drawing was prohibited. Various detainees mention a Jordanian or Iraqi art trainer, who, we might reasonably assume, had no art-therapy training.[12] The bulk of the Guantánamo paintings are variations on a few themes most likely assigned by a teacher—still lifes, hands holding flowers, and so on.

The only fully original work, and the only abstract painting, is Anmar Al-Baluchi's *Vertigo at Guantánamo*, which the artist painted in an attempt to explain to his lawyer the vertigo he suffers after a traumatic brain injury sustained during interrogation at a CIA black site before being transferred to Camp 7 at Guantánamo (plate 5).

As the show's title makes clear, the majority of paintings portray the sea, which is also evoked by Moath Al-Alwi's sculptures of a ship and a gondola, all creatively fabricated from found materials such as cardboard, bottle caps, and glue-stiffened T-shirts sourced at the detention site. Of all the works held by lawyers and human rights groups, about a third depict the sea. A catalogue essay by Adayfi, who was imprisoned at Guantánamo for fourteen years, offers an explanation for the prevalence of the motif. Walls of tarpaulins and fences block Camp Delta's prisoners' views: "It was hard not seeing the sea," writes Adayfi,

> despite its being only a few hundred feet away from us. At the recreation area, if we lay on our stomach, we could get glimpses of the sea through small openings below the tarp. When the guards found out, they blocked the openings. In some cells, in some blocks, we could stand on the windows at the back of our cells to see the sea, but that was risky, because the guards punished us every time they saw us standing and looking out. Whenever any of us wanted to look at the sea, we needed to ask one of the other detainees to watch for the guards and warn us if they came around the block. It wasn't long before the administration made higher covers, blocking us from seeing the sea.[13]

For a few days, however, after reports of an approaching hurricane, the tarps were removed and then "each of us found a way to escape to the sea," writes Adayfi. "The sea means freedom no one can control or own, freedom for everyone," he says, a sentiment echoed by the curators, who also treat the sea as a symbol of freedom.[14] But this interpretation of the motif is misleading, and it is contradicted by other works in the show. For example, the introductory painting, by Muhammed Ansi, reproduces a widely circulated 2015 news photo of the body of Alan Kurdi, the little boy who drowned at the edge of the Mediterranean while fleeing Syria. Djamel Ameziane's watercolor of a shipwrecked boat reflects the artist's remark to his lawyers that at his "worst moment" he felt like "a boat out at sea, battered by successive storms."[15] Even the catalogue blurb contests the association of the sea and freedom, observing that Ameziane's painting expresses anxiety about the future.[16] Ameziane was right to be worried. Having fled as a refugee from Algeria before being detained for eleven years at Guantánamo, he was returned to Algeria over his lawyers' objections. Not particularly optimistic representations of the sea are also found in two paintings of the *Titanic*, known to the detainees because the movie about the ship's sinking was screened at Guantánamo. Finally, Ibraham Al-Ribaish's title poem reads: "O sea! You taunt us in our captivity / You have colluded with our enemies and you cruelly guard us."[17]

The catalogue treats the Guantánamo works primarily as a form of therapy that helps detainees cope with stress and traumatic experiences and increases their self-awareness. It follows that the writers, seeking to uncover the artists' hidden feelings and messages, tend to interpret individual works as vehicles of self-expression. Here are two examples, both describing paintings by Ahmed Rabbani:

> (*Untitled (Still Life of Glassware)*, 2015: Upon first glance, this works seems to be the result of a still life assignment that could have been given in any painting class. But the empty vessels also serve as an oblique reference both to the absence of Rabbani's family but to his self-denial and resistance.

> (*Untitled (Binoculars Pointing at the Super Moon)*. 2016: Initially, this appears to be simply a memento of the Super Moon, a much reported cosmic event in November 2016. However, it is difficult to ignore Rabbani's parallels with the moon: the countless unseen eyes at the end of binoculars seem to represent the authorities who scrutinize every aspect of Rabbani's life without, as he claims, understanding it at all.[18]

Of course, self-expression is a crucial aspect of the detainees' artmaking. As Theodor Adorno writes in the context of another atrocity, "perennial suffering has as much right to expression as a tortured man has to scream."[19] Yet everyone, artists and commentators alike, agrees that the exhibition of the Guantánamo works has a broader purpose: to show the world, especially Americans, that the works' creators are human beings. That they are might seem obvious, but, given the massive dehumanization detainees have suffered at the camp and in Western media and propaganda, it is a significant goal. "To be detained at Guantánamo is to be dehumanized," reads the introduction to Paglen's catalogue essay. "Creating artworks is one of the few ways for detainees to fight this dehumanization, by expressing emotions and a love of beauty."[20] "Let the sea remind you we are human," writes Adayfi.[21] "We are not extremists, we do not hate nice things," says al-Alwi. "I want [an American audience] to think about us in this way."[22] Djamel Ameziane communicates through his lawyer:

For many years we Guantánamo prisoners were pictured by many US govern-ment officials as monsters, the evilest people on earth, the worst of the worst, and I am sure many Americans believed that. Displaying the artwork is a way to show people that we are people who have feelings, who are creative, that we are human beings. We are normal people and not monsters.[23]

What exactly is the connection between the quest to establish the hu-manness of the artists in *Ode to the Sea* and the effort to obtain justice for Guantánamo detainees, an effort implicit in if not emphasized by the exhi-bition and catalogue? Had the curators engaged explicitly with this ques-tion, they might have framed the exhibition not only within a rhetoric of individual emotional expression that offers evidence of human status but also as a collective declaration of what Hannah Arendt called the "right to have rights," which, in democratic societies, is a correlative of human sta-tus.[24] When individuals or groups are counted as human beings, they be-come eligible for human rights. But they do not simply "have" rights; they must *claim* them, for, as theorists of radical democracy argue, rights, like democratic society itself, have no transcendental or immanent foundation. We don't simply possess rights that belong to us by Nature or are bestowed by God or conform to Supreme Reason. Precisely because of the lack of ex-trasocial guarantees, democratic rights and democratic society are open to debate. Rights must be claimed within the social world and against a so-cial order that excludes certain groups of people.[25] In situations of injustice, then, proving humanness and claiming rights happen together. As Thomas Keenan, director of the human rights program at Bard College, notes, in such situations claimants have had to say, "I am a human being."[26] Con-sider, as one of numerous examples, the slogan of striking Memphis sanita-tion workers in 1968: "I am a man." Viewed as a rights claim made by people with no rights except those bestowed on them by their captors, *Ode to the Sea* gave Guantánamo detainees a voice, allowing them to claim, via their previ-ously unseen artworks, precisely this: "We are human beings," or, interrog-atively, "Are we not human beings?" In this way, as speakers, they made an appearance in the democratic public sphere.

A rights claim is an address to others whom the speaker seeks to per-suade. What, then, is the relationship between the detainee art in *Ode to the Sea* and the metropolitan viewers, largely American, who have received it—at the exhibition, in mass media, and now in *Artforum?* A photograph of a man looking at one of the paintings while wearing a jacket with "USA" em-blazoned across the back evokes the same question (fig. 8.1). A claim requires

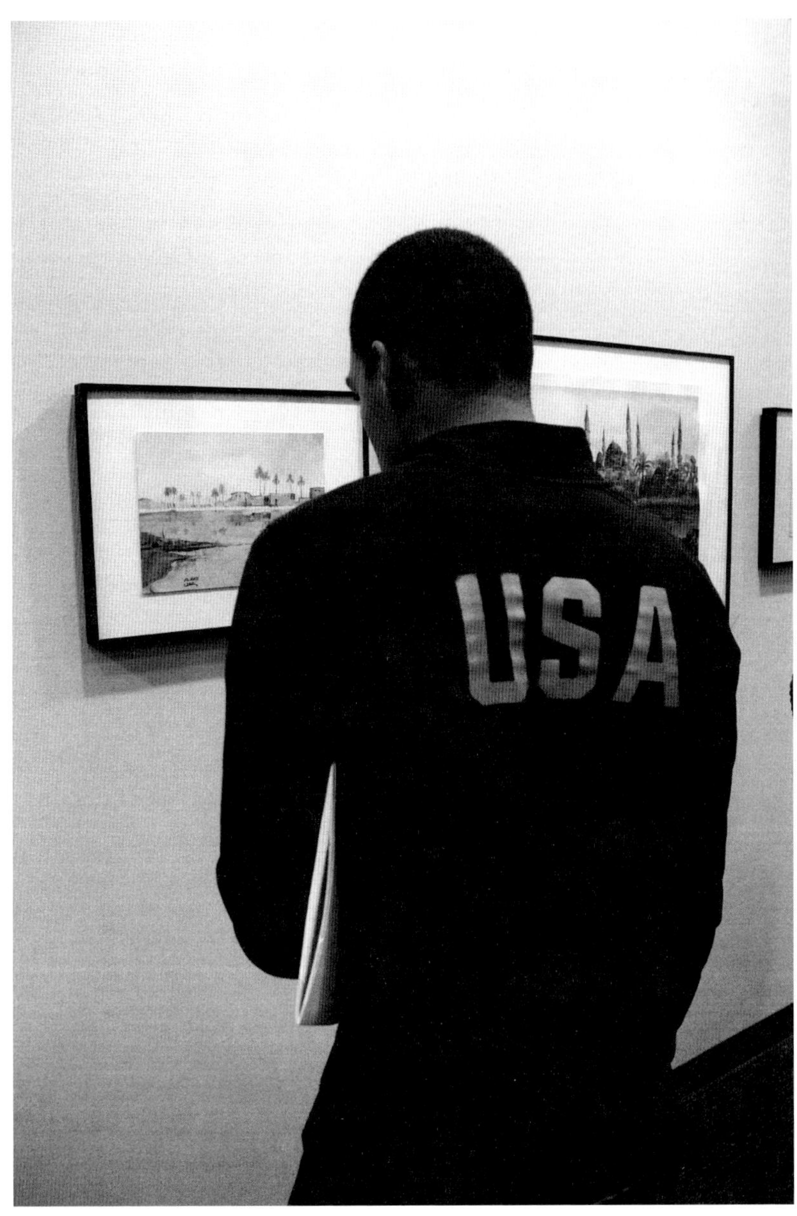

8.1 Visitor at *Ode to the Sea: Art from Guantanamo Bay*, 2017–18, President's Gallery, John Jay College of Criminal Justice, New York. Courtesy Art from Guantanamo Bay and John Jay College.

evidence—in this case, art—and calls on addressees to respond. Judging by the catalogue texts and various articles about *Ode to the Sea*, the predominant response has been to endorse the assertion that the detainee artists are human. However, respondents tend to cast their definition of humanity in classically humanist terms: Humanity's unifying essence, embodied in art, is a love of beauty, truth, and goodness. But despite the fact that the English word *humanity* stands for both "the human race" and "the quality of being humane; kindness; benevolence," to equate the first definition with the second is a fantasy that flies in the face of historical evidence. "Part of being human is the inhumanity of it," says the narrator of Romain Gary's *The Kites*. "As long as we refuse to admit that inhumanity is completely human, we'll just be telling ourselves pious lies."[27] The very existence of Guantánamo attests to such a lie.

It is true that ever since the French Assembly's 1789 Declaration of the Rights of Man and Citizen, human rights have been conceptualized in the name of something all humans share. No subject is ruled out a priori, even if they might be excluded in fact, says Lynn Hunt, author of *Inventing Human Rights* (2007).[28] This is the bright side of Enlightenment universalism. What is more, Hunt argues, the declaration did not offer specific qualifications for people to become subjects of rights, and this lack of definition allowed new groups to claim that "we are like those who are eligible for rights," leading to the ongoing extension of rights.[29] But there is another side to universalism. To assert that metropolitan viewers and Guantánamo artists share a common humanity can function to conceal and thereby legitimate the starkly uneven social conditions of the two groups. Can humanness be detached from barbarically unequal circumstances of existence? Or are humanity and social circumstances inseparable, as the African-American writer Morgan Jerkins argues in a 2018 *New York Times* essay titled "Not Just 'Human.' Black"[30] "I cannot be grouped under simply 'human,'" says Jerkins, "because that default is 'white,' and, I have come to understand, some white people do not seem concerned with my protection or safety."[31] Can we then dismiss, under the cover of abstract humanity, the social relationship that brought together American viewers and Guantánamo detainees at *Ode to the Sea*? Occupying the privileged position in that relationship, we may deplore the imbalance, but we are hopelessly embedded in it.

Instead of responding to the detainees' rights claim with assertions of a supposed common humanity, one unified by its search for the goodness and beauty manifested in art, we might opt for a more difficult, politico-ethical response, one that assents to the claim but acknowledges that we in the US are inevitably entangled in what cultural theorist Bruce Robbins calls "the discourse of the beneficiary":

> The contradictory situation of someone denouncing a system that he finds intolerable but to which he nevertheless continues to belong, from which he continues to derive certain benefits and privileges, from which he may have no possibility of making a clean break—and which he can only denounce to others who also continue to belong to it. I will call talk like this the discourse of the beneficiary.[32]

We benefit from the violent injustices of a US-dominated transnational economic system that causes untold suffering and breeds the resentment that adds to the appeal of terrorism, which is then mobilized by the security state to justify its perpetual "war on terror." There is, in other words, a causal connection between the Guantánamo art and the places Americans see it from. Agreeing that the Guantánamo artists are just like us does not keep us from being beneficiaries. As Robbins concludes, there is no good way to be a beneficiary—even by recognizing the humanity of nonbeneficiaries— "except by trying not to be one," a task that can only be accomplished by "trying to do away . . . with the stark geometry of global injustice by which beneficiaries are defined."[33]

Reasonable Urbanism

Neil Bartlett's beautiful novel *Ready to Catch Him Should He Fall* is a love story whose main characters include two men and a city.[1] The lovers are Boy and O (short for The Older Man), and, as these names suggest, the couple has the quality of an allegorical image, evoking an entire world and history of homoerotic relationships. The city is London, which, like the story's human characters, is larger than itself. Bartlett portrays it as a city of Eros: setting of love, object of love, and site of encounters with exquisite strangers—the passing strangers that Walt Whitman, celebrating the urban nature of gay life and the erotic nature of urban life, called "lovers, continual lovers."[2] One might say of Bartlett's London what Apollinaire said of Paris, that it was created by love.[3] For Eros is not only the thematic content but also the driving force of the narrative, at least the comprehensive Eros that, for the Greeks, surpassed passionate attachment to one's own things and inspired the search in life for the good and the just.

Ready to Catch Him Should He Fall can, then, be read as a story—a myth really—about ethics, justice, and urbanism, where "urbanism" refers, in a broad political sense, not simply to the way of life of those in urban areas but to our manner of living together in the city. This is the story, from a novel rich in stories, that I will read and weave together with certain strands of urban theory. My main purpose is to question two phenomena that currently threaten democratic urbanism. One consists of the moralistic attitude and the animus against rights and equality that dominate public discourse in cities throughout the United States, including New York—the city where I live. The other is the prevailing framework of urban debates, which sets up a division between homogenizing and particularistic politics, either relativizing differences by encompassing all people within a complete social totality or asserting absolute differences in the form of autonomous group identities. Neither position interrogates the exclusionary operations that simultaneously affirm and prevent the closure of identity; neither makes its exclusions available for contestation. Common to both is an orientation toward protecting those who are like "us." This framework makes no room for a politics tied to the capacity for what Emmanuel Levinas calls "non-indifference to the other," a capacity he considers "the essence of the *reasonable* being in man."[4] Secondarily, I use Bartlett's novel to explain why I believe that attempts to understand what a *reasonable*—rather than *moralistic*—urbanism might mean are impeded by a tendency among critical urban scholars to limit urban reality to that which be fully seen or known and to relegate anything else to the realm of the merely, even dangerously, fictional.

Bartlett's London is not only an amorous city but also a menacing one. Gay men and other outsiders—immigrants, blacks, and ethnic minorities—are knifed, beaten, arrested, and verbally abused in the city's public spaces nearly every night. Accounts of these attacks punctuate the story, like gathering clouds. They refer to actual incidents of homophobic and xenophobic violence in London. But they also create a mental landscape for the reader that recalls scenes in classical myths or in Handel's "magic operas," when an approaching earthquake, thunderstorm, or some other natural or—what in this case amounts to the same thing—supernatural event warns a community of danger, portending great disasters or highly marvelous happenings. What danger hangs over London in *Ready to Catch Him Should He Fall*? Put schematically, my answer is this: the fact that members of certain social groups are treated as detestable strangers with no "right to the city"—the phrase, to which we shall return, is, of course, Henri Lefebvre's—and are, as a consequence, threatened in the city by its "rightful" citizens, places the city itself in peril.

An anonymous narrator tells most of the story in the form of a memoir, performing a role akin to that of Socrates in the dialogues of Plato. The novel invites this comparison with classical tradition in its opening paragraph, as the narrator sets the scene and introduces the characters, beginning with Boy:

> This is a picture which I took of him myself. He was so beautiful in those days—listen to me, *those days*, talking like it was all ancient history. It's just that at the time it all seemed so beautiful and important, it was like some kind of historical event. *History on legs*, we used to say; a significant pair of legs, an important stomach, legendary . . . *a classic of the genre. Historic.* Well it was true, all of it.[5]

Ancient history, legendary, a classic of the genre—three times he alludes to the antique world. In addition, the story recalls a particular classic of the genre: Plato's *Republic*, one of the serio-comical dialogues that Mikhail Bakhtin calls "the novels of their time."[6] According to Bakhtin, the early serio-comical genres distinguished themselves from the epic by portraying "the subject of serious literary representation . . . without any distance, on the level of contemporary reality."[7] The serio-comical story is explicitly memoirist. Told as a belated narrative, it places its author on the same temporal plane as the events he recounts, bringing him into a "zone of contact" with the depicted world.[8] At the same time, it brings both the text and the distant past it portrays "into contact with the spontaneity of the inconclusive present."[9]

In this novelistic spirit, Plato's *Republic* and Bartlett's *Ready to Catch Him Should He Fall* examine civic life. Both depict quests for justice in the city, interrogate conventional morality and the nature of love, and "found" imaginary cities, though, to be sure, quite different ones. Both take the form of a story within a story, which is told in a conversational style by a narrator who, as J. Hillis Miller writes about Plato, "probably made the whole thing up anyway."[10] Bartlett's narrator says as much. A few pages into an eyewitness account of Boy's first appearance on London's gay scene, he equivocates: "Actually, I am not sure that I was there on that night of his arrival" (16). Toward the end of the book, after describing a final photograph of the lovers, he says, "Oh how I wish there really was a picture like that for me to give you" (310). At such moments he calls attention to the role of desire in narrative, to the inseparability of memory and fantasy, to his status as an authorial image rather than the actual author, and, above all, to his story's artifice. Yet he neither breaks its spell nor disqualifies it as a reference to reality. On the contrary, he insists that "it was true, all of it."

Does the fact that he is lying make the story unreal? Or, as Oscar Wilde asks in "The Decay of Lying," one of his own Socratic dialogues about art, is "lying"—the term that Wilde favored over "imagination"—the only way to make a story real?[11] More to the point of this essay, does the ambiguity about fiction and reality expressed by Bartlett's narrator mean that the urban space to which his story refers is "unreal"?

Real and Unreal Space?

Today, many critical urban scholars would no doubt answer "yes," especially those reacting against the strong influence that cultural theories of representation have exerted on urban studies over the last two decades. Cultural critics have treated discourses as social spaces and social spaces as discursive constructions, and insisted that both imply a human subject, thereby calling into question the foundations that mark off the boundaries of established spatial categories. Against these ideas, certain neo-Marxist geographers have issued a call to order in spatial thought, trying to maintain a traditional division between what they call "material" or "concrete" space, on the one hand, and "metaphorical" or "discursive" space, on the other. They designate the first "real," the second "unreal."[12] Frequently they add the adjective "social" to the "material" and "concrete" pole of the division and in this way place discourse outside the social world. The social/nonsocial division in critical urban theory repeats an opposition that critical social theory has traditionally drawn between political and nonpolitical, public and private, space. Ultimately, the argument is this: concrete, material, or real—that is, social—spaces are proper objects of political struggle; metaphorical, discursive, or unreal—that is, nonsocial—spaces divert attention from politics. Like other inside/outside dichotomies, the concrete/metaphorical space polarity stabilizes the identities of the political and the nonpolitical while making it seems as through these identities are discrete entities that stabilize themselves.

What exactly do these geographers mean by "concrete space"? Their definitions can be bewildering, testifying to an underlying disavowal that categories of social space are themselves sociospatial productions. One thing is clear, however: they do not simplistically equate concrete space with the physical space of the build environment. Indeed, a major achievement of radical geography, which emerged in the late 1960s as a critique of what Lefebvre calls "traditional spatial knowledge," was its refusal to detach spatial forms from social relations. Geographers and other spatial theorists defined urban space as the materialization of social processes and urbanization as the spatial component of social change, arguing that transformations in spatial organization are not the effect of inevitable evolutions—natural, supernatural, social, or technological—but go hand in hand with the restructuring of the oppressive social relations of capitalist society. Space is socially produced and therefore political. Traditional spatial knowledge supports existing power relations by endowing spaces with proper uses that seem dictated by natural or objective truths. It engages in and conceals "the politics of space." The neo-Marxist critique investigated the socioeconomic conflicts that produce seemingly coherent spaces.

During the same period, changes taking place across a host of disciplines began challenging the social theory that informed radical geography. These changes included the assertion that social reality is not independent of language; the calling into question of the orthodox Marxist idea that society is governed by a single, economic antagonism; the proposal, first made by Ernesto Laclau and Chantal Mouffe, that society, in the sense of a closed entity, is "impossible" insofar as it is constituted by an outside that not only affirms, but also threatens its closure;[13] psychoanalytic notions that social space is entangled with the psychical processes of the human subject; and feminist explorations of the role played by totalizing images of social space in producing and maintain masculinist subjects, whose orientation toward completion represses differences.

Often, geographers themselves helped bring about these changes, enlarging the critique of spatial politics so that it now extended to, among other things, the power relations that structure the space of geographical knowledge. In short, scholars explored the spatial politics of the discourse about spatial politics and investigated the production of the space of politics itself.[14] But some geographers tried to steel Marxist geography against innovations in the conceptualization of space by shoring up the real/unreal space dichotomy and an equally rigid subject/object division. In this way, "objective," external space was safeguarded from contamination by its "subjectivization" in other disciplines.

Still other geographers, perhaps inadvertently, go a step farther. They not only polarize discourse and reality or the spaces to which discourse refers, but also take it for granted that the field of discourse—of uses of language—can itself be so divided, calling certain *conceptions* of space material, hence real, and others metaphorical, or unreal.[15] With this slippage, they couple "real space" with "real language" and imply that both must be protected from the supposed "distortions" of figuration—of, that is, "unreal," or metaphorical, language. Indeed, this protective attitude, though not explicitly stated, is embedded in the assumptions underlying a great deal of the literature about real and unreal space. Many geographers use the adjectives "real," "concrete," and "social" interchangeably to designate a space they construe as the materialization of oppressive economic relations, which in turn unify emancipatory political struggles that are presupposed to be independent of discourse. They presume, in other words, that real political space is extradiscursive and that real political discourse uncovers and analyzes this space, while unreal discourse ignores it and so colludes with oppression, endangering real politics, real space, and real discourse. Demanding a literal use of language, these authors beg the question of reference and, in the name of order, breed confusion. For what they forget is that space itself never speaks directly through discourse, and what they refuse to avow is that to say this is not to deny the existence of a world external to thought but, rather, to acknowledge that in the field of representation, as Bakhtin points out—in appropriately spatial terminology—"the boundaries between fiction and non-fiction . . . are not laid up in heaven."[16]

It is precisely the laying down of boundaries—in the social world, not heaven—that is at issue when Bartlett's narrator exposes the artifice of his story while insisting upon its truth and, in so doing, raises important questions about reference: how does a story refer and thus give access to reality—in this case, urban reality? Is the text's relation to reality measured, as in the simplest realist model, by its references to an urban world that can be seen or, if invisible, understood? Is "urban space" the ground rather than the effect of a discourse that not only knows its object but also knows itself? As in all boundary disputes, the stakes in debates about these questions are political. How and by whom are the boundaries of reality established? What and who are forced into unreality, which political struggles are abandoned as unreal, and, most important, how do epistemologies that treat their exclusions as self-evident fortify their realities against democratic contestation? While urban critics sometimes invoke the simple realist model of reference in unmasking the political conflicts that produce seemingly harmonious spaces, it is important to remember that the model itself can be a powerful political tool, masking its own identity as representation, devalorizing whatever challenges its mastery, and depleting reality of that which cannot be made fully visible or known.

Reading the City, Ethically

There are of course more complex ways to think about reference. Cathy Caruth, in an essay about the relationship between texts and reality, counters the accusation that deconstruction is unconcerned with reference. Deconstruction, she says, does not do away with, but offers a different model of, reference. Caruth approaches reference as a response to realities that cannot be encountered from a position of full understanding. Reference refers to "the ways in which texts render legible those realities that may not be available to preconceived notions of language and the world."[17] A case in point, one that concerns urban reality, is *Ready to Catch Him Should He Fall*. The novel presents a topography of London, mapping empirically identifiable features of the city's physical and social landscapes—specific monuments, buildings, and parks—as well as generic spaces of homosexual culture and homophobic violence. But cityscapes have features that are not so easily mapped. These include, as Lefebvre writes, the residua of earlier people and events: "Nothing disappears completely . . . nor can what subsists be defined solely in terms of traces, memories, or relics. In space, what came earlier continues to underpin what follows. The preconditions of social space have their own particular way of enduring and remaining actual within that space."[18] "What came earlier" often survives in physical form, as ruins, traces, or preserved objects. For Lefebvre, however, social space cannot be extricated from the "mental space" of the human subject. That which is empirically observable he calls "spatial practice," designating that aspect of social relations that is materialized in the organization of physical space. But spatial practice is only one facet of social space. Another is "representational space," or space as psychologically "lived."[19] Both are moments in what Lefebvre famously calls "the production of space."

Insofar as ruins or traces are objects of meaning, what came earlier is inseparable from the relationship the human subject in the present has to them. Spatial practice thus exhibits the same combination of spatial immediacy and temporal anteriority as the serio-comical memoir with which I have associated Bartlett's book. The sense of what came earlier provoked by spatial practice also resembles what Roland Barthes calls the *"having-been-there"* quality of the photograph, the type of visual image that Bartlett's narrator repeatedly longs to show us and makes the object of the reader's desire.[20] In the absence of physical traces, however, what came earlier may persist solely in the subject's psychical relationship to spatial practice. Moreover, what came earlier came only in relation to what did *not* come earlier, what *might* have come, and what has not *yet* come. Social space thus eludes mapping inasmuch as it contains these events that never took place as phenomenal happenings. Indeed, Michel de Certeau contends that it is just such events that produce "space." He proposes that any "place"—which is to say, any clearly demarcated, seemingly coherent interior that serves as a base for managing relations with an outside—contains such events, which destabilize it, no matter how solid and univocal it appears.[21] Bartlett, as we shall see, mobilizes dreams, memories, hopes, repressions, and possibilities that interrupt and put into question the city's present existence, troubling it from the moment of its founding. Are these unreal? Is narrating them not an act of reference? Is the truth of the city separable from what might have been and still might be true? How do we refer to a reality-in-the-making, a making that is, moreover, directed toward no known ideal but is, precisely, unknowable?

For Bakhtin, this is the reality to which fiction refers. When the novel, departing from the conventions of the epic, placed the author in the field of representation and made contemporary reality its starting point, the past world to which the novel referred was opened to history.

Every event, every phenomenon, every thing, every object of artistic representation loses its completedness, its *hopelessly* finished quality. . . . No matter how distant this object is from us in time, it is connected to our incomplete, present-day, continuing temporal transitions, it develops a relationship with our unpreparedness, with our present. But meanwhile our present has been moving into an inconclusive future. And in this inconclusive context all the semantic stability of the object is lost; its sense and significance are renewed and grow as the context continues to unfold.[22]

Further: "Reality as we have it in the novel is only one of many possible realities; it is not inevitable, not arbitrary, it bears within itself other possibilities."[23]

A past brought into a present, which by its very nature demands continuation and moves into a future; a reality that contains other possible realities; a quality of "unfinish" that is the condition of hope: these features characterize the city of London in *Ready to Catch Him Should He Fall*. The book refers to a space—and is itself such a space—inhabited by "the force of what is not known . . . the powerful effects of the ill-understood and not-yet-known in human experience,"[24] by that force which founds every reality.

The problem of reference opens onto the tension between "revealing" and "creating" that is inherent in mapping, writing, or any means of representing the cityscape. J. Hillis Miller argues that the very term "topography" contains this tension. Topography has two dictionary definitions: first, the representation of a landscape using the conventional signs of a system of mapping, and second, that which is mapped, the landscape "as such," with no reference to representation. Discourse about landscape frequently elides the difference between the two, but the relationship of the first to the second is never direct: "The landscape 'as such' is never given, only one or another of the ways to map it."[25] While critical urban theory often maps the oppressive social relations hidden by traditional spatial knowledge, the social landscape portrayed in alternative maps is also never given as such. Alternative maps—which are different from critical maps—also conceal events, especially those that cannot be assimilated to phenomenal reality and that, because they do not take the form of identifiable entities, cannot be mapped but only narrated. Are these narrations, then, untrue? Lynne Tillman, in a superb essay on Bartlett's work, answers this way: "Fiction's 'truth' is verisimilitude, an appearance of truth, of likelihood."[26]

What inhabits the topography of London in *Ready to Catch Him Should He Fall*? If, as I have suggested, the spirit of the *Republic* haunts Bartlett's London, it is only one of many spirits, a whole crowd of books and plays, musical and literary forms, artists and writers that populate the novel and the city it depicts. Prominent among this spectral group is Oscar Wilde, whose imprisonment in 1895 for indecent behavior with men, precipitated by his affair with Lord Alfred Douglas, is remembered and reimagined in the book. In a way, Bartlett undoes Wilde's fate; he gives O a Boy worthy of love, their relationship turns out well, and the lovers prevail over the city's homophobic moralism. The very title of Bartlett's book alludes to Wilde, who is described in the first few lines of Richard Ellmann's classic biography as "refulgent, majestic, ready to fall."[27] The evocation of Wilde also embeds the novel more firmly in the Greek context. Wilde admired Plato and mimicked the dialogue form in his own essays. What is more, Wilde, like Socrates, conducted "in the most civilized way, an anatomy of society, and a radical reconsideration of its ethics,"[28] and this interrogation of conventional morality led each man to his trial and downfall.

"Haunts," however, is not quite the right word to describe the relationship between *Ready to Catch Him Should He Fall* and the *Republic*. It would be more accurate to say that Bartlett breathes life into Plato's dialogue. This act of animating Plato exemplifies the trope of "prosopopoeia," a term that also reaches us from the Greeks. Following Paul de Man, the literary theorist Kenneth Gross defines prosopopoeia as "the often hallucinatory figure by which poets lend a voice, face, or apparent subjectivity to things in themselves inanimate, absent, or lost—the wind, a dead child, a past self, an ideal of liberty."[29] Apart from Bartlett's specific resuscitation of the *Republic*, his very use of prosopopoeia raises the spirit of Plato. Plato's dialogues are narrated by Socrates, who, when Plato wrote them, was already dead, and therefore, as Miller writes, the dialogues are one extended prosopopoeia.[30]

Miller makes this point in an essay about Plato's *Protagoras*. He demonstrates how the dialogue at once uses and comments on prosopopoeia. Socrates recounts his encounter with Protagoras. While narrating the meeting, he twice quotes Homer's *Odyssey*. Both citations are from the account of Odysseus's visit to the underworld. Miller argues that, in quoting Homer at the point where Socrates meets Protagoras, Plato places Socrates's entire narrative under the aegis of Odysseus's visit, which is "the original myth on which all prosopopoeias depend or of which they are miniature imitations."[31] When Plato repeats the myth told in the *Odyssey*, a myth that, incidentally, is also a subtext of the *Republic*, he directs the reader's attention to prosopopoeia, which, says Miller, may be "the fundamental poetic power" and "is certainly the power that makes narrative possible."[32]

> All prosopopoeias are visits to the underworld. They depend, in a shadowy
> way on the assumption that the absent, the inanimate, and the dead are wait-
> ing somewhere to be brought back to life by the words of the poet or orator.[33]

Miller links prosopopoeia to ethical responsibility: by following his argument and bringing it together with ideas about democracy, freedom, and
rights, we can illuminate the way this literary figure bears on issues of urbanism.

To begin with, Miller connects prosopopoeia to ethical thought and action and to struggles against forgetfulness by maintaining that in acts of
prosopopoeia a writer assumes "the responsibility the living have to the
dead."[34] Moreover, responsibility informs not only the act of storytelling
but also that of reading, in which the reader ascribes "a face, a voice, and a
personality to those inanimate black marks on a page."[35] He adds, "The moment no one anywhere is reading Plato, all the figures in his dialogues will
die again."[36] Prosopopoeia is therefore a way of telling stories and of keeping stories and people alive.

Past events, stories, and people are not simply in danger of being forgotten, however, but, as Walter Benjamin famously warns, of being remembered in a manner that turns them into "a tool of the ruling classes."[37]
Throughout history tradition has been constructed as the tradition of the
victorious, burying what Benjamin calls "the tradition of the oppressed,"[38]
which is to say, the tradition of fighting against oppression. Tradition
ceaselessly falls prey to a petrifying conformism, and "Only that historian
will have the gift of fanning the spark of hope in the past who is convinced
that *even the dead* will not be safe from the enemy if he wins."[39]

Miller's discussion of prosopopoeia is part of his broader theory of "the
ethics of reading," a phrase that refers to that aspect of reading in which
the reader opens herself to something unknown, responds to a call in a text,
and, further, takes responsibility for the effects of her act of reading.[40] Responding differs from, indeed interrupts, understanding. For reading is
ethical when we expose ourselves and answer to the other—an other that
is not a transcendent entity but something that manifests itself precisely
as that which is not an object for understanding. Emmanuel Levinas names
this other "the face," a term that designates the other human being who
both looks at and "concerns me," who matters "to me as someone for whom
I am answerable."[41] Ethical responsibility appears, then, when certainty disappears. It emerges with the proximity of the face—not that which is literally near to me but that which addresses itself to me as something that
is "not mine" and which therefore disrupts a world construed as an object

for the "self." Responsibility is incompatible with moral discourses that posit unassailable, substantive grounds of the norms they seek to enforce. Rather, it presses us to interrogate conventional morality and, in this way, resembles Sin, about which Wilde wrote, "In its rejection of the current notions about morality, it is one with the higher ethics."[42]

Like responsibility, democracy is also constituted by uncertainty. Claude Lefort, in his generative work on democracy, argues that the bourgeois political revolutions of the eighteenth century shifted the site of power. The monarchical state referred its sovereign power to a source outside society—God or Supreme Justice—a transcendent source that also guaranteed social unity. With the Declaration of the Rights of Man, however, state power derives from "the people"; it is located within the social. But with the abandonment of references to a transcendent ground of power—with "the dissolution of the markers of certainty"—reference to an unconditional ground of the social order disappears as well. We are exposed to others, but the "basis of relations between *self* and other"[43] is indeterminate. Put differently, indeterminacy exposes us to others, and, with this exposure, democracy is invented. While the markers of certainty legitimated absolute power, their dissolution legitimates debate about what is socially legitimate and what is illegitimate. Because the ground of our commonality is uncertain, has no fixed point, no external guarantee, it is open to interrogation through the declaration of rights, a process in which the meaning and unity of society are perpetually negotiated. Social questions may well be decided, and conflicts settled, but to be democratic, society itself must remain an unsolved problem.[44]

With the collapse of the ground, the social world becomes an enigma and slips from the grasp of the subject. The image of social space as an object totalized by a substantive foundation, an object that transcends partiality and is independent of all subjectivity, positions the subject as the external point of complete or, more often, potentially complete knowledge. Democratic society does not, however, present itself as an object for the subject. The removal of its ground pluralizes society—not by fragmenting it into self-contained, conflicting groups but by making it incompletely knowable and therefore "not mine." Far from dividing a substantially unified humanity—a frequently expressed fear—the collapse of the ground makes us what Levinas calls "reasonable" human beings, beings defined by the capacity to be "non-in-different to the other."[45] And since the dissolution of the markers of certainty is simultaneous with the founding of the rights of man, these rights imply a "consciousness of the rights of the other, for which I am answerable."[46] Democratic rights can then be understood not simply as the freedom *of* the self but as freedom *from* the self, "from its ego-tism." Through non-indifference of the one for the other, "the justice of the rights of man takes on an immutable significance and stability, better than those guaranteed by the state."[47] Levinas's conception of rights casts doubt on an ethics that would link rights to the unified identity of a political group, such as the nation-state, since this would only sanction indifference. As Julia Kristeva points out, a national political conscience normalizes the notion of foreigners, which it defines as "people who do not have the same rights as we do."[48]

With the idea of non-indifference, we can again take up the discussion of Bartlett's novel and of ethical reading, whose prerequisite is precisely the capacity to respond to a world that does not belong to me, in which *I* am a foreigner. Tillman captures this connection beautifully: "The resistance to reading fiction may be a refusal to enter into another world, a strange place, where one must suspend one's own world, which may be ignored. A novel speaks: 'This is a world not of your making.'"[49]

Moving Statues

Bartlett animates Plato, just as Plato rejuvenated Socrates, who has been seen as the first philosopher "to call philosophy down from the heavens and set her in the cities of men."[50] Yet this invocation of the origins of political philosophy signals no adherence to substantive notions of the good society, no simple nostalgia. *Ready to Catch Him Should He Fall* deals with *contemporary* urban-political issues, specifically those that began to threaten London in the 1980s, when an aggressive homophobia surfaced as an emblematic urban problem. This problem has manifested itself in moralizing antisex campaigns, legislation aimed at censoring pornography, a censorship system that, as Simon Watney writes, "regards all references to homosexuality as such to be intrinsically indecent and/or obscene,"[51] and the press's construction of homosexuality "as an exemplary and admonitory sign of Otherness . . . in order to unite sexual and national identifications amongst readers over and above all distinctions of class, race and gender."[52] The violence that erupts at key moments in Bartlett's London encapsulates these threats. But there is another striking feature of the cityscape, another danger that has occasioned and legitimated homophobia and which, though never named, may lie at the secret heart of the novel—the AIDS epidemic that began to devastate London in the 1980s, as it did so many other cities.

Boy and O walk all over this city. They meet when Boy has finished a journey so exhausting that it seems as though he has wandered out of the past and across vast territories. He arrives at The Bar, where O, another "man with a past" (68), is a regular patron and where much of the novel takes place. In a way, Boy's arrival is a homecoming. The narrator, a longstanding denizen of The Bar, describes it as a very strange place that "to us" was "as normal as home" (23). Run by Mother, who helps educate Boy about gay history and culture, The Bar is both a shelter from the homophobic city and itself a kind of city (a metropolis or mother-city), one in which gay men can walk, have sex, get engaged, be promiscuous, and dance all night without fear, subject only to "our own rules" (30). The Bar is a fictional amalgam of different types of spaces—bars and sex clubs—in which gay men have developed a public culture. In The Bar, gays, who live in what Bakhtin, writing about medieval carnival, calls a "two-world condition," have "built a second world and a second life outside of officialdom."[53] Evoking the rituals of play associated with both carnival folk culture and modern urban traditions of gay male performance, Bartlett's narrator describes dramas that are staged each night at The Bar against painted backdrops representing foreign countries. Sometimes Mother feels that the men under her care need a more drastic change of scenery and she redecorates the whole place to look like another city: Amsterdam or Paris or just London—"our own dear city"—in an earlier era (27). But whichever city The Bar resembles, "whatever city we were all supposed to be in," one element remains constant: the ceiling, painted black and inlaid with hundreds of tiny lights forming constellations. "And on a good night," says the narrator, "the stars would seem to brighten; if you looked up, it was like a clear winter's night in the city" (28–29).

Outside The Bar is a homophobic city of fear; inside, a city of homoerotic refuge. Yet Bartlett cancels the opposition as much as he affirms it. While The Bar is a city nested within London, London is also nested within The Bar. The Bar is big and "contained in a way the streets of the whole city, there were men there from all the different parts of it" (33). And while The Bar permits a kind of eroticism prohibited in the city, it also brings the eroticism of urban space—wanderings, chance meetings, encounters with strangers, dark corners, public intimacies, bodies coming together and moving apart—into its interior. The Bar reiterates and transforms the features of the city so that, as Henry Urbach writes about gay sex clubs, "once contested sites are voided of homophobia to become enclaves of queer sexual practice."[54] Toward the end of *Ready to Catch Him Should He Fall*, the conditions of The Bar prevail in the larger city when, in a carnivalesque reversal, traditional sociospatial hierarchies are suspended for a single night, and Boy and O walk freely through the streets of London.

Boy appears on the threshold of The Bar like a herald of this marvelous event. "Boy was truly beautiful, when he came to us," recalls the narrator. "I can see him now standing there in the door" (15). At the exact moment of Boy's arrival, a man from The Bar is stabbed four times in the city outside. Only later does the narrator connect the two events. First he describes Boy and, immediately afterward, a second image: "I have this postcard depicting an allegorical figure of Strength." The figure "is naked like a statue," and "in the palm of his raised, right hand he holds out to you a miniature city, complete with dome, bridges and towers, the freedom of which he is offering you and which he has promised to protect" (15). The narrator compares Boy's beauty to that of a civic statue watching over the city. Perhaps the description was inspired by Wilde's homoerotic and ethical fairy tale *The Happy Prince*, in which a gilded and bejeweled statue of a prince, perched on a hillside "high above the city," is overcome with sorrow at the inequality and misery he sees. Aided by a male swallow, with which he falls in love, he is able to alleviate the sufferings of the oppressed by giving away his gold and precious stones.[55] In addition to painting a picture of Boy, Bartlett's passage about the statue gives us an image of the novel's *own* activity, of the way it, too, will protect the city's freedom. Like *The Happy Prince*, the passage is an example of ekphrasis, the literary description of a real or imagined work of visual art. *Ready to Catch Him Should He Fall* contains numerous ekphrases. Indeed, the entire book is ekphrastic: it begins by describing Boy's photograph and ends with a phantasmagoria of images of Boy, O, Mother, and all The Bar's inhabitants in a variety of cities that have been liberated from totalitarian or tyrannical regimes. Like prosopopoeia, ekphrasis transfigures object, submitting the inanimate artwork "to languages of conversion"[56] or to conversions wrought by language. Ekphrastic texts do not uncover original, unchanging meanings of art objects. They rediscover the fact that political struggles constitute the meaning of an object. Ekphrasis thus figures the way in which ideas, language, and images are reanimated—through practices of use.

Among the silent, immobile objects that can be brought to life and lent a voice through ekphrasis and prosopopoeia are the things of the city—buildings, monuments, streets, parks, and the built environment as a whole. Midway through *Ready to Catch Him Should He Fall* something astonishing, though not miraculous, occurs: the clouds that have been gathering over London break, and, in the ensuing storm, the city speaks. It happens at the climax of Boy and O's courtship. On this night, Mother has staged a play at The Bar. The dramatis personae are The Son (Boy), The Father (O), and The Lover (also played by O). In the play's final scene, The Son defies The Father and runs off with The Lover.[57] The curtain falls and then rises again at midnight. Gary, The Bar's pianist, strikes twelve notes as Mother steps onto the stage, leads Boy and O toward the footlights, and joins their hands "in public." "And that was it," recounts the narrator, "I had tears in my eyes, and they were engaged" (167–68).

Shouts, applause, and a joyous, drunken celebration follow, drowning out the thunderstorm that has struck London. The storm's proportions are epic; it nearly wrecks the city. But it also interrupts the city's violence. No gay men are attacked that night. Moreover, London becomes the setting of a drama, which, like that performed inside The Bar, publicly announces and commemorates the male couple's love. As the narrator puts it, "the city itself had celebrated O and Boy's engagement, but in the strangest fashion" (168). As the storm hits the city's power lines, extinguishing streetlights and illuminated clocks, time is suspended and the theater darkened. The statues of London begin to move and talk. Their speech is operatic, stretched to the expressive limits of the human voice.

> They beckoned to each other, their arms upraised against the winds in benediction, exhortation, jubilation; and when the rain finally came, just before morning, the stone and metal of those limbs, which had become warm, almost as warm as flesh, in the heat of the long summer day and evening, seemed to take on a sort of life. Of course none of the statues was actually seen to move; that would have been a miracle; but as the rain fell they seemed, though immobile, to live. The Temple dragon in the Strand mewed a clear poison which dripped from under his forked tongue. The great, stupid, sleeping lions in the square drooled saliva and seemed about to rise and roar; a kind of clear blood ran down the blade of the uplifted scimitar with which the Allegory of Fortitude protected her naked child from the snake pinned beneath her foot at the Aldwych; there was so much blood it ran over the handle of the scimitar and down over her wrist. The wings of the Victory alighting atop the arch at Park Lane found a wind at once adequate to their size, weight and fury; her horses reared at the lightning and were lathered in sweat. On the parapet of the cathedral at Ludgate, St. Agatha expressed a single drop of milk from the nipple of her stone breast. And on churches, tombstones, banks and derelict theatres, all the angels of London wept; tears dripped down their metal cheeks and trickled from under their stone eyelids. Since their faces did not move, their reasons for crying on this occasion remained hidden . . . Michael, Prince of all the city's angels, wept on the porch of St. Peter, Cornhill. And above them all the great golden figure on the Old Bailey, Justice herself, blindfolded and armed just as Love is armed and blind, Justice herself was seen to move; she rocked and swayed in the storm. (169–70)

This is the most elaborate and overt prosopopoeia in *Ready to Catch Him Should He Fall*. Like the earlier description of the postcard of a civic statue, the passage about the storm has affinities with *The Happy Prince*. In Wilde's story, too, a statue weeps, and the swallow that loves the prince at first mistakes his tears for rain. Like Wilde's fairy tale, Bartlett's thunderstorm scene epitomizes a recurrent literary fantasy: the dream of the moving statue, which Kenneth Gross analyzes in his book of the same name. The salient characteristics of statues are silence and immobility, yet they have, Gross argues, the power to transfigure the spaces they share with us. Indeed, it is the very silence of statues that makes them sites of contest, though silence can also serve as an image of "what seems to exist outside the deformations of human language"[58] and is therefore *incontestable*. While the fantasy of their animation turns statues into literal figures of speech—figures that speak—it, like ekphrasis, also "turns our attention away from the artifact itself and toward the complex act of reading it."[59] The fantasy thus emphasizes the figurative, rather than literal, nature of language. Perhaps this is one reason that signs of life in statues can be frightening and are frequently warded off by countervailing fictions of stability. "Works of sculpture are such solid wises," says Gross, "or vehicles of a wish for things that *are* solid," that they "are more than usually subject to the fate that threatens any work of figuration—that of becoming literalized."[60] The insistence on literalism kills statues—by, paradoxically, rendering them statuesque—just as, in Miller's words, it "strikes language dead."[61] Conversely, the dream of the speaking and moving statue can keep alive not only the statues but also language, and, particularly in the case of civic statues, the cities we inherit.

This capacity for revitalization depends not only on the content but also on the form of the statues' speech. Bartlett makes it clear that his statues are neither literally alive nor animated from within: "Of course none of the statues was actually seen to move; that would have been a miracle; but as the rain fell they seemed, though immobile, to live." The scene is realistic, though it does not purport to convey meanings inherent in the external world, in things themselves. Rather, it dramatizes the emergence of meaning at the object's surface, its point of contact with an outside.

Bartlett thus avoids the danger to which the urban theorist Raymond Ledrut alerts us: making the city speak "in such a way that it will seem as if the city itself were speaking."[62] In a 1973 essay, "Speech and the Silence of the City," Ledrut combines semiological and sociological analyses to investigate the city as a signifying practice. How, he asks, are the things of the city made meaningful? How, that is, do they learn to speak? The answer depends in turn on what we mean by "the city." Ledrut rejects the technocratic notion that the city is a spatial framework created *for* users by powers that surpass them, and suggests that "the city is truly the city only insofar as it is an environment formed *by* users.[63] It is "an object charged with meaning by . . . the use men make of it."[64] To make the city speak in a way that makes it seem as if the city itself is speaking is to give the impression that the organization and uses of urban space are dictated by the objective needs of a uniform society. This has the effect of erasing the operations that produce urban meaning by claiming that a pregiven reality speaks for itself. For Ledrut, as for all critical urban scholars, the city is more than a built environment. But he does not de-fetishize the city by revealing the socioeconomic relations materialized in space only to re-fetishize it by fixing its meaning in those relations. Rather, Ledrut implies that the built environment is a city only insofar as it is a term in a relationship with a subject.

Bartlett also restores the subject to the city. The fantasy he weaves of speaking statues works not so much to supply a lack as to release the statues from a spell—a state of petrifaction—that has been cast over them to avoid the apprehension of a lack, of, that is, their incompletion. His statues are civic monuments. More than figures *in* the city, they are figures *of* the city, images of the city as a social form. Like the Florentine statues analyzed by Mary McCarthy in *The Stones of Venice*, the statues of London might be viewed as "formalized civics lesions" and "even a group of ideal stone citizens."[65]

Throughout history, political revolutions have demolished such symbols, as when the Paris Commune toppled the Vendôme Column, calling it "a permanent insult to the vanquished by the victors."[66] Does the monument scene in *Ready to Catch Him Should He Fall* join this tradition of political iconoclasm? Yes and no. One the one hand, the thunderstorm that shakes the statues in a celebration of gay love has the vehemence of a rebellious political force that, like the Commune, challenges the authority the monuments represent. Also like the Commune, the storm contests urban geography, challenging the exclusionary operations of a city that leaves certain social groups—in the first case, workers, in the second, gay men—with few "expectations of space."[67] The storm undoes an urban space in which, to borrow Michel de Certeau's works, "there is no longer any alternative to disciplinary falling-into-line or illegal drifting away, that is, one or another of prison and wandering outside the pale."[68]

On the other hand, where the Vendôme Column commemorates imperialist conquest, Bartlett's statues are figures of saints, angels, Fortitude, and "above them all the great golden figure on the Old Bailey, Justice herself." And the storm that makes them tremble and weep is allied *with*, not *against*, them. Historically, of course, such sculptural figures have legitimated conquest, transposing it into a civilizing mission. But the animated statues of *Ready to Catch Him Should He Fall* perform differently. In the first place, the thunderstorm scene is set within a story that has the quality of a fairy tale, one of fiction's forms that, according to Freud, makes strangeness less real, less threatening, and therefore less susceptible to rejection or conquest.[69] In *Strangers to Ourselves*, Julia Kristeva brings Freud's investigation of the unconscious—what she calls the "small truth" that there is foreignness within us[70]—and of the uncanny feeling of strangeness—which Freud defined as "that class of the frightening which leads back to what is familiar"[71]—to bear on ethico-political concerns about living with others in a contemporary world characterized by an unprecedented mixing of foreigners, a term Freud does not use.[72] The archaic, narcissistic self, Kristeva argues, constructs "the strange" by projecting "out of itself what it experiences as dangerous or unpleasant in itself."[73] One form of uncanny projection is the creation of doubles: statues, for example. The strange, then, is the product of repression, which never fully succeeds. Kristeva suggests that encounters with people from foreign countries or societies can provoke confrontations with our own foreignness, our own unconscious. We at once reject and identify with the foreigner, and this ambivalence troubles our sense of boundaries, of being itself.

Freud speculates that the obvious, generalized artifice of literary forms such as the fairy tale eliminates the reader's uncertainty about whether what is strange is real, "whether things . . . regarded as incredible may not, after all, be possible."[74] In the fairy tale, strangeness is not uncanny since it is set in an imaginary space that seems definitively separated from reality. Strangeness becomes less familiar, more acceptable, even pleasurable, and we can confront it, which is to say detect it in ourselves, with less apprehension. For Kristeva, consciousness of our own otherness is the precondition of "being *with* others"[75] without either expelling them or obliterating them by transforming them into ourselves: "The foreigner comes in when the consciousness of my difference arises, and he disappears when we all acknowledge ourselves as foreigners, *unamenable* to bonds and communities."[76] Kristeva reserves the term "foreigner" for a person who is not a citizen of the nation in which she resides. But her analysis can, I think, apply to other groups that, diverging from social norms, interrupt the image of society as a unitary, organic whole—ultimately an idealized self-image. Any "disruptive" group can appear as the actualization of early, fantasized dangers to the integrity of the self. Bartlett's thunderstorm scene, in which civic monuments come to life and speak on behalf of non-normative sexualities, can be read as a theatricalization of the stranger, which, like the fairy tale, offsets the impulse to conquest that such monuments often represent.

A second way in which the thunderstorm scene differs from traditional political iconoclasm is that instead of destroying the statues it gives them a role in the ethical, political, and historical education of a troubled city. It casts them as democratic citizens—actors in a contest over the meaning of the urban community they symbolize and the ideas, values, customs, and beliefs they allegorize. It is no accident that the scene reaches its climax with the "movement" of Justice on top of the Old Bailey, the courthouse where in 1895 the statue witnessed a different scene as the first trial of Oscar Wilde opened, also with a theatrical air: "There was the sense that a great legal battled was to be fought, and a crowd watched the arrival of the principals."[77] It is not by chance that in Bartlett's rewriting of the scene Justice is aligned *with*, rather than *against*, Love.

Like most civic monuments, Bartlett's statues signify power, but on the night of the thunderstorm they also signify the right to question the basis of power. As Lefort argues, democracy is "inspired by a demand for freedom which destroys the representation of power as standing above society and as possessing an absolute legitimacy." This demand "has the effect of challenging the omnipotence of power,"[78] which can no longer appeal to a substantial basis. Bartlett's statues could not make this demand for freedom were they, too, not liberated from the assumption that "they have a self-presence or transparency alien to the domain of the figurative."[79] For just as the indeterminacy of society is the starting point of democratic politics, just as the question at the heart of democratic society makes it possible to question society, so the indeterminacy of works of figuration—in this case, the things of the city—opens them to subversion and resignification. All monuments, to vary an idea from Alois Riegl, are "unintentional"[80]—open to their own historicity and to unintended meanings. Iconoclasm is inscribed in their very being.

The scenes in which weeping citizens—men and monuments—celebrate Boy and O's love assume their poignancy in the context of a homophobic society where nonstandard intimacies are denied, denigrated, and violently attacked. One night, on their way to The Bar, Boy and O are threatened by a group of homophobic men. Overcoming his fear, O protects Boy. As in the folk tradition of carnival, when the destruction of fear turns everything into gaiety, and light replaces darkness,[81] the lovers join a crowd assembled for a public ritual in which the city is lighted for Christmas. They walk and dance together freely until dawn. "For this one night they went out," Bartlett has said, "and instead of the world being the city where you're walking down the street, after just having made love, and someone says to you 'Queer'— and that's it, it's all taken away from you. In *Ready* the reverse happens, the city is turned into a carnival, and for once the city seems to be operating on their laws."[82] After this incident, Mother closes The Bar, and in the book's penultimate scene the narrator imagines a third magical transformation of the city—"one final picture" he ardently wants to show us (312). In this image, Mother stands with Boy and O on a stage in a public square, "against the backdrop of some grand historical event" (310), and speaks the opening words to "All of Me," the love song she had sung repeatedly on the stage in The Bar;

> Your goodbyes,
> Left me with eyes that cry,
> How can I go on, dear, without you?

At this point, "from the great crowd comes rising the whispered chorus, a great, strong, slow, gentle sound, everyone now holding up a candle or just a hand or a photograph of a person who couldn't be here tonight" (312). This account summons images of the candlelight vigils held for AIDS victims in London and other cities in the 1980s. Coupled with the book's less overt references to AIDS—for example, when the narrator compares Boy to an allegorical statue, he says that "it is him who will attend our funerals"—this scene makes it possible to read *Ready to Catch Him Should He Fall* as an extended prosopopoeia that lends a voice to, among others, those silenced by AIDS.

The fantasy of the moving statues, in which the figures of the city celebrate the survival of Boy and O's relationship and of the collective gay world that fostered it, throws into relief the city's actual reaction to AIDS: punitive policies against its victims, moralistic indictments of homosexuality— and, by implication, of those who have died—harassment of gays in public places, and restrictions on gay sexual culture. The statues come to life at a Benjaminian "moment of danger,"[83] when the city is employing images of the dead to overpower tradition with sexual conformism—in addition to the political and economic conformism about which Benjamin wrote. At this moment, memories "flash up,"[84] including the memory of Wilde, reminding us that today's victors descend from those who nearly a hundred years ago, in the highest moral tone and calling on the "common sense of indignation,"[85] condemned Wilde. Seizing hold of this memory, "fanning the spark of hope in the past," Bartlett uses the symbols of civic tradition to wrest it from the victors. His monuments reenter a dialogue with "the tradition of the oppressed" and therefore with history, including the history of the search for justice in the city, a search stretching back to the classical tradition that makes up the past of the monuments themselves.

Placed within the tradition of the oppressed, the statues' speech does more than publicly announce Boy and O's love or protest the cruelty of a moralizing, heteronormative culture. It also declares rights, itself a kind of prosopopoeia, since claiming rights keeps democracy alive. Patricia Williams, describing how the discourse of rights animates oppressed peoples, who at the same time give life to the notion of rights, compares rights to alchemical transformations:

> Give to all of society's objects and untouchables the rights of privacy, integrity, and self-assertion; give them distance and respect. Flood them with the animating spirit that rights mythology fires in this country's most oppressed psyches, and wash away the shrouds of inanimate-object status, so that we may say not that we own gold but that a luminous golden spirit owns us.[86]

Williams's alchemy of rights, poetically distinguished from interests, resembles Hannah Arendt's notion of "a right to have rights."[87] Discussing the long history of struggles against oppression that have been framed as demands for new rights, Lefort asks, "Are these various rights not affirmed by an awareness of right without objective guarantees, and equally with reference to publicly recognized principles which are partly embodied in laws and which must be mobilized in order to destroy the legal limits that restrict them?"[88]

Bartlett's monuments set rights in motion, for each new rights claim repeats the initial democratic demand for a "public inscription of freedom and equality."[89] Democracy depends on this continual revitalization since the lack of guarantees that is its condition means that in declaring rights we do not lay claim to something that belongs to us by nature. More radically, in referring power to society, the democratic invention relocates rights from a transcendent to a political realm. The declaration of rights generates democracy, and rights themselves are invented only when they are declared. They are coextensive with, not prior to, politics so that democracy affirms what Balibar calls "a *universal right to politics*,"[90] the right to engage in struggle by . . . declaring rights.

This entanglement of rights and politics undermines distinctions between the rights of man—the supposedly private, nonpolitical individual—and the rights of the citizen, that person whose activity connotes politics. Balibar writes:

> The declaration of the rights of man and the citizen is a radical discursive operation that deconstructs and reconstructs politics. It begins by taking democracy to its limits, in some sense *leaving* the field of instituted politics . . . but in order to mark, immediately, that the rights of man have no reality and no value except as political rights, rights of the citizen, and even as the unlimited right of all men to citizenship.[91]

The radical discursive operation contains an ambiguity. On the one hand, the invention of democratic rights is tied to the logic of the unified political group or nation, separating "man" and "citizen" and naturalizing the assumption that some people have fewer rights. On the other hand, the declaration erodes the citizen/man distinction by politicizing rights and expressing "an essential limitlessness characteristic of democracy."[92] While social questions are decided, no one can be forever excluded from politics. The problem of society can never be finally settled. Therefore, the rights of man imply conflicts over attempts to gain respect for *different* rights.

Bartlett's monuments intervene in such conflicts. Exercising the right to constitute and question—to constitute by questioning—the social order that they represent, they publicly claim liberties for gays: the right, say, to walk in the city or the right to a publicly accessible sexual culture. In so doing, they no longer present themselves as either "ideal" or "stone" citizens. Unlike the citizens posited in classical theories of the public sphere or citizenship, they do not claim or aspire to the status of abstract, impartial beings that, upon entering the public sphere, transcend race, gender, and sex and remain untouched by history and undivided by an unconscious. They cast off the pretense, inherent in the ideal of the abstract citizen, of sexlessness that every normalization of sexuality protects. As sexualized actors in the public sphere, the statues awaken from their confinement to what Lauren Berlant calls "dead citizens": beings that, like certain common metaphors—her example is "the legs of a table"—have become "so conventionalized as to no longer seem figural, no longer open to history."[93]

Although Bartlett's monuments divest themselves of abstract personhood, they do not assume the alternative disguise of a specific, fundamental identity. They do not, that is, retreat from public space, the sphere where, in the absence of a pre-political "basis of the relation between *self* and *other*," we negotiate social identities and the identity of society.[94] But while the rights the statues claim have no ground in an *essential* human nature, they do lay claim to *universality*, if by this we mean that they demand an equal right to politics for all people.[95] The civic statues demand precisely this equality and this freedom,[96] proclaiming on behalf of non-normative sexualities "the right to the city," to use Lefebvre's famous phrase.

The Right to the City

What kind of rights claim is this, which has inspired urban social movements and compelled the attention of critical urban theory but still remains so vaguely theorized? For some time now, radical urban scholars, following Lefebvre, have invoked the right to the city against the capitalist domination of space. Some equate opposition to capitalist space with the defense of "authentic" owners and uses of space. The Paris Commune has been described, for example, as an exercise of the right to the city, defined not only as the contestation of spatial exclusion but as the reclamation of space by its proper owners—in this case, the workers of Paris—or as a step toward restoring an originary spatial wholeness, a true identity given by the "use-value" of space. Major aspects of Lefebvre's theory support this interpretation, especially his conception of power, which ultimately reduces oppressive social relations to those of class and of a state in the service of capitalism, and, further, his references to a once integrated, non-alienated sociospatial condition.

In a different vein, urban scholars invested in dividing metaphorical and concrete spaces often claim Lefebvre's mantle. Linking material space with real politics, they loosely associate both with struggles for the right to the city. Explicitly or implicitly, they suggest that debating the discursive construction of space or investigating the spatial politics of discourse ignore—and thus prevent us from engaging in—struggles over the right to the city. The argument, though rarely articulated in any clear fashion, is this: theories about the politics of subjectivity in discourse, images, and representation divert attention from, and are therefore complicit with, social oppression and violence.[97] Yet once we ask what kind of claim is made in declaring "the right to the city" and once we pose the question *in a democratic manner*—which is to say, once we dispense with appeals to external guarantees of meaning—we have to acknowledge that the answers we propose depend on our images of the city and of rights, and this in itself erodes the dichotomy between social-concrete and metaphorical-discursive spaces and, with it, easy divisions between real and unreal politics.

How can we formulate an ethical and emancipatory conception of the right to the city that does not appeal to proper owners and users of space? A right to the city that does not idealize traditional city spaces as "authentic" and dismiss new spatial arrangements as unreal, thus abandoning them as new spaces of political action? It is possible to locate in Lefebvre support for this other formulation. For while he sometimes deploys a vocabulary of "restoration," he also contends that the right to the city is not a return to traditional cities but a right "to appear on all the networks and circuits of communication, information, and exchange."[98] Far from a right to something known but not yet achieved or a naturally given right of which one has been dispossessed, the right to the city is "a right in the making,"[99] a right to urban society, to, that is, a heterogeneous and nonsegregated social space[100] of "encounter" and "simultaneity." Lefebvre claims the right to the city against the suppression of this form of society, and for him the democratic character of a regime can be measured by its attitude toward "urban freedoms."[101]

Reinventing the concept of the right to the city is the task of another essay, but the urgency of this undertaking is increasingly apparent in cities such as New York, whose conditions distressingly resemble those of Bartlett's London. In making rights inseparable from democratic urbanism, the notion of the right to the city challenges the ease with which those who are hostile to rights now present themselves as guardians of urban life. For hostility toward rights is a hallmark of moral crusades, which are guided by the precept that today's urban problems spring from a decline in adherence to conventional moral values.[102] In New York, this moralizing attitude is currently embodied in campaigns to improve "the quality of life," a term that has become the centerpiece of public discussion about the city, though its genealogy in urban discourse awaits critical investigation. Since the early 1990s, policy intellectuals at the conservative Manhattan Institute have promoted a quality-of-life agenda at elite conferences and in their magazine *City Journal*.[103] In 1993, Rudolph Giuliani, influenced by the Institute and building on the foundation laid down during the Reagan-Bush-Koch years, adopted the term as the slogan of the first of his successful mayoral campaigns, and his administrations have mobilized it to legitimate authoritarian policies. They equate quality-of-life initiatives with the imperatives of urban comfort, beauty, and utility—all considered to be benign and to lie outside the limits of the political. Within this framework, interrogating notions of "comfort," "beauty," and "utility" becomes tantamount to repudiating them. Questioning their deployment signals an embrace of discomfort, ugliness, and dysfunction, which, by the very nature of things, endanger the city.

Quality-of-life initiatives have of course been criticized, often on the ground that they trivialize urban problems. But actually, they have deadly serious effects. Residents made homeless during the 1980s by changing employment patterns, cutbacks in social services, and city government's support of real estate interests, are now removed to undisclosed locations. People apprehended for quality-of-life violations are likely to be arrested if they do not live in the neighborhoods in which they commit their offenses. Public space is increasingly controlled by the housed residents of neighborhoods and conceded to corporations, real estate, and nonaccountable entities representing private profit, such as Business Improvement Districts. And the conditions of gay public life are endangered: Times Square is being redeveloped into a family entertainment area; the Hudson River piers, a refuge for gays, where "we can hold hands without being harassed,"[104] are fenced off for redevelopment; gay bars and dance clubs are harassed and closed; and in 1995 a new zoning law was passed, which threatens to eliminate the vast majority of legal sex businesses in Manhattan, businesses that have long provided public venues for gays to meet in a homophobic city.[105] The zoning law restricts sex businesses to remote—frequently unusable— sites, makes them less visible by limiting the size, placement, and illumination of signs, and isolates them by allowing no adult business within five hundred feet of another.

In these circumstances, certain gay writers, such as Gabriel Rotello, author of *Sexual Ecology: AIDS and the Destiny of Gay Men*, have recently blamed urban gay sexual culture for causing AIDS and continuing to spread HIV infection.[106] In contrast, the organization Sex Panic! was formed in 1997 both to promote safer sex and, taking a stand against the city's quality-of-life campaign, to defend the rights of gays to a publicly accessible sexual culture.[107] Sex Panic! takes the position that sex businesses have been major sites of safer-sex education and that higher rates of HIV transmission will result from trying to cope with the complexity of human sexual behavior by sorting it into a few moral categories, encouraging shame, and, in Walt Odets's words, taking "no account of the reality of the gay men most susceptible to HIV infection, the young ones" who are exploring their sexuality.[108] Arguing against Sex Panic!, Rotello claims that while he does not necessarily support quality-of-life regulations, they do not specifically target gays since they are applied almost universally.[109] This is a mistake. It is true, as Rotello says, that New York's quality-of-life campaign benefits real estate— this is one of its principal functions. Gays are not isolated victims. But this increases, rather than mitigates, the danger of making common cause with sanitizing crusades. In *Ready to Catch Him Should He Fall*, Mother takes a different approach when she urges the men in The Bar to understand the connections between homophobic, xenophobic, and racist violence.

It is also true that the presumption of universality embedded in the singularity of the term "quality of life" gives the impressions that the regulations apply equally to all residents. But in fact, they are only neutral on their face and fall with disparate impact on different social groups. For instance, the criminalization of sleeping, bathing, and urinating in public has little relevance for housed New Yorkers. Likewise, as the queer theorist Michael Warner points out in a 1995 essay, "Zones of Privacy," gays are particularly vulnerable to initiatives such as the new zoning bill since, with few publicly accessible resources, they have constructed a shared world largely through sex businesses: "Extinguish sexual culture, and almost all *out* gay culture will wither on the vine."[110]

In claiming the right of gays to a public sexual culture against the city's attempt to privatize sexuality, "Zones of Privacy" diverges sharply from the more familiar arguments for sexual liberties based on the right to privacy. Warner places his claim under the rubric "the right to the city," which, however, he mentions only in passing, without elaborating its meaning. Nonetheless, his use of the term is consistent with and even enlarges Lefebvre's notion. Warner affirms the right to a public sexual culture against the power of city government and real estate to isolate and exclude gay sexuality. Similarly, Lefebvre invents the right to the city to challenge the segregating and isolating ambitions of the state and private enterprise. Although Warner invokes the right to the city as the right of access to pregiven spaces, he does so while posing the question of what an urban space is and, in answering, moves closer to Lefebvre's explanation. "The *right to the city*," says Lefebvre, "legitimates the refusal to allow oneself to be removed from urban reality by a discriminatory and segregative organization."[111] Warner observes that the zoning bill isolates, hence privatizes, sexual culture by mandating three changes in the organization of sex businesses: from concentration to dispersal, from conspicuousness to discretion, and from residential to remote sites.[112] Where Warner maintains that the zoning bill promotes a particular vision of urban life, Lefebvre might conclude that, by virtue of its isolating strategies, it suppresses urban life. In the end, Warner agrees. He argues that the zoning scheme advances an ideology of neighborhood that defines urban space as a community of shared interest based on residence and property, and he asserts that this ideology is anti-urban: "Urban space is always a host space. The right to the city extends to those who use the city. It is not limited to property owners."[113] For Lefebvre, of course, the right to the city does not extend to but is declared against private property ownership. Still, Warner's proposal is in keeping with the spirit, if not the letter, of Lefebvre. Calling the city a host space is similar to defining urban life in terms of encounter and simultaneity. True, Warner's rejection of neighborhood control may contradict Lefebvre's support of community self-management, and, more important, the categorical nature of Warner's dismissal seems politically counterproductive. In failing to differentiate among neighborhoods on the basis of, say, their socioeconomic and racial character, to take account of historical contingencies, including the legacy of environmental racism, or to give any weight to people's attachment to the places where they live, Warner disregards the possibility that under certain circumstances, struggles for neighborhood control may resist, rather than support, spatial domination. In no way, however, does this obviate the question he poses. In New York, today, "neighborhood" is deployed to evict homeless people from the city, deprive gays of public venues, and support social service cutbacks. Jane Jacobs's famous celebration of neighborhood in *The Death and Life of Great American Cities*[114] is cited ubiquitously, not, as she intended, against urban renewal and anti-urbanism but against heterogeneity and the rights of others, and, as Jacobs was accused of doing, to treat the city "as an organization for the prevention of crime."[115] In this situation, there is reason to take very seriously the ways in which the discourse of neighborhood, far from saving the city, threatens urban life, and may even be unneighborly.

Historically, of course, defending neighborhood has hardly been the only way of challenging sociospatial power. Michel de Certeau, for one, proposed something different: "walking in the city," that is, using space to elude the discipline imposed by urban development. If Lefebvre's right to the city is at odds with current invocations of neighborhood, it is compatible with Certeau. Consider *Ready to Catch Him Should He Fall*. The book declares a right to the city that might be interpreted as, precisely, the right to walk in the city. Walking is a recurrent motif in the novel and, as the object of a rights claim, might refer to literal freedom of movement for gays—no insignificant demand, indeed, as Bartlett makes clear, a matter of life and death. If, however, we approach the city as a form of society, the right to walk in the city assumes broader and more radical implications. What happens, for instance, if we define the city not as a city of neighborhoods but as, in Certeau's words, an "immense social experience of lacking a place," an experience brought about by "the moving about that the city multiples"?[116] The right literally to walk in the city becomes part of a more comprehensive freedom, the freedom to use the constructed spatial order in a way that not only actualizes but also transforms it. Certeau likens walking in the city to figurative uses of language. Both drift from the proper meanings of the spatial systems within which they operate—urban and linguistic. Both introduce tension and differences and found within those systems "a legitimate *theater* for practical *actions* . . . a field that authorizes dangerous and contingent social actions."[117] Both take the risk of creating a public space.

Bartlett's drama of the moving statues, which I have read as a figure of democratic urbanism, animates the city by walking and animates democracy by declaring rights. The two practices converge in the right to the city. We might now reanimate this right—modifying, perhaps discarding, some of Lefebvre's ideas and articulating them with ideas from other sources—to assert it against the cruel and unreasonable urbanism that currently travels under the slogan "the quality of life." Proponents of this urbanism treat those who diverge from moral norms as representatives of the city's outside and adopt punitive measures against them, remaining indifferent to the possibility that, to paraphrase Oscar Wilde, one of moralism's saddest victims, "the habitual employment of punishment" may brutalize a city as much as the occurrence of crime.[118]

War Resistance

: **10** :

Un-War: An Aesthetic Sketch

Attempts to abolish war—not a particular war but war as a social institution—are often dismissed as utopian idealism, wild fantasies far removed from the realm of real politics. War, we are told, is inevitable. Humans are territorial and predatory beings. Besides, there has always been war. Who can forget the opening pages of Kurt Vonnegut's *Slaughterhouse-Five*, wherein the narrator says that he is writing an antiwar novel and his interlocutor replies, "You know what I say to people when I hear they're writing antiwar books? . . . I say, 'Why don't you write an anti-*glacier* book instead?'" "What he meant, of course," the narrator explains, "was that there would always be wars, that they were as easy to stop as glaciers. I believe that, too."[1] (Of course, that was before global warming.)

Still, Krzysztof Wodiczko fearlessly pursues perpetual peace in an ongoing aesthetic project titled *Arc de Triomphe: World Institute for the Abolition of War* and in a book, *Abolition of War*, that documents, contextualizes, and theorizes the project. Introduced in *Harvard Design Magazine* in 2010, *Arc de Triomphe* is a proposal to attach a transparent scaffold-like structure to the Arc de Triomphe in Paris (fig. 10.1, plate 6).[2] Traditional historical monuments such as the Parisian Arc embody what Friedrich Nietzsche called "monumental history" and Walter Benjamin famously denounced as the history of the victors—the past narrated as a progression of supposedly eternal "great" moments.[3] Therefore, all traditional monuments, whether or not they overtly commemorate war, can be considered war memorials. Wodiczko has long treated them as such in public projections that animate and destabilize monumental structures, for example, the *AT&T Long Lines Building Projection*, the *Homeless Projection*, the *Hirschhorn Museum Projection*, and the *San Diego Museum of Man Projection*, all realized in the 1980s. The

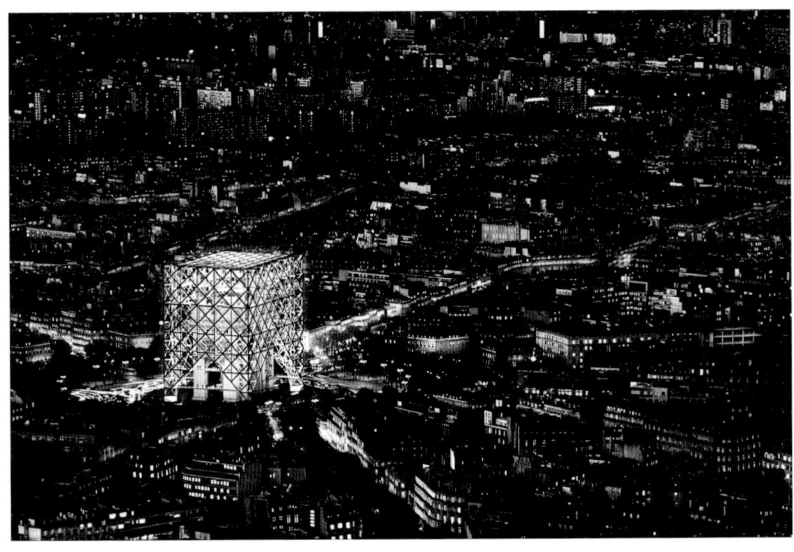

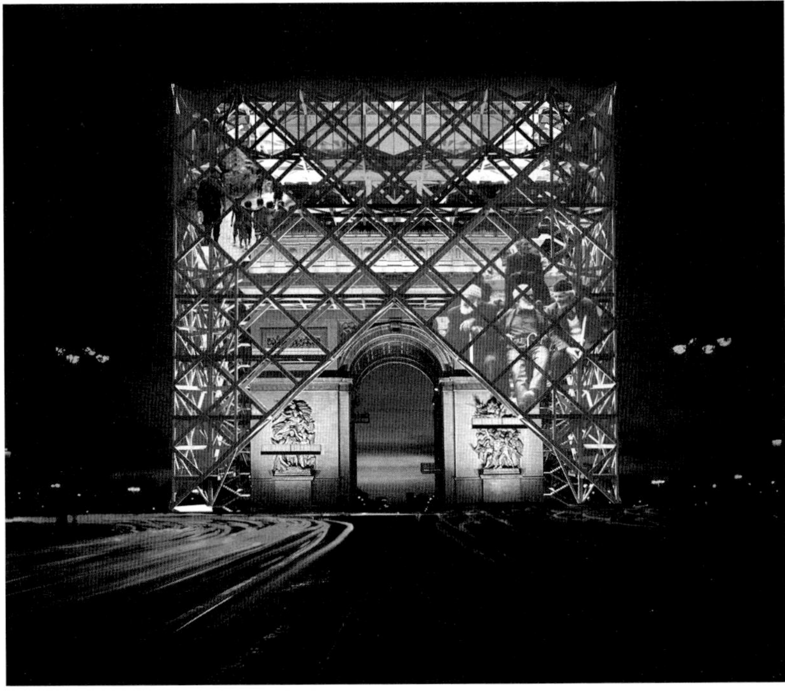

10.1 Krzysztof Wodiczko, *Arc de Triomphe: World Institute for the Abolition of War*, 2010–present. Digital rendering. Courtesy the artist and Galerie Lelong, New York.

projections infiltrate buildings and sculptures with images that awaken memories of those groups that have been defeated in the conflicts that produce social space.

However, the neoclassical Arc de Triomphe, the scene and object of Wodiczko's new activity (itself a kind of projection[4]), is not only an explicit war memorial—"a permanent insult to the vanquished by the victor," as the Paris Commune called the Vendôme Column before destroying it—but an especially hyperbolic example of the genre. Until 1982, the Arc de Triomphe was the largest triumphal arch in the world, and its immensity, coupled with its patriotic messages, made it the standard for modern public monuments. Commissioned in 1806 and completed in 1836, modeled on the Roman Arch of Titus, the Arc glorifies Revolutionary and Napoleonic conquests. For many years, it served as the rallying point of French troops parading after successful military campaigns. As the linchpin of the city's sequence of monuments and grand thoroughfares known as the Historical Axis—also a visualization of monumental history—the Arc now occupies a central place in both Paris and the European Union as a symbol of Western triumphalism. Beneath its vault lies the Tomb of the Unknown Soldier from World War I—"the war to end all wars"—installed on Armistice Day in 1920, accompanied by the first eternal flame lit in Europe since the fourth century and by a typically nationalistic inscription: "Here lies a French soldier who died for the fatherland, 1914–1918." The Arc is adorned with thirty shields inscribed with the names of ninety-six Revolutionary and Napoleonic military victories, allegorical friezes, an engraved list of French victories, an engraved list of 660 soldiers and generals who fought in French victories, and four enormous sculptural reliefs, including, most strikingly, François Rude's bellicose *La Marseillaise*, which features a wild-eyed Winged Victory wearing a helmet crowned by Furies. The chronological order of the reliefs, advancing from *Departure* to *Triumph* to *Resistance* to *Peace*, suggests that war can produce peace (fig. 10.2).

Wodiczko approaches the Arc de Triomphe not only as a symbol but also as a symptom of our culture of war.[5] "The motivation to fight and die in war," he writes,

> is perpetuated by a Culture of War that manifests itself through uniforms, war games, parades, military decorations, and war memorials (including statues and shrines, triumphal arches, cenotaphs, victory columns, and other commemorations of the dead); the creation of war art and military art, martial music, and war museums; and the popular fascination with weap-

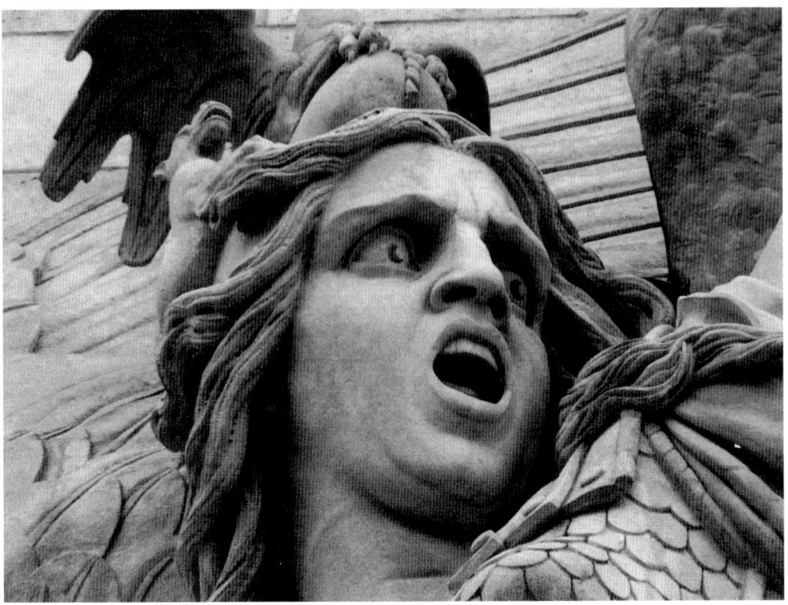

10.2 François Rude, *The Departure of the Volunteers of 1792* ("La Marseillaise"), 1833–36. Detail. Photo: Krzysztof Wodiczko.

ons, war toys, violent video and computer games, battle reenactments, collectibles, and military history and literature.[6]

These undisguised expressions of warlike culture are only the tip of the iceberg, however. For, as Virginia Woolf demonstrated in *Three Guineas*, her feminist antiwar essay of 1938, the culture of war (though she didn't use the term) takes more insidious and therefore more dangerous forms. It is perpetuated, for instance, in the customs of the most esteemed professions of men, manifested by distinctions of dress that indicate rank or titles placed before or after names, both of which establish superiority, provoke competition, and encourage a warlike disposition: grandiose, vain, egoistic, possessive, combative.[7]

Enclosed within Wodiczko's new structure, the *World Institute for the Abolition of War*, the Arc de Triomphe undergoes a Brechtian transformation into an extraordinary object. Remaining fully visible but appearing isolated and entrapped, it metamorphoses into a gigantic specimen, as Wodiczko describes it, even a pathogen, producing war as "collective madness."[8] *World Institute*'s objective is to disarm the Arc. Combining commemorative, investigatory, educational, and activist functions, it would, if built, allow the public as well as scholars from a variety of disciplines to examine the memorial from new viewpoints. The institute would also house a wide array of activities devoted to peacemaking, or what Wodiczko calls "un-war," the term he prefers to "peace."[9] Peace, after all, has long coexisted with preparedness for war. According to the American philosopher William James, writing in the first decade of the twentieth century,

> "Peace" in military mouths today is a synonym for "war expected." The word has become a pure provocative, and no government wishing peace sincerely should allow it ever to be printed in a newspaper. Every up-to-date dictionary should say that "peace" and "war" mean the same thing, now *in posse*, now *in actu*. It may even be reasonably said that the intensely sharp *preparation* for war by the nations is the *real war*, permanent, unceasing; and that the battles are only a sort of public verification of the mastery gained during the "peace"-interval.[10]

Un-war, by contrast, implies disarmament, a process of un-doing war, which, as we shall see, the artist understands not only as military preparedness and combat but also as an individual and collective state of mind.[11]

Wodiczko's plan for a project to disarm the Arc and the larger culture of war exhibits the same combination of practicality and vision that distinguishes his earlier works of "interrogative design" such as *The Homeless Vehicle* of 1988 or the immigrant instruments of the 1990s. Like the interrogative-design projects, which invent equipment to fulfill the urgent needs of excluded and oppressed groups while questioning the societies that produce such needs, *World Institute for the Abolition of War* incorporates meticulous technical drawings and other architectural renderings into a work of imagination. It may therefore be tempting to describe it as a work of "visionary architecture." Yet the project also resists such a categorization. For one thing, Wodiczko insists that his designs on paper are meant for actual use; the institute is to be built. And while the project is certainly "imaginative," it is not unrealistic or impossible. Rather, it deals creatively with realities that often go unseen and anticipates a cultural condition that may yet come to pass. Renderings of the proposed institute present a system of ramps, elevators, horizontally moving walkways, and vertically moving viewing platforms that intersect along the outside and through the inside of the Arc (fig. 10.3). The circulation system, if realized, would allow visitors to study the Arc's iconography and diagnose the war pathologies that war culture tries to repress. For instance, when standing on a platform to view at eye level the female representation of Victory at the top of Rude's *La Marseillaise*, one could detect just how crazed she is. External and internal

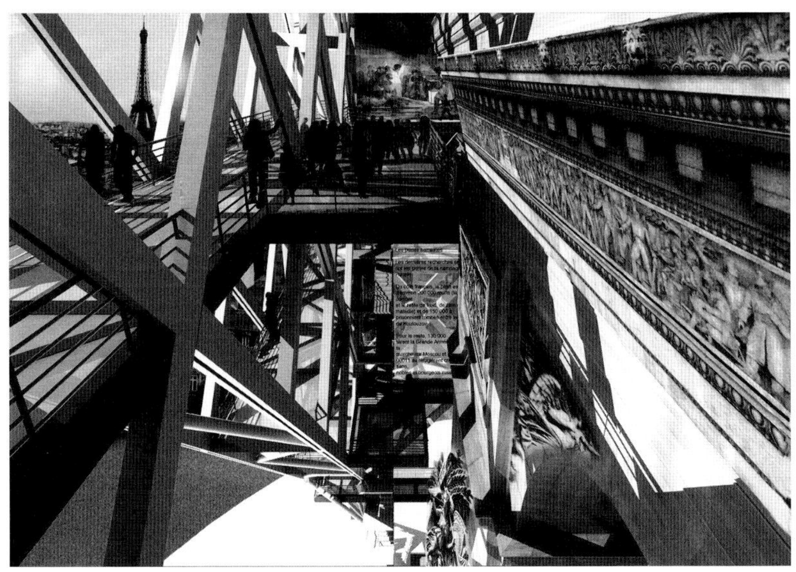

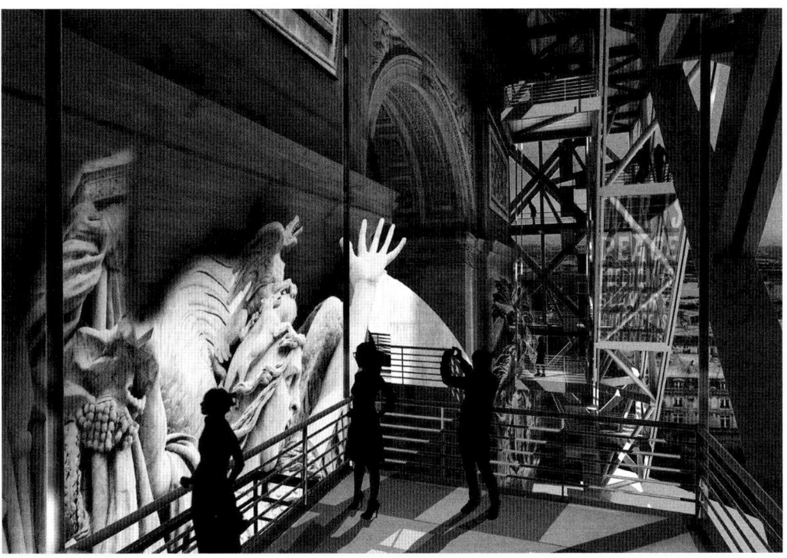

10.3 (*above and facing page*) Krzysztof Wodiczko, World Institute displays, projections, media environments, and installations, 2010. Digital renderings. Courtesy the artist and Galerie Lelong, New York.

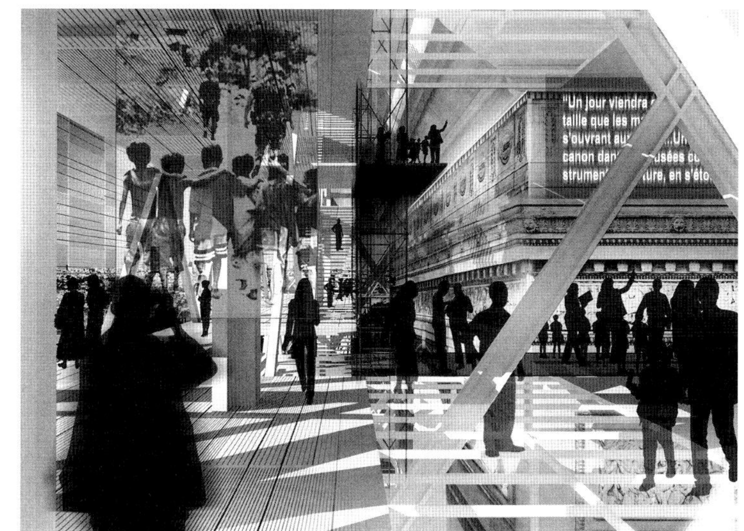

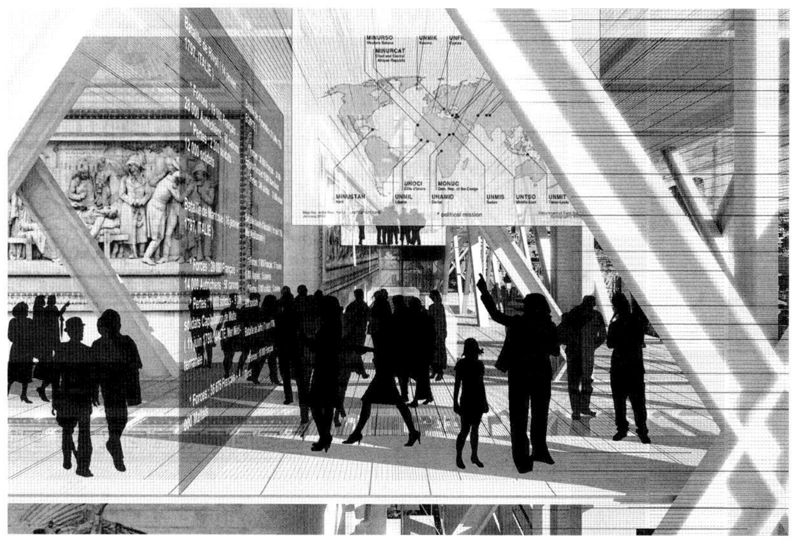

plasma screens and pixel boards installed throughout the scaffolding would display programs related to the institute's work and encourage visitors to stop to join discussions. Parallel to the main frieze of the Arc, a continuous strip of media-display panels would enumerate all recorded wars, campaigns, battles, and military assaults on civilians and list direct and indirect human casualties. Similarly, parallel to each relief honoring a Napoleonic battle would stand a list of killed and wounded soldiers, prisoners of war, and civilians.

Currently, there are several different designs for the *World Institute*. Likewise, the institute's program is provisional. Wodiczko foresees the division of the structure's top floors into four informational zones, each containing audiovisual, interactive, telepresent, and immersive displays and environments. The zones, suggests the artist, might be devoted to information about past and present peace-building efforts, the disarmament process, the present state of world armament, multidisciplinary theoretical discourses in peace-related fields past and present, and cultural, artistic, and pedagogical projects that have contributed to the discourse of war resistance. Wodiczko's program also provides for a World Situation Map located in the area above the roof of the Arc, in the central horizontal section of the upper level of the structure. Displaying the changing global dynamics of wars, conflicts, and post-war, post-conflict, and peace zones, the map overhangs a large hall bearing the name of the Discursive Forum for the Abolition of War, a highly mediatized space that hosts special events and global conferences. The area surrounding the Discursive Forum contains facilities for what is called the Cross-Disciplinary Center for Global Peace Projects, which develops and implements practical programs to abolish war.[12]

The *World Institute for the Abolition of War* aims to render the Arc de Triomphe inoperative in promoting war, but, Wodiczko says, it is not enough to disarm the external culture of war. Un-war projects must also disarm the individual. One of the premises of *World Institute*, then, is that abolishing war is an individual responsibility. Wodiczko's call for individual responsibility arises not from moralism but from the conviction that we are each accountable for war because, as psychoanalysis teaches us, war is hidden in our unconscious minds. "We are ourselves inner war memorials," the artist writes,[13] unwittingly echoing Gertrude Stein, who in 1947 observed that while there is certainly war outside, there is also war inside: "What is there inside in one that makes one know all about war," she asked.[14] As if in response to Stein, Wodiczko makes research into the psychoanalytic dimensions of war an indispensable part of his project's agenda.[15]

Of course, war is, above all, a collective phenomenon, so the notion that we are "inner war memorials" raises the vexed question of the relationship between internal wars and external wars—between, that is, the psychical and the social realms: is violence instilled in us from within or from without? In an essay devoted to the location of violence, especially sexual violence, Jacqueline Rose, quoting Wilhelm Reich, poses the question this way: "Where does the misery come from?"[16] For Reich, violence is imposed on the individual's psyche by a strictly external social world that is itself untouched by psychic processes.[17] Rose observes that Reich's social-determinist theory "pits inside and outside against each other in . . . deadly combat" and, in doing so, "wipes out any difference or contradiction on either side."[18] This polarizing structure—one that, we might note, is warlike—is shared with the seemingly opposing yet equally determininistic view that strictly internal psychic processes cause social violence.[19] Consequently, both approaches evade what Rose calls the radical ambiguity of the inside-outside, psychical-social relationship.[20] The relationship is ambiguous because, among other reasons, the psychoanalytic subject itself is social, which is to say, it is formed through relationships and its emergence is one and the same with its entry into the social field, so that subjectivity exceeds the level of the individual. Therefore, there can be no bright line, no secure boundary, between internal and external worlds. In addition, psychoanalysis has theorized complex connections between individual and social subjectivity, particularly in its study of group psychology, which is based on the premise, as Freud wrote, "that in the individual's mental life someone else is invariably involved, as a model, as an object, as a helper, an opponent"; therefore, "from the very first individual psychology . . . is at the same time social psychology as well."[21] In 1952, the British analyst W. R. Bion combined Freud's researches with those of Melanie Klein to elaborate on the idea that groups such as armies and churches are driven by unconscious forces.[22] Psychoanalytically speaking, then, the idea that war exists inside each of us does not mean, as sociologically oriented thinkers tend to assume and as Wodiczko sometimes seems to suggest, that a purely external culture of war imposes war on our minds. Neither does it mean that a purely external power—the state—forces individuals to go to war, though of course the state does so. Rather, it means that unconscious aggressivity—a tendency toward destructive, hostile attitudes and behavior, a tendency springing from the individual's formative relationships—abides in human subjects, persisting throughout our lives and playing a significant role in wars outside us. For this reason, each individual is responsible for war in the sense of being its agent, and in an ethical universe, each individual is responsible for war in the sense of being accountable for abolishing it.

Responsibility

Psychoanalytic literature offers many ideas about the psychic dimensions of the war phenomenon. In 1915, for example, during World War I, we find

Freud struggling to understand the connection between internal and external violence. Expressing shock at the extreme cruelty of the war and the participating nations' lack of respect for the laws of war, Freud speculated that war depends on a regression to infantile barbarism. Regression, he writes, is possible because in the development of the human mind, earlier stages persist alongside later ones: "Succession also involves co-existence."[23] Normally, the capacity for barbarous deeds is held in check, even transformed, by external factors—the community and the state, which forbid wrongdoing. Freud hypothesizes that the state does so "not because it desires to abolish [wrongdoing], but because it desires to monopolize it, like salt and tobacco."[24] In times of war, however, the state sanctions rather than prohibits barbarism.

As far as I am aware, the most thoroughly elaborated psychoanalytic theory of war was drafted by Franco Fornari, who was president of the Italian Psychoanalytic Society, a member of Psychoanalysts against Nuclear War, and the person who introduced the ideas of Melanie Klein to Italy. In 1964, he published *The Psychoanalysis of Nuclear War*, following it two years later with *The Psychoanalysis of War*, which greatly influenced Wodiczko.[25] *The Psychoanalysis of War*, the only one of Fornari's books translated into English, is out of print, despite the fact that the important French psychoanalytic thinker André Green apparently called the author's thoughts on war "the most important work on the subject since Freud's *Civilization and Its Discontents*."[26] Fornari wants to return war to the unconscious of the individual subject while, like Freud, avoiding reductive approaches to the inside/outside relationship. He reassures his readers that psychoanalytic exploration "is not a matter of a conflict between the traditionally recognized, external causes (economic, demographic, political, ideological, etc.) of war and its unrecognized internal causes, but rather of a shift of emphasis from the former to the latter" and that the mobilization of the psychological factors of war requires the intervention of specific historical realities.[27] For Wodiczko, too, fighting on the scale of war materializes when virulent patriotism, collective hatred, and other cultural values draw on unconscious aggression. At the same time, however, Fornari insists that investigations into social phenomena that separate social facts from the concrete individuals who form society are obscurantist and lend a pseudoscientific pretext to the renunciation of responsibility.[28] In Fornari's theory, war mobilizes—indeed resolves—unconscious depressive and persecutory anxieties and conflicts that, as Klein taught, arise from the major role played by aggression in infantile mental life. For Klein, the infant's rudimentary ego experiences conflict between loving and destructive impulses. The conflict is aroused by and experienced in relation to external objects, such as the mother's breast, which, as the infant's first love-object, stands for the principle of the outside world. Terrified by its internal destructiveness, which it believes can destroy the love object, the infant rids itself of the terror by means of the unconscious mechanisms of splitting and projection. Splitting the external world into good and bad objects, the infant projects its own destructiveness into the bad ones, which it experiences as persecutory and destructive of the love-object. Building on Freud's notion that early stages of mental life persist in and are available to the adult psyche, Fornari argues that the individual subject's projection of its internal terror—what he calls the Internal Terrifier—onto external enemies operates in war, with the difference that in adult life, the love-object that needs protection has become a group or nation. Projection, motivated by terror and love, allows us to express aggressiveness without guilt. As a result, war defends people against deep-seated anxieties about internal enemies by finding real enemies to kill. But, says Fornari, with the advent of the nuclear situation, war enters a state of crisis. It ceases to operate as a defense because nuclear war destroys the love-object along with the enemy.

With regard to the question of responsibility, the most important part of Fornari's theory is his idea that the individual subject gets rid of its violence, which is prohibited by law, by investing or alienating it in the state, the social institution that monopolizes violence. Fornari returns war to the subject precisely in order to "rouse" individuals from their alienation in the state and thereby motivate them to take responsibility for war. In a passage that Wodiczko spotlights in *The Abolition of War*, Fornari writes:

> It is we ourselves who desire war, and the alienation of our aggressiveness into the state serves us simply to be able to say that it is not we who desire war but that the state forces us to make war. In this manner, we convince ourselves that the state is responsible for war in order not to feel responsible for it ourselves. To escape from our alienation in the state, therefore, means to be personally responsible for war, just as we feel personally responsible for inter-individual crimes.[29]

"I deem it important," he says, "to insist on the thesis that in tracing the war phenomenon to the unconscious of each man we arrive at considering each man responsible for war."[30]

Taking responsibility for abolishing war begins, then, with taking responsibility for war, which is one and the same act as taking responsibility for the unconscious. And taking responsibility for the unconscious means tolerating what Freud taught us: that in our unconscious, as Mignon Nixon has remarked, "we are very bad."[31] Since the alternative to tolerating badness is self-deception, which includes externalizing aggressivity in the form of the external enemy against whom we wage war, to take responsibility for the unconscious is to embrace what the psychoanalyst Anthony Sampson, following Jacques Derrida, calls "a courageously disillusioned Freudian politics," one that acknowledges what is most troubling about the human subject.[32] "It is a central tenet of psychoanalysis," says Jacqueline Rose, that if we can tolerate what is most disorienting—disillusioning—about our own unconscious, we are less likely to act on it, less inclined to strike out in a desperate attempt to assign the horrors of the world to someone, or somewhere, else. It is not . . . the [aggressive] impulse that is dangerous but the ruthlessness of our attempts to be rid of it.[33]

In an uncharacteristic moment, Wodiczko promises that un-war projects will eventually turn "our formerly bloody, self-destructive minds" into a thing of the past and make our "souls" war-free.[34] With this statement, he steps back from the psychoanalytic principles he otherwise espouses. For Freud did not underestimate the enduring power of the forces he grappled with, making clear that, in reality, there is no such thing as eradicating psychic violence.[35] According to the British analyst Hanna Segal, recognizing such psychic facts is "the psychoanalytic stand."[36] Naive idealism—the charge frequently leveled at those who want to abolish war—inheres, then, not in working for a world without war but, rather, in failing to face the difficulty of the goal, a difficulty that arises because opposition to abolishing war comes "not only from others but also has its roots in ourselves."[37] Yet today, in an era of perpetual war, not to mention sexualized torture, intellectuals on the left continue to resist psychoanalytic insights into the war phenomenon and therefore to refuse responsibility for the unconscious, frequently expressing the belief that psychoanalytic ideas about subjectivity are a distraction from politics. In this manner, some antiwar leftists may worry that reflecting on individual responsibility will automatically divert attention from the need for collective action. For those whose antiwar politics are courageously disillusioned, however, the reverse has been the case: Precisely because we are warlike, they argue, a less violent world requires the establishment of new social institutions and, in particular, international institutions. Consider, to begin with, Immanuel Kant's 1795 essay "Perpetual Peace: A Philosophical Sketch," one of the earliest modern proposals for an international peacemaking institution. Kant believes that "the warlike inclination of those in power," the "savagery" of European and American states, is integral to human nature: "A state of peace among men living together is not the same as the state of nature, which is rather a state of war."[38] What he elsewhere calls "radical evil"—a wickedness of the human heart that is innate insofar as it cannot be gotten rid of and that is displayed, on the level of the state, in war—makes peace difficult; "thus," Kant concludes, "the state of peace must be *formally instituted*."[39] Kant's reasoning about the relationship between evil and social institutions applies equally if we view war psychoanalytically: because of our ineradicable "badness," our unconscious aggressivity, un-war must be formally instituted. Fornari, invoking the Kleinian notion of our ability to recognize and make reparation for destructive impulses,[40] says as much:

> The purpose of the psychoanalytic disclosure of the individual responsibility for war is to prepare the ground for new social institutions which would allow the individual concretely to express his responsibility on the politico-social level. . . . If it is I who am responsible it is I who must make amends; but if I must make amends, I must have concrete political instruments through which my reparative wishes may be concretely expressed.[41]

Believing that responsibility for unconscious wishes can become a social force, Fornari proposes such a reparative political instrument, one he names the Omega Institution. Integrating individual forces into social reality was the purpose of the institution, to which we shall return.

Cosmopolitics

In designing the *World Institute for the Abolition of War*, Krzysztof Wodiczko becomes heir to the modern legacy of international peacemaking, placing his work within the field of cosmopolitan politics, or, as it is sometimes called, cosmopolitics. Modern cosmopolitanism, an embattled term going back to the eighteenth century, encompasses a variety of moral and political views and is currently the subject of vigorous debates.[42] I use it here to refer to a global political consciousness that, though not necessarily post-nationalist, responds to the suffering of those who live beyond its own geographic and cultural borders and is adversarial in relation to global patriarchy and capitalist cosmopolitanism, which is what Marx calls exploitation on a world scale through a global mode of production. Equally contentious is cosmopolitanism's correlative term *universalism*. In contrast to depoliticizing, generalizing universalisms that cast differences and particularities into privacy and constitute one aspect of Enlightenment thought, another kind of "universalism" names a practice dedicated to extending the demand for justice and equality, which, along with nationalism, was also a facet of the Enlightenment. The demand for justice requires, in Etienne Balibar's words, "the affirmation of a *universal right to politics*," the right to, that is, constitute the social order and put it at risk.[43] Joan Copjec advocates the second kind of Enlightenment universalism in a superb essay on radical evil: "The Kantian universal is neither an underlying principle that informs individual beings, nor a superior instance that subsumes our particularity; it is rather, the focal point of our actions."[44]

Focusing on "perpetual peace," by which he means the cessation not only of hostilities but of the threat of their breaking out, Kant believes that the only rational way to bring this peace about is by establishing an international state. Realizing, however, that at the time such a state was not the will of nations, he proposes a "negative substitute": a federation of nations that would create a system of international law based on principles of right.[45] For his part, Fornari agrees with Bertrand Russell, one of many influential figures who after 1945 thought that a single world government was the only alternative to the extinction of the human race, but like Kant, though for different reasons, he envisions obstacles to its formation. However, Fornari also emphatically rejects Kant's substitute: a union of states, an organization like the United Nations, in which "each member nation [is] above all jealous of preserving its own sovereignty."[46] World government, Fornari insists, presupposes the abolition of state sovereignty. But "who will abolish it?" Arguing that the abolition of sovereignty "from above," by international agreements between nations, would only arouse the persecution and castration anxieties that lead to heightened vindictiveness, Fornari maintains that state sovereignty must first be abolished "from below," when individual citizens reappropriate the violence they have alienated in the state. In so doing, individuals do not themselves become violent or exonerate the state's violence; rather, they take responsibility for war by withdrawing their consent to—protesting against—state violence. Returning to the subject, then, is the starting point for the sovereign state to evolve toward the nonsovereign state, one subject to the same laws as it citizens, and is also the foundation of the Omega Institution, a judicial institution operating on a *national* level that would inaugurate the evolution by establishing laws prohibiting the nation's aggression against other groups and instituting penalties for the exportation of violence. Omega Institutions would, to borrow Wodiczko's term, "detoxify" national cultures and group identities[47] and, according to Fornari, pave the way to world government.[48]

Wodiczko's *World Institute for the Abolition of War* diverges from more classical paradigms of international peacemaking because, unlike Kant's and Fornari's proposals, it is not grounded in the model of the nation-state. Instead, it stresses multilateral, nongovernmental alliances in the form of the Discursive Forum for the Abolition of War and the Cross-Disciplinary Center for Global Peace Projects. Neither does *World Institute* refer to world government. *World Institute*, then, participates in the construction of a *new* cosmopolitics, one responsive to Jacques Derrida's exhortation to cultivate the spirit of the cosmopolitan tradition by questioning its limits and adjusting it to our own time.[49] For Derrida, this means, in addition to assuming responsibility before the stranger,[50] recognizing that justice is not fully exercised within the framework of the nation-state or the boundaries of law—that the law cannot encompass ethical life.[51] While Wodiczko, like Derrida, may support international law as a means of helping to expand justice universally, *World Institute* is not a law-making or judicial institution but, rather, a public and cultural one—"public" not in the sense of state-related or open to a preexisting audience but because, in a Kantian spirit, it cultivates a public sphere of critical speech and democratic, agonistic discourse. Perhaps the very debate about war might help bring about un-war, for, as Chantal Mouffe writes,

> the novelty of democratic politics is not the overcoming of [the] us/them distinction—which is an impossibility—but the different way in which it is established. . . . The aim of democratic politics is to construct the "them" in such a way that it is no longer perceived as an enemy to be destroyed, but an "adversary," i.e., somebody whose ideas we combat but whose right to defend those ideas we do not put into question.[52]

World Institute, unlike previous peacemaking proposals, aims to dismantle the culture of war and institutionalize a new transnational un-war culture, challenging the oft-expressed notion that emotional ties, identifications, and shared responsibilities can only be forged on local and national scales. Bruce Robbins, a scholar of cosmopolitanism, notes that "though the concept of culture emerged historically in close connection with nationalism, it does not belong inevitably or definitively on the side of nation, inheritance, or locality." The reason, he explains, is that although throughout most of human history "both habitual knowledge of others and habitual opportunities to affect others' lives were very limited in space," social organizations and communication technologies have now expanded and, along with them, possibilities for international common cultures and modes of belonging.[53] To realize one such possibility, Wodiczko mobilizes sophisticated communication and information technologies, in order to bring about an antiwar instance of what Robbins calls "global feeling."[54] *World Institute* thus exemplifies what Robbins has more recently called "a *newer* cosmopolitanism," which, in the wake of the localizing, pluralizing tendency of certain new cosmopolitanisms of the 1990s, reconsiders "the virtues of cosmopolitanism's universalist impulse" and, like the Omega Institution, makes it a priority to oppose the military aggression of one's own country, especially if that country is the United States.[55]

In the preface to "Perpetual Peace," Kant remarks on the practical politician's condescending attitude toward political theorists. "The worldly-wise statesman," he writes, believes that the theorist is a mere academic who cannot endanger the state. "It thus follows," he concludes, "that if the practical politician is to be consistent, he must not claim, in the event of a dispute with the theorist, to scent any danger to the state in the opinions which the theorist has randomly uttered in public. By this saving clause, the author of this essay will consider himself expressly safeguarded, in correct and proper style, against all malicious interpretation."[56]

Kant casts himself as a hopeless idealist, detached from practical matters, trading in fantasies—the role frequently assigned to those who assume responsibility for abolishing war. Kant's preface is ironic, however, because, as the ethico-political philosopher Allen W. Wood writes, Kant actually rejected the notion that "historical hopes must never be entertained . . . as though we could not devote ourselves to final ends of humanity . . . unless we see clear signs that humanity is on the brink of fulfilling them."[57] *World Institute for the Abolition of War* makes clear that the same is true of Wodiczko, who, in a time of perpetual war, allows the historical hope of un-war to enter the public space of appearances, establishing it as a reality.

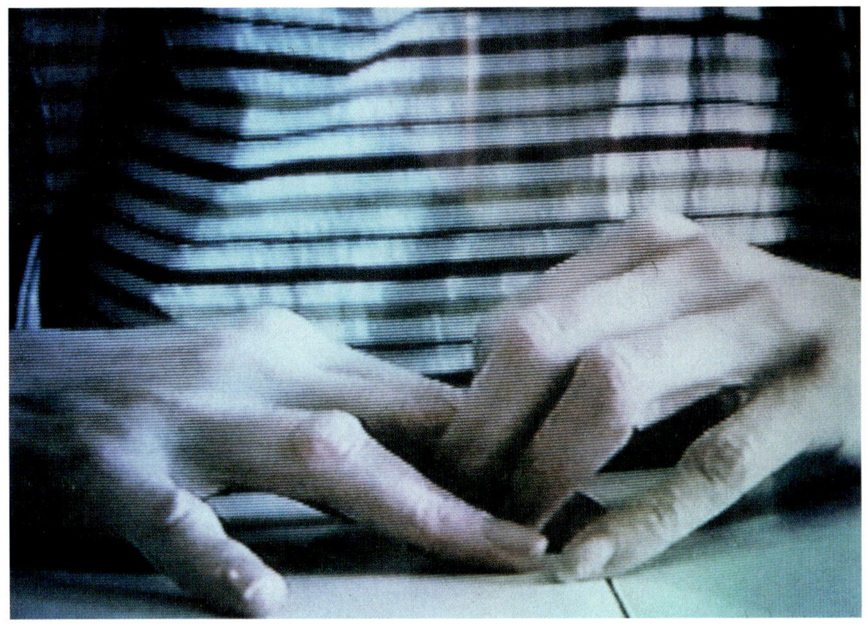

PLATE 1 Silvia Kolbowski, *an inadequate history of conceptual art*, 1998–99. Still, video and audio installation. Courtesy the artist.

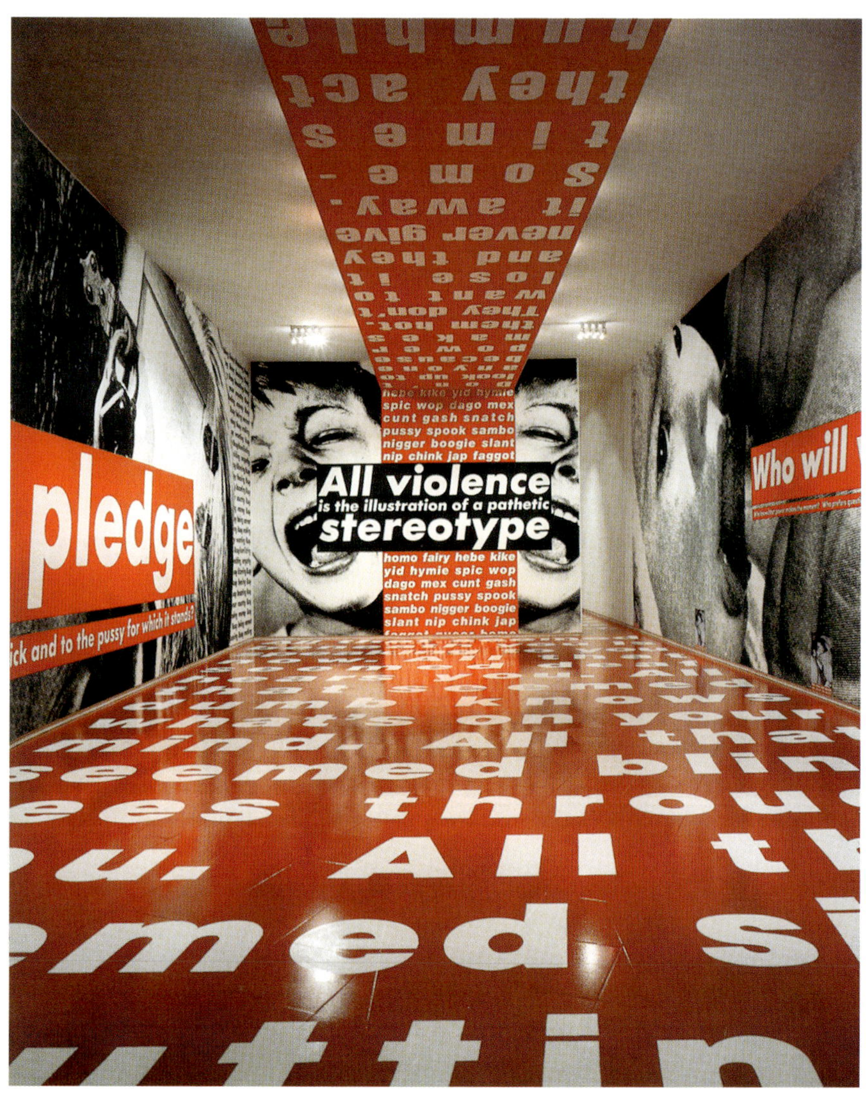

PLATE 2 Barbara Kruger, *Barbara Kruger*, 1991. Installation view, front room, Mary Boone, New York. Courtesy the artist.

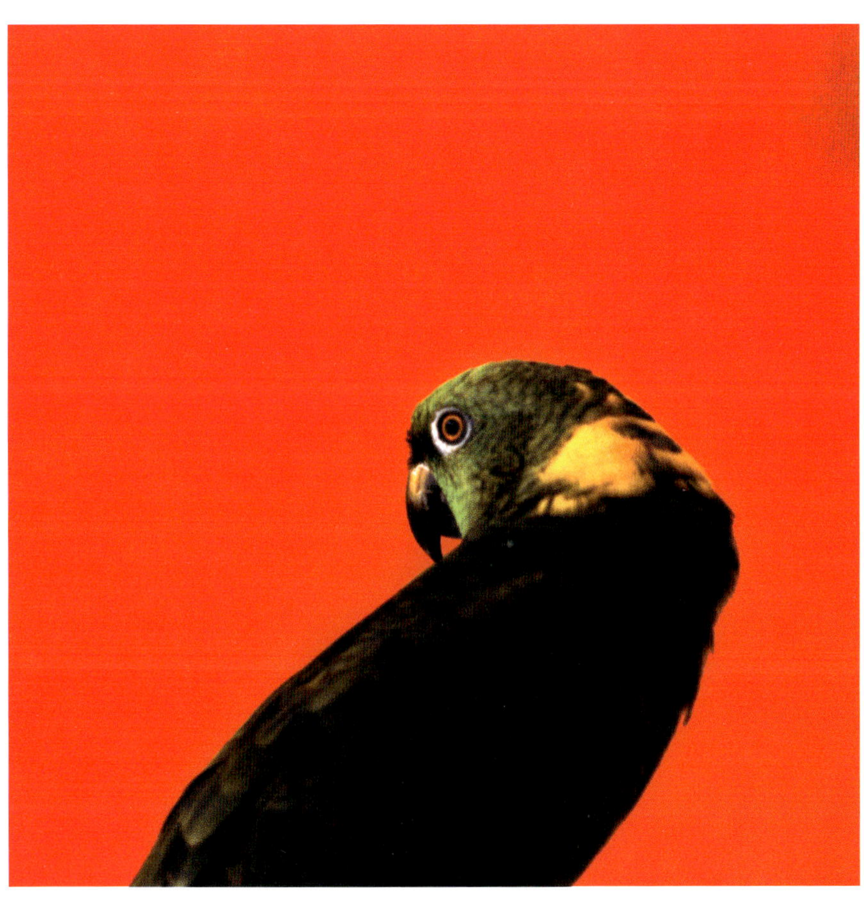

PLATE 3 Louise Lawler, *Portrait*, 1982. Silver dye bleach print. Courtesy of the artist and Metro Pictures, New York.

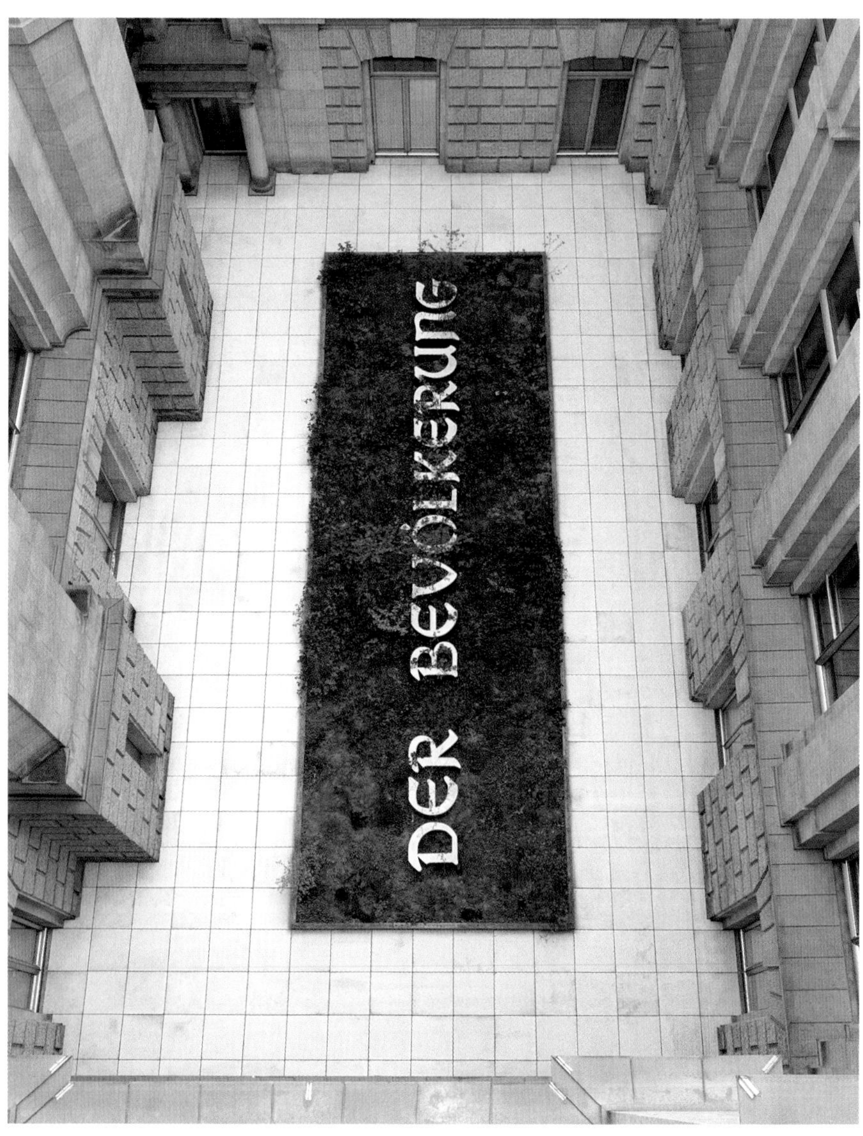

PLATE 4 Hans Haacke, *DER BEVÖLKERUNG* (*To the Population*), 2000. Biotope in the northern atrium of the Reichstag (German Parliament Building), Berlin. Photo: Stefan Müller, 2006. Courtesy the artist and Paula Cooper Gallery, New York. © Hans Haacke/ Artists Rights Society (ARS), New York.

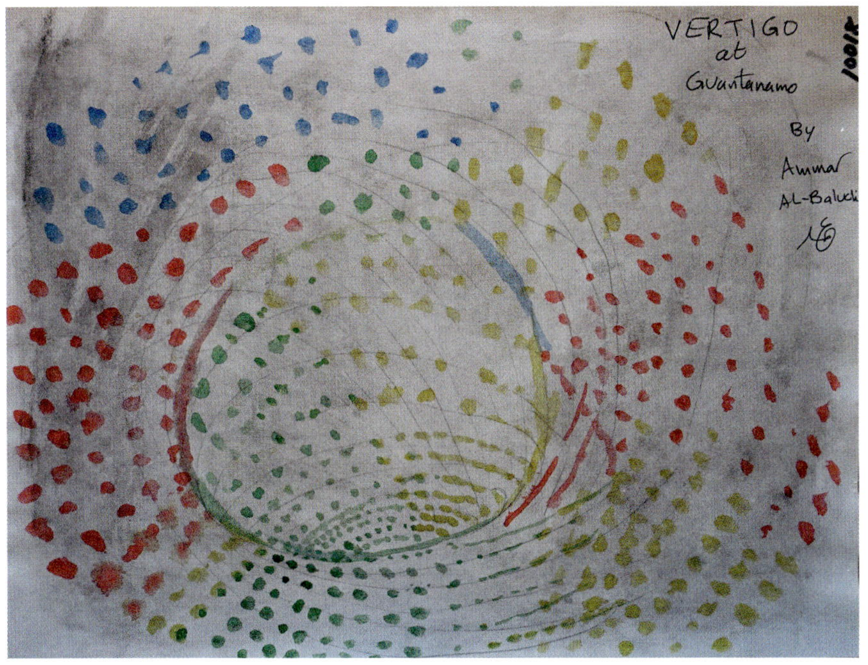

PLATE 5   Ammar al-Baluchi, *Vertigo at Guantanamo*, 2016. Graphite and watercolor on paper. Courtesy the artist.

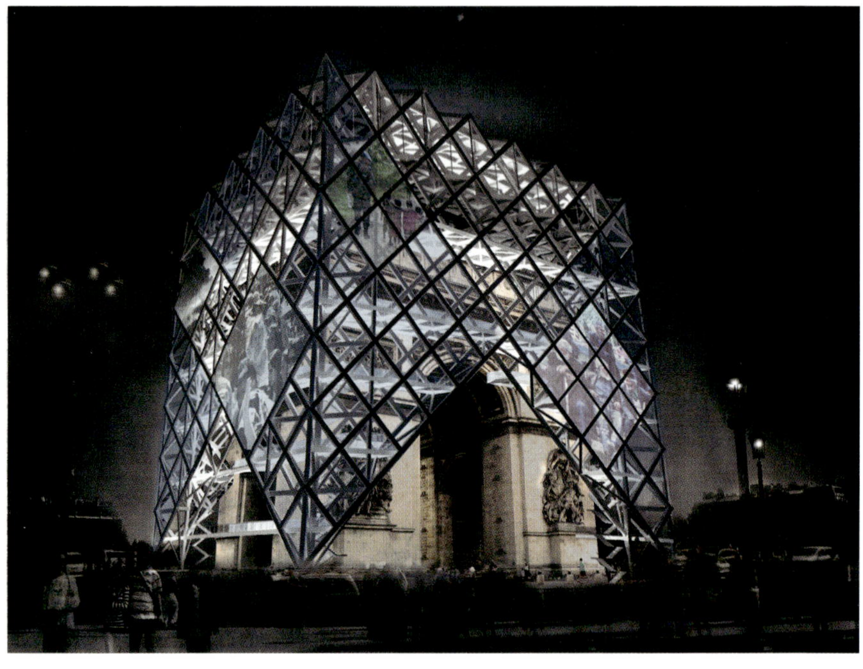

PLATE 6 Krzysztof Wodiczko, *Arc de Triomphe: World Institute for the Abolition of War*, 2010–present. Digital rendering. Courtesy the artist and Galerie Lelong, New York.

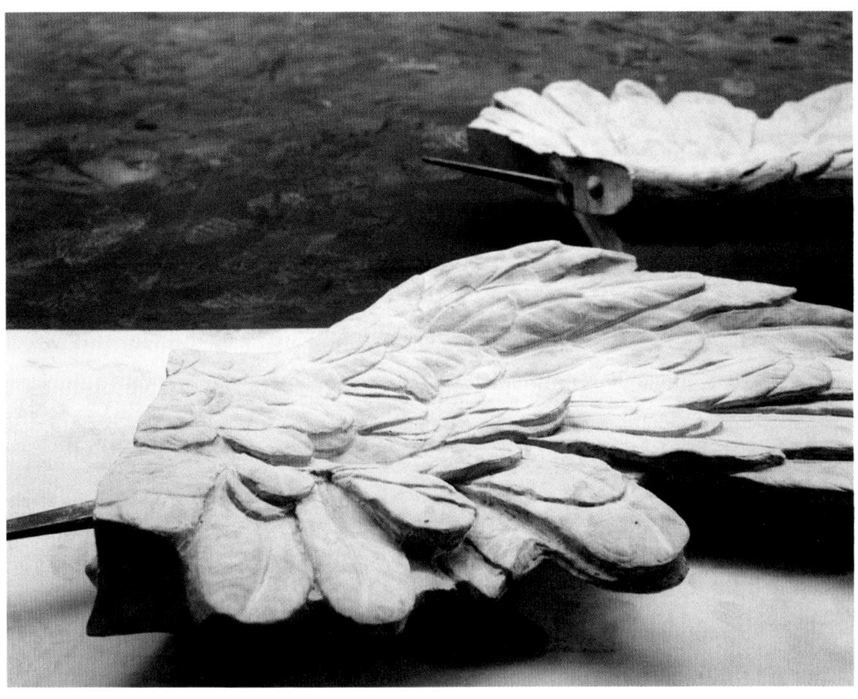

PLATE 7 Louise Lawler, *Grieving Mothers—Still*, 2005/2008. Silver dye bleach print. Courtesy of the artist and Metro Pictures, New York.

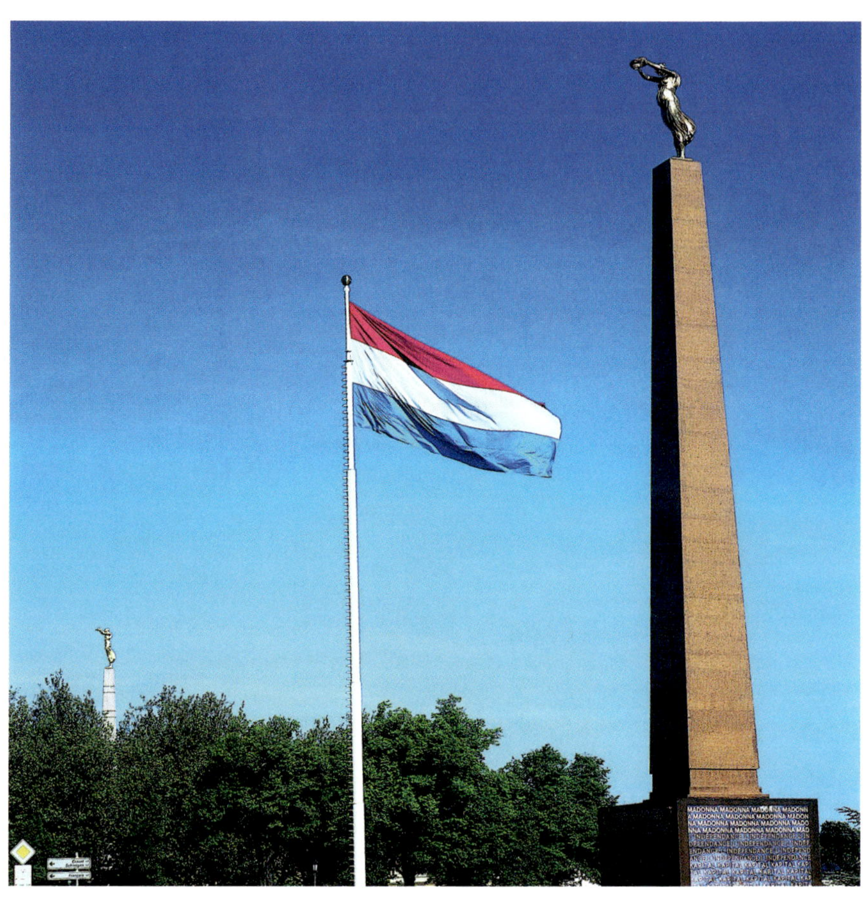

PLATE 8 Sanja Iveković, *Lady Rosa of Luxembourg*, 2001. Gilded polyester, wood, and printed text. Photo: Christian Mosar. Courtesy the artist.

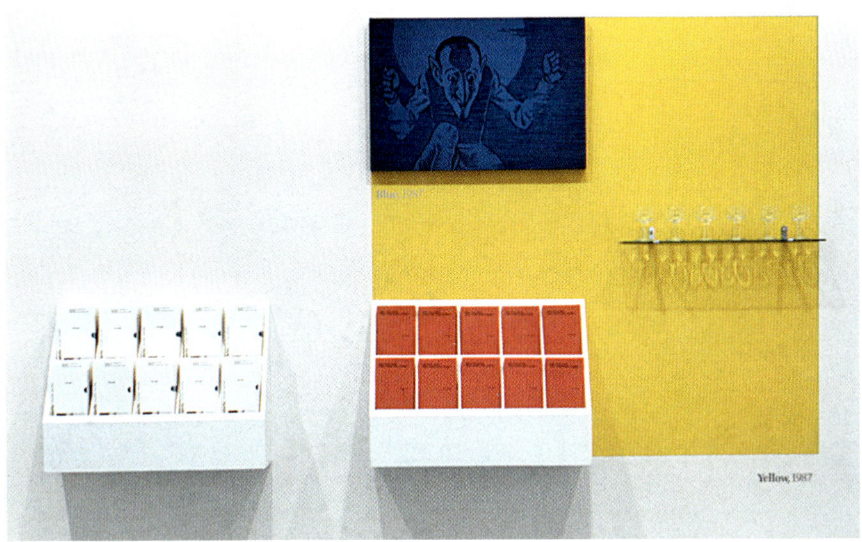

PLATE 9 Louise Lawler, *Enough. Projects: Louise Lawler*, the Museum of Modern Art, New York, September 19–November 10, 1987. Installation view. Works shown (left to right): Blue, 1987. Silver dye bleach print; Enough, 1987. Six cordial glasses on glass shelf; Exhibition brochure. Courtesy of the artist and Metro Pictures, New York.

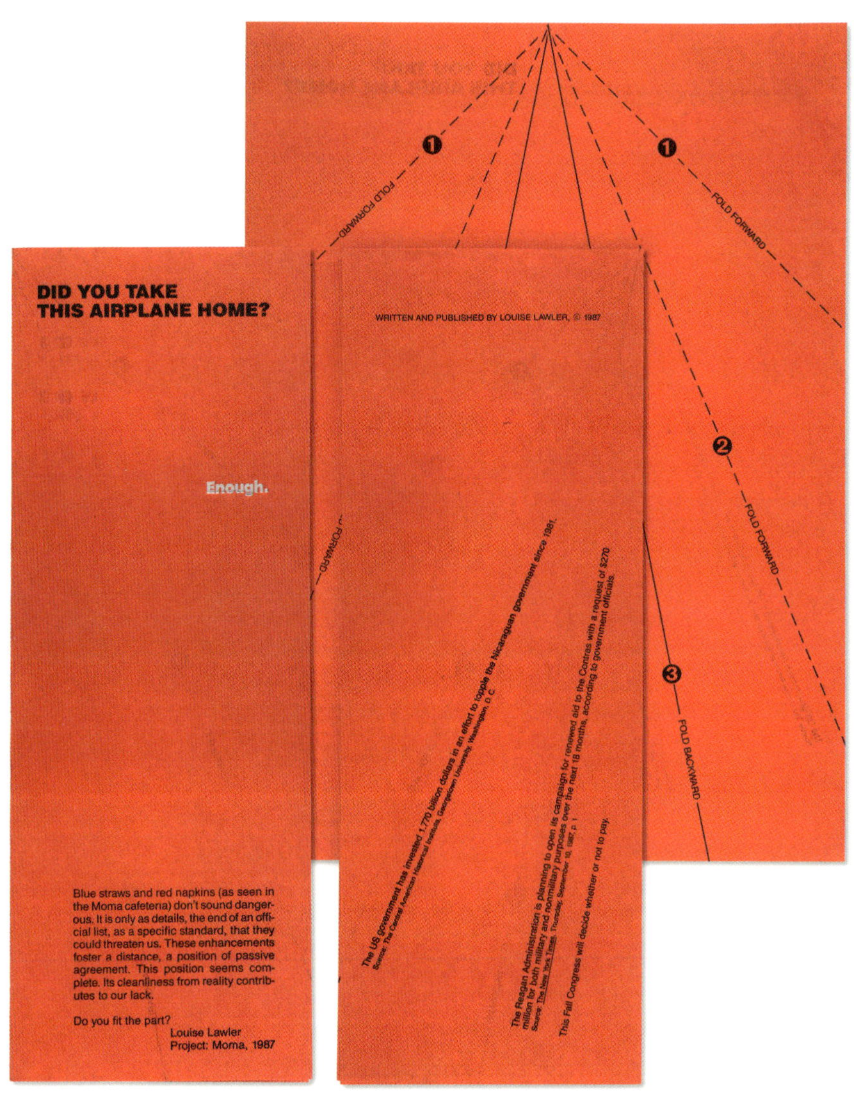

PLATE 10 Exhibition brochure for *Enough. Projects; Louise Lawler*, The Museum of Modern Art, New York, September 19–November 10, 1987. Printed paper, folded. Courtesy of the artist and Metro Pictures, New York.

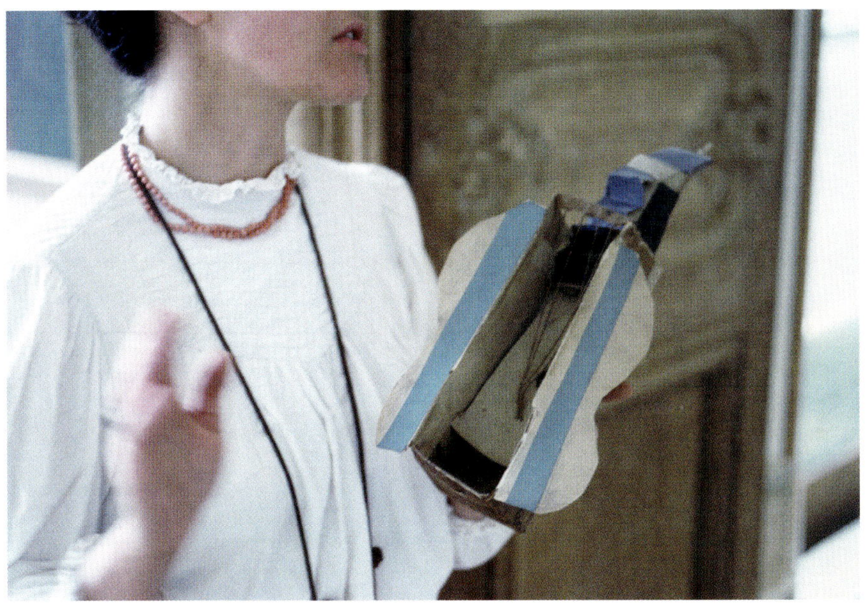

PLATE 11 Louise Lawler, *Woman with Picasso*, 1912, 1986. Silver dye bleach print. Courtesy of the artist and Metro Pictures, New York.

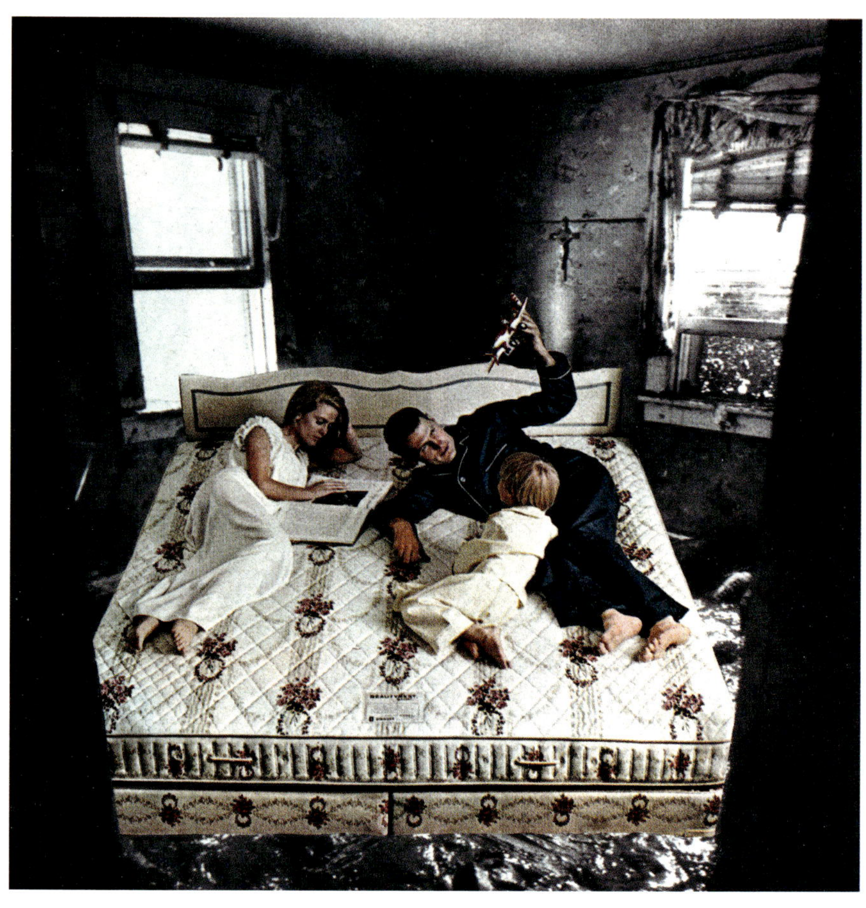

PLATE 12 Martha Rosler, *Beauty Rest*, from the series *House Beautiful: Bringing the War Home*, ca. 1967–72. Photomontage. Courtesy the artist.

:11:

Museum of Innocence

Before analyzing the recently opened National September 11 Memorial Museum, let us remember its prehistory—the memorial proposals that were never considered, the museums that were censored. In 2002, for example, sociologist Andrew Ross suggested that the best tribute to the victims of the terrorist attack on the World Trade Center would be "a new, genuinely mixed-income neighborhood that could capture, in the hustle and bustle of the living, the full sociological variety of those who died on 9/11."[1] Ross's idea was eminently reasonable and humane, but, given the nature of the economic forces that have long dominated the organization and use of space in New York, it was also doomed to obscurity. For, as could already be predicted in November 2001—when the rebuilding of downtown was turned over to the Lower Manhattan Development Corporation (LMDC), a new superagency with condemnation authority and the power to circumvent local regulations—the current redevelopment carries forward the process initiated in the late 1950s and '60s with the construction of the original WTC, which spearheaded attempts to shape Lower Manhattan in the interests of global finance and local real estate.

The censored museums were the International Freedom Center (IFC) and the Drawing Center, both selected by the LMDC in 2004 to occupy a proposed World Trade Center Memorial Cultural Complex on the southwest quadrant of the memorial plaza. The IFC was to be a new institution that its planners hoped would fulfil one of the goals professed in the memorial's mission statement: "to strengthen our resolve to preserve freedom."[2] The center intended to sponsor discussions about the "foundations of free and open societies" and document worldwide struggles for civil and human rights. Topics would have included the genocide of Native Americans, slavery and racism in the United States, and, according to at least one report, information about the curtailment of civil liberties in the US since 9/11.[3] It may well be true, as one opponent of the museum argued, that 9/11 was not about freedom, but the IFC promised to provide substance to a word that, in the wake of the attack, was being evacuated of meaning, made banal and reduced to a synonym for free trade. The Drawing Center, a nonprofit museum under the astute directorship of Catherine de Zegher, would have relocated from SoHo to the memorial site. The LMDC described it as an organization "committed to the discipline of drawing, one of the most elemental and universal forms of human expression."[4]

In 2005, both museums fell victim to the very erosion of rights the IFC had aimed to challenge. In early June, a red-baiting campaign mounted by a group called Take Back the Memorial and launched by an op-ed piece in the *Wall Street Journal* accused the IFC of disturbing the purity of sacred ground and therefore of insulting the dead and their families.[5] On June 24, the front page of the New York *Daily News* declared that the presence of the Drawing Center at Ground Zero would be a "disgrace" because the museum had shown art critical of the US, particularly of its occupation of Iraq and practice of torture.[6] The museum, the *News* said, would "violate" us "again."[7] That same day, Governor George Pataki announced that "we will not tolerate anything on that site that denigrates America, denigrates New York or freedom, or denigrates the sacrifice or courage that the heroes showed on September 11th."[8] The Drawing Center withdrew under pressure just before the governor, mobilizing the logic of the state of exception—protecting freedom by restricting it—barred the IFC from the WTC site in order to make it possible to create "an inspiring memorial." To honor the dead properly, we were told, we must surrender our democratic right to critical speech and subjugate ourselves to official discourses of truth.

The National September 11 Memorial Museum complies with this demand. As a result, the memory it constructs conceals a massive forgetting—which, from a Freudian viewpoint, is no unintentional failure of remembrance but rather an active process of omitting, which is to say, repressing. The museum's repressions are so manifold, the story it tells so circumscribed, that it seems driven by a passion for ignorance. To an extent, it forgets by means of the kind of reaction to traumatic loss that Eric L. Santner, writing about the German politics of memory, calls narrative fetishism—"the construction and deployment of a narrative consciously or unconsciously designed to expunge the traces of the trauma or loss that called that narrative into being in the first place." The narrative fetish tries to deny trauma by "simulating a condition of intactness" or by conveying uplifting, self-serving messages.[9]

In this light, consider Pataki's insistence on an "inspiring" memorial. Or the museum's assertion on its website that it "attests to the triumph of human dignity over human depravity."[10] Consider also the strategic placement of three of the museum's artifacts, two of them the most monumental in its collection. Visitors enter the museum, which occupies the former location of the Twin Towers, at ground level, passing through a glass pavilion designed by the Norwegian architecture firm Snøhetta. Proceeding from the entrance hall to the underground Davis Brody Bond building that houses the museum, they descend first to the lobby and then, via a sloping ramp, to original WTC bedrock, where the main exhibits, divided into a memorial section and a three-part historical section, are located. The very first exhibit, visible from the entryway, consists of two immense steel trident columns from the facade of the North Tower (fig. 11.1). A placard describes them as symbols of the savagery of the attack and, by virtue of their survival, of "fortitude in the face of tragedy." The lobby showcases a model of Fritz Koenig's 1971 bronze sculpture *The Sphere*, originally located between the Twin Towers. Damaged on 9/11 but structurally intact, it, too, is interpreted as "a lasting symbol of resilience." Halfway down to bedrock, the ramp turns at a sharp right angle to form a balcony that overlooks an exposed section of the original WTC's slurry, or perimeter, wall, which rises sixty feet from Foundation Hall, the museum's largest space and the one where, it is imagined, "visitors will end their Museum experience, contemplating the themes of strength and endurance" (fig. 11.2). Built to keep the Hudson River from leaking into the WTC's basement, still standing though in need of repair, and described as "a testament to survival and determination," the wall is accompanied by an unpersuasive comment from the new WTC's master planner, Daniel Libeskind, likening it to "the Constitution itself asserting the durability of Democracy and the value of individual life."

Despite these idealizing assertions of the WTC's symbolic wholeness, the museum is dominated by displays of the buildings in fragments. Mangled, shattered, and pulverized architectural remains hang from ceilings and walls and sit on platforms and pedestals, some in vitrines: an elevator motor, a crushed segment of the North Tower's radio and TV antenna, a fuel-tank remnant, steel from floors ninety-six to ninety-nine of the North Tower, a South Tower column, a single windowpane, a river-water valve, and a set of box-column remnants that mark the footprints of the towers. As the director, Alice M. Greenwald, reminds us, the museum does not simply house artifacts but is built within an architectural artifact itself. The amount of space allotted to the Twin Towers' architecture far exceeds that devoted to "In Memoriam," the memorial exhibition where visitors look at

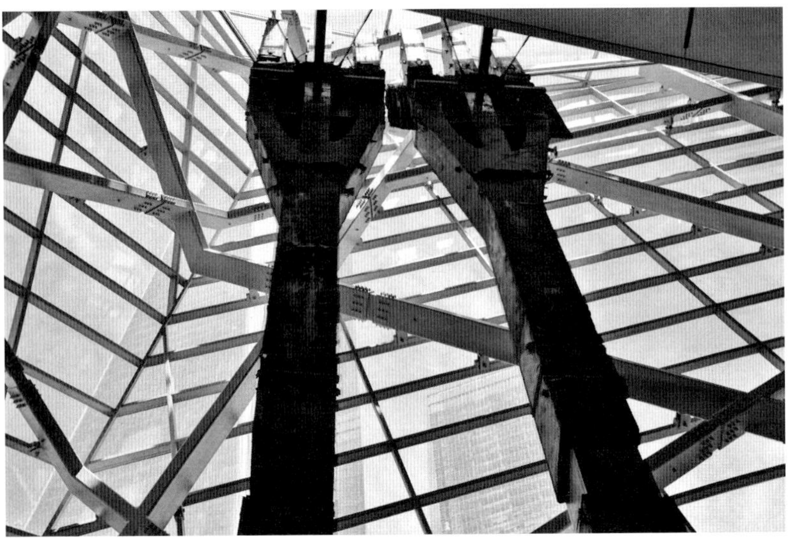

11.1 World Trade Center trident columns, National September 11 Memorial Museum, New York, 2014. Photo: Augie Ray. Courtesy Augie Ray.

photographs of the human victims and listen to recorded verbal testimonies in relative isolation from the architectural displays.

Elsewhere, however, the museum does not separate the buildings and their former human occupants but erodes the division between the two. In part, this reflects the physical reality of the attack, which, like the atomic bombing of Hiroshima, rendered people to dust—producing, as architect and scholar Mark Wigley has observed, "an unprecedented blurring of traditional distinctions" between human and architectural remains.[11] But insofar as monumental buildings are objects of identification by human subjects, such physical blurring has a psychic counterpart. Wigley, examining "the intense fantasies people have about buildings in general and the twins in particular"—the way "we use buildings to construct an image of what we would like the body to be"—elucidates how terrifying it was when, on 9/11, collective-unconscious associations between body and building were literalized in an event that destroyed both, the consequence of which was a traumatic loss of the nation's illusion of invulnerability and geographic exceptionalism with regard to violence.[12] The museum protects itself against the loss not only by simulating the WTC's intactness but by soliciting viewers' identification with it as a victim, an identification made possible by endowing the structure with the innocence of the human victims.

Perhaps the desire to turn away from the trauma by reidealizing the

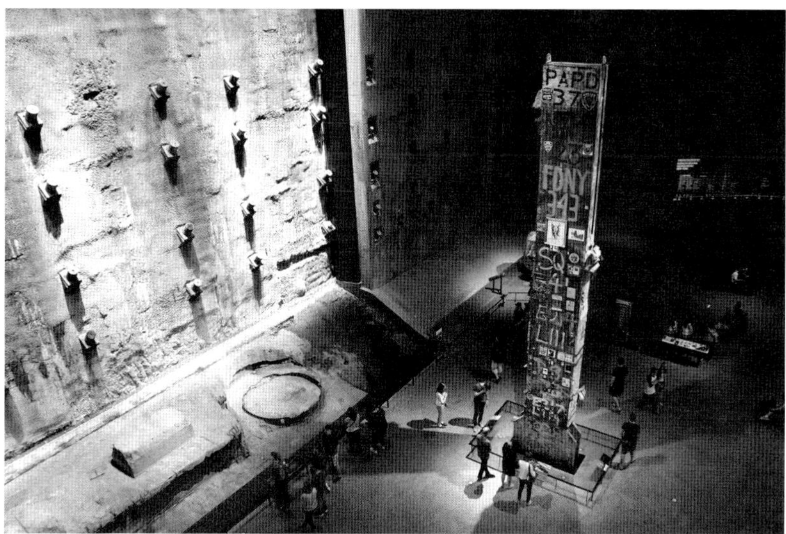

11.2 World Trade Center, slurry wall and the "last column," National September 11 Memorial Museum, New York, 2014. Photo: Augie Ray. Courtesy Augie Ray.

buildings as pure victims explains the enormous amount of attention focused on their anatomy. It is surely responsible for the astonishing omissions in the museum's history of the WTC. The towers are largely portrayed as technical feats: the elevator motor was part of an "innovative" elevation system, the slurry wall an engineering triumph. A sign informs us that "the novel engineering and architectural solutions [the developers] devised revolutionized skyscraper construction." Repeated emphasis on the towers' height and massiveness is exemplified by a chart showing the "World Trade Center by the Numbers": sixteen acres of land, 110 stories, 1,730 feet from street level to the top of the television mast, 43,600 windows, twelve million square feet of office space, etc.

Part two of the three-part historical exhibition is titled "Before 9/11" and, according to official descriptions, explores "the background leading up to the events." Its opening display is an original presentation model of the WTC. Featured quotations describe it as an icon of New York, which it was, and also, in former Port Authority director Austin Tobin's words, as the "United Nations of Commerce." With the exception of one photograph depicting a protest by small-business owners against the WTC, the museum ignores the buildings' social history—which includes the obliteration of an Arabic neighborhood, known as Little Syria, that once occupied the site; strong local opposition to the construction of the complex; the displacement of about eight hundred small businesses and tens of thousands of employees; the local government's subsidization of private profit; and, encompassing all of these, the fact that the WTC project ushered in a period of unprecedented social polarization that was engineered by New York's transformation into a corporate city, a polarization whose most visible symptom was the appearance of masses of homeless people on the city's streets. In the same way, the museum avoids recognizing that, for many of the world's peoples, the towers symbolized not freedom but the cruelties of US-dominated neoliberal capitalism and especially its financial system. The towers, that is, were not only targets but agents of destruction, both local and global.

The museum's prodigious amnesia is repeated in its approach to other topics in the historical exhibition. For example, aside from sketchy biographies of Osama bin Laden and other individual terrorists, the section about Al Qaeda in part two divulges only the barest facts: militant Islamism began during the Soviet occupation of Afghanistan; bin Laden founded Al Qaeda and, following the Persian Gulf War, began to advocate against American troop presence in Saudi Arabia, home to the holiest Muslim sites. No mention is made of the long history of US intervention—invasions, bombings, assassinations, coups—in the Middle East, which reaches back to the 1920s and picks up speed after 1949, when the CIA backed a military coup in Syria. Part three deals with "the aftermath and continuing implications of 9/11" but provides virtually no information about the "war on terror," the Afghanistan and Iraq wars, dead and wounded Afghan and Iraqi civilians and US soldiers who are also victims of 9/11, remote-controlled killings, the persecution of Muslims and other Arab immigrants, America's production of a population of "detainees" who have no rights, restrictions on civil liberties, and increasing government surveillance and secrecy. Several large rooms display documents and artifacts related to rescue, recovery, and relief operations in the wake of the attack and to sympathetic responses from other countries. The problem of "how we understand [9/11's] significance and place in history," however, is confined to a small alcove that concludes the historical exhibition. There, six questions are posed: How do we know what happened? Who should be held accountable? How are victims identified? What are the ongoing health effects? How should we remember? How can America protect its citizens? Below each question is a small, haphazard display of documents including, under "How can America protect its citizens?," a couple of photographs of soldiers in Iraq and Afghanistan, an antiwar flyer, and a photo of President Bush signing the USA PATRIOT Act, with, however, no accompanying information about the wars or the act.

What are the ethico-political consequences of all this forgetting? Likening psychic repression to a censor's alteration of the text of a book, Freud says that the aim of both is to defend against danger by "actively modifying reality." Such modifications are "not in the interests of truth." Repression in the individual can therefore itself become dangerous, producing "an ever-growing alienation from the outside world."[13] The National September 11 Memorial Museum's collective repressions are similarly pathogenic. For although it claims that it wants "to inspire an end to hatred, ignorance, and intolerance,"[14] the museum constructs a narcissistic memory that impedes its own goal. Hiding 9/11's traumatic disturbance of the nation's self-image, the museum concerns itself only with the violence *we* have suffered and supposedly triumphed over and, turning away from the rest of the world, resists trying to understand (which is not the same as forgiving or justifying) the psychic, political, economic, and cultural conditions of religious terrorism that contributed to the barbaric attack. By contrast, a *critical* memory, one that is not fully identificatory and so can pursue such understanding, is the basis of responsible action toward answering what is surely the most important question raised by 9/11, the one the museum does not ask: how to make the world less violent for everyone.

12

"We don't need another hero": War and Public Memory

At the height of World War I, the British author Ivor Gurney wrote a poem that illustrates the relationship between memorialization and repression. Titled "To His Love," Gurney's poem is a homoerotic monologue in which a soldier addresses the lover of another soldier, one who has been killed in the war. "To His Love" begins as a traditional pastoral elegy:

> He's gone, and all our plans
>> Are useless indeed.
> We'll walk no more on Cotswold
>> Where the sheep feed
>> Quietly and take no heed.

The second stanza mentions the dead soldier's body: it "was so quick" but "Is not as you | Knew it | You would not know him now." Yet the next few lines banish the sinister reference:

> But still he died
> Nobly, so cover him over
>> With violets of pride
>> Purple from Severn side.

Nothing prepares us for the desperation of the final stanza:

> Cover him, cover him soon!
>> And with thick-set
> Masses of memoried flowers—
>> Hide that red wet
>> Thing I must somehow forget.

Two transformations take place in the course of Gurney's poem. The soldier's body that "was so quick" turns into "that red wet | Thing"—a mutilated body. And a commemorative tribute—"violets of pride," which, by virtue of their association with kingship, symbolize the nobility of death in war—becomes an instrument of deception: "thick-set | Masses of memoried flowers" conceal the ghastly corpse.

The urgent plea of Gurney's soldier, that his friend's mangled body be driven from memory, may be understandable as a personal way of coping with traumatic loss, a symptom of pathological, or what the French philosopher Paul Ricoeur calls "wounded," memory.[1] But the imperatives of public remembrance extend beyond mourning, and even beyond commemoration, directing these activities toward a larger purpose. It is a commonplace to assert that one of the major purposes of memorializing human-inflicted disasters, such as war, is to prevent their recurrence. Routinely, we are told that a memorial, simply by its presence, will help build a better, less violent world. Yet, like Gurney's "violets of pride," conventional war memorials stress the righteous cause, the virtuous sacrifice, the great victory and, in this way, divert attention from the war-wrecked body. As a consequence, they doom their ostensibly future-oriented projects to failure. For the repression of the wounded body not only disposes of the true war memorial—the hurt body in which the record of war survives. Nor does it only turn away from the meaning of war, which, as Elaine Scarry writes, resides in "the incontestable reality of the body—the body in pain, the body maimed, the body dead and hard to dispose of," the body in which the nation has literally inscribed itself.[2] But, even more dangerously, the censorship of the wounded body resurrects the very condition that, according to Sigmund Freud, makes war possible: regression to the fantasy of the invulnerable body, or, as Freud calls it, heroism.

Two years before Gurney wrote "To His Love," Freud, too, reflected on the horrors of World War I, arguing that the secret of heroism in war is lack of belief in one's own death. This disbelief represents a withdrawal from reality and a move toward the phantasmatic security of primary narcissism, which children use to protect themselves during the process of self-formation. "The rational grounds for heroism," says Freud, "rest on a judgment that the subject's own life cannot be so precious as certain abstract and general goods. But more frequent, in my view, is the instinctive and impulsive heroism which knows no such reasons, and flouts danger in the spirit of . . . 'Nothing can happen to *me*.'" "The heroic reaction," Freud explains, "corresponds to the unconscious," which does not acknowledge death.[3] Recently, a United States Marine captain unwittingly confirmed

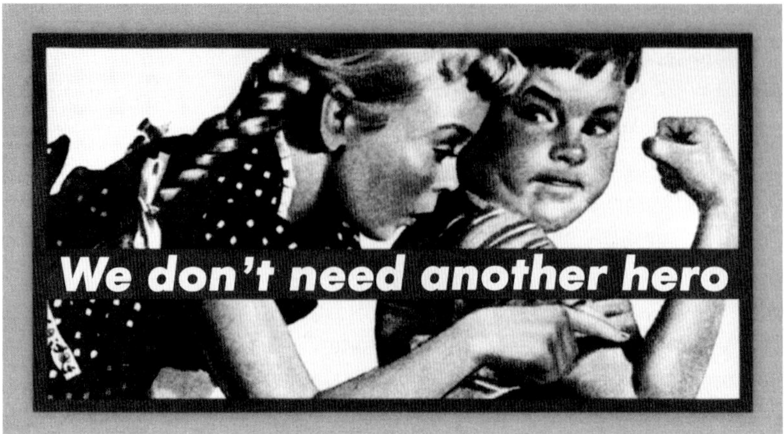

12.1 Barbara Kruger, *Untitled (We don't need another hero)*, 1987. Photographic silkscreen on vinyl. Gift from the Emily Fisher Landau collection. Courtesy the artist and Whitney Museum of American Art. Image © Whitney Museum of American Art. Licensed by Scala/Art Resource, NY.

Freud's analysis when he recalled that until one of his own men was killed, "our deployment in Afghanistan had been exhilarating because we felt invulnerable. This invulnerability in an environment of death was the most powerful sensation I'd ever experienced. I felt favored and possessed with the power to do anything."[4]

Anyone who seriously hopes to make the world less warlike would do well to begin by reading Virginia Woolf, who, as Roger Poole suggests, may be "[war's] greatest theoretician."[5] The same year that Freud psychoanalyzed heroism and twenty-three years before her own *Three Guineas*, a radically feminist antiwar polemic, which attributes war to the infantilism and grandiosity of patriarchal behavior, Woolf published her first novel, *The Voyage Out*. Early in the book, a group of vacationers spots a fleet of British warships and at lunch afterward talks about valor in battle, praising the magnificence of British admirals. "No one liked it," then, when Helen Ambrose, the feminist among them, remarks, "as for dying on a battle-field, surely it was time we ceased to praise courage."[6] About seventy years later, during the period leading to the US-led Operation Desert Storm in Iraq, Barbara Kruger, channeling Tina Turner, echoed Ambrose's sentiment in a work that linked escalating militarism to masculinism. Kruger overlays an old, cropped Coppertone advertisement with a text that declares, "We don't need another hero" (fig. 12.1). Especially when he flexes his phallic biceps. As we've seen, Ivor Gurney expressed similar feelings. Precisely by demonstrating that memorialization covers the reality of war, Gurney uncovered it and, in doing so, attacked an entire heroic tradition of World War I poetry. "To His Love" embodies a shift in British poetry, "from Keatsian lyricism to raw, aghast reportage," observes Glyn Maxwell. In the poem's last line, we hear "the sound of a culture's poetic history cracking in half."[7]

Today, in an era of perpetual war, poets no longer exalt death in war, though American politicians do. The United States has "forgotten the meaning of war," writes Tony Judt, and "is the only advanced democracy where public figures glorify and exalt the military, a sentiment familiar in Europe before 1945 but quite unknown today."[8] Heroism still figures in pro-war propaganda, especially when it perpetuates the longstanding poetic tradition of linking war to the struggle for liberty and, in this way, transforms it into something beautiful, no matter how hellish. Just as on the eve of World War I, Germany's chancellor proclaimed, "We are not driven by the desire for conquest" but by the highest principles, so in 2003 President Bush gave the invasion of Iraq what Rosa Luxemburg calls "a democratic halo," describing it as a mission to bring freedom and justice to Iraq.[9] Vice-President Cheney strengthened Bush's depiction by banning media coverage of American bodies returning from Iraq.

Memory exercised in the interests of power is what Walter Benjamin had in mind when he wrote that "*even the dead* will not be safe from the enemy if he wins."[10] Paul Ricoeur calls this kind of memory "instrumentalized memory."[11] Like the pathological memory of Gurney's traumatized soldier, instrumental memory seeks to conceal the reality of war, only it does so by placing war within the narrative of greatness that Nietzsche dubs "monumental history"—the history of the victors.[12] Resistance to war requires that we remember differently, that we commemorate war by uncovering "that red wet / Thing." Gurney uses this phrase to refer to the shocking body of his dead comrade and to the horrors of war more generally. But insofar as it stands for all the dark things repressed by instrumental memorialization, "that red wet / Thing" denotes not only war's awful consequences but its dark, irrational causes as well. While the political, economic, demographic, and ideological causes of war are well recognized, almost no one wants to think about the role played by what Leo Bersani describes as the "intractable destructiveness intrinsic to being human."[13] Acknowledging unconscious aggression—the passion to injure—profoundly disillusions us about ourselves. We can no longer believe that violence always belongs to someone else. Yet, as Jacqueline Rose writes, "the subterranean aspects of . . . the human . . . play their part in driving the world on its course."[14] They must therefore be faced if we want to establish a better future. In this regard, art has something to contribute to the antiwar project, something other than ag-itprop activities. For if, as Judith Barry argues, art can make a space for a "hitherto *unthought* configuration of reality,"[15] it can also make a space for the unsettling realities we do not want to think about. Contemporary artists have assumed the responsibility of bringing to the surface the darkest aspects of war, and some, as we shall see, have done so by entering into a dialogue with the traditional commemorative forms that repress the red, wet thing.

Modern warfare severely challenges the fantasy of the invulnerable body on which war depends. Gurney's depiction of a soldier's dead body is a far cry from the one that King Priam voices in Homer's *Iliad*:

> For a young man killed in battle
> It's seemly to lie dead, cut about by the sharp bronze,
> Nothing, even in death, that's visible is repugnant.[16]

In Priam's view, the dead body, though wounded, remains intact. Yet in Gurney's, it is an unrecognizable thing. It is likely that Gurney's compatriot was killed by one of the Great War's technologically advanced weapons, which destroyed bodies on an unprecedented scale. He may have been hit by an artillery shell "that tore bodies to pieces or produced deep, wide perforations," or by a high-speed, dome-tipped bullet that "reduced the soft tissues and blood vessels to a devitalized pulp."[17] Inside the body, "the bullet may have 'somersaulted,' tearing tissues, shattering bones, and leaving ragged-edged exit wounds."[18] The gruesome injuries of World War I prefigure those of later wars. Ann Jones reports that in Afghanistan, for instance, IEDs produce blasts so strong that they rise "into the perineal area, where the two legs meet, to smash genitals and into the pelvic cavity to pulverize soft tissue and sever intricate bodily systems." Sometimes, they disintegrate the body "into such tiny fragments that it returns to earth in a snowfall of flesh" and soldiers "crawl around the blast site, scraping at the soil with their fingernails for some remains of their vaporized comrade to put in the body bag with which they came equipped."[19]

In the aftermath of World War I, widely publicized medical, surgical, and bodybuilding campaigns labored to reconstruct the male body. At the same time, a frenzy of commemoration sought to revive the masculinist dream of corporeal inviolability. Classical ideals became a vehicle of both attempts. Classicizing memorials, while functioning as sites of mourning, were also designed to transform memory, a transformation conducted in the name of "healing," commonly a euphemism for shifting attention from the war-ruined body toward discourses of nobility, glory, honor, and sacrifice. Monumental classicism, says Ana Carden-Coyne in her encyclopedic study of World War I memorials, "created an alternative architectural body."[20] Classical architectural structures replaced the fragmented bodies of those whose names were inscribed on them with a beautiful, unified, whole body.[21] Not surprisingly, "commemorative forms never honoured the disabled—and still don't."[22]

One of the most popular motifs decorating World War I memorials is the winged figure of Nike—Greek goddess of victory, companion of Roman emperors, and, in later centuries, a visible manifestation of triumph. Best-known is the marble Nike of Samothrace, which, since its discovery in 1863, has become a cultural icon that crystallizes," in Marina Warner's words, "the concept of classical Victory for the contemporary public more than any other" and exerts "an immeasurable effect on the public iconography of glory."[23] A photograph by Louise Lawler depicts the detached wings of this Nike—or, as the protruding pin makes clear, the wings of a plaster version of this Nike, one of countless copies in museums around the world. Lawler shot Nike's wings in 2005, when they were lying on blocks on the floor of the National Gallery in Oslo during the reinstallation of the museum's plaster cast collection. Lawler had visited the city more than a decade earlier and at that time took a picture of several plaster statues, including Nike, using it in one of her paperweight works. In 2005, however, the US was waging wars in Afghanistan and Iraq, wars launched as part of a post-9/11 campaign, comparable to the one following World War I, to reconsolidate the nation's heroic masculinity. Lawler captioned her 2005 image *Grieving Mothers (Attachment)* (fig. 12.2), following it in 2008 with a smaller crop named *Grieving Mothers—Still*. By that time Nike's wings were no doubt reattached to her torso, but the "war on terror" continued (plate 7).

In the 1980s, in what now appears as a precedent for *Grieving Mothers*, Lawler produced a group of photographs of classical and neoclassical statues in museum settings. Some of the figures are conquering heroes. Works like *The Rude Museum* (1987) and *Statue before Painting, Perseus with the Head of Medusa, Canova* (1982) testify to Lawler's long-standing war-consciousness.[24] With bold cropping, oblique angles of vision, and witty, suggestive juxtapositions, these works attack the integrity of militarized male bodies, subjecting their phallic pretensions to ridicule. Although the *Grieving Mothers* photographs picture a female statue, they nonetheless belong to this group. Nike, like Perseus, materializes a desire for conquest, and images of female perfection function as idealized self-images of the masculinist subject—that is to say, they are fetishes. Like the classical sculptures that populate Lawler's earlier works, the statue of the goddess is a symbol of the wished-

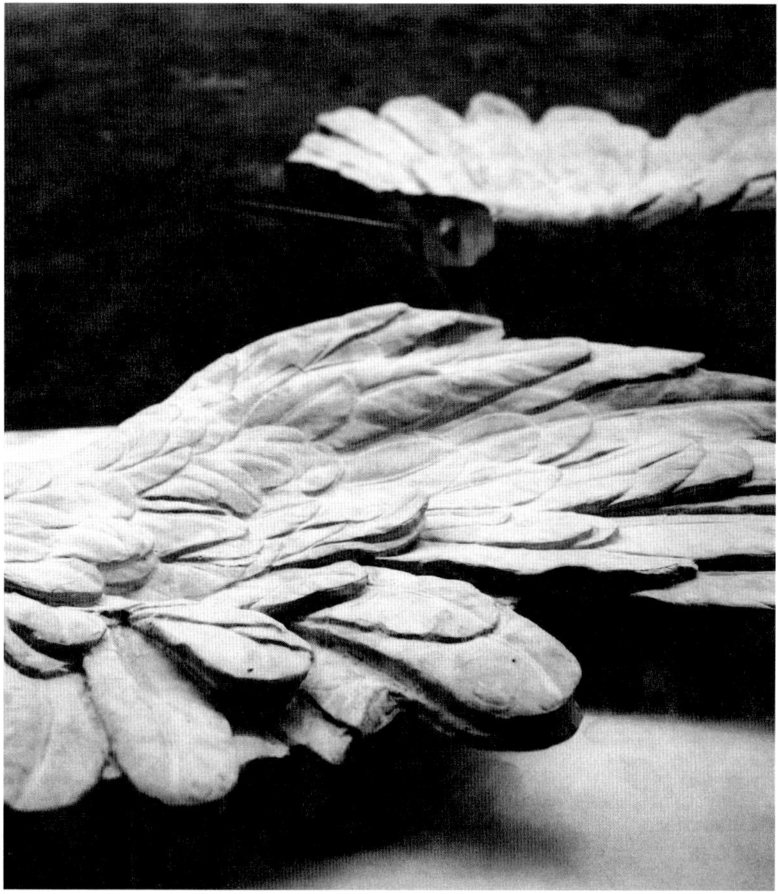

12.2 Louise Lawler, *Grieving Mothers (Attachment)*, 2005. Silver dye bleach print. Courtesy of the artist and Metro Pictures, New York.

for presence that will guarantee wholeness—a phallus, and a flying one at that, a larger version of the flying phallus charms hung around the necks of Roman generals.

The relationship of Lawler's captions to the images they accompany are generally ambiguous, and the title *Grieving Mothers*, reinforcing the image's association with war, is especially rich in interpretive possibilities. Do the detached wings symbolize the grieving mothers? Or do they stand for fallen soldiers that the mothers are attached to and grieve for? Are they severed limbs of wounded soldiers? Perhaps Nike herself has metamorphosed into a grieving mother, as she did in certain World War I memorials that portray her not as a belligerent figure but as a nurturing one. One example is the

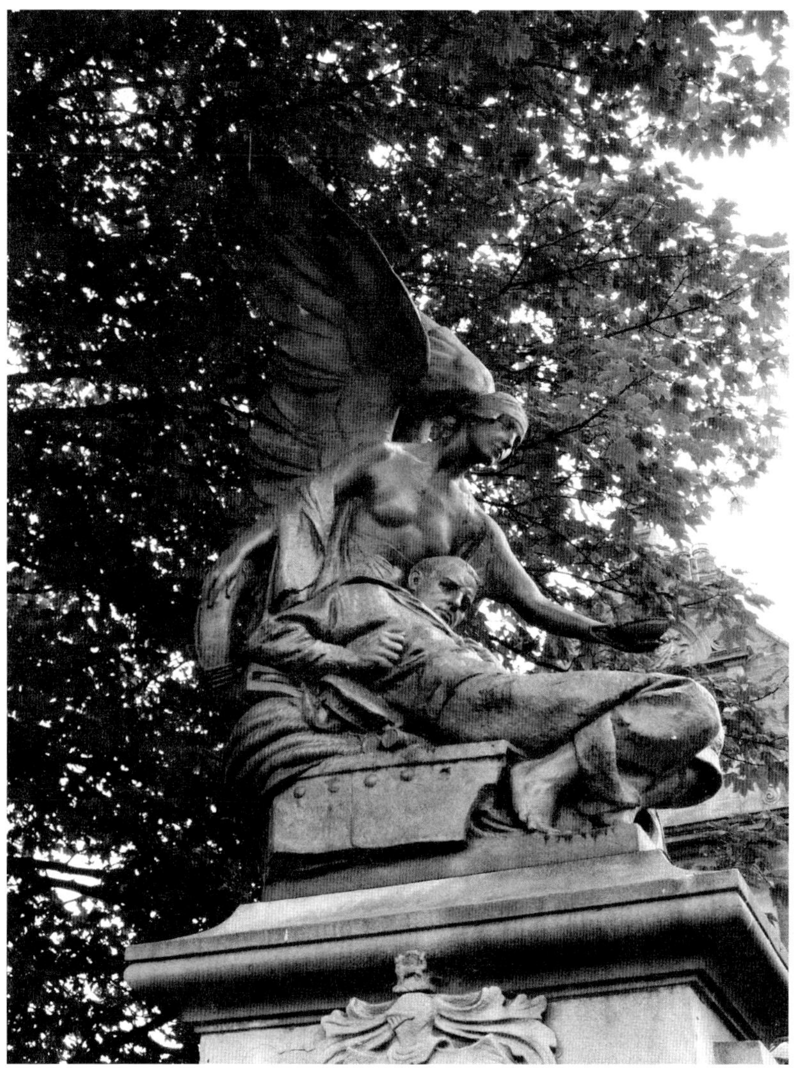

12.3 Unknown photographer, Stalybridge War Memorial, Greater Manchester, England, October 18, 2013. Courtesy Repton1x, Wikimedia Commons.

statue on the British Stalybridge War Memorial, which maternalizes Nike, albeit in her Christian incarnation as an angel of victory (fig. 12.3). Likewise, the sculptor of the figure on the Folkestone Memorial intended his Nike-like statue to represent motherhood while, at the same time, embodying the triumphant, intact nation. A Nike faithful to her classical origins, however, cannot represent both maternal grief, which places her in the company of

women, and manly heroism since, in the ancient world, the two were opposing practices. As part of its regulation of civic memory, the Athenian political community strictly monitored women's mourning, limiting it as far as
possible to the private home, for sorrow, especially sorrow over sons killed
in war, might turn into the "memory-wrath" that the Greeks called *mênis*.
Relentless in its refusal to forget and capable of evolving into defiance,
mênis threatened the continuity of the polis.[25] By contrast with such unfor-
getting mothers, the maternal Nikai at Stalybridge and Folkestone typify
the amnesiac reaction to traumatic loss that Eric L. Santner calls "narrative
fetishism"—"the construction and deployment of a narrative consciously
or unconsciously designed to expunge the traces of the trauma or loss that
called that narrative into being in the first place." The narrative fetish tries
to deny trauma by "simulating a condition of intactness" or by conveying
uplifting, self-serving messages.[26]

In this manner, Nike was occasionally conscripted into the story of
World War I as a paradigm of grieving that also stands for victory, patriotism, peace, and sacrifice. Her presence exalted grief as service to the nation. In fact, World War I propaganda equated the sacrifice of mothers with
that of heroic soldiers, recruiting the image of grieving mothers for the war
effort, as in a poster that states, "Women of Britain Say . . . Go!" and shows
potential grieving mothers watching their sons march off to battle. A more
flagrant exploitation of mothers appeared in a 1916 letter sent to the editor of the *Morning Post* from "A Little Mother." "Women," writes the Little
Mother, "are created for the purpose of giving life, and men to take it. Now
we are giving it in a double sense." She notes, "It is we who 'mother the men'
who have to uphold the honour and traditions not only of our Empire, but
of the whole civilised world."[27] The Little Mother letter elicited grateful tes-
timonials, like the one from "A Bereaved Mother": "I have lost my two dear
boys, but since I was shown the 'Little Mother's' beautiful letter a resignation too perfect to describe has calmed all my aching sorrow, and I would
now gladly give my sons twice over."[28] Clearly, maternal grief does not in itself challenge instrumental war memory. Mourning is not the universal affective and expressive practice depicted in traditional humanist accounts
but, rather, a plural and contested—which is to say, political—one that can
be mobilized for divergent political ends.[29]

Although it deeply touched the queen consort, the Little Mother letter
was a fake, probably written by an editor at the *Post* and widely distributed
as a propaganda pamphlet to counter calls for peace negotiations. But in
2005, the year that Lawler produced *Grieving Mothers (Attachment)*, a genuine grieving mother refused induction into the war propaganda machine

and became, instead, an agonistic actor. Cindy Sheehan's son Casey had been killed in Iraq. Sheehan regretted allowing him to be buried as a soldier and built an alternative memorial in the form of an extended antiwar protest outside President Bush's Texas ranch, naming it Camp Casey.[30] She demanded accountability from the president about how he had conducted the wars in Afghanistan and Iraq. "I want to ask George Bush, Why did my son die?" she told reporters. "I don't want him to use my son's name or my family name to justify any more killing. . . . If he even starts to say freedom and democracy, I'm gonna say, bullshit." Recollecting her journey "through heartache to activism," she recommends that mothers stand up and say, "No, I am not giving my child to the fake patriotism of the war machine, which chews up my flesh and blood to spit out profits."[31]

Sheehan's words have a quality that is frequently ascribed to Lawler's art: poignancy, a term that, as Douglas Crimp points out, means both "moving" and "pointed."[32] The caption gives *Grieving Mothers (Attachment)* its poignancy, but so does the artist's treatment of the work's thematic content—the detached wings of Nike, which are laden with symbolic connotations: brokenness, harm, fragmentation, suffering, incapacitation, castration. Like all war memorials, Lawler's photograph is inhabited by a tension between the presence and absence of a body, echoing what Carden-Coyne calls the "marked unease" "between the absent bodies memorialized and the colossal signs"—such as Nike—"directing the memory process."[33] Its iconography, title, and melancholic, gray tonality also endow *Grieving Mothers* with a memorial mood. But Lawler reverses the way Nike is deployed in World War I memorials: instead of displacing mutilated bodies with one that is complete, she turns Nike herself into a wounded body, maybe an injured soldier. Nike of Samothrace is already disarmed, of course, but now she has lost the body part that ensures her divinity. Listen to Socrates in Plato's *Phaedrus*: "The natural property of a wing is to raise that which is heavy and carry it aloft to the region where the gods dwell: and more than any other bodily part it shares in the divine nature."[34] Nike is divine because, like God, material rules do not apply to her; but in Lawler's photographs they do. Dusty footprints, legible in the smaller version of *Grieving Mothers*, cover the floor of the Oslo Museum on which Nike's plaster wings rest, underscoring her earthbound condition. However, the background of the first version is out of focus, and the blurriness, coupled with the absence of a horizon line, transforms the floor into a cloudy, celestial realm—the region where the gods dwell, Nike's proper home. Yet the allusion to a heavenly sky doesn't mitigate the goddess's plight. Instead, it provides an idealized norm against which the gravity of her injury is heightened. Akin to the protagonist of a Greek tragedy at the moment of the plot's reversal, Nike has undergone a change of fortune—from security to vulnerability. As in Greek tragedy, the violence has occurred offstage, and Nike's fall stems from a fatal flaw in her character—overconfidence, hubris, the belief that "nothing can happen to me." Especially in her monumental sculptural forms, Nike symbolizes the wish to solidify the heroic feeling. In this reading, Lawler's *Grieving Mothers* evokes the grievous consequences of the violence caused by disavowing the fact that, like plaster and even marble, we are susceptible to being wounded.

Because the heroic fantasy originates in a defense against the losses that constitute us as human subjects, and because in phallocentric culture the female body signifies symbolic castration, it is hardly surprising that one of the fantasy's most grievous consequences is cruelty toward women. "It would seem," writes Jacqueline Rose, "that women's bodies are there to be punished, that the mere sight of them is in itself a punishable offence."[35] In 2015, the chief prosecutor for the International Criminal Court criticized the inaction of the UN Security Council in securing the arrest of rapists in Darfur. "Women and girls continue to bear the brunt of sustained attacks on innocent civilians," said the prosecutor, "but this council is yet to be spurred into action. Victims of [war] rapes are asking themselves how many more women should be brutally attacked for this council to appreciate the magnitude of their plight."[36] World War I monuments also failed to attend to female victims of war, never commemorating them.[37] No Nike, not even a maternal one, protected women or grieved for their suffering.

The goddess's neglect might have been partially rectified in 1998 had the Croatian artist Sanja Iveković been allowed to execute a work that, like *Grieving Mothers*, would have initiated a dialogue with an existing war monument. Iveković was invited to participate in Manifesta 2, the European Biennial of Contemporary Art, which was being held that year in Luxembourg City, capital of the state of Luxembourg. In the center of the city, in Constitution Square, stands a sixty-nine-foot-tall granite obelisk erected in 1923 to memorialize Luxembourg citizens who fought against the Germans in World War I. At the foot of the obelisk, two bronze statues represent Luxembourg soldiers who volunteered to serve in the French army during the German occupation of their own country. One, who died for the fatherland, lies on a pedestal; a seated compatriot mourns him. Topping the obelisk is a larger-than-human-size, gilded bronze neoclassical statue of a wingless yet still triumphant Nike, crowning the nation with a laurel wreath—Greek symbol of victory, Roman symbol of triumph, and Christian sign of Christ's victory over death. In October 1940, Germans, who were again occupying the country, pulled down the monument, which was rebuilt in the 1950s and now also commemorates Luxembourgers killed in World War II and the Korean War. The Nike sculpture gives the monument its popular name—*Gëlle Fra*, the Golden Lady—and because she stands for Luxembourg's independence from two occupations, she is also called the "Queen of Freedom."

For her contribution to Manifesta 2, Iveković submitted a proposal to remove the Nike statue from the *Gëlle Fra* and reinstall it on the premises of the city's shelter for abused women. In her new location, Nike would have defended female victims of violence and, at the same time, highlighted the disparity between the idealizing treatment of women's bodies in allegorical representations and the degrading treatment of actual women's bodies. The work might have suggested that both uses of the female body deprive women of agency. Considered too controversial, Iveković 's proposal was rejected.

Fortunately, three years later, Iveković resumed her conversation with the *Gëlle Fra*, this time provoking an even fiercer controversy, which took place on television and in newspaper headlines, articles, internet discussions, and two parliamentary debates. Invited back to Luxembourg to take part in an exhibition dealing with national identity, Iveković created a same-size replica of the *Gëlle Fra*, installing it within walking distance of the original (plate 8). In addition to using less permanent materials—wood and gilded polyester—Iveković changed the monument in three ways. First, the Nike at the top of her obelisk, though otherwise an exact copy of the *Gëlla Fra* sculpture, is visibly pregnant. Second, whereas the plinth of the *Gëlle Fra* is inscribed with quotations celebrating national war heroes, each side of Iveković 's plinth is divided into three horizontal registers containing reiterated words. Two registers display French or German terms, the majority of which denote concepts historically conceived of as masculine but symbolized by allegorical female figures—*La Résistance, La Justice, La Liberté, L'Indépendence, Kapital, Kunst, Kultur*. Either a degrading or an idealizing English term for women—Madonna, Virgin, Whore, Bitch—fills a third register, so that the monument's base, instead of commemorating war heroism, literalizes heroism's misogynistic foundation (fig. 12.4). Read in conjunction with the words on the plinth, the pregnant woman at the top of Iveković 's memorial, emerging from the very figure that epitomizes the idealization of women, brings to mind the widespread, long-standing result of war for real women—rape.

Iveković 's third change to the *Gëlle Fra* was to rename it *Lady Rosa of Luxembourg*. While this gesture doesn't physically move Nike, as the artist had hoped to do in her first proposal, it symbolically resituates her, bringing her

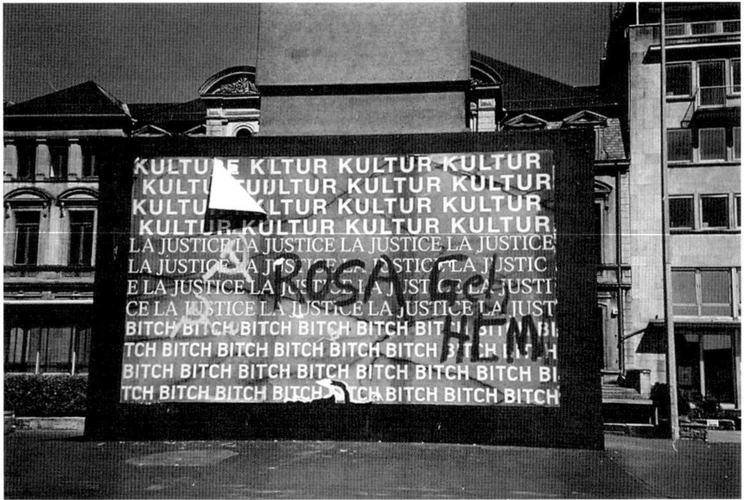

12.4 Sanja Iveković, *Lady Rosa of Luxembourg*, 2001. Detail. Gilded polyester, wood, and printed text. Photo: Christian Mosar. Courtesy the artist.

down from an "abstract allegorical context into concrete historical circumstances."[38] Her new situation transforms the *Gëlle Fra* into an antiwar memorial and Nike into a political activist, for the Marxist philosopher Rosa Luxemburg, to whom the new name obviously refers, vehemently opposed World War I; she spent most of the war in prison for organizing antiwar demonstrations and encouraging conscientious objection to military conscription. Luxemburg's *The Crisis in the German Social Democracy* (the "Junius" Pamphlet), written in jail in 1915 and smuggled out in 1916, excoriates the German Social Democratic Party for supporting an imperialist war in the name of national defense. The interests of the bourgeois nation and of the international proletariat, Luxemburg insists, are not the same: "In the present-day imperialistic milieu there can be no national wars of defense, and any socialist policy which … lets itself be governed merely by the isolated viewpoint of a single country is doomed in advance." Luxemburg also indicts war more generally, calling it "methodical, organized, gigantic murder … possible only when a state of intoxication has been previously created."[39] In a later text on the Russian Revolution, Luxemburg criticized Lenin's support of the right of nations to self-determination and in this context wrote her most famous line: "Freedom is always and exclusively freedom for the one who thinks differently."[40]

Iveković was impressed by the fact that Luxembourg residents view the *Gëlle Fra* as a symbol of freedom, but in dedicating her memorial to Rosa

Luxemburg, she questions the notion of freedom that the monument celebrates. Following in Rosa Luxemburg's footsteps, Iveković lifts freedom—and with it, the war memorial—out of a restricted nationalist framework, quoting Benedict Anderson's description of the nation as a "fraternity that makes it possible . . . for so many millions of people, not so much to kill, as willingly to die for . . . limited imaginings."[41] *Lady Rosa* thus contests the collective narcissism of state-sanctioned memorials, which are concerned only with the violence "we," as a nation, have suffered and supposedly triumphed over. Bojana Pejić suggests that Iveković intervenes in narcissistic memory in yet another way, one that troubles the nation's would-be unity. Noting that sexual violation can cause women to remember wars differently than men, Pejić says that the pregnancy of *Lady Rosa* brings to mind "women of the 'other' side," who were "violated and raped in . . . wars" yet "scarcely honored as 'fallen heroines.'"[42]

Enemies, of course, were never honored in official World War I memorials. In Mark Twain's *War Prayer*, an antiwar parable written in the early years of the twentieth century, an entire community agrees that it makes no sense to acknowledge, let alone mourn, the enemy's suffering.[43] Twain's story takes place on a Sunday morning during a time of war, when a packed church asks God to watch over its nation's soldiers and ensure their victory. A "fervent appeal" from the preacher concludes his long prayer: "Bless our arms, grant us the victory, O Lord our God, Father and Protector of our land and flag!" At this point, an aged stranger, who has entered the church, takes the minister's place, claiming to bring the worshippers a message from god. He then informs them of the unspoken part of their prayer, voicing what they are really asking for when they pray for victory:

> help us to tear their soldiers to bloody shreds with our shells . . . to drown the thunder of the guns with the shrieks of their wounded, writhing in pain . . . to wring the hearts of their unoffending widows with unavailing grief . . . to turn them out roofless with their little children . . . blast their hopes, blight their lives. . . . We ask it, in the spirit of love, of Him Who is the Source of Love and Who is the ever-faithful refuge and friend of all that are sore beset and seek His aid with humble and contrite hearts. AMEN.

Afterward, everyone believes that "the man was a lunatic, because there was no sense in what he said."

In 1970, the French Fluxus artist Robert Filliou made a work that recalls the words of Twain's stranger and that, even more emphatically than *Lady Rosa*, repudiates nationalism in order to commemorate losses on the other side. *COMMEMOR*, first installed at the Neue Galerie in Aix-la-Chapelle, not

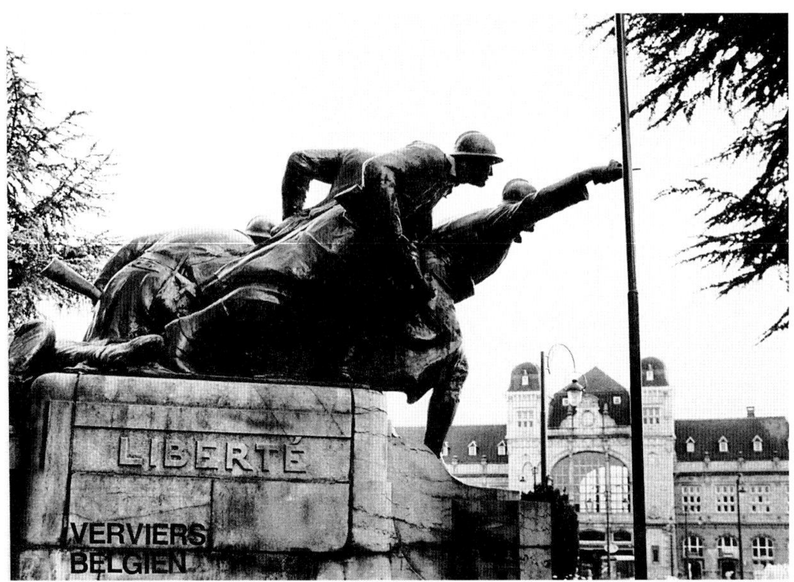

12.5 Robert Filliou, *COMMEMOR*, *Verviers, Belgium*, 1970. Black-and-white photograph on chipboard. Photo: Horst Kolberg, Neuss. Courtesy Museum Kunstpalast, Düsseldorf, and the Estate of Robert Filliou/Peter Freeman, Inc. © Museum Kunstpalast, Horst Kolberg, ARTOTHEK.

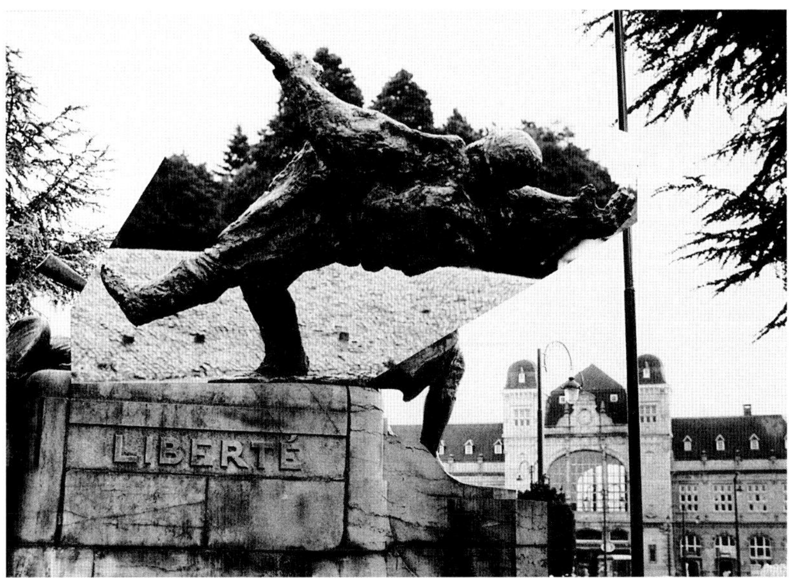

12.6 Robert Filliou, *COMMEMOR*, *Verviers, Belgium*, 1970. Black-and-white photomontage on chipboard. Photo: Horst Kolberg, Neuss. Courtesy Museum Kunstpalast, Düsseldorf, and the Estate of Robert Filliou/Peter Freeman, Inc. © Museum Kunstpalast, Horst Kolberg, ARTOTHEK.

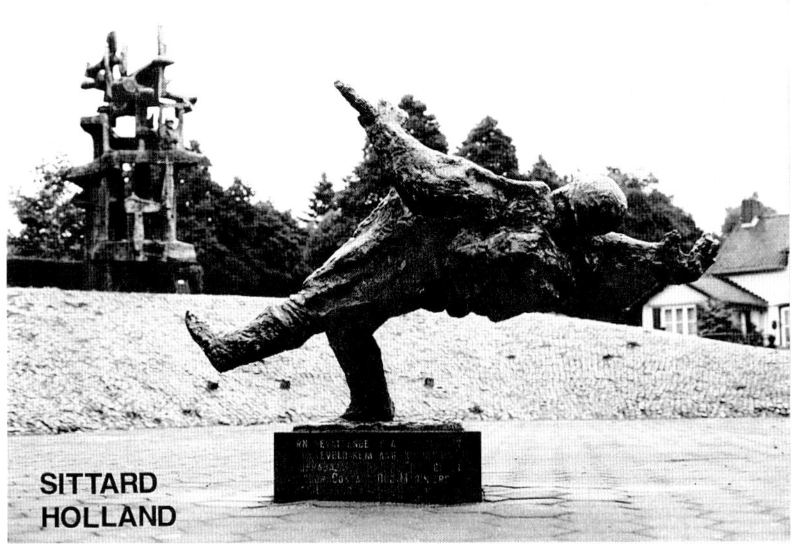

12.7 Robert Filliou, *COMMEMOR*, *Sittard, Holland*, 1970. Black-and-white photograph on chipboard. Photo: Horst Kolberg, Neuss. Courtesy Museum Kunstpalast, Düsseldorf, and the Estate of Robert Filliou/Peter Freeman, Inc. © Museum Kunstpalast, Horst Kolberg, ARTOTHEK.

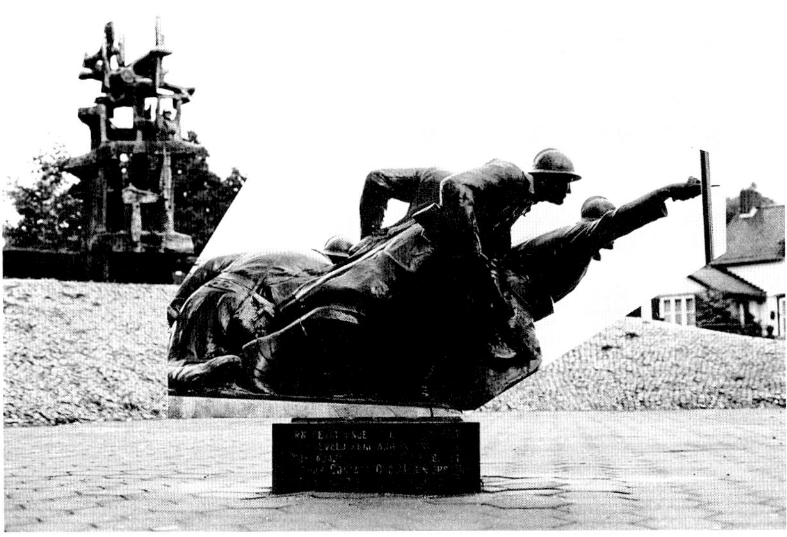

12.8 Robert Filliou, *COMMEMOR*, *Sittard, Holland*, 1970. Black-and-white photomontage on chipboard. Photo: Horst Kolberg, Neuss. Courtesy Museum Kunstpalast, Düsseldorf, and the Estate of Robert Filliou/Peter Freeman, Inc. © Museum Kunstpalast, Horst Kolberg, ARTOTHEK.

only talks with existing war monuments but puts them into dialogue with one another. The key element of Filliou's conceptual work is a text in French and English that begins with a "PROCLAMATION OF INTENT":

> In order to:
> - seal the reconciliation of the nations of Europe through a single powerful act
> - create a precedent that will spread one day to all the continents,
> - honour truly the memory of this century's war victims
> - remind future generations of the futility and obscenity of nationalism
> - decisively bring together European towns and villages
> - transform the pompous, revengeful style history bequeathed us into a new and generous expression of our destiny.

To achieve these goals, the text continues,

> IT IS SOLEMNLY PROPOSED TO THE EUROPEAN PEOPLES THAT THEY BEGIN EXCHANGING THEIR RESPECTIVE WAR MEMORIALS
>
> To this end the creation of a Joint Commission for the Exchange of War Memorials (COMMEMOR) is suggested, whose activities will be accompanied by meditation and rejoicing.[44]

A final sentence turns Filliou's antiwar memorial into what Eric Baudelaire calls an ante-war, in the sense of before-war, memorial:[45]

> COUNTRIES WHICH NOWADAYS ARE THINKING OF GOING TO WAR ARE SUMMONED TO EXCHANGE THEIR WAR MEMORIALS BEFORE AND INSTEAD OF MAKING IT.[46]

Filliou illustrated his proposal with playful collages constructed from photographs of war monuments in Holland, Germany, and Belgium, which the artist cut out and swapped (figs. 12.5–12.8).

A year later, Filliou produced a related project—a portfolio of silkscreen prints titled *7 Childlike Uses of Warlike Material* that outlines a kind of play therapy for overly aggressive adults. On the cover is a proposal, in which—on the left—the artist lists everyday objects that could be used to represent tools of war: "a saw could be a submarine, a nail could be a missile, a shirt could be a uniform, an old can could be a tank, sticks of wood could be guns, old newspapers could be bureaucratic documents, something burnt out could be a bonfire." Then, in the right-hand column, he outlines a plan to banish the war apparatus to imagined places: "I can put the submarine on the mountains, the missile on the moon, the uniforms around the stars, the tank in the desert, the guns into the ocean, the bureaucratic documents into outer space. I can set the war academy on fire." "It will," he says, "become A CONTRIBUTION TO THE ART OF PEACE." He then plans to place these transformed objects along the Rhine, take photographs, and make prints.

Filliou's earlier work, *COMMEMOR*, likewise transforms war material in order to imagine what could be. But, in calling on nations to exchange war memorials, *COMMEMOR* also promotes the exercise of memory on an ethico-political level. Paul Ricoeur calls ethico-political memory "the duty of memory." He cautions, however, that the term does not refer to the "obsession with commemoration" that characterizes our historical moment. In fact, for Ricoeur, following Pierre Nora, current enthusiasm for commemoration is an abuse of the duty of memory because it "short-circuits the work of critical history."[47] But if the duty of memory can epitomize abuse in the exercise of memory, it can also exemplify the "good use" of memory—if, that is, it adds to mourning and to memory the imperative of justice.[48] What conception of justice gives it ethical force? Ricoeur responds to this question in three steps: first, the duty of memory is the duty to do justice, through memories, to an other than the self; second, the duty of memory as the duty of justice helps repay a debt to "those who have gone before us"; and finally, "among those to whom we are indebted, the moral priority belongs to the victims," and "the victim at issue . . . is the other victim, other than ourselves."[49] "Justice," says Ricoeur, "turns memory into a project," giving it the form of an imperative and of the future.[50]

COMMEMOR is a project that invites us to confront the memory of those we have injured, challenging claims of innocence and goodness on "our side" and encouraging accountability for our violence. It brings the death of the enemy out of isolation, eroding the rigid separation of self and other. And it seeks to prevent impending violence. Placing the work of memory and of mourning under an ethical idea of justice, Filliou offers a glimpse of what might inspire genuine hope for a less warlike future.

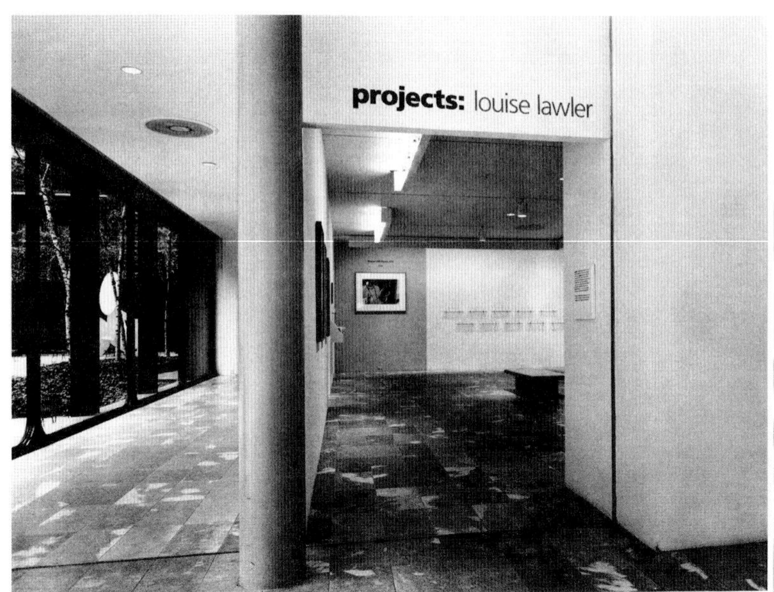

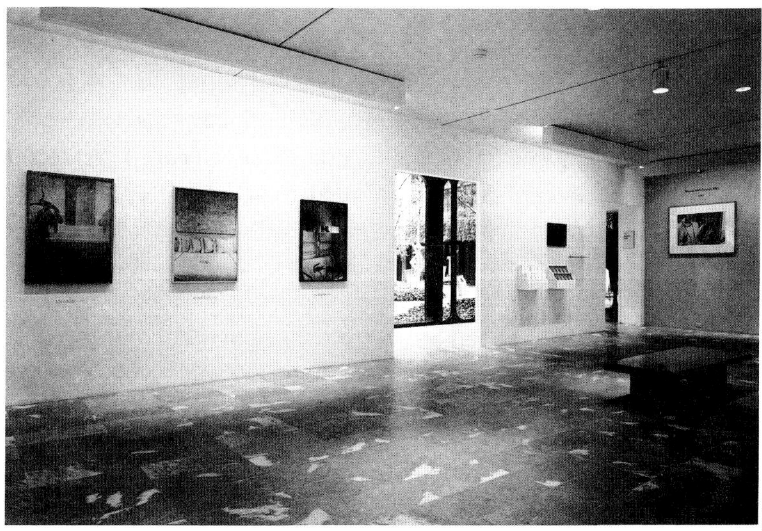

13.1 Louise Lawler, *Enough. Projects: Louise Lawler*, Museum of Modern Art, New York, September 19–November 10, 1987. Installation view. Courtesy of the artist and Metro Pictures, New York.

13

Louise Lawler's Play Technique

Louise Lawler first exhibited at the Museum of Modern Art in 1987, when she was featured in *Projects*, a series devoted to the work of young, emerging artists. Three years earlier, the museum had reopened after a lavish renovation by the architecture firm of Cesar Pelli & Associates. Its collections had also been reinstalled, once again separated into departments based on traditional mediums—painting and sculpture; drawings, prints, and illustrated books; architecture and design; photography; and film. It was the height of the critical postmodern era; artists and critics were challenging such neutralizing classification systems, which embody the doctrine that medium specificity guarantees the autonomy of the work of art.[1] Yet MoMA, the world's preeminent institution of modern art, persisted, as Douglas Crimp has observed, in imposing an idealist aesthetic vision that removes art objects from the social and historical worlds.[2]

Lawler's *Projects* exhibition took place in a small room off the museum's enormous new lobby and across from its expanded sculpture garden (fig. 13.1).[3] But Lawler resisted confinement, transgressing MoMA's categorical boundaries by bringing the entire museum, nearly all its departments, into her allotted space. To begin with, she assembled several of her photographs, taken between 1984 and 1987, that depict works by artists who figure prominently in MoMA's version of twentieth-century art history. Side by side on one wall, for example, she mounted *Untitled, 1950–51* (1987), three identical silver dye bleach prints of a large painting by Joan Miró that was on display at the time on the museum's second floor (fig. 13.2). Boldly cropped, shot from an oblique vantage point, showing only part of the Miró, the photographs exemplify Lawler's tactics in the works she gathers under the overarching rubric "arrangements of pictures": photographs of artworks in the circumstances of their existence—display, storage, transport, and so on. These suggest that the meaning of a work of art is largely determined not by its individual contents but by its institutional frames. Claude Gintz has put it well: "While shifting to reframe a fragment of a work to include a piece of its outside, the eye of [Lawler's] camera negates the very notion of individual work as totality, and the emphasis is put on the field of inscription . . . within which it is shown."[4] The Miró photos include one such piece of the artwork's outside—a bench that MoMA had placed in front of it, thereby establishing it as a "masterpiece" worthy of prolonged contemplation. The polished surface of the depicted bench reflects the painting, symbolizing the inseparability of work and context; the bench itself makes concrete the generally invisible ways in which, as part of its arrangement of artworks, the museum also arranges the museumgoer.

Lawler makes perfectly clear that her photographs of arrangements are themselves arranged. In the case of the Miró images, she fragmented the painting and highlighted its alignment with the bench. She exhibited the images as a triptych and hung them below eye level. Mimicking a museological tool for designing the viewer's experience of art, she painted a section of the wall behind the photographs gray. The color block, on which Lawler printed "1950–51, 1987," the dates of Miró's work and of her photograph of it, in discrete silver type, consolidated the Miró photographs into a subgroup, a work within the larger installation. The marble floor in the pictures duplicated the one on which the viewer of the exhibition actually stood. In addition, Lawler placed a real museum bench in front of her photographs. As MoMA did, she invited viewers to pause and reflect—not, however, on a work of art but on their own role in the museological situation. By encouraging spectators to step out of a prescribed position, Lawler suggested that the art institution, as Andrea Fraser has written, "is a field of social relationships"; as such, "it is inside of us, and we can't get outside of ourselves."[5]

Throughout the exhibition Lawler distributed additional photographic arrangements of pictures, likewise organized into subgroups, each portraying a painting or sculpture by a major artist in MoMA's canon—Pablo Picasso, Robert Rauschenberg, Jasper Johns, Jackson Pollock, Donald Judd. Some of the works are depicted on display in private homes, others in American and European museums. To the right of the Miró prints, sandwiched between sheets of Plexiglas, was a small, original photograph of Paul Cézanne's garden in Aix-en-Provence annexed to a label of equal size, which mimicked American museum signage. The image and text referred to the artist MoMA positions as the founding father of modernism and to the museum's own garden, while also hinting that museumgoers may spend

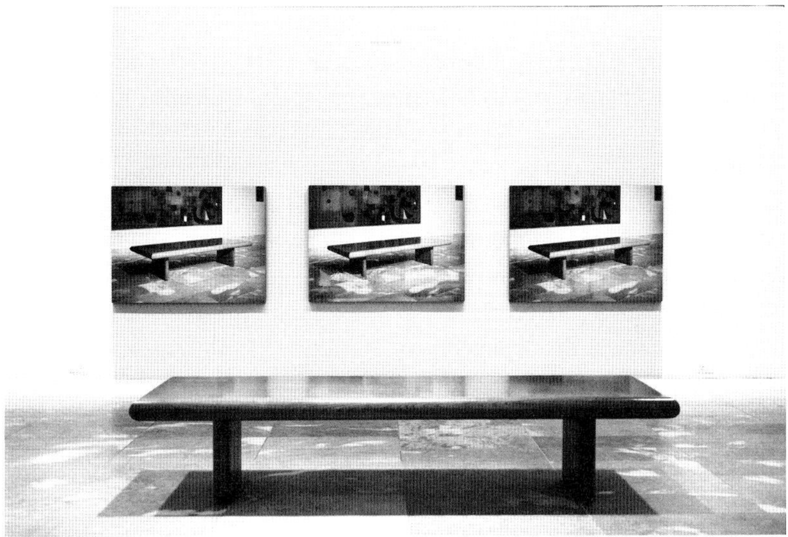

13.2 Louise Lawler, *Enough. Projects: Louise Lawler*, Museum of Modern Art, New York, September 19–November 10, 1987. Installation view. Work shown: *Untitled, 1950–51*, 1987. Three silver dye bleach prints and transfer type on painted wall: "1950–1951, 1987." Courtesy of the artist and Metro Pictures, New York.

as much time looking at labels as at works of art. Glass shelves mounted at several locations in the installation held sets of transparent drinking glasses reminiscent of the modernist objects in MoMA's design collection and gift shop. Finally, Lawler included two photographs she shot from a book of Mother Goose nursery rhymes published in 1915, near the beginning of World War I.

The individual elements of the show did not easily cohere into a unity—associations between them were too free—thus inviting curiosity and authorizing viewers to become investigators, not only of the artist's work but of the museum that it staged. Lawler titled the exhibition *Enough*.

∷

I play, therefore I think. . . .
Julia Kristeva, *Melanie Klein*

As an adjective, "enough" means "sufficient to satisfy desire." As an adverb, it denotes "in a quantity or degree that satisfies desire; sufficiently or fully." Although there was no authoritative starting point for Lawler's exhibition,

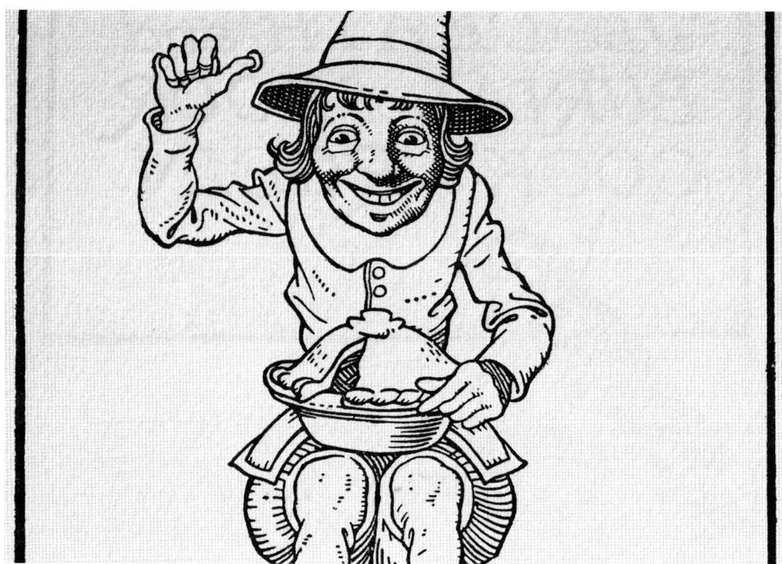

13.3 Louise Lawler, *Yellow*, 1987. Silver dye bleach print. Courtesy of the artist and Metro Pictures, New York.

one of the Mother Goose pictures can, by virtue of its location, serve to introduce the questions condensed in the show's title. Lawler placed this photograph on the exterior of one of the walls enclosing her exhibition space, a side adjacent to a passageway leading to MoMA's Garden Cafe (fig. 13.3). Printed in sunny yellow and titled *Yellow*, the photograph shows a cropped version of an illustration for "Little Jack Horner," who, according to Mother Goose,

> Sat in a corner,
> Eating a Christmas pie;
> He put in his thumb,
> And he took out a plum,
> And said, "What a good boy am I!"

The triumphant, grinning boy holds up the plum, the discovery of which has produced the satisfaction—the *self*-satisfaction—suggested in the color of the photograph and expressed in the rhyme's final line, which links the plum to the object of extreme desire that Freud called a "token of triumph": the fetish, the penis substitute, whose presence in the fantasy life of patriarchal culture denies castration anxiety and reassures the subject that it is whole, enough, a good boy.[6] Like other phantasmatic objects of gratification, the fetish reinforces feelings of omnipotence.[7]

Jack Horner's gesture mimics the art museum's principal activity—the presentation of idealized objects. *Yellow* suggests, then, that childhood fantasies and object relations operate in the adult world of the museum, which may itself be a fantasy with infantile roots. Fraser has speculated that "art institutions don't simply exhibit scenes of fantasy . . . they *are* themselves fantasies in the sense that they are scenes of satisfaction."[8] If so, neither boy child nor museum is innocent. Fetishism, springing from a misperception of the female body as castrated, does not merely name an individual object choice; rather, as certain feminisms have taught us, it designates a representational economy, in which the masculinist desire for wholeness—a desire that is not restricted to male persons—achieves satisfaction by conquering difference.

If *Yellow* introduced *Enough* in an allegorical way, another element inside Lawler's exhibition space pointed explicitly to the show's theme: the modern art museum's ideological promise of plenitude—not just culinary but, more important, visual—and the relation of that promise to violence. Lawler often locates her work in textual components of the art institution's presentational apparatus—labels, press releases, exhibition announcements—infiltrating them with unexpected content that diverts them from their normal functions. For *Enough*, she created a takeaway brochure imitating MoMA's well-designed informational leaflets, printed on red paper in the exact size and shape of the museum's handout. Lawler put her brochures in a wall-mounted dispenser identical to the one holding the museum's leaflets, which hung directly to the left. To the right, a glass shelf held six cordial glasses, each inscribed with the word "Enough," and above her brochures, hung Lawler's second Mother Goose photograph, this one titled *Blue*. A yellow square painted on the wall framed the red leaflets, glasses, and *Blue*, organizing them into a group and distinguishing them from MoMA's brochures even as Lawler used the same primary colors—the building blocks of modern design—deployed by the museum (plate 9). *Blue* depicts an illustration for the nursery rhyme about the Man in the Moon, who, with upraised fists and a malevolent smile reminiscent of Little Jack Horner, eagerly jumps to earth and, unlike Jack, burns his mouth by, inexplicably, "eating cold pease porridge" (although some versions say "cold plum porridge). His injury results from a search for satisfaction and, as we shall see, anticipates a danger Lawler warned against in her brochure.

In capital letters at the top of the leaflet's front page, Lawler directly addressed viewers, posing what at first seemed a cryptic question: "DID YOU TAKE THIS AIRPLANE HOME?" The exhibition title appeared in silver type farther down. A message from the artist near the bottom of the leaflet concluded with another question:

> Blue straws and red napkins (as seen in the Moma cafeteria) don't sound dangerous. It is only as details, the end of an official list, as a specific standard, that they could threaten us. These enhancements foster a distance, a position of passive agreement. This position seems complete. Its cleanliness from reality contributes to our lack.
>
> Do you fit the part?[9]

The straws and napkins in the nearby Garden Cafe were finishing touches that would lend coherence to MoMA's visual environment. But Lawler warned that the fiction of such spectatorial plenitude, which, like the fetish, supposedly protects against loss, actually wounds us. Weakening our grasp on external reality, it produces, as Freud remarked about the sanitizing aims of psychic repression, "an ever-growing alienation from the outside world."[10] Lawler's question "Do you fit the part?" asks viewers (who might be better described as recipients of the artwork's communication) to perceive the invisible grip of the museum's ideology, the way it fosters a position of passive agreement or, in psychoanalytic terminology, identification.[11]

In his reading of the structuralist Marxist Louis Althusser, the political philosopher Étienne Balibar stressed that ideology reproduces oppressive social relations by means of subjectivation, a mechanism of simultaneous subject-formation and subjection that depends on identification. Critiques of ideological domination, said Balibar, must contain two components: a description of subjectivation "*and* a 'performative' gesture allowing for a 'subject' to become located . . . within the ideological mechanism itself in order to reveal its coherence and insecurity."[12] The performative move implicates the subject, making it aware of its own identifications. Althusser believed that certain works of art, specifically theatrical ones, can enact the performative gesture, and Judith Butler, in a dialogue with Balibar about Althusser's ideas on dramaturgy, articulated perfectly, if unwittingly, the manner in which *Enough*'s theatricalization of the museum does so: when the "forms of enthrallment that persist throughout ordinary life are explicitly staged so that they can become an object of critical reflection. . . . Such a reflection involves self-reflection, namely the recognition of how one is in a daily way implicated in that form of consciousness without recognizing it as such."[13] The epic theater of Bertolt Brecht, Butler continued, allows viewers to see themselves as a product of the political character of their society while at the same time disidentifying with it: "I can ask: what propels me to identify in this way?"[14]

Lawler broached this question with a distinctive artistic technique, one with the potential to call forth somewhat different answers than those solicited by Althusser or Brecht: she gave museumgoers a toy to play with. Upon opening Lawler's brochure, viewers discovered that, by following the instructions printed inside, they could fold the brochure, along numbered, converging lines, into a paper airplane, turning it into a literal flyer. But in the act of playing with the brochure and creating an airplane, viewers also found, printed along folds on the brochure's recto side, two surprising, even startling, texts:

> The US government has invested 1.7770 billion dollars in an effort to topple the Nicaraguan government since 1981.
> Source: The Central American Historical Institute, Georgetown University, Washington, D.C.

> The Reagan Administration is planning to open its campaign for renewed aid to the Contras with a request of $270 million for both military and non-military purposes over the next 18 months, according to government officials.
> Source: *The New York Times*, Thursday, September 10, 1987

> This Fall Congress will decide whether or not to pay. [plate 10]

Suddenly the airplane began to resemble a bomber instead of a harmless toy, transporting viewers to the reality of United States military support for the Contras—the counterrevolutionary forces then carrying out multitudinous human rights abuses and terrorist attacks in an attempt to overthrow the left-wing Sandinista government of Nicaragua, which had come to power in 1979.[15]

Like the Mother Goose images, Lawler's airplane brochure alluded to the infantile character of the fantasies inhabiting the museum. But now the triumphalism latent in the nursery rhymes surfaced in undisguised facts about military conquest. The insertion of the topic of war into seemingly innocent contexts (a familiar tactic, which Lawler also used with champagne glasses in *Enough*)—paper airplane and museum—implied that the adult worlds of war and of the idealized art institution might have common childhood origins. We can investigate this possibility by associating the paper airplane to another aircraft on display at MoMA—the Bell-47D1 helicopter, a design object unveiled with great fanfare at the inauguration of the renovated museum in 1984 (fig. 13.4). Designed by Arthur Young in 1946, the Bell-47D1 was manufactured by a division of Textron, a US defense contractor. As Douglas Crimp pointed out in 1984 in an essay about the new MoMA, an essay for which Lawler provided photographs, Textron supplied helicopters for deployment in El Salvador, Honduras (i.e., Nicaragua), and Guatemala.[16] For Crimp, the Bell helicopter, which originally hovered above the escalator in the atrium of the Pelli building and today hangs over part of the main lobby, exemplifies not only the "corporate idea of art" that he felt informed the new MoMA but also the effects of the museum's aesthetic ideology, which, in focusing on the aircraft's functionalist design, drew attention away from its social function as a vehicle and symbol of imperialist violence, and away from Textron's role in perpetuating such violence. Consider the current description on MoMA's website:

> While the Bell-47D1 is a straightforward utilitarian craft, its designer, Young, who was also a poet and a painter, consciously juxtaposed its transparent plastic bubble with the open structure of its tail boom to create an object whose delicate beauty is inseparable from its efficiency. That the plastic bubble is made in one piece rather than in sections joined by metal seams sets the Bell-47D1 apart from other helicopters. The result is a cleaner, more unified appearance.[17]

MoMA selected a "good" helicopter to epitomize the virtues of modern design, one whose primary uses, at least according to the museum, were civilian—crop dusting and spraying. In reality, beginning in late 1946, variants of the Bell-47D1 entered military service under different designations. Idealizing the aircraft, however, requires separating it from highly dangerous "bad" helicopters; thus the museum split the helicopter, a process analogous to the unconscious psychic mechanism in which a subject denies unwanted characteristics of its objects by dividing those objects into good and bad ones.[18] Splitting not only provides an alibi for a war profiteer—"We weren't killing civilians; we were dusting crops"—but, more insidious, allows MoMA to disavow the connection between its idealizing mission and destructiveness.

Lawler's airplane brochure is part of her long-standing protest against US military aggression and, more broadly, war as a social institution. Resistance to war has informed her art as far back as the early 1980s, when photographs such as *Statue before Painting, Persesus with Head of Medusa, Canova* (1983) questioned the relationship of the art museum to patriarchal militarism.[19] An announcement for Lawler's exhibition at Metro Pictures, New

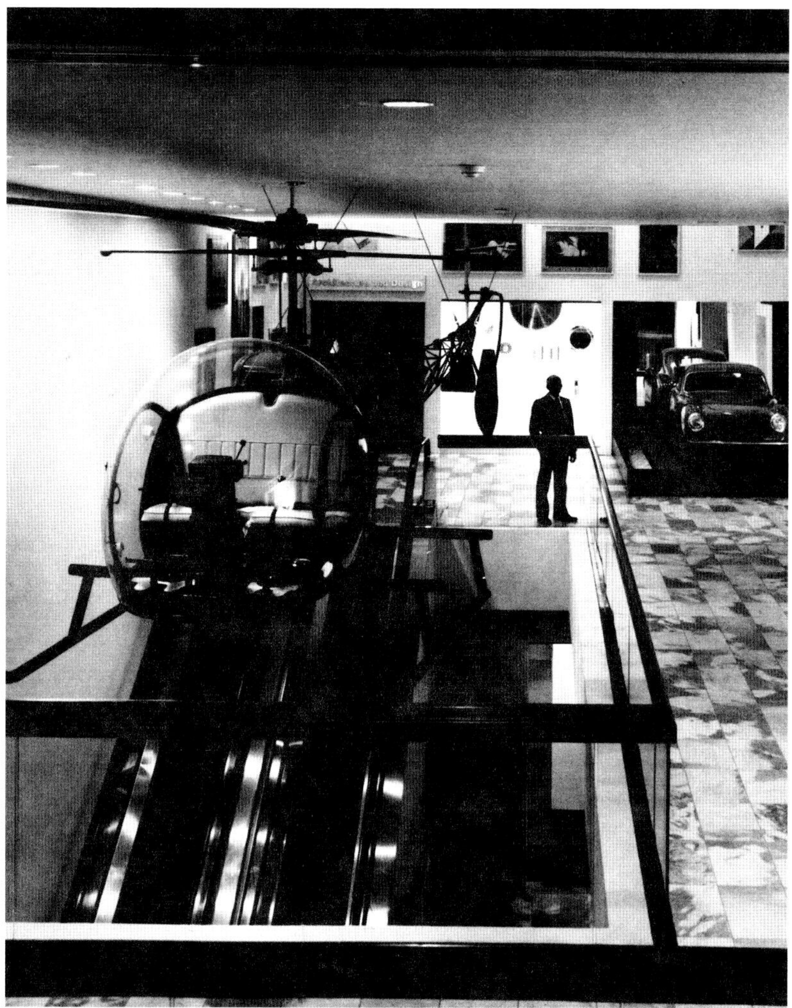

13.4 Installation view of Arthur Young, Bell-47D1 Helicopter, in *Selections from the Permanent Collection, Architecture and Design*, May 17, 1984. Photographic archive, Museum of Modern Art, New York. Courtesy Museum of Modern Art Archives. Image © The Museum of Modern Art. Licensed by SCALA/Art Resource, NY.

York, in 2003 declared, "No drinks for those who do not support the anti-war demonstration." *WAR IS TERROR* (2001/2003), a photograph of a domestic interior, suggests of course that war affects everyday life, but it goes further, suggesting also that the patriarchal values organizing everyday life *cause* war—or, as Virginia Woolf, a portrait of whose mother appears in *WAR IS TERROR*, wrote, war is "a preposterous masculine fiction."[20] Lawler's war consciousness continues today in various works titled *No Drones*—an installation, a set of glasses—which, as heirs to the paper airplane, challenge the current version of American warfare from the sky.[21]

Lawler inherits the legacy of earlier artists who have previously exposed war-related activities at MoMA. In 1969, when the American war in Vietnam was escalating, the Guerrilla Art Action Group performed its antiwar action *Blood Bath*, distributing leaflets that outlined the involvement of members of the Rockefeller family in corporations manufacturing napalm and other chemical and biological weapons and called for "the immediate resignation of all the Rockefellers from the Board of Trustees of the Museum of Modern Art." The following year, the exhibition *Information* included Hans Haacke's *MoMA Poll*, another pioneering work of institutional critique. Haacke revealed the presence of power—military, political, cultural—in the supposedly neutral museum by asking viewers to cast a vote for or against the activities of the Rockefellers: "Would the fact that Governor Rockefeller has not denounced President Nixon's Indochina policy be a reason for you not to vote for him in November?" But whereas Haacke addressed viewers as sociological subjects with conscious political opinions, Lawler's "you" was also psychoanalytic, a desiring subject of unconscious fantasy.

Fantasy plays a defensive role by producing feelings of gratification that are independent of reality. But it is also a way of gaining insight into reality. Therefore, as Julia Kristeva has remarked, "fantasy is the one true object of every analyst," who at the same time encourages "the patient's encounter with reality."[22] Kristeva made this observation in a book about the Austrian-British psychoanalyst Melanie Klein, the inventor of the play technique in child analysis. Klein equipped her consulting room with small, simple, nonmechanical toys because, as she explained, play uses the same symbolic language as dreams and is equally bound up with fantasies and wishes: "It was by approaching the play of the child in a way similar to Freud's interpretation of dreams that I found I could get access to the child's unconscious."[23] Unlike the Surrealists, who believed that play liberates utopian aspects of the psyche, and unlike D. W. Winnicott, for whom play was a creative process only minimally invested with aggression, Klein observed, participated in, and interpreted children's play in order to pursue the implications of Freud's death drive—the subject's unconscious destructive impulses. "The room," she wrote, "generally becomes a battlefield."[24] The play technique also strengthened Klein's belief in the centrality of aggression in adult mental life, which goes back to childhood and which, given the right historical circumstances, can be drawn upon to wage war.

Klein's ideas developed in the context of war. *Narrative of a Child Analysis*

(1961) recounts her four-month treatment of ten-year-old Richard during the German bombing raids carried out on London in World War II.[25] Richard was very anxious about the war, whose course he followed in three newspapers and which he reenacted in analytic sessions by drawing pictures and playing with a fleet of tiny warships. Klein interpreted his play not only as a reflection of external destructiveness but also as an expression of his own aggressive thoughts, feelings, and fantasies: an airplane might stand for a destructive part of himself and a particular kind of fish for a part that regretted the destruction he caused.[26] As his anxiety lessened somewhat, Richard tried to defeat his own destructive tendencies instead of exulting in the victory of the Allies over German troops, towns, and ships, for which he began to show compassion. One day, he was visibly moved upon learning that Berlin and Munich, which had been bombed the previous night, were beautiful cities.[27] Most important, Klein used play to analyze the *interaction* or, better, *ambiguity* between internal and external destructiveness—between what Gertrude Stein calls "war inside" and "war outside"—an ambiguity that, Klein said, "persists throughout life."[28] Richard's play confirmed Klein's earlier belief that "fears derived from external sources increase anxieties about internal dangers and the other way round."[29] For Klein, internal danger arises from the subject's destructive feelings toward its objects, feelings that provoke anxiety about retaliation. The anxiety can lead the subject to deny its objects' unwanted characteristics by conjuring ideal objects, a mechanism linked to splitting. It can also result in the projection of destructive impulse onto others, a psychic device that produces fears of persecutory aggression from external enemies, who must then be annihilated.[30] Idealization and war, as I have already suggested, have at least one common origin as defenses against the anxiety produced by inner aggression.

Enough, like the work of many artists who are critical of institutions, eroded the division between the inside and the outside of the art institution. At one point, having run out of brochures, Lawler told a member of MoMA's Professional and Administrative Staff Association, the union that represents many of the museum's curatorial and administrative workers and which was itself leafleting outside the museum, that the union could put flyers in her dispenser, although it never did. But it was by rendering ambiguous a different inside/outside relationship, between internal and external destructiveness, that Lawler's airplane brochure was, I think, truly Kleinian: the brochure literally folded destructiveness in the form of war into a plaything that asked viewers to look into themselves. Imitating one of MoMA's own design objects, it performed the museum's idealizing operations while simultaneously intruding on viewers' identificatory fascination with specular perfection. The airplane became a symbol—something to play and think with.

Kristeva has observed that for Klein, unlike for Anna Freud or D. W. Winnicott, the goal of "interpretation-in-the-context-of play" was to encounter sexuality, especially, we might add, its connection to aggression. In Klein's playroom a train was not just a train; it stood for Daddy's penis.[31] A train crash or battle might represent sexual intercourse between, or with, parents. Similarly, in *Enough*, Jack Horner's plum is a penis-substitute and also stands for the fetishized work of art. Toy airplanes are associated particularly with boys. And all of *Enough*'s photographic "arrangements of pictures" depict art made by men, MoMA's "masters." Gintz has singled out, for its obvious sexual connotations, *Pollock and Tureen* (1984), a photograph in which a fat globule of porcelain decorating the cover of a fancy tureen seems to have dripped from the Pollock action painting hanging above it.[32]

But one image in Lawler's exhibition featured a female protagonist, and a "real" one at that—*Woman with Picasso, 1912* (1986). Displayed on a section of wall that was painted pink, next to shelves with sixty champagne glasses inscribed "*Apres la Guerre*" and "After the War," the photograph shows a woman holding in her left hand a paper guitar construction by Picasso from 1912 (plate 11). Only the woman's upper torso, neck, and lower head are visible, and she remains unidentified, despite the lanyard around her neck that seems as if it might carry an official ID card, were it not cropped from the picture. Perhaps she is a curator or conservationist—though not at MoMA, for her architectural environment is distinctly nonmodern. Besides, the sculpture she handles does not belong to the museum. MoMA does, however, own a painting by Picasso from the same period as the guitar. Titled *Ma Jolie (Woman with a Guitar)*, it is one of the highlights of the museum's collection and, like the guitars, was crucial to the artist's development of Analytical Cubism (fig. 13.5).

By 1912, Picasso had nicknamed his lover Marcelle Humbert *Ma Jolie*—"my pretty one"—words inscribed at the painting's lower edge. According to the museum website, the painting "takes apart a traditional subject—a woman holding a guitar."[33] Gintz has interpreted Lawler's photograph as a comment on the artwork as fetish, the exclusion of the woman's eyes from the picture indicating that the "gaze" belongs solely to the "male subject."[34] Yet *Woman with Picasso, 1912* does not merely describe the masculinist relations of sexuality that structure the art institution. It also tells a feminist joke, one that, by giving prominence to a woman, takes away the authority of the "great male artist" and of the museum that constructs him.[35] With her caption, Lawler plays on the title *Woman with a Guitar*, and in her

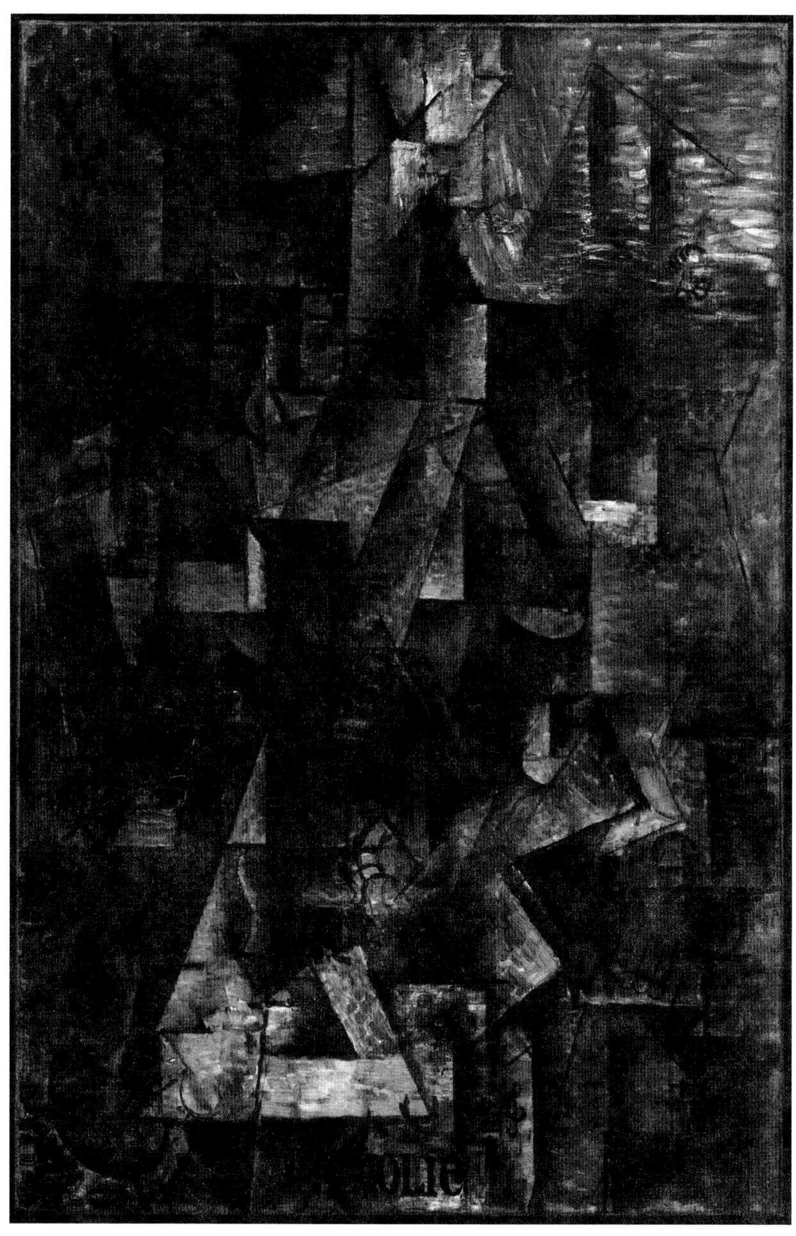

13.5 Pablo Picasso, *Ma Jolie*, Winter 1911–12. Oil on canvas. Acquired through the Lillie P. Bliss bequest. © 2021 Estate of Pablo Picasso/Artists Rights Society (ARS), New York. Image © The Museum of Modern Art. Licensed by Scala/Art Resource, NY.

photograph she appropriates the painting's radical aesthetic innovations as a metaphor for the sexual politics of art making and viewing. Whereas Picasso abstracted his mistress's body, making her disappear and replacing her with words that mark her as his possession, Lawler returns the body of the woman, still fragmented but partially recomposed, to the picture. Now it is Picasso who is replaced by an art object, a substitution emphasized by the removal of the indefinite article "a" in the caption, *Woman with Picasso*. The deletion turns the artist's name into a metonym for his body and his body of work. Of course, as Gintz has pointed out, the artwork itself is a substitute, a fetish, but one that in yet another reversal is fondled and looked at by a woman.

∷

To restrain iniquity entails renouncing the restitution of innocence.
PAOLO VIRNO, "ANTHROPOLOGY AND THEORY OF INSTITUTIONS"

Some artists and critics charge institutional critique with obsolescence and failure because, they say, it "can analyze and problematize the institution of art but cannot imagine an alternative to, or an outside of, its framework."[36] Surely there is nothing wrong with artists adopting what Alexander Alberro has referred to as "exit strategies," choosing to work outside art institutions.[37] But drawing a bright line between problematizing the institution, on the one hand, and imagining an alternative, on the other, is misleading at best. For even as an exhibition like *Enough* inhabited the museum, it performed what the philosopher Sonja Lavaert calls "an exercise in exodus."[38] Lavaert, writing about the ideas of the Italian political theorist Paolo Virno, noted that the biblical story of Exodus is a "metaphor for liberation and revolution . . . a judicial-theological text intended for analogous application"—for "trying at home," like Lawler's airplane.[39] Virno has argued that because human beings are dangerous animals, we need institutions to protect us, but institutions that profess to be innocent of aggression are themselves dangerous.[40] They refuse to acknowledge that destructive impulses are an ineradicable aspect of being human and therefore of human institutions—a disillusioning recognition, to be sure, but one that is necessary to at least partly divest such impulses of their potential to emerge in violent acts. In fact, Virno has said, quoting Aristotle, "institutions protect us if, and only if . . . they exhibit at each and every moment their belonging to the category of '*that which can be different than it is*.'"[41] If, that is, they expose themselves to perpetual change.

As an interjection, "enough" expresses impatience and frustration. It can issue a call to change a situation—in Lawler's case, the situation of art. "Enough" could even serve as a catchword for institutional critique more generally, insofar as the purpose of the practice, in the astute words of Fraser, who has likened it to psychoanalytic treatment, is to transform social relations by engaging with them "in their enactment."[42] In harmony with Virno's proposal, *Enough* did not merely send viewers into a supposedly external reality. By opening MoMA to its negation, Lawler's installation imagined and temporarily *made* an alternative institution—one that performed an apotropaic function against human destructiveness and countered the "rather menacing ways" in which the museum had previously sought to protect us.

: 14 :

Mary Kelly's Attunement

Any kind of political project must have the "making and using" of mood as part and parcel of the project; for, no matter how clever or correct the critique or achievable the project, collective action is impossible if people are not, so to speak, in the mood.
JONATHAN FLATLEY, *Affective Mapping*

In two large-scale art projects, first exhibited between 1974 and 1989, Mary Kelly explored the construction of feminine subjectivity. *Post-Partum Document* dealt with the maternal woman; *Interim*, the woman in middle age. Then Kelly turned to masculinity. Or, to be more precise, what she calls "pathological masculinity," also known as "phallic" or, more popularly, "toxic" masculinity. I use the term "masculinism," by which I mean the relentless pursuit of mastery, dominion, and control over others—and otherness in the self. Trinh T. Minh-ha names it "victory disease."[1] It is not surprising, then, that *Gloria Patri (Glory Be to the Father)*, unveiled in 1992, is not only Kelly's first work about masculinity but also her first about war (fig. 14.1).

Gloria Patri is a theatrical installation consisting of three horizontal rows of elements hung one above the other. Each row consists of a particular form of triumphalist iconography—six trophies, five shields, twenty discs silkscreened with militarist and nationalist logos. All are flat and stand two inches away from the wall. All are made of highly polished aluminum. Carefully positioned spotlights sometimes allow viewers to read the work's texts and at other times catch viewers in their glare, making them a part of the work. The trophies' bases bear aggressive phrases culled from television appearances by military men—". . . NOT ENOUGH GEES AND GOLLIES TO DESCRIBE IT!" ". . . LETTING LOOSE AND HITTING 'EM WITH ALL WE GOT," "CUT IT OFF AND KILL IT," ". . . BUSTING OUR BUTTS TO GET IT RIGHT," ". . . MORE FIRES DOWN THERE THAN I CAN COUNT," "KICK ASS" (fig. 14.2). Etched into the surfaces of the shields are third-person narratives about displays of masculinism—or, more accurately, about masculinism *as* display. Here is one story:

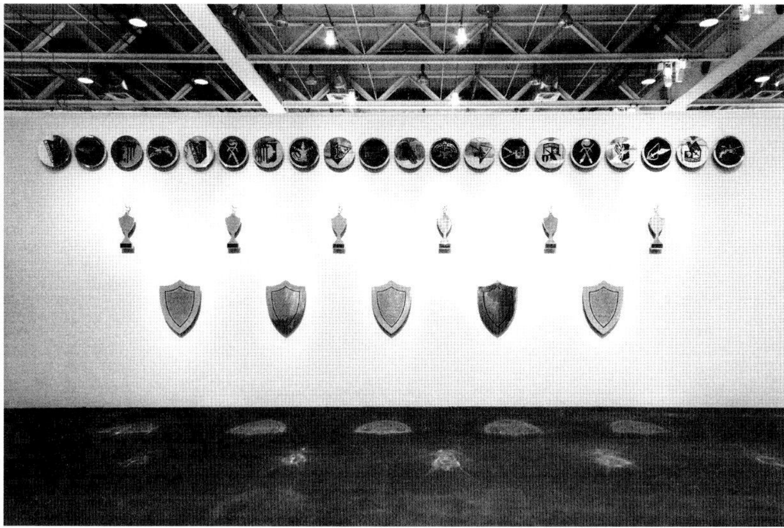

14.1 Mary Kelly, *Gloria Patri*, 1992. Installation view, Art Basel 2016. Etched and polished aluminum. Photo: Dawn Blackman. Courtesy the artist and Vielmetter Los Angeles.

Audio receiver, track one. He adjusted the frequency level and and pushed away the tray.

A clump of collard greens sat resolutely in the center of a white plate. Any moment, she would ask him when he was going to eat it. He could see the look on her face describing a long list of catastrophes: the inevitable outcome of deficiencies in vitamins A and C. He fed more bass to the speaker B. *Head like a hole, black as your soul*, the room reverberated. Green as his guilt. It's not that I don't like what you make, Mom. He would apologize, maybe later. Later he'd be outta there. Hang with the guys. Throw Arnie on the boob tube and pull some bong. In anticipation of the bongish bliss, he altered the state of his surround sound to *Theater* and imagined a stage in his life when he could go out in the cold without a coat, lose his glasses, pick his nose or his ass or fart if he felt like it, leave the blinds down and the toilet seat up and, above all, eat whatever he damn well chose. He recalled her sitting next to him, her hand on his; the soft skin, frail and translucent, loosely draped over her prominent veins, studded with drab patches and scored with tiny creases. It made him queasy. At the same time, it made him want to please her, to risk everything to order salad even in the presence of his beefy bros, to announce his queerness with each leafy forkful. And finally, when the green stuff had gone to his brain, he would oppose the war. Only girls would be on

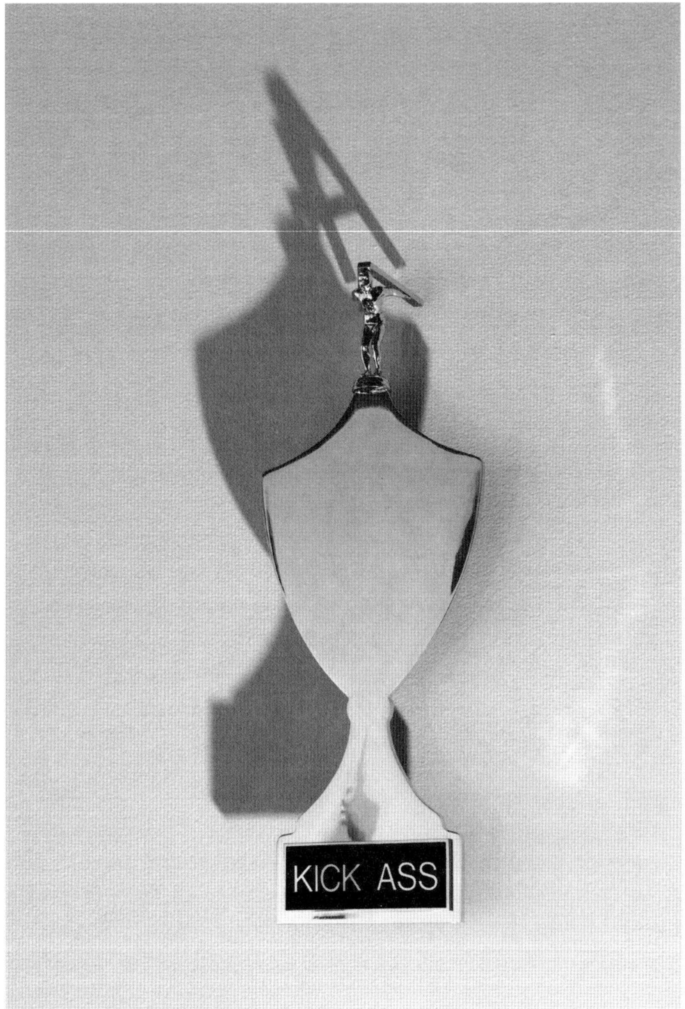

14.2 Mary Kelly, *Gloria Patri*, 1992. Detail, one of six trophies, etched aluminum. Photo: Jeff McLane. Courtesy of the artist and Vielmetter Los Angeles.

his side. All the flesh-eaters would say, "Just bomb the hell out of 'em." She would pry: What's wrong? Shut up bitch, get off my case, he'd want to say. Instead he's hit the volume. *Bow down before the one you serve, you're going to get what you deserve.* The song ended and his resolution waned. You're going to eat the fucking greens aren't you, he sneered. (fig. 14.3)

This story discloses matrophobia, misogyny, and homophobia as well as the subterranean conflicts and vulnerabilities that prompt the erection of the

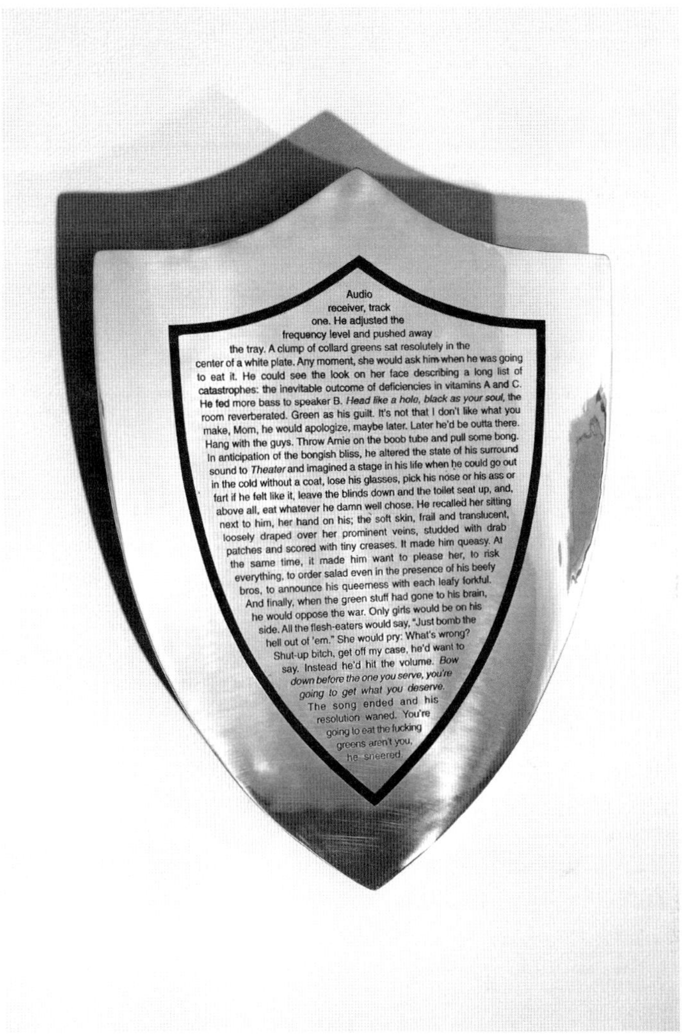

14.3 Mary Kelly, *Gloria Patri*, 1992. Detail, one of five shields, etched aluminum. Photo: Jeff McLane. Courtesy of the artist and Vielmetter Los Angeles.

protagonist's masculinist facade or, put differently, his assumption of masculinist armor.

But one shield tells a story with a female protagonist:

First she made sure the thigh pads were in the right position, then she went into a funk. Where was the lever and why was she sweating before she even started. She despised it. Despised the woman-thing, the soft thing that sev-

ered her will before a hard thing, hard to do, hard to touch, hard to understand, like the machine in front of her. If only she could cut it off; cut off her
sequacity and kill it. . . . Her body tensed, muscles hardened, resolve harden-
ing. Search and destroy. . . . Yes, fast and hardheaded, she'd think in tough
metaphors. Deploy her assets. . . . Project power. . . . Hardhearted? Not at all,
she told herself: It was a hard life. What she had was hard-earned and, if anyone objected, well, that was, she spat on the floor, hard luck. (fig. 14.4)

By including a woman among her characters, Kelly makes clear that while,
historically, men have occupied the masculinist position in social relationships, it is perfectly possible for women to identify with that position, which is neither an essential quality of nor confined to male persons.
Women, that is, can play the role of a representative man, as when they demand "the right to go to the front, to wear the uniform, to kill the enemy."[2]

Although *Gloria Patri* was a departure from *Post-Partum Document* and
Interim, there was also an important connection between it and the two
earlier works. In the artist's words, the later project "suggests a kind of
underside, a repression of the feminine that [had] been the topic of the
work before." After completing *Gloria Patri*, Kelly made a similarly dialecti-
cal move, once again shifting her focus, this time to the war-related atrocities inflicted by the militarized masculinity she had just investigated. Her
next installation, *Mea Culpa*, appeared in 1999. Despite the thematic link to
Gloria Patri, however, the inherent properties and symbolic connotations
of the materials could hardly be more different. In sharp contrast to *Gloria
Patri*'s polished aluminum, Kelly fabricated *Mea Culpa* from compressed
gray lint gathered from the filter of her home dryer, in which she had dried
many loads of black and white clothes. By attaching vinyl letters to the
dryer's filter screen, Kelly was able to produce intaglio words in the lint.
She then joined together the units of lint, each retaining the dimensions
and curved shape of the filter, to form five sixteen- to twenty-foot-long,
horizontal panels. Each panel is matted and framed as a separate work,
and each is titled with the site of a historical, collective, politically motivated trauma—*Johannesburg; Buenos Aires; Beirut; Sarajevo; Phnom Penh*.
With the exception of *Johannesburg*, which was made first, the panels relate stories about traumatic events involving women and children. The
stories come from the testimonies of primary witnesses—those who lived
through the events—which were given as evidence before war crimes tri-
bunals and human rights commissions. An anonymous narrator narrates
the stories told by the original witnesses, who are referred to in the third

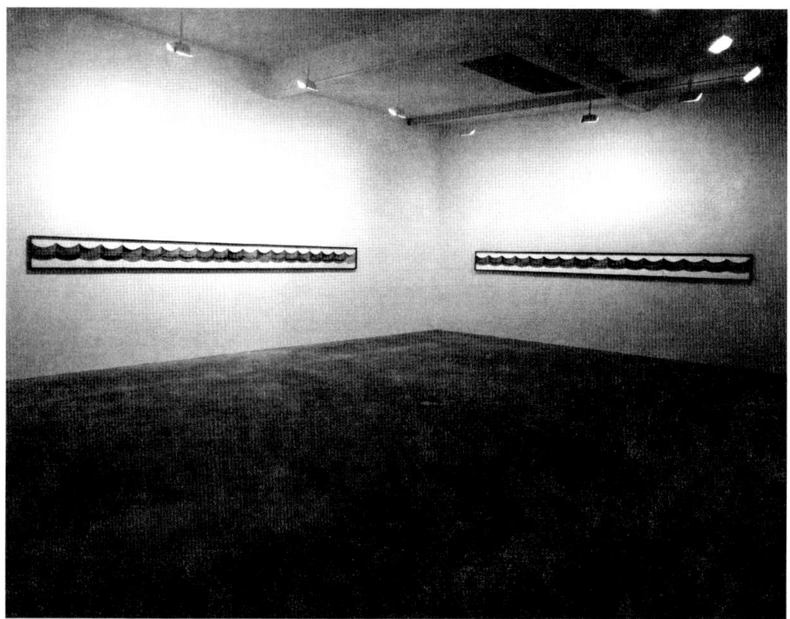

14.4 Mary Kelly, *Mea Culpa*, 1999. Installation view. Courtesy the artist and Mitchell-Innes & Nash, New York. © Mary Kelly.

person, as "she." The narrator is, then, a secondary witness, one who observed, heard, or read the testimonies and who, by bearing witness, attaches herself to what the scholar of historical memory Marianne Hirsch calls a "testimonial chain."[3] The panels' titles include the dates of the testimonies.

This is the story told in *Johannesburg 1997*:

> In the courtroom she heard him describe the routine of releasing activists so that they could be picked up again outside the station, driven to a specified location blindfolded, sedated and shot in the head just behind the left ear. Then we burned the bodies, turning them frequently, he added, and buried the remains.

Sarajevo 1992:

> A few bathroom tiles and the smell of burning: nothing else left. Probing the ashes, she retrieved a family photograph, the faces scratched out with a drill bit. She rocked back and forth on her heels. What will we do? Slit their throats, said her four-year-old son (fig. 14.5).

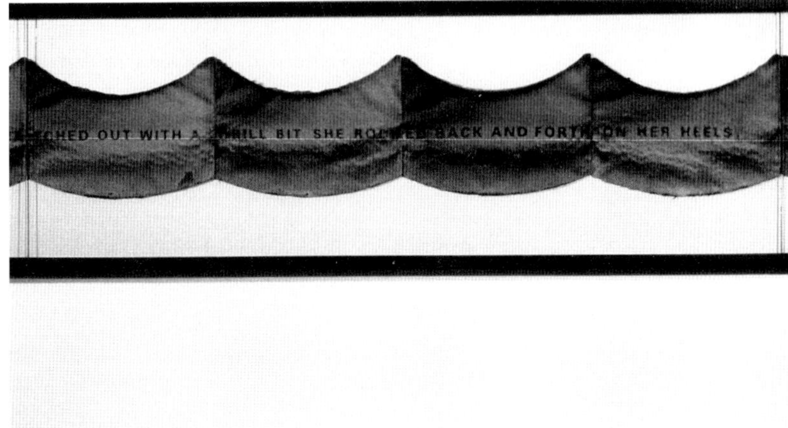

14.5 Mary Kelly, *Mea Culpa*, 1999. Detail, *Sarajevo 1992*. One of four panels, compressed lint. Courtesy the artist and Mitchell-Innes & Nash, New York. © Mary Kelly.

Buenos Aires 1976:

> The interrogation was systematic, almost clinical. They played music to drown out her screams. When the time came, she was chained to a bed and gave birth to a boy with black hair, pale skin, almond eyes. No name was recorded.

Beirut 1982:

> No running water. She washed dishes near the pump and listened. Rockeye cluster bombs dispensed their submunitions: 247 8-inch dart grenades, 262.4 pounds of high-density explosives, 200,000 shrapnel fragments. Armed with an aluminum pan, 4 unmatched plates, 2 glasses, 3 spoons and a kitchen knife, she held her child and waited (fig. 14.6).

Phnom Penh 1975:

> She watched the soldiers in a rice paddy beat her daughter with the butts of their rifles until she was dead. Then she had headaches and trouble with her eyes. To distract herself, she worked at the bridge of her nose with a knife. When the pain subsided she could no longer see.

Phnom Penh provides explicit evidence of psychic trauma, of, that is, the way the Cambodian genocide was lived in the mind of a survivor later on. "The

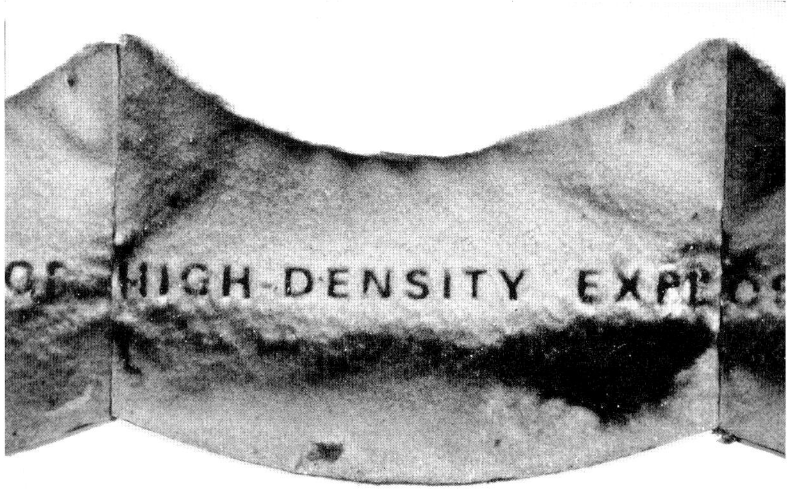

14.6 Mary Kelly, *Mea Culpa*, 1999. Detail, compressed lint. Courtesy the artist and Mitchell-Innes & Nash, New York. © Mary Kelly.

story of trauma," writes Cathy Caruth, "as the narrative of a belated experience . . . attests to the traumatic event's endless impact on life."[4] Indications of such belated patterns of suffering were one of Kelly's criteria for selecting *Mea Culpa*'s five testimonies.

In a psychoanalytic sense, trauma is a disruption that occurs when the human psyche is presented with external stimuli so powerful that they cannot be dealt with in the usual ways. Most significantly, trauma entails the psychic consequences of that disruption. Sigmund Freud speculates that the conscious mind operates as a barrier defending individuals against stimuli coming from the outside world. Traumatic excitations, however, are so powerful that they break through the barrier, producing a wound that allows stimuli to deposit permanent memory traces in the psychic system "lying next within"—which is to say, the unconscious mind.[5] Because traumatic stimuli are too overwhelming to be grasped as they are received and are therefore not fully experienced, they evade the victim's understanding. Consequently, Freud approaches trauma as a paradox: the victim cannot remember the past but is possessed by it. Unable to remember, or remembering incompletely, the traumatized person tends to compulsively repeat the event in some way—in dreams, for example. The repetition-compulsion is the form of traumatic memory. Influenced by his observation of a game played by a young child—the famous *fort-da* game—which he interprets as the child's attempt to repeat and master the trauma of separation from the mother, Freud speculates that the repetition-compulsion in survivors of accidents, childhood incest, or war represents an effort to retroactively work through a traumatic event that was not comprehended in the moment.[6]

Caruth supplements Freud by arguing that traumatic repetition is not only an attempt at working-through but also an address—a cry for the psychic wound to be witnessed. Kelly's *Mea Culpa* invites viewers to respond to such cries. Its texts materialize voices, which imply receiving ears. "The voice," as Kelly puts it, "is libidinally 'attached' to the ear" of the receiver,[7] who is thus called upon to assume the responsibility of witnessing the distress of others. Kelly also points out that the repeated curves of the lint panels resemble phrases of a musical composition, one whose libretto tells of traumatic loss. In this regard, *Mea Culpa* practically illustrates Julia Kristeva's assertion that artistic creations can bear witness to sadness by transposing affect into rhythms, signs, and forms.[8] Unlike emotion, which connotes something internal to an individual, affect is expressed and/or observed emotion. As the literary theorist Jonathan Flatley writes, "One *has* emotions; one is affected *by* people or things." Affect is relational and transformative, a point to which I shall return.

Gloria Patri's material is reflective, durable, and seemingly hard, while *Mea Culpa*'s is absorbent, ephemeral, and soft. Given that *Gloria Patri* treats its subject matter, phallic masculinity, as defensive display, it is not difficult to understand the artist's decision to make the work from shiny metal (although, interestingly, in light of Kelly's emphasis on masculinism's vulnerability, aluminum is actually a soft metal, one that readily succumbs to fatigue failure). But what explains the "peculiar" material and method of *Mea Culpa*—to borrow Kelly's own adjective?[9] Why dryer lint and a dryer turned into a printmaking machine to transmit voices that attest to human-inflicted catastrophes?

Wanting to make a work about war-related atrocities, Kelly inevitably faced what Theodor Adorno, writing about images of the Holocaust, calls "the problem of suffering"—the ethico-politial dilemma of the representing subject's relation to the suffering of oppressed and persecuted others.[10] Adorno poses the problem like this: "The . . . artistic representation of the . . . pain of people contains . . . the power to elicit enjoyment out of it. The moral of this art, not to forget for a single instant, slithers into the abyss of its opposite"—which is to say, forgetting.[11] Can artworks concerned with the pain of others avoid the fate that Adorno envisions? Can they counteract the sensationalizing and simultaneously numbing effects of mass media, in which images of suffering generally appear to us? How can such works affect readers and spectators in a way that differs from the effects of political and administrative documents, which, according to the historian Saul Friedlander, often neutralize the concreteness of despair and death?[12] Is it possible to portray the suffering body without figuration, which, while not prohibited, can elicit sentimental, exploitative, even sadistic modes of viewing? Can artistic representations of suffering fulfill the task that Marianne Hirsch calls "retrospective witnessing by adoption"?[13] Hirsch coined the term *postmemory* to designate a kind of memory exercised by those a generation removed from a traumatic event, which they know only through stories, images, and other forms of representation. The simplest example is the relationship of the child of a Holocaust survivor to the trauma of its parents. More broadly, however, postmemory is an intersubjective space that opens up when someone who is temporally or geographically distant from a traumatic event identifies bodily with its victims. Finally, can art help prompt collective action to prevent the recurrence of politically motivated traumas, thereby constituting its audience into a public?

Kelly's accounts of the gestation of *Mea Culpa* reveal her struggle with questions like these. After *Gloria Patri*, she decided to focus on "the vilification and dehumanization of the other that functions in the time of war."[14] From magazines, newspapers, websites, and other sources, she assembled an archive of visual and verbal representations of war crimes. At some point, while working in her kitchen, she overheard a televised report about the brutality of South African police during the country's apartheid regime. A voice speaking of suffering reached her from a distance. The experience caused her to reflect on the effect of such information as it filters into the everyday lives of people in metropolitan centers—when suffering is simultaneously near and far away. Like psychic trauma itself, the simultaneity blurs rigid divisions between internal and external worlds, public and private spheres, here and there. Inspired by a magazine photograph of a scene from the Sarajevo massacre, Kelly had herself photographed as a dead body shrouded in voluminous sheets. Upon viewing the photo, she noted how the contours and forms of her body were displaced to the folds of the sheets. The observation made her think about the material she would use for a work about victims of atrocities: it should be "something decomposed, like dust or ashes."[15] This thought led her, by means of free association, to the idea of using lint from her clothes dryer.

Kelly describes her associative process as "rather mysterious,"[16] but in retrospect it is quite logical. For like the folds of the sheets under which the artist lay, dryer lint bears a trace of the body, of its closeness. Lint is a residue of clothes that have been physically intimate with their wearers. In a study of a later work by Kelly, Griselda Pollock writes that "lint has a tenuous link with the human body, which these textile fibers once touched."[17] When, in addition, lint is merged with texts about collective traumas, it functions metonymically, as a symbolic residue of social as well as individual bodies. Kelly's lint, then, is a figure of the elements that individuals and groups—say, nations—seek to expel in order to construct and maintain the boundaries of their supposedly pure, unitary identities. In its most monstrous manifestation, expulsion takes the form of genocide, such as Serbian ethnic cleansing, to which, as others have remarked, *Mea Culpa*'s process alludes. Like any filter, a dryer screen is an apparatus that preserves boundaries, protecting something against contamination. Lint from a specifically domestic dryer that bears witness to war crimes also links war to the home, which war filters into and affects, as it did in the incident that inspired Kelly to create *Mea Culpa*. But Virginia Woolf attributes the *causes* of war to the home, to the infantilism, egoism, vanity, combativeness, and grandiosity of patriarchal behavior, which, says Woolf, manifests itself in the domestic realm, where it is exhibited by private, not just public fathers. "The public and the private worlds are inseparably connected," writes Woolf, "the tyrannies and servilities of the one are the tyrannies and servilities of the other."[18]

Pollock refers to psychic trauma as an "affective residue."[19] This description implicitly associates lint, insofar as it too is a residue, with the unconscious mind, wherein, according to Freud, the mnemonic remains of an individual's traumatic history reside. When lint is integrated with testimonies to war crimes, it connotes the affective residue of collective traumatic histories as well. Dominick LaCapra bases his work as an historian on the premise that no binary opposition can be drawn between individual and social worlds. As Freud writes, "In the individual's mental life someone else is invariably involved, as a model, as an object, as a helper, as an opponent." Therefore, "from the very first, individual psychology . . . is at the same time social psychology."[20] LaCapra likens the writing of history to the collaboration between patient and analyst, who, together, represent and work through the past.[21] LaCapra stresses further that counterhistories, those that assume responsibility for bringing back what is repressed by dominant, official histories, must confront individual voices, using testimonies or other archival traces.[22] Kelly does this in *Mea Culpa*, where, engaging in a dialogue with the recent past, she embraces the revolutionary memory exercised by Walter Benjamin's counterhistorian.[23] Seizing hold, quite literally, of images of suffering, Kelly rescues them from the neutralizing ways they generally come into our view, and from "instrumentalized memory," Paul Ricoeur's term for the type of memory that conceals the reality of war

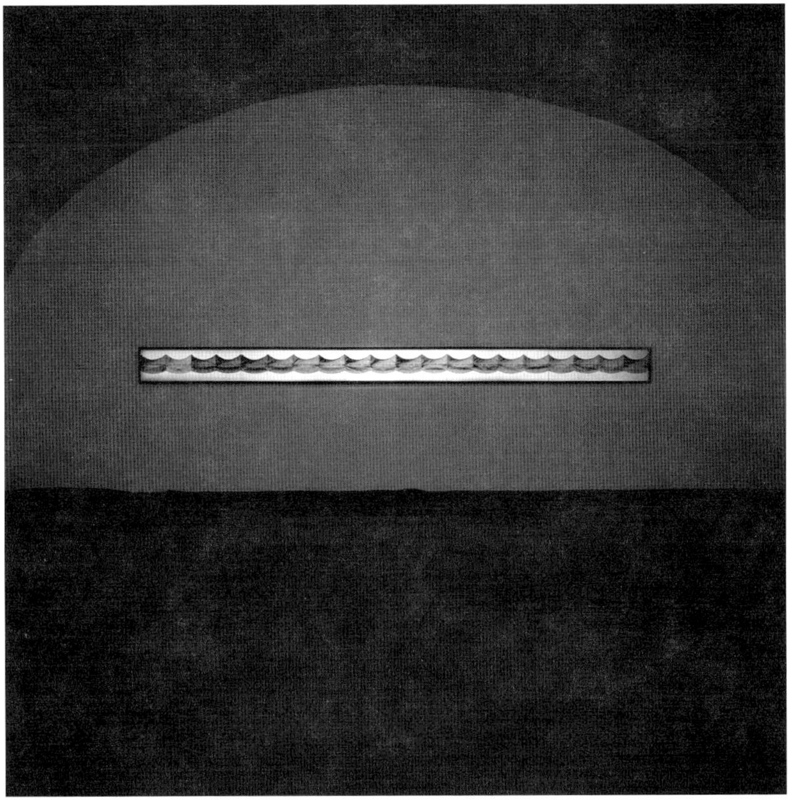

14.7 Mary Kelly, *Mea Culpa*, 1999. Installation view, Centre for Contemporary Art, Ujazdowski Castle, Warsaw. Courtesy the artist and Mitchell-Innes & Nash, New York. © Mary Kelly.

by placing it within monumental narratives of glory and greatness—the history of the victors.[24]

When a visitor enters the space of *Mea Culpa* in its entirety, as I did when the work was first shown at New York's Postmasters Gallery,[25] she is surrounded by undulating, scroll-like panels, whose soft gray tonality and stories of loss and death create a melancholic mood (fig. 14.7). Voices address her as the inherently relational being that Martin Heidegger calls *Dasein*, his name for the distinctive mode of existence realized by human beings. Dasein means "being-there" and can also be interpreted as being-open. To be Dasein means to be-with, to be "thrown" into a network of historically and culturally conditioned involvements that are shared with those whom one is among. As a result, Dasein is capable of becoming affected.[26] This is especially true given Dasein's distinctive spatiality, which, according to Heidegger, is marked by "de-severance"—the ability to bring something close, to make farness vanish.[27] (Given that a televised report about atrocities in South Africa contributed to Kelly's creation of *Mea Culpa*, it is interesting to note Heidegger's 1926 remark that the radio—an earlier communication technology—has pushed Dasein toward the "conquest of remoteness," accomplishing a de-severance of the "world."[28]) Heidegger chooses the word *Stimmung*, or "mood," to refer to Dasein's way of belonging to the world.[29] We are always in one mood or another. But Heidegger's mood is not an inner, subjective state superimposed on an objective world. Moods do not arise in the interior of individuals. Nor are they strictly external. Rather, a mood is a shared cultural climate, an environment that moves through us. A mood is not just in us; we are in a mood, a "state of readiness for some affects and not others," an "atmosphere in which . . . particular affects can attach to particular objects."[30] The condition for being in a mood is *Befundlichkeit*, which has been variously translated,[31] including as "attunement," "receptiveness," "disposedness," all terms that signify openness to the world.[32] Affirming our inseparability from the world in which we live, the concepts of Stimmung and Befundlichkeit mediate between the social and the personal. Heidegger writes that "only because the 'senses' belong ontologically to an entity whose kind of Being is Being-in-the-world with a [receptive or attuned] state-of-mind, can they be 'touched' by anything or have a sense for something in such a way that what touches them shows itself as an affect."[33]

In his book *Affective Mapping*, cultural theorist Jonathan Flatley draws on Heidegger to speculate about how art can represent concrete historical situations.[34] Flatley's account elucidates the political possibilities of a work like *Mea Culpa*. With Heidegger's help, Flatley reworks Freud's ideas about a particular mood: depressive melancholia or inconsolable mourning for lost objects. For Freud, melancholia causes sufferers to withdraw from the world around them.[35] But Flatley argues that there are also nondepressive attachments to lost objects and that these attachments can, conversely, cause people to become interested in the world. Non- or even antidepressive melancholia, that is, can produce knowledge of others, with whom similar attachments are shared. Flatley suggests that artists are uniquely qualified to provide new objects of affective attachment and, in doing so, to transform a depressive cultural mood into a politicized melancholic one. An artwork, says Flatley, can create "a kind of mood atmosphere with its own objects and thereby bring affects into existence in forms and in relation to objects that otherwise might not exist."[36] When art does this, it follows Heidegger's exhortation to produce a "counter-mood," one that changes the dominant mood: "*Dasein* can, should, and must, through knowledge and will become master of its mood," writes Heidegger. "When we master a mood, we do so by way of a counter-mood."[37]

Mea Culpa has the potential to create a community of nondepressive melancholics—a community of loss. As Andrea Geyer notes in a conversation with Kelly, viewing an artwork in a gallery or museum is not just an individual experience; it "is at the same time a collective one . . . you know that many people before you have seen this work and many will see it in the future and you become part of a group of people who share this experience."[38] With *Mea Culpa*, Mary Kelly made a group of visual and verbal objects that invite viewers to establish affective relationships with victims of distant atrocities, thereby attaching themselves to a global testimonial chain. Ours may be a depressing historical moment, but a work like *Mea Culpa* can help transform the current mood in a politicized direction, an ever more urgent task in our time of perpetual war, itself an atrocity.

: 15 :

Martha Rosler's Unrest

Let feminism be the place where the most painful aspects of our inner world do not have to hide from the light, but are ushered forth as handmaidens to our protest.
JACQUELINE ROSE, *Women in Dark Times*

On a cold night in December 2016, just before she was scheduled to speak to an audience filling the lobby of New York's Whitney Museum, Martha Rosler told me that she "just [couldn't] seem to recover from it."[1] She was referring, of course, to the recent election of Donald Trump as president of the United States. Many in the crowd felt the same way. Moments later, however, on stage with the museum's director, Adam Weinberg, and without, so far as I remember, explicitly mentioning the election, Rosler conveyed a sense that possibility—the possibility of a less cruel and violent world—is not impossible, that, in Theodor Adorno's words, "education and enlightenment can still manage a little something" against barbarism.[2] Was it hope—an emotion in crisis—she offered that evening? It was certainly not the fraudulent hope that Ernst Bloch describes as a dangerous form of wishful thinking.[3] Neither was it the "negative" kind that, according to Georges Bataille, writing in the wake of the atomic bombing of Hiroshima, limits sensibility and turns attention away from dark realities.[4] For Bataille, fully living disaster requires the suppression of such hope. What struck me at the Whitney was, if not the appearance of hope, exactly, the steadfastness of Rosler's commitment to the art of critique—to art as a form of critique—as an element of social change. Rosler exhibited the same enduring resolve to interrogate authoritarian discourses of truth that has driven her work for more than fifty years.[5] From her student days in the late 1960s and early 1970s, during the American war in Vietnam, through decades of permutations in ideas about critique, to the current moment of perpetual war and protofascism, Rosler's resistance continues unabated. She has held out, maintaining a presence close to what Bloch calls "informed discontent," which the philosopher regarded as an aspect of hope.[6]

Like many critical theorists, Rosler links social change to transformations in human subjectivity, which, for the ardent feminist she has always been, is in turn inseparable from the construction of alterity and sexual difference. Recall Simone de Beauvoir's *Second Sex*, a book that Rosler read in the 1960s along with more contemporary feminist writings and that, as she puts it, "was always glittering there in our consciousness."[7] "Humanity is male," writes Beauvoir, "and man defines woman not in herself but as relative to him . . . she is the incidental, the inessential as opposed to the essential. He is the Subject, he is the Absolute—she is the Other."[8]

In a series of photomontages created between 1967 and 1972, Rosler brought together the theme of gendered subjectivity with the theme of imperialist war. Both are as urgent today as when the works were produced, a principal reason the artist self-reflexively reprised them in 2004, in the middle of the American war in Iraq, which continues the tradition of United States warfare from the sky. More than thirty years after she distributed the original series at antiwar protests and in underground newspapers, around the time it was first shown in an art gallery, Rosler named it *Bringing the War Home: House Beautiful*, which she more recently reversed to *House Beautiful: Bringing the War Home*, in part to resonate with the title of a contemporaneous and closely related series, *Body Beautiful: Beauty Knows No Pain*. The subtitle *Bringing the War Home* appropriates the words of John Jacobs, a member of the Weathermen faction of Students for a Democratic Society, during the Days of Rage antiwar protests in 1969. For Jacobs, who was echoing Lenin, bringing the war home meant turning the imperialist war in Vietnam into an American civil war. But by the time Rosler read the phrase (probably in a publication called *Prairie Fire*), "bring the war home" had become a slogan of the broader antiwar movement, an exhortation to engage in struggles against injustices in the United States. All the photomontages that make up *House Beautiful* protest war, but most bring the war home in a somewhat different sense, lodging it literally in the space of the American home. Rosler edited together mass-media images, mostly from *Life* magazine, of American combat and destruction in Vietnam and mass-media images, primarily from *House Beautiful*, of idealized homes designed for middle- and upper-class white heterosexual Americans. The war was already known as the living-room war, a phrase invented by the media critic Michael Arlen to describe the first war in which battle footage was televised nightly.[9] Arlen felt that the televising of the war affected popular morality, but Rosler brought the American war and the American home together not only to examine the war's effects on the home but to stage the intimacy that already existed between the two. The problem was not simply the television set *in* the home, Beatriz Colomina writes in *Domesticity at War*, but that "in [Rosler's] remarkable works, the image on the TV screen becomes the image in the picture window. The house is placed on the battlefield. . . . The suburban American house becomes an inhabited television set."[10] Rosler wanted to touch the viewers of her montages closely, where they live, at home.

House Beautiful: Bringing the War Home is justly famous and has elicited a robust critical literature. Writers have illuminated the connections Rosler reveals between rampant consumerism, especially of goods for the home and of the home itself, and the war, both of which, at the time, were treated ideologically as evidence of American freedom.[11] Commentators have also emphasized Rosler's erosion of public/private divisions, her disclosure of links between war and everyday life, and her challenge to the illusion that the home enjoys immunity from military atrocities—from the atrocity of war. Feminist critics have argued that the idealized domesticity depicted in *House Beautiful* cannot be detached from male domination in the nuclear family. "The house," writes Mark Wigley, "is a mechanism for the domestication of women," a process that simultaneously produces masculinity. seen as control in an uncertain world.[12] The idealized home is inseparable from what Trinh T. Minh-ha terms the "victory-crazed" mentality pictured in Rosler's appropriated combat photographs.[13] Victory-crazed is an apt synonym for masculinism, insofar as the latter denotes a drive toward ideals of mastery.

Sigmund Freud uses the word "home" to stand for the human subject. Presenting his ideas to a lay audience, Freud speculates that psychoanalysis deals a bitter blow to humanity's craving for grandiosity because the exposure of unconscious motivations for feelings, attitudes, and actions proves to "each one of us that he is not even master in his own house."[14] Frequently, art historians and critics claim that the shocking juxtapositions emerging from the seemingly cohesive imaginary spaces in Rosler's *House Beautiful* series make viewers uneasy by destabilizing their conscious identifications. It is true that for American middle-class spectators the work stages, Brechtlike, the relationship between fantasies of plenitude, which propel consumption, and willingness to go along with barbarism. Rosler's theatricalization of the relationship encourages viewers to recognize and at the same time reflect on their own everyday implication in an ideological form of consciousness. However, the nuclear family home is not only a site of consumption and male domination, but also the realm of transmission between the unconscious formation of subjectivity and broader society, and in this regard Rosler brings the war home in a particularly dark sense.

Virginia Woolf, whose lifelong war consciousness parallels Rosler's, goes deep into the darkness when she investigates the family psychic dynamics that are called upon not only to wage war but also to cause war. In her post–World War I novels and other writings, Woolf shows how civilian blindness to war perpetuates myths about war. In her feminist antiwar essay *Three Guineas*, written on the eve of World War II, she attributes war to patriarchal attitudes and behavior—egoism, grandiosity, vanity, competitiveness, patriotism, and so on.[15] Connecting the political and the psychical, Woolf argues that patriarchy is a form of society that protects what she calls, following Freudian theory, an unconscious "infantile fixation," a combination of unconscious fear, shame, and destructive anger whose consequence is authoritarianism. First, Woolf examines a report of the Archbishops' Commission on the Ministry of Women. The commission refused to admit women to the Anglican priesthood even though a philosopher had testified that psychologists recognize male dominance but not male superiority. Because the members of the commission ignored psychology's affirmation of women's equality with men, the philosopher concludes that their "strength of feeling . . . is clear evidence of the presence of powerful and widespread subconscious motive" that "has its background in infantile conceptions," which "survive in the adult."[16] Woolf recounts three examples of the infantile fixation as manifested in nineteenth-century fathers' destruction of their daughters' lives—acts, says Woolf, excused by society: "Society it seems was a father, and afflicted with the infantile fixation, too," and in the later nineteenth and early twentieth century, as fathers in private yielded to women's demands, "the fathers in public . . . were even more subject to the fatal disease."[17]

Only two of the homes pictured in *House Beautiful: Bringing the War Home* explicitly include American children—*Boys' Room* and *Beauty Rest*. The children are all boys (fig. 15.1). A third home contains a trace of what might have been a child's party.[18] But idealized images of the American family home generally imply the existence of idealized American children.[19] *Beauty Rest*, the single image showing an entire nuclear family, is a chilling update on Woolf's notion of the infantile fixation as a determinant of war (plate 12). The framing elements that appear to be a doorway, but given their position cannot be one, lead the eye to the photomontage's central image, a color photograph depicting a mother, father, and small boy relaxing on a Beautyrest mattress. The mother peruses a large-format magazine, an emblem of the domestic presence of mass media that Rosler attends to in the series as a whole. Bedrooms, of course, are the most intimate room in what Jürgen

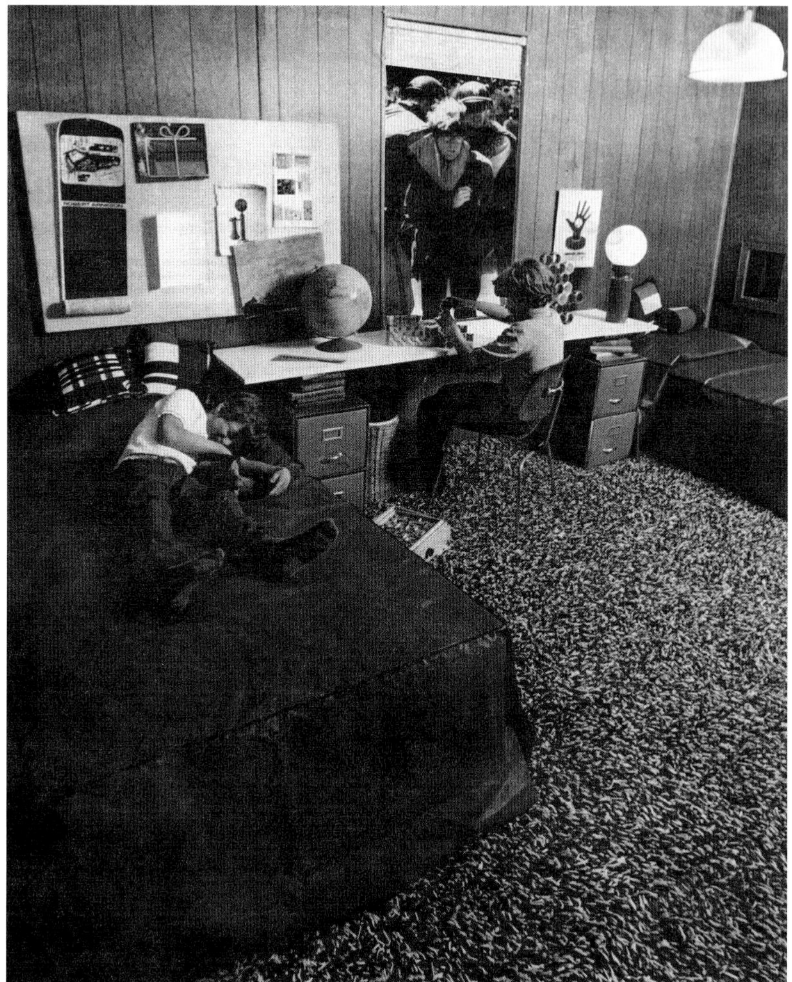

15.1 Martha Rosler, *Boys' Room*, from the series *House Beautiful: Bringing the War Home*, ca. 1967–72. Photomontage. Courtesy the artist.

Habermas calls "the intimate sphere." In the household, writes Habermas, bourgeois males view themselves as independent beings capable of entering into the political public sphere with no special interests.[20]

But in *Beauty Rest* the supposedly autonomous intimate sphere is opened up to the external world—shown in black and white—as the bed floats on the flooded floor of a ruined room. Rosler did not use any actual war imagery in this montage, but in the context of the series as a whole, *Beauty Rest*'s scene of destruction by flood can reasonably be interpreted as a surrogate for a scene of destruction by war. Outside the windows lies more extensive devastation. Fittingly, the central image includes a toy airplane. Though the plane does not appear to be a military craft, the father holds it aloft in a downward attack position, a motif that elicits, especially given the association of conjugal family bedrooms with (suppressed) sexuality, a link between the violence of war and male sexual violence, so often unleashed in war rape. The image alludes to the passing on of phallic masculinity from father to son, whose eyes focus on the plane. But because it is the father who plays with the toy, *Beauty Rest* also points to the infantile roots of such masculinity. Around the time that Woolf published *Three Guineas*, during and after German bombing raids carried out on London, Melanie Klein used toys, including toy planes, to psychoanalyze her child patients because, as she argues, play allowed her to gain access to the unconscious destructive impulses that arise from early relations to their objects, mother and father in particular.[21] Klein claims, as does Rosler's photomontage, that such impulses survive in adults.[22]

Toward the end of *Three Guineas*, Woolf sets an imaginary visual image before the reader: "It is the figure of a man; some say, others deny, that he is Man himself, the quintessence of virility, the perfect type of which all the others are imperfect adumbrations. . . . His body, which is braced in an unnatural position, is tightly cased in a uniform. Upon the breast of that uniform are sewn several medals and other mystic symbols. His hand is upon a sword. He is called in German and Italian Führer or Duce; in our own language Tyrant or Dictator. And behind him lie ruined houses and dead bodies—men, women, and children."[23] The father figure in Rosler's image wears pajamas and is neither Hitler nor Mussolini. But Woolf says that she conjures the tyrant, who in reality is often a family man, to argue that "we cannot dissociate ourselves from that figure but are ourselves that figure. It suggests that we are not passive spectators doomed to unresisting obedience but by our own thoughts and actions can ourselves change that figure."[24] Rosler makes the same argument—a plea, really—and, in doing so, offers hope in dark times, the kind of hope whose condition is the ability to look into ourselves.

Acknowledgments

I am very grateful to Susan Bielstein, who acquired *Not-Forgetting* for University of Chicago Press, and whose expert guidance brought it to fruition. Many thanks to my team at the press: Dylan Joseph Montanari, Adrienne Meyers, Joel Score, and Rae Ganci Hammers. Their unfailing skill and congeniality made the process of producing this book a truly pleasurable and rewarding experience.

I thank *Not-Forgetting*'s anonymous reviewers for their comprehensive and erudite evaluations, which helped me clarify the scope of the book and improve the introduction.

Thanks to Barnard College for awarding me two Faculty Research Grants that allowed me to complete this project; to Jonathan Reynolds, chair of the Art History Department, who supported my application for the grant; and Elisabeth Sher, who administered it with such good will during the difficult period of the COVID-19 pandemic.

Sincere thanks to the curators, scholars, editors, museums, and galleries that invited me to write the essays that are included in *Not-Forgetting*: Johanna Burton, Joan Copjec, Ann Goldstein, Roxana Marcoci, Helen Molesworth, Michael Sorkin, David Velasco, the Jewish Museum, and Mitchell-Innes & Nash. Also, to Kaira Cabanas, professor of Art History at the University of Florida, Gainesville, Scott McLeod, programmer of the Urban Field Speaker Series at Prefix Institute of Contemporary Art in Toronto, and the Stanford University Department of Art and Art History for inviting me to deliver talks that developed into the essays "Mary Kelly's Attunement" and "Christopher D'Arcangelo's Elliptical Interruptions."

Heartfelt thanks to the wonderful undergraduate and graduate students at Barnard and Columbia, on whom I tested many of the ideas in this book and who taught me so much.

The ethically and politically conscious artists whose work inspired these essays include Christopher D'Arcangelo, Robert Filliou, Sanja Iveković, Mary Kelly, Silvia Kolbowski, Barbara Kruger, Louise Lawler, Martha Rosler, James Welling, and Krzysztof Wodiczko. Thanks to all of them. It has been a privilege to think in their company.

I greatly appreciate the assistance of Cathy Weiner, who read a draft of the essay about her former partner Christopher D'Arcangelo, made important corrections, and offered significant historical information.

I owe a considerable debt to Leah Pires, my former PhD student and now a valued colleague, who served as my research assistant on this project. It was reassuring to have her by my side, tracking down images, obtaining permissions, and conducting research on Christopher D'Arcangelo, all with her characteristic good humor, efficiency, and intelligence. In consultation with Cathy Weiner and me, she took the lead in questioning how best to caption the photographic documentation of D'Arcangelo's museum "actions," a decision that, as she insisted, is crucial to how the artist's work is understood.

Thanks to Mignon Nixon and Ann Reynolds for their careful reading of and astute comments about *Not-Forgetting*'s introduction.

Many thanks to Jane Weinstock for our weekly get-togethers and expeditions, to Robert Millner and Stephen Stanczyk for taking me away from it all to observe owls and sit by campfires in the country, to Lynne Tillman, who always offers solace and sage advice.

Profound thanks to Aaron Metrikin. My work with him has helped me to stay sane and enjoy life.

For warm support, intimate conversation, intellectual exchange, good food, and lots of fun over the more than twenty years in which I wrote these essays, I sincerely thank the following friends, family members, and colleagues (and one cat): Alexander Alberro, Naiyah Ambrose, Judith Barry, Morgan Bassichiss, Robert Benton, Gregg Bordowitz, Greg Bryda, Charlotte, Marielle Cohen, Shane Cohen-Mungan, Bryn Cohen-Mungan, Rita Dennis, Jonathan Flatley, Isabel Freeman, Martha Gever, Rebecca Harrington, Jennifer Hayslett-Ubell, Thornton Hayslett, Ella Hayslett-Ubell, Benjamin Hayslett-Ubell, Elizabeth Hutchinson, Adam Kaplan, Silvia Kolbowski, Louise Lawler, Susan Laxton, Simon Leung, Emily Liebert, Elizabeth Miller, Stevens Miller, Fordon Miller, Nadja Millner-Larsen, Matt Mungan, Mignon Nixon, Leah Pires, Yvonne Rainer, Gerard Roman, Ann Reynolds, Marc Siegel, Jon Smit, Carol Squiers, Susanne Sachesse, Janet Wolff, and Krzysztof Wodiczko.

For years, my friend and colleague Douglas Crimp encouraged me to publish a collection of my recent essays. I always assumed that when I got around to doing so he would write a preface. By the time I acted on his advice, however, it was too late. By then, he was in hospice care, dying of multiple melanoma, though still urging me to get started on the book. I promised him that I would. Douglas's spirit hovers over *Not-Forgetting*, which is dedicated to him, with love.

My gratitude to Robert Ubell is beyond measure. Thank you, Bob, for everything.

Notes

Introduction

1. The fifteen texts collected here were written between 1999 and 2020. The majority have been previously published in disparate journals, catalogues, and anthologies, many of which are out of print or difficult to find. These are reprinted in their original versions with slight, mostly grammatical modifications and a standardized citation format. Updates to endnotes are contained in brackets. Two texts—"Mary Kelly's Attunement" and "Christopher D'Arcangelo's Elliptical Interruptions"—which were first given as lectures, appear here for the first time.

2. Christina Lamb, *Our Bodies, Their Battlefields: War through the Lives of Women* (New York: Scribner, 2020), 132. The court's official name is the International Criminal Tribunal for the former Yugoslavia.

3. Paul Ricoeur, *Memory, History, Forgetting*, trans. Kathleen Blamey and David Pellauer (Chicago: University of Chicago Press, 2004), 87. As I explain in "We don't need another hero," Ricoeur's "duty of memory" combines mourning and memory with the imperative of justice.

4. Sigmund Freud, "Analysis Terminable and Interminable" (1937), in *Therapy and Technique*, ed. Philip Rieff (New York: Macmillan, 1963), 254–56.

5. Alain Badiou, *Ethics: An Essay on the Understanding of Evil* (London: Verso, 2001), 41–52.

6. Badiou, *Ethics*, 41. Badiou warns that an ethics of truths brings with it the danger of making truths absolute, allowing them to harden into dogma, and imposing them as a total power, a danger he calls Evil.

7. As I write in "Not-Forgetting: Mary Kelly's *Love Songs*," Badiou does not mention feminism as an event, and in *Metapolitics* fails even to include it in an outline of the last forty years of French politics. Badiou, *Metapolitics* (London: Verso, 2005), xxxiv–xxxv.

8. Simone de Beauvoir, *Memoirs of a Dutiful Daughter*, trans. James Kirkup (New York: Harper & Row, 1958), 94.

9. Virginia Woolf, *Three Guineas* (New York: Harcourt, Brace & World, 1938), 75.

10. See Griselda Pollock, "What's Wrong with 'Images of Women'?" (1977), in *Framing Feminism: Art and the Women's Movement 1970–1985*, ed. Pollock and Roszika Parker (Lon-

don: Pandora, 1987), 132–38; Elizabeth Cowie, "Woman as Sign," *m/f*, no. 1 (1978), 49–63; and Theresa de Lauretis, *Alice Doesn't: Feminism, Semiotics, Cinema* (Bloomington: Indiana University Press, 1984).

11. Laura Mulvey, "Visual Pleasure and Narrative Cinema" (1975), in *Visual and Other Pleasures* (Bloomington: Indiana University Press, 1989), 14–26.

12. Kimberly Drew, "Carrie Mae Weems: The Legendary Photographer on Becoming and Exploring Personhood through Art," in *Carrie Mae Weems*, ed. Sarah Elizabeth Lewis, October Files 25 (Cambridge, MA: MIT Press, 2021), 95. Weems has made clear that *Kitchen Table Series* is not only about the Black woman but woman more generally. In addition to Weems, Adrian Piper, Lorna Simpson, Ellen Gallagher, and others have engaged in a critique of representations of the Black female body using postmodern tactics such as appropriation, the staging of images, image-text combinations, and direct address. I am grateful to Oluremi Cecilia-Anne Onabanjo for discussions about the woman-as-image discourse in relation to race.

13. Craig Owens, "The Discourse of Others: Feminists and Postmodernism," in *Beyond Recognition: Representation, Power, and Culture* (Berkeley: University of California Press, 1992), 166–90.

14. By including coloniality, a term not yet coined during the heyday of postmodernism, among the objects of postmodern critique, I do not mean to equate postmodernism and decoloniality. However, the two discourses' descriptions of the mode of being human produced by the West are approximate. For example, the Jamaican author and philosopher of decoloniality Sylvia Wynter argues that all current struggles are aspects of the struggle against "our present ethnoclass (i.e., Western bourgeois) conception of the human, Man, which overrepresents itself as if it were the human itself." While this is the same Man targeted by postmodernism, which, like Wynter, called for the recognition of Man's construction by symbolic, representational systems, Wynter draws on Aimé Césaire and Frantz Fanon to propose a redescription of the human that will secure the well-being not of Man but of the human species in its entirety. Wynter, "Unsettling the Coloniality of Being/Power/Truth/Freedom: Towards the Human, after Man, Its Overrepresentation—An Argument," *New Centennial Review* 3, no. 3 (Fall 2003): 257–337.

15. Ernesto Laclau, "Politics and the Limits of Modernity," in *Universal Abandon? The Politics of Postmodernism*, ed. Andrew Ross (Minneapolis: University of Minnesota Press, 1988), 63.

16. I attended the Graduate Center at the City University of New York, where the poststructuralist project took place under the leadership of Rosalind Krauss. When Linda Nochlin joined the faculty, the PhD students began to articulate that project with feminism.

17. Cicero, *Tusculan Disputations*, trans. J. E. King, book V.iv, Loeb Classical Library (Cambridge, MA: Harvard University Press, 1927; rev. 1945), 435.

18. See Jacques Derrida, *Writing and Difference*, trans. Alan Bass (Chicago: University of Chicago Press, 1978), 279.

19. Christopher Bollas, "Generational Consciousness," in *Being a Character: Psychoanalysis and Self Experience* (London: Routledge, 1992), 247–76.

20. Jacques Lacan, "The Function and Field of Speech and Language in Psychoanalysis," in *Écrits: A Selection*, trans. Alan Sheridan (New York: W. W. Norton, 1977), 86.

21. I am grateful to one of my anonymous readers for emphasizing this point in my work.

22. Gayatri Chakravorty Spivak, *The Post-Colonial Critic: Interviews, Strategies, Dialogues,* ed. Sarah Harasym (New York: Routledge, 1990), 19; Jean-François Lyotard, *The Postmodern Condition: A Report on Knowledge,* trans. Geoff Bennington and Brian Massumi, Theory and History of Literature, volume 10 (1979; Minneapolis: University of Minnesota Press, 1984), xxv.

23. Emmanuel Levinas, "Being-for-the-Other," in *Is It Righteous to Be? Interviews with Emmanuel Levinas,* ed. Jill Robbins (Stanford, CA: Stanford University Press, 2001), 114.

24. Homi Bhabha, "A Good Judge of Character: Men, Metaphors, and the Common Culture," in *Race-ing Justice, En-gendering Power: Essays on Anita Hill, Clarence Thomas, and the Construction of Social Reality,* ed. Toni Morrison (New York: Pantheon, 1992), 242 (emphasis added). Bhabha defines masculinism in the context of the 1991 hearings to confirm Clarence Thomas's nomination to the US Supreme Court. Thomas had been accused of sexual harassment by the lawyer Anita Hill. During his testimony, he called the hearings and attendant media coverage "a high-tech lynching," thereby deploying antiracist language to dismiss the black feminist discourse represented by Hill's testimony. Bhabha calls Thomas's claim to stand for the entire race masculinist but explains that in using the term he is not attacking men.

25. Bhabha, "Good Judge of Character," 242.

26. Trinh T. Minh-ha, *Lovecidal: Walking with the Disappeared* (New York: Fordham University Press, 2016), 71.

27. Claude Lefort, "The Question of Democracy," in *Democracy and Political Theory,* trans. David Macey (Minneapolis: University of Minnesota Press, 1988), 9–20.

28. Sigmund Freud, *A General Introduction to Psychoanalysis* (New York: Simon and Schuster, 1935), 252.

29. Freud, *General Introduction,* 252 (emphasis added).

30. Freud writes about the capacity for regression and ineradicable destructiveness in relation to war in "Thoughts for the Times on War and Death," *The Standard Edition of the Complete Psychological Works of Sigmund Freud,* ed. James Strachey (London: Hogarth Press, 1953–74), 14:275–300.

31. Judith N. Shklar, *Ordinary Vices* (Cambridge, MA: Harvard University Press, 1984), 7–44. I am grateful to Henry Abelove for introducing me to this brilliant book.

32. Jacques Derrida, "Psychoanalysis Searches the States of Its Soul: The Impossible Beyond of a Sovereign Cruelty (Address to the States General of Psychoanalysis)," in *Without Alibi,* trans. Peggy Kamuf (Stanford, CA: Stanford University Press, 2002), 239–40.

33. Judith Barry, "The Space That Art Makes," in *A Dynamic Equilibrium: In Pursuit of Public Terrain,* ed. Sally Yard (San Diego: Installation Gallery, 2007), 48, 47.

34. Claudia Rankine, *Just Us: An American Conversation* (Minneapolis, MN: Graywolf Press), 329.

35. This interdependence is also responsible for some repetitions that readers will encounter in *Not-Forgetting.*

36. See Rosalyn Deutsche, response to "Questionnaire," *October,* no. 123 (Winter 2008), 38–40, and *Hiroshima after Iraq: Three Studies in Art and War,* Wellek Library Lectures (New York: Columbia University Press, 2010), 1–5.

37. Rosalyn Deutsche, *Evictions: Art and Spatial Politics* (Cambridge, MA: MIT Press, 1996).

38. David Harvey, *The Condition of Postmodernity: An Enquiry into the Origins of Cultural Change* (Oxford: Basil Blackwell, 1989); Edward W. Soja, *Postmodern Geographies: The Reassertion of Space in Critical Social Theory* (London: Verso, 1989); Fredric Jameson, "Postmodernism, or the Cultural Logic of Late Capitalism," *New Left Review*, no. 146 (July/August 1984), 53–92.

1: Not-Forgetting

Originally published in *Grey Room*, no. 24 (Summer 2006). Reprinted in catalogue of Mary Kelly exhibition at CCA Ujazdowski Castle, Warsaw (2008), and in *Mary Kelly*, ed. Mignon Nixon, October Files 20 (Cambridge, MA: MIT Press, 2015).

1. Giorgio Agamben, *State of Exception*, trans. Kevin Attell (Chicago: University of Chicago Press, 2005), 14.

2. Wendy Brown, "Resisting Left Melancholia," in *Loss*, ed. David L. Eng and David Kazanjian (Berkeley: University of California Press, 2003), 458–65.

3. Brown, "Resisting Left Melancholia," 460, 462–63.

4. Brown, "Resisting Left Melancholia," 460.

5. Retort (Ian Boal et al.), *Afflicted Powers: Capital and Spectacle in a New Age of War* (London: Verso, 2005).

6. Brown, "Resisting Left Melancholia," 460.

7. Alain Badiou, *Ethics: An Essay on the Understanding of Evil* (London: Verso, 2001).

8. Julia Kristeva, *Revolt, She Said*, trans. Brian O'Keeffe (Los Angeles: Semiotexte(e), 2002), 104.

9. Badiou, *Ethics*, 41–42.

10. Badiou, *Ethics*, 50.

11. Feminism is absent from Badiou's 2005 outline of the last forty years of French politics; see *Metapolitics* (London: Verso, 2005), xxxiv–xxxv.

12. Badiou, *Ethics*, 72.

13. Drucilla Cornell, "Rethinking the Time of Feminism," in Seyla Benhabib et al., *Feminist Contentions: A Philosophical Exchange* (New York: Routledge), 152.

14. Josh Tonsfeldt, unpublished term paper, 2005.

15. Sasha Archibald, "Care and the Psyche: An Interview with Mary Kelly," in *At the Mercy of Others: The Politics of Care*, catalogue of exhibition organized by the Helena Rubinstein Curatorial Fellows of the Whitney Museum of American Art Independent Study Program at the Whitney Museum of American Art, New York, May 18–June 25, 2005, 26.

16. Archibald, "Care and the Psyche," 26.

17. Jacqueline Rose, *The Haunting of Sylvia Plath* (Cambridge, MA: Harvard University Press, 1992).

18. Rose, *Haunting of Sylvia Plath*, 144.

19. On a BBC broadcast, Plath introduced this poem by saying, "Abstractions, by definition, are withdrawn from life and formulated in spite of life's minute and vital complexities. In this poem, 'Magi,' I imagine the great absolutes of the philosophers gathered

around the crib of a newborn baby girl who is nothing *but* life." Sylvia Plath, *The Collected Poems* (New York: Harper & Row, 1981), 289–90n130.

20. Rose, *Haunting of Sylvia Plath*, 149.

21. Cornell, "Rethinking the Time of Feminism," 152.

22. Jacques Lacan, "The function and field of speech and language in psychoanalysis," in *Écrits: A Selection* (New York: W. W. Norton, 1977), 86.

23. Walter Benjamin, "Theses on the Philosophy of History," in *Illuminations*, ed. Hannah Arendt, trans. Harry Zohn (New York: Schocken, 1969), 255.

24. Cornell, "Rethinking the Time of Feminism," 155.

2: Inadequacy

Originally published as "Inadequacy" in *Silvia Kolbowski: inadequate . . . Like . . . Power* (Vienna: Secession, 2004). Reprinted in *Silvia Kolbowski: Nothing and Everything* (Montréal: Leonard and Bina Ellen Art Gallery, Concordia University, 2009).

1. *L'art conceptuel, une perspective*, Musée d'Art Moderne de la Ville de Paris, November 22, 1989–February 18, 1990.

2. The full text of Asher's proposal is the following: "*L'art conceptuel, une perspective* is as much a view of Conceptual Art as it is a perspective of the institutions used for the maintenance and historical production of that practice. What are the forces and conditions driving the historical analysis which are beyond conceptual art practice's own definition of its historical context and production procedures? Historical objectification ought to be accelerated while there is still a collective experience and memory which can assist in the clarity of an analysis, simultaneously opening up a space to ask fundamental questions regarding history making. To look at this question further, I propose as my contribution to *l'art conceptuel, une perspective* that separate groups of historians be notified by an announcement of this exhibition in the below journals that a new historical perspective is being mapped on to conceptual art practice. *M.A. Apollo, Art History, Daidalos, The Journal of Aesthetic and Art Criticism, La Revue du Louvre et des musées de France, Romagna Arte e Storia*, and *Simiolus*."

3. Asher, proposal.

4. The artists included Victor Burgin, Sarah Charlesworth, Mary Kelly, Sherrie Levine, Cindy Sherman, Gretchen Bender, Louise Lawler, and Laurie Simmons, among others. In mounting a feminist critique of vision, these artists also questioned theories of postmodernism, which at that point remained indifferent to sexuality and gender. On this blindness, see Jane Weinstock, "A Laugh, a Lass and a Lad," *Art in America*, 71, no. 6 (Summer 1983): 8; and Craig Owens, "The Discourse of Others: Feminists and Postmodernism," in *The Anti-Aesthetic: Essays on Postmodern Culture*, ed. Hal Foster (Port Townsend, WA: Bay Press, 1983), 57–82.

5. *Difference: On Representation and Sexuality*, organized by Kate Linker and Jane Weinstock at the New Museum of Contemporary Art, New York, 1985.

6. Roberta Smith, "Beyond Gender," *Village Voice*, January 22, 1985, 103.

7. Simon Leung, "Contemporary Returns to Conceptual Art: Renée Green, Silvia Kolbowski, and Stephen Prina," *Art Journal*, Summer 2001, 57–58.

8. Quoted in Mignon Nixon, "*She-Fox*: Transference and the 'Woman Artist,'" in *Women Artists at the Millennium*, ed. Carol Armstrong and Catherine de Zegher (Cambridge: MIT Press/October Books, 2006).

9. Jacqueline Rose, *Why War? Psychoanalysis, Politics, and the Return to Melanie Klein* (Oxford: Blackwell, 1993), 36.

10. Hayden White, "The Value of Narrativity in the Representation of Reality," *Critical Inquiry* 7, no. 1 (1980).

11. Joan Wallach Scott, *Gender and the Politics of History* (New York: Columbia University Press, 1988), 26.

12. Claude Gintz, "'*L'art conceptuel, une perspective*': Notes on an Exhibition Project," in *L'art conceptuel, une perspective*, 19.

13. *Global Conceptualism: Points of Origin, 1950s–1980s*, Queens Museum of Art, 1999; *Reconsidering the Object of Art: 1965–1975*, Museum of Contemporary Art, Los Angeles, October 15, 1995–February 4, 1996.

14. See, for example, Alexander Alberro and Blake Stimson, eds., *Conceptual Art: A Critical Anthology* (Cambridge, MA: MIT Press, 1999); Peter Osborne, *Conceptual Art* (London: Phaidon, 2002); and Michael Corris, ed., *Conceptual Art: Theory, Myth, and Practice* (Cambridge: Cambridge University Press, 2004).

15. Lucy Lippard, *Six Years: The Dematerialization of the Art Object from 1966 to 1972* (Berkeley: University of California Press, 1997).

16. Alexander Alberro, *Conceptual Art and the Politics of Publicity* (Cambridge, MA: MIT Press, 2003); Benjamin Buchloh, "Conceptual Art 1962–1969: From the Aesthetic of Administration to the Critique of Institutions," *October*, no. 55 (Winter 1990).

17. Leung, "Contemporary Returns," 66; Kolbowski, conversation with the author, November 12, 2003.

18. Leung, "Contemporary Returns," 54.

19. For another description of these two tendencies, see Paul Wood's discussion of the term "conceptualism" in *Conceptual Art* (New York: Delano Greenidge Editions, 2002), 8–9.

20. Alexander Alberro, "Silvia Kolbowski," *Artforum* 38, no. 4 (December 1999) 148–49.

21. Alberro and Stimson, *Conceptual Art*, 5.

22. Buchloh, "Conceptual Art 1962–1969," 107.

23. Griselda Pollock, *Vision and Difference: Femininity, Feminism and the Histories of Art* (London: Routledge, 1998), 53.

24. Buchloh, "Conceptual Art 1962–1969," 143.

25. Buchloh, "Conceptual Art 1962–1969," 137.

26. Buchloh, "Conceptual Art 1962–1969," 105.

27. As early as 1984, Victor Burgin theorized the connection between Conceptualism and feminism in "The Absence of Presence: Conceptualism and Postmodernism," in *The End of Art Theory: Criticism and Postmodernity* (Atlantic Highlands, NJ: Humanities Press International, 1986), 29–50.

28. Quoted in Silvia Kolbowski, "an inadequate history of conceptual art," *October*, no. 92 (Spring 2000), 53.

29. Alberro, "Silvia Kolbowski," 149.

30. Kolbowski, "Interview: A Conversation Between," in *Flash Art*, no. 103 (November–December 1988), 103.

31. Silvia Kolbowski, *XI Projects* (New York: Border Editions, 1992), 60–61.

32. Kolbowski, *XI Projects*, 60–61.

33. Kolbowski, *XI Projects*, 60

34. Fredric Jameson, *The Political Unconscious: Narrative as a Socially Symbolic Act* (Ithaca, NY: Cornell University Press, 1981), 19 (emphasis added).

35. Jameson, *Political Unconscious*, 86.

36. "An Interview with Fredric Jameson by Anders Stephanson on Postmodernism," *Flash Art*, December 1986–January 1987, 69.

37. Owens, "Discourse of Others," 63.

38. Marianne Hirsch and Valerie Smith, "Feminism and Cultural Memory: An Introduction," *Signs* 28, no. 1, special issue, "Gender and Cultural Memory" (Autumn 2002): 11.

39. Juliet Flower MacCannell, "Language," in *Feminism and Psychoanalysis: A Critical Dictionary*, ed. Elizabeth Wright (Oxford: Blackwell, 1992), 210 (emphasis added).

40. MacCannell, "Language," 211.

41. Dominick LaCapra, "History and Memory: In the Shadow of the Holocaust," in *History and Memory after Auschwitz* (Ithaca, NY: Cornell University Press, 1998), 19.

42. LaCapra, "History and Memory," 19.

43. Saul Friedlander, *Memory, History and the Extermination of the Jews of Europe* (Bloomington: Indiana University Press, 1993), 97.

44. Friedlander, *Memory, History*, 97.

45. Friedlander, *Memory, History*, 97.

46. Michel de Certeau, *The Writing of History* (New York: Columbia University Press, 1988), 287.

47. Rose, *Why War?* 16.

48. Owens, "Discourse of Others," 62.

3: Darkness

Originally published in *James Welling: Abstract* (Brussels: Palais Royale; Toronto: Art Gallery of York University, 2002).

1. Metro Pictures was founded in 1980 by Helene Winer and Janelle Reiring, who still run the gallery in another location. James Welling exhibited at Metro Pictures from its opening until 1986. [Metro Pictures closed in 2021.]

2. Roland Barthes, "The Structuralist Activity" (1963), in *Critical Essays* (Evanston, IL: Northwestern University Press, 1972).

3. "Artist's Biography," in *James Welling: Photographs 1974–1999*, ed. Sarah J. Rogers (Columbus, OH: Wexner Center for the Arts, 2000), 125.

4. Barthes, "Structuralist Activity," 218.

5. James Welling in conversation with Trevor Fairbrother, *BiNational: American Art of the Late '80s* (Boston: Institute of Contemporary Art and Museum of Fine Arts; Cologne: DuMont Buchverlag, 1988), 219.

6. [See plate 2 and figure 4.2 in this volume.]

7. See Louise Lawler, *An Arrangement of Pictures* (New York: Assouline, 2000), in particular the introductory text, "Prominence Given, Authority Taken: An Interview with Louise

Lawler by Douglas Crimp," which is reprinted with a new introduction by Crimp (that is, rearranged) in *Grey Room*, no. 4 (Summer 2001), 70–81. [Also see figures 5.2, 5.5, 13.1, 13.2, 13.3, and 13.5 and plate 10 in this volume.]

8. Gayatri Spivak, "The Post-modern Condition: The End of Politics?" (1984), in *The Post-Colonial Critic: Interviews, Strategies, Dialogues*, ed. Sarah Harasym (New York: Routledge, 1990), 18.

9. Michael Fried, "Art and Objecthood," in *Minimal Art: A Critical Anthology*, ed. Gregory Battcock (New York: Dutton, 1968), 147.

10. Michael Fried, "James Welling's Lock, 1976," in Rogers, *James Welling: Photographs 1974–1999*, 28 (emphasis added).

11. Walter Benn Michaels, "Photography as Art," unpublished paper, 1992.

12. Walter Benn Michaels, "The Photographic Surface," in *James Welling: Photographs 1977–90* (Bern: Kunsthalle Bern, 1990).

13. Allan Sekula, "The Traffic in Photographs," in *Photography against the Grain: Essays and Photo Works* (Halifax: Press of the Nova Scotia College of Art, 1984), 82.

14. Michaels, "Photographic Surface."

15. Eduardo Cadava, *Words of Light: Theses on the Photography of History* (Princeton, NJ: Princeton University Press, 1997), 42.

16. Walter Benjamin, *One-Way Street, and Other Writings*, trans. Edmund Jephcott and Kingsley Shorter (London: New Left Books, 1979), 357; quoted in Cadava, *Words of Light*, 42.

17. Michaels, "Photographic Surface."

18. Rosalind Krauss, "Photography and Abstraction" (New York: Bertha and Karl Leubsdorf Art Gallery, Hunter College, 1989), 66.

19. James Welling, "Abstract," *Effects: Magazine for New Art Theory*, no. 2 (1984), 18. All quotes in this paragraph are from this source.

20. Welling, "Abstract," 220.

21. David Joselit, "Surface Histories: The Photography of James Welling," *Art in America* 89, no. 5 (May 2001): 137–38.

22. Joselit, "Surface Histories," 138

23. Joselit, "Surface Histories," 141.

24. Joselit, "Surface Histories," 140.

25. Jacqueline Rose, "Why War?" in *Why War? Psychoanalysis, Politics, and the Return to Melanie Klein* (Oxford: Blackwell, 1993), 37.

26. Cadava, *Words of Light*, 66

27. Sarah J. Rogers, "James Welling: Photographs 1974–1999," in Rogers, *James Welling: Photographs 1974–1999*, 71.

28. Craig Owens, "Photography en abyme," *October*, no. 5 (Summer 1978). Reprinted in Owens, *Beyond Recognition: Representation, Power, and Culture* (Berkeley: University of California Press, 1992), 17.

29. Owens, "Photography en abyme," 28.

30. Batchen uses Daguerre's words as the title of a book on the role of desire in the invention and meaning of the medium. Gregory Batchen, *Burning with Desire: The Conception of Photography* (Cambridge, MA: MIT Press, 1997), viii.

31. Krauss, "Photography and Abstraction," 65.

32. Krauss, "Photography and Abstraction," 65.

33. Roland Barthes, "Rhetoric of the Image," in *Image, Music, Text*, trans. Stephen Heath (New York: Hill & Wang, 1977), 44.

34. Mikhail Bakhtin, "Epic and Novel: Toward a Methodology for the Study of the Novel," in *The Dialogic Imagination*, trans. Caryl Emerson and Michael Holquist (Austin: University of Texas Press, 1981), 22.

35. Cadava, *Words of Light*, 24.

36. Walter Benjamin, "The Storyteller," in *Illuminations*, ed. Hannah Arendt (New York: Schocken, 1969), 101.

37. Fried, "James Welling's Lock, 1976," 26.

38. Fried, "James Welling's Lock, 1976," 26.

39. Fried, "James Welling's Lock, 1976," 26.

4: Breaking Ground

Originally published in *Thinking of You: Barbara Kruger* (Los Angeles: Museum of Contemporary Art, 1999), 77–84.

1. Some critics single out Kruger's work in outdoor spaces and endow it with the status of a democratic activity by labeling it "public art." This label consigns work in galleries and museums to privacy and "elitism" and fails to acknowledge the ways in which outdoor urban spaces are privatized. But the category "public art" is a space, too, and, as she does with other spaces, Kruger displaces its boundaries, challenging rigid divisions between public and private space. The publicness of her art is not tied to location but, rather, resides in the performance of an operation—the use and undoing of spaces defined by power relationships.

2. Mark Wigley, "Editorial," *assemblage*, no. 20, special issue, "Violence/Space" (April 1993), 7.

3. See Michel de Certeau, "'Making Do: Uses and Tactics," in *The Practice of Everyday Life*, trans. Steven Rendell (Berkeley: University of California Press, 1984), 29–42.

4. Jacques Derrida, *Positions*, trans. Alan Bass (Chicago: University of Chicago Press, 1981), 94.

5. The exhibitions were held at the following galleries: Fred Hoffman, Los Angeles (1989); Rhona Hoffman, Chicago (1990); and Mary Boone, New York (1991).

6. Roland Barthes, "The Rhetoric of the Image," in *Image, Music, Text*, ed. and trans. Stephen Heath (New York: Hill & Wang, 1977). 32–51.

7. Craig Owens, "The Medusa Effect, or, The Specular Ruse," in *We won't play nature to your culture* (London: Institute of Contemporary Arts, 1983), 6; reprinted in Owens, *Beyond Recognition: Representation, Power, and Culture* (Berkeley: University of California Press, 1992), 192.

8. Norman Bryson, "The Logic of the Curatorial Gaze," in *Still, the Museum* (Rotterdam: Boijmans Van Beuningen Museum, 1997), 32.

9. Julia Kristeva, *Strangers to Ourselves*, trans. Leon S. Roudiez (New York: Columbia University Press, 1991), 17.

10. Barbara Kruger, "Untitled" (1987), in *Remote Control: Power, Cultures, and the World of Appearances* (Cambridge, MA: MIT Press, 1993), 230.

11. Oscar Wilde, "The Critic as Artist" (1891), reprinted in *The Artist as Critic: Crit-*

ical Writings of Oscar Wilde, ed. Richard Ellmann (Chicago: University of Chicago Press, 1968), 360.

12. For a brilliant discussion of the ethico-political, see Thomas Keenan, *Fables of Responsibility: Aberrations and Predicaments in Ethics and Politics* (Stanford, CA: Stanford University Press, 1997).

13. *Newsweek,* June 8, 1992, cover.

14. Kruger, "Untitled," 230.

15. The installation was mounted at Mary Boone Gallery, New York, October 31–December 20, 1997.

16. Sigmund Freud, "Fetishism" (1927), in *Sexuality and the Psychology of Love,* ed. Philip Rieff (New York: Collier Books, 1963), 214–19.

17. Jacqueline Rose, "Sexuality in the Field of Vision," in *Difference: On Representation and Sexuality* (New York: New Museum of Contemporary Art, 1985), 33.

18. Slavoj Žižek, *For They Know Not What They Do: Enjoyment as a Political Factor* (London: Verso, 1991), 174n38.

19. [Kruger exhibited *Untitled (No Radio),* made in 1988, at the beginning of her 1991 installation at Mary Boone Gallery, which is described above. New York City at the time was experiencing a rash of smash-and-grab thefts of car radios. People put signs on their cars reading "No Radio" in an effort to prevent such violations, which I am reading as a symbol of the violation of the female body in visual representation.]

20. Jacqueline Rose, "Why War?" in *Why War? Psychoanalysis, Politics, and the Return to Melanie Klein* (Oxford: Blackwell, 1993), 37.

5: Louise Lawler's Rude Museum

Originally published in *Twice Untitled and Other Pictures (Looking Back)* (Columbus, OH: Wexner Center for the Arts; Cambridge, MA: MIT Press, 2006). Reprinted in *Art and Contemporary Critical Practice: Reinventing Institutional Critique,* ed. Gerald Raunig and Gene Ray (London: MayFly Books, 2009), transform.eipcp.net/transversal/0106, and *Louise Lawler,* ed. Helen Molesworth with Taylor Walsh, October Files 14 (Cambridge, MA: MIT Press, 2013).

1. Virginia Woolf, *Three Guineas* (New York: Harcourt, Brace & World, 1938), 6.

2. As Silvia Kolbowski asks about the rejection of psychoanalysis in current criticism: "Is psychoanalysis too feminine? i.e. too 'weak' to serve political analysis?" Kolbowski, "Diary of a Buren Spectator," *October,* no. 115 (Winter 2006), 89.

3. Woolf, *Three Guineas,* 75.

4. Mignon Nixon, *Fantastic Reality: Louise Bourgeois and a Story of Modern Art* (Cambridge, MA: MIT Press, 2005), 67.

5. Sigmund Freud, *Jokes and Their Relation to the Unconscious* (New York: W. W. Norton, 1960), 123–25.

6. Woolf, *Three Guineas,* 19.

7. Woolf, *Three Guineas,* 19.

8. Woolf, *Three Guineas,* 19.

9. Homi K. Bhabha, "A Good Judge of Character: Men, Metaphors, and the Common

Culture," in *Race-ing Justice, En-gendering Power: Essays on Anita Hill, Clarence Thomas, and the Construction of Social Reality*, ed. Toni Morrison (New York: Pantheon, 1992), 242. Bhabha writes, "'Masculinism' as a position of social authority is not simply about the power invested in the recognizable 'persons' of men. It is about the subsumption or sublation of social antagonism; it is about the repression of social divisions; it is about the power to authorize an 'impersonal' holistic or universal discourse on the representation of the social that naturalizes cultural difference and turns it into a 'second'-nature argument."

10. Walter Benjamin, "Theses on the Philosophy of History," in *Illuminations*, ed. Hannah Arendt (New York: Schocken, 1969), 256.

11. Woolf, *Three Guineas*, 63.

12. Linda Nochlin, "Why Have There Been No Great Women Artists?" *Art News*, January 1971, 22–39, 67–71. Zoffany's painting is alternatively titled *Academicians of the Royal Academy*.

13. Naomi Schor, *Reading in Detail: Aesthetics and the Feminine* (New York: Methuen, 1987), 17.

14. Schor, *Reading in Detail*, 5.

15. Laura Mulvey, "Visual Pleasure and Narrative Cinema" (1975), in *Visual and Other Pleasures* (Bloomington: Indiana University Press, 1989), 14–26.

16. It could also be argued that Lawler entered the artistic profession differently insofar as she has been reticent "about taking on the conventional role of the artist." See "Prominence Given, Authority Taken: An Interview with Louise Lawler by Douglas Crimp," in Lawler, *An Arrangement of Pictures* (New York: Assouline, 2000).

17. [This chronology of institutional critique, which I divide along the line of gender, is too simplistic. Now, I would include such feminist women artists as Mierle Laderman Ukeles and Martha Rosler within the first generation, although dominant histories of the practice focus on Asher, Broodthaers, Haacke, and Buren.]

18. Hal Foster, Rosalind Krauss, Benjamin H. D. Buchloh, and Yve-Alain Bois, *Art since 1900: Modernism, Antimodernism, Postmodernism*, vol. 2 (New York: Thames & Hudson, 2004), 624.

19. Andrea Fraser, "In and Out of Place," *Art in America*, June 1985, 123.

20. Kate Linker, "Rites of Exchange," *Artforum*, November 1986, 99.

21. Birgit Pelzer, "Interpositions: The Work of Louise Lawler," in *Louise Lawler and Others* (Basel: Kunstmuseum Basel, Museum für Gegenwartskunst; Ostfildern-Ruit, Germany: Hatje Cantz, 2004), 32. Pelzer is referring specifically to the portfolios of photographs that Lawler has published in books and magazines.

22. Kenneth Gross, *The Dream of the Moving Statue* (Ithaca, NY: Cornell University Press, 1992), 198. [For more on Gross's book, see chapter 9 in this volume.]

23. Peter Bürger, *Theory of the Avant-Garde*, trans. Michael Shaw (Minneapolis: University of Minnesota Press, 1984), 22.

24. Kathleen Howard, ed., *The Metropolitan Museum of Art Guide* (New York: Metropolitan Museum of Art, 1983/1994), 265. A photograph in the *Guide* documents the museum's arrangement of *Perseus*.

25. Howard, *Metropolitan Museum of Art Guide*, 186.

26. Sigmund Freud, "Medusa's Head" (1922), in *Sexuality and the Psychology of Love* (New

York: Collier Books, 1968), 212–19; Laura Mulvey, "Fears, Fantasies and the Male Unconscious, *or* 'You Don't Know What Is Happening, Do You, Mr. Jones?'" (1973) and "Visual Pleasure and Narrative Cinema" (1975), in *Visual and Other Pleasures*, 6–13, 14–26.

27. Hélène Cixous, "The Laugh of the Medusa" (1975), in *New French Feminisms: An Anthology*, ed. Elaine Marks and Isabelle de Courtivron (New York: Schocken, 1981), 245–64.

28. Mulvey, "Fears, Fantasies," 13.

29. Nixon, *Fantastic Reality*, 66, 236. Nixon's thesis differs from mine insofar as, using Melanie Klein, she argues that Bourgeois, Jasper Johns, Yayoi Kusama, and Eva Hesse posed the phallus as, specifically, a part-object—a literal body part.

30. Crimp and Lawler, "Prominence Given, Authority Taken."

31. Nixon suggests that Bourgeois did something similar when, in 1982, she posed with her sculpture *Fillette* (1968) for a portrait produced by Robert Mapplethorpe for her retrospective exhibition at the Museum of Modern Art. *Fantastic Reality*, 71.

32. Jacques Lacan, "The mirror stage as formative of the function of the I, as revealed in psychoanalysis" (1949), in *Écrits*, trans. Alan Sheridan (New York, W. W. Norton, 1977), 1–7 (emphasis added).

33. Christian Metz, "Photography and Fetish," in *Overexposed: Essays on Contemporary Photography*, ed. Carol Squiers (New York: New Press, 1999), 217.

34. To the list of fetishes that Lawler highlights, we could add Perseus's feet in the winged sandals that Athena and Hermes lent him to aid in the conquest of Medusa. Recall that Freud speculated that the foot fetish originates in the fact that the woman's feet are the last thing the child sees before he catches sight of her genitals. The foot fetish represents the male subject's denial of the traumatic sight.

35. Lawler has used the phrase "prominence given, authority taken," and it is the title of an important interview she did with Douglas Crimp, cited above. The phrase can be read as a description of the way the museum positions the artists or, conversely, of Lawler's resistance to that positioning.

36. Georges Bataille, "Musée," in *Oeuvres Complètes*, 12 vols. (Paris : Gallimard: 1971–88), 1:239.

37. Freud, *Jokes*, 125.

38. The twenty artists are Vito Acconci, Carl Andre, Richard Artschwager, John Baldessari, Robert Barry, Joseph Beuys, Daniel Buren, Sandro Chia, Francesco Clemente, Enzo Cucchi, Gilbert & George, Dan Graham, Hans Haacke, Neil Jenney, Donald Judd, Anselm Kiefer, Joseph Kosuth, Sol Lewitt, Richard Long, Gordon Matta-Clark, Mario Merz, Sigmar Polke, Gerhard Richter, Ed Ruscha, Julian Schnabel, Cy Twombly, Andy Warhol, and Lawrence Weiner.

39. E-mail correspondence with the artist, April 22, 2005.

40. Lawler, in conversation with the author, February 26, 2005.

41. Stephen W. Kress, *Bird Life: A Guide to the Behavior and Biology of Birds* (New York: St. Martin's Press/Golden Guides, 1991), 80.

42. Crimp and Lawler, "Prominence Given, Authority Taken."

43. Crimp and Lawler, "Prominence Given, Authority Taken."

44. Peter Marler and Christopher Evans, "Birdcalls: Just Emotional Displays or Something More?" *Ibis* 138, no. 1 (1996): 26–33.

45. Fernando Nottebohn, "Hitting the Right Note," review of *Nature's Music: The Science of Birdsong*, ed. Peter Marler and Hans Slabbekoorn, *Nature* 435 (May 12, 2005), 146.

46. Michel Foucault, *Discipline and Punish: The Birth of the Prison*, trans. Alan Sheridan (New York: Random House, 1979), 200.

47. Crimp and Lawler, "Prominence Given, Authority Taken."

48. Douglas Crimp, "The Art of Exhibition," in *On the Museum's Ruins* (with photographs by Louise Lawler) (Cambridge: MIT Press, 1993), 238.

49. Lawler was not invited to participate in *Documenta 7*, but Jenny Holzer and the alternative gallery Fashion Moda asked her to contribute to their collaborative work: a trailer stationed at the entrance to the show, which would sell objects and souvenirs. For an account of the stationery that Lawler ended up selling at Fashion Moda's installation, see Crimp, "Art of Exhibition."

50. Lawler wanted to sell the record at Jenny Holzer and Fashion Moda's trailer, which was installed at the entrance to *Documenta 7*. See note 49.

51. Artist's brochure distributed at "Projects: Louise Lawler," *Enough* (Museum of Modern Art, New York, September 19–November 10, 1987).

52. A recent photographic work by Lawler repeats the warning, which has become especially urgent at a time when the Bush administration has banned media images of coffins returning from the Iraq War and has treated certain, particularly Arab, deaths as ungrievable. Lawler's image, depicting the detached wings of a classical statue of Nike, goddess of victory, is titled *Grieving Mothers*. [For a discussion of this work, see chapter 12 in this volume.]

6: Christopher D'Arcangelo's Elliptical Interruptions

Published here for the first time, this essay is a substantially modified version of a lecture first delivered in the Urban Field Speaker Series at Prefix Institute of Contemporary Art, Toronto, and in the Fred Weintz and Rosemary Weintz Art Lecture Series at Stanford University, Department of Art and Art History, both in 2019.

1. Godfre Leung, "Christopher D'Arcangelo's Occupations," *Toronto Review of Books*, June 20, 2012.

2. Martin Heidegger, "Building Dwelling Thinking," in *Poetry, Language, Thought*, trans. Albert Hofstadter (New York: Harper & Row, 1971), 145–61.

3. Peter Bürger, *Theory of the Avant-Garde*, trans. Michael Shaw (Minneapolis: University of Minnesota Press, 1984), 22.

4. Bürger, *Theory of the Avant-Garde*, 22.

5. Craig Owens, "From Work to Frame, or, Is There Life after 'The Death of the Author'?" (1987), in *Beyond Recognition: Representation, Power, and Culture* (Berkeley: University of California Press, 1992), 122–39.

6. Sigmund Freud, "Repression" (1915), in *The Standard Edition of the Complete Psychological Works of Sigmund Freud*, ed. James Strachey (London: Hogarth Press, 1953–74), 14:147 (emphasis in original).

7. Freud, "Repression," 14:151.

8. Sigmund Freud, "Civilization and Its Discontents" (1930), in *Standard Edition*, 21:59–148.

9. See Jacqueline Rose, "Femininity and Its Discontents," *Feminist Review* 14 (Summer 1983): 5–21.

10. W. H. Auden, "In Memory of Sigmund Freud (d. Sept. 1939)" (1939), in *W. H. Auden: Collected Poems*, ed. Edward Mendelson (New York: Random House, 1991), 273–76.

11. Sigmund Freud, *A General Introduction to Psychoanalysis* (New York: Simon and Schuster, 1935), 252.

12. Mary Boone Gallery, New York, 1991. [For a longer account of Kruger's installation, see chapter 4 in this volume.]

13. Henri Lefebvre, *The Survival of Capitalism*, trans. Frank Bryant (1973; New York: St. Martin's Press, 1976), 86.

14. Sigmund Freud, "Thoughts for the Times on War and Death" (1915), in *Standard Edition*, 14:279.

15. Paolo Virno, "Anthropology and Theory of Institutions," trans. Alberto Toscano, *Transversal*, May 2007, eipcp.net/transversal/0407/virno/en/print.

16. Virno, "Anthropology and Theory of Institutions."

17. Virno, "Anthropology and Theory of Institutions."

18. Christopher D'Arcangelo, Whitney Statement, 1975, series I, box 3, folder 24, Christopher D'Arcangelo Papers, Fales Archives and Special Collections, New York University, New York.

19. The New York exhibitions were *Anarchism without Adjectives: On the Work of Christopher D'Arcangelo (1975–79)*, curated by Dean Inkster and Sébastien Pluot, Artists Space, September 10–October 16, 2011, and *The Christopher D'Arcangelo Homage*, Algus Greenspon Gallery, October 11–29, 2011. *Anarchism without Adjectives* also appeared at several international venues: the CAC Brétigny-sur-Orge, France (July–August 2011); Centro Cultural Montehermoso, Vitoria-Gasteiz, Spain (December 2011–January 2012); Extra City Kunsthal, Antwerp, Belgium (September 2012); and the Leonard and Bina Ellen Art Gallery, Concordia University, Montreal, Canada (September 4–October 26, 2013).

20. D'Arcangelo, Whitney Statement, 1975.

21. Writing statements by Cathy Weiner, "The Whitney," 1975, series I, box 3, folder 25, Christopher D'Arcangelo Papers.

22. Jeffrey Deitch, "Christopher D'Arcangelo," in *Anarchism without Adjectives: On the Work of Christopher D'Arcangelo (1975–1979)*, 13.

23. Writing statements by Cathy Weiner, "The Modern," 1975, series I, box 3, folder 25, Christopher D'Arcangelo Papers.

24. Leung, "Christopher D'Arcangelo's Occupations."

25. Deitch, "Christopher D'Arcangelo," 16. Deitch notes that, at the same time, D'Arcangelo's body looked frightening.

26. Writing statements by Cathy Weiner, "The Guggenheim," 1975, series I, box 3, folder 25, Christopher D'Arcangelo Papers.

27. Norman Bryson, "The Logic of the Curatorial Gaze," in *Still, the Museum* (Rotterdam: Boijmans Van Beuningen Museum, 1997), 32.

28. Judith Butler, *The Force of Non-Violence* (London: Verso, 2020), 101.

29. Christopher D'Arcangelo, "When I State That I am an Anarchist" stencil, undated, oversize series I, box 9, Christopher D'Arcangelo Papers.

30. Christopher D'Arcangelo, letter, 1978, series I, box 3, folder 5, Christopher D'Arcangelo Papers.

31. Leah Pires, "'A [____] space is something that has been made room for . . .': Christopher D'Arcangelo, 1975–79," unpublished paper, 2013, 5–6.

32. Reiring in statement for Artists Space exhibition

33. Lawler recalls that she and D'Arcangelo had "spoken quite a bit before the show," indicating that D'Arcangelo may have influenced her design for the new logo.

34. George Woodcock, *Anarchism: A History of Libertarian Ideas and Movements* (2004; Toronto: University of Toronto Press, 2009), 91.

35. Pierre-Joseph Proudhon, *What Is Property?* (1840), ed. and trans. Donald R. Kelley and Bonnie G. Smith (Cambridge: Cambridge University Press, 1994), 209.

36. Copies of D'Arcangelo Notebook, undated entry, series II, box 4, folder 4, Christopher D'Arcangelo Papers.

37. Christopher D'Arcangelo, Artists Space Writings, 1978, series I, box 1, folder 4, Christopher D'Arcangelo Papers.

38. Copies of D'Arcangelo Notebook, December 27, 1975, entry, series II, box 4, folder 4, Christopher D'Arcangelo Papers.

39. Jacques Derrida, *Writing and Difference*, trans. Alan Bass (Chicago: University of Chicago Press, 1978), 295.

40. Derrida, *Writing and Difference*, 297.

41. Dean Inkster, "What's in a Name and Why It Matters," in *Anarchism without Adjectives: On the Work of Christopher D'Arcangelo (1975–1979)* (New York: Artists Space, 2011).

42. Fernando Tarrida del Mármol, "Anarchism without Adjectives," trans. Nestor McNabb, *La Révolte* 3, no. 51 (September 6–12, 1890), https://theanarchistlibrary.org/library/fernando-tarrida-del-marmol-anarchism-without-adjectives.

43. George R. Esenwein, *Anarchist Ideology and the Working-Class Movement in Spain, 1868–1898* (Berkeley: University of California Press, 1989), 136.

44. Derrida, *Writing and Difference*, 296.

45. The literary theorist Victor Li has written about Derrida's use of the two meanings of ellipsis in the context of explaining Derrida's preference for the term "mondialisation" rather than "globalization." The main title of my essay is borrowed from Li. See Li, "Elliptical Interruptions; or, Why Derrida Prefers Mondialisation to Globalization," *CR: The New Centennial Review* 7, no. 2 (Fall 2007): 141–54.

46. Jacques Derrida, *Rogues: Two Essays on Reason* (2003), trans. Pascale-Anne Brault and Michael Naas (Stanford, CA: Stanford University Press, 2005), 1.

47. Derrida, *Writing and Difference*, 296.

48. Derrida, *Rogues*, 1.

49. Derrida, *Rogues*, 86. Derrida introduced the term "democracy to come" in *Specters of Marx: The State of the Debt, the Work of Mourning, and the New International*, trans. Peggy Kamuf (New York: Routledge, 1994).

50. Oscar Wilde, "The Soul of Man under Socialism" (1891), in *In Praise of Disobedience* (London: Verso, 2018), 15

51. Derrida, *Rogues*, 87.

52. Claude Lefort, "The Question of Democracy" and "Human Rights and the Welfare

State," in *Democracy and Political Theory*, trans. David Macey (Minneapolis: University of Minnesota Press, 1988), 9–20, 21–44. For a more detailed account of Lefort's theory, see "Reasonable Urbanism," chapter 9 in this volume.

53. Christopher D'Arcangelo, Letter to *Libération*, 1978, series I, box 3, folder 5, Christopher D'Arcangelo Papers.

54. Jennifer Licht, *Eight Contemporary Artists* (New York: Museum of Modern Art, 1974), 21.

55. Licht, *Eight Contemporary Artists*, 21.

56. Daniel Buren, "Function of the Museum" (1970), in *Five Texts* (New York: John Weber Gallery; London: Jack Wendler Gallery, 1973), 60.

57. Lefebvre, *Survival of Capitalism*, 89.

58. Butler, *Force of Non-Violence*, 201.

59. Christopher D'Arcangelo, Open Museum Proposal, 1975, series I, box 3, folder 7, Christopher D'Arcangelo Papers.

60. Christopher D'Arcangelo, "LAICA as an Alternative to Museum," in *LAICA: Journal of the Los Angeles Museum of Contemporary Art*, no. 13 (1977), 31.

61. Christopher D'Arcangelo, text for Rosa Esman Gallery, 1978, series I, box 2, folder 1, Christopher D'Arcangelo Papers.

62. Christopher D'Arcangelo, "Look Out for What You Look At," 1978, series I, box 2, folder 1, Christopher D'Arcangelo Papers.

63. Guerilla Art Action Group, "A CALL FOR THE IMMEDIATE RESIGNATION OF ALL OF THE ROCKEFELLERS FROM THE BOARD OF TRUSTEES OF THE MUSEUM OF MODERN ART" (1969), in Alexander Alberro and Blake Stimson, eds., *Institutional Critique: An Anthology of Artists' Writings* (Cambridge, MA: MIT Press, 2009), 86.

7: The Art of Not Being Governed Quite So Much

Originally published in *Hans Haacke: For Real—Works 1959–2006* (Hamburg: Deichtorhallen Hamburg; Berlin: Akademie der Künste, 2007). Reprinted in Pelin Tan and Sezgin Boynik, eds., *Olasiliklar, Duruşlar, Müzakere* (Istanbul: Santralistanbul, 2007), in translation; *What Is the Political* (Bat Yam, Israel: Bat Yam Museum of Art, 2010); Marc James Léger, ed., *Culture and Contestation in the New Century* (Bristol, UK: Intellect, 2011); and *Hans Haacke*, ed. Rachel Churner, October Files 18 (Cambridge, MA: MIT Press, 2015).

1. Claude Lefort, "The Question of Democracy" and "Human Rights and the Welfare State," in *Democracy and Political Theory*, trans. David Macey (Minneapolis: University of Minnesota Press, 1988).

2. Etienne Balibar, "'Rights of Man' and 'Rights of the Citizen': The Modern Dialectic of Equality and Freedom," in *Masses, Classes, Ideas: Studies on Politics and Philosophy Before and After Marx* (New York: Routledge, 1994), 49.

3. Michel Foucault, "What Is Critique?" in *The Politics of Truth*, ed. Sylvère Lotringer, trans. Lysa Hochroth and Catherine Porter (Los Angeles: Semiotext(e), 1997), 28.

4. Press release for *Hans Haacke: State of the Union*, Paula Cooper Gallery, New York, November 5–December 23, 2005. Haacke's full statement reads, "Experience tells us that one should never leave politics to the politicians. Aside from the trouble this can get us into,

such abdication would also be in conflict with generally held notions of democracy. But it would also be dangerous for art. Shutting out the social world would reduce it to a self-consuming 'art for art's sake.'"

5. Pierre Bourdieu and Hans Haacke, *Free Exchange* (Stanford, CA: Stanford University Press, 1995), 52.

6. Walter Grasskamp, "Kassel New York Cologne Venice," in *Hans Haacke: Obra Social* (Fundació Tàpies de Barcelona, 1995), 17.

7. Judith Butler, "Commemoration and/or Critique? Catherine de Zegher and the Drawing Center," *Texte zur Kunst*, June 2006, 197–200.

8. Giorgio Agamben, *State of Exception*, trans. Kevin Attell (Chicago: University of Chicago Press, 2005).

9. Agamben, *State of Exception*, 2.

10. Agamben, *State of Exception*, 21.

11. Agamben, *State of Exception*, 3–4.

12. Douglas Feiden, "Violated . . . Again," *Daily News*, June 24, 2005.

13. Yates McKee, "Suspicious Packages," *October*, no. 11 (Summer 2006), 100.

14. Douglas Feiden and Joe Mahoney, "Zero Tolerance at WTC," *Daily News*, June 25, 2005, 7.

15. Hans Haacke, "Speaking Freely" transcript, recorded February 27, 2001, New York, First Amendment Center, www.firstamendmentcenter.org/about.aspx?id=12351. For accounts of De Zegher's resignation from the Drawing Center, see Butler, "Commemoration and/or Critique?" and Carol Armstrong, "Back to the Drawing Board," *Artforum*, Summer 2006, 133–34.

16. Bourdieu and Haacke, *Free Exchange*, 98.

17. T. W. Adorno, "Politics and Economics in the Interview Material," in Adorno et. al, *The Authoritarian Personality* (New York: W. W. Norton, 1950), 655.

18. Adorno, "Politics and Economics," 655.

19. To say that Haacke radically changed direction with the polls is not to say that they have no continuity with past works. For an excellent discussion of the continuities, see Walter Grasskamp, "Real Time: The Work of Hans Haacke," in *Hans Haacke* (London: Phaidon, 2004), 28–81. Haacke himself partially encouraged the notion of a "natural" progression of his work. For example, in a statement accompanying *Gallery-Goers' Birthplace and Residence Profile* (1969) he failed to differentiate among physical, biological, and social systems. In a 1972 text about the cancellation of his 1971 Guggenheim exhibition, he writes, "Having stepped from the perceptually oriented and culturally controlled imagery of the visual arts to the presentation or interference in physical and/or biological systems in real time, the need arose to complete the areas of my activities with work also in the sociopolitical field. . . ." In the next sentence, however, Haacke counters this description of his development when he attributes the new direction in his work in 1969 to "the general political awakening that followed the years of absolute apathy after World War Two." He goes on to differentiate social from natural systems. "Provisorische Bemerkungen zur Absage meiner Ausstellung im Guggenheim Museum, New York," in *Hans Haacke: Werkmonographie*, ed. Edward Fry (Cologne: Verlag M. Dumont Schauberg, 1972), 64.

20. Grasskamp, "Real Time," 33.

21. Theodor Adorno, *Negative Dialectics*, trans. E. B. Ashton (New York: Continuum, 1999), 365; originally published as *Negative Dialektik* (Frankfurt am Main: Suhrkamp Verlag, 1966).

22. It is also possible to think of *Recording of Climate in Art Exhibition* of 1969–70 [figure 7.1] as Haacke's first work of institutional critique. Grasskamp ranks it "among the artist's first explicitly institution-related pieces" ("Real Time," 45). Likewise, the various versions of *News* (1969–70), in which teletype machines printed out messages transmitted by different news services during the Vietnam War, certainly attempted to open up the art institution to social and political events and could lay claim to the title of Haacke's first institution-critical work. A version of *News* was installed at the Jewish Museum's *Software* show. Another version was installed at Haacke's exhibition *State of the Union*, held at Paula Cooper Gallery in New York City in 2005 during the ongoing Iraq War.

23. Bourdieu and Haacke, *Free Exchange*, 97

24. Rosalind E. Krauss, *Passages in Modern Sculpture* (Cambridge, MA: MIT Press, 1977), 73.

25. For an account of Haacke's Guggenheim exhibition and of his two real-estate pieces, which were also responsible for the cancellation, see my "Property Values: Hans Haacke, Real Estate, and the Museum," in *Evictions: Art and Spatial Politics* (Cambridge, MA: MIT Press, 1996), 159–92.

26. Three other exhibitions are closely related to the polls but did not themselves take the form of polls. In 1970, at Galerie Paul Maenz in Cologne, Haacke displayed photographs of 732 building facades in Manhattan. The buildings were those that had been designated as residences by participants in *Gallery-Goers' Birthplace and Residence Profile*. In 1976 and 1977, at the Frankfurter Kunstverein and the Badischer Kunstverein in Karlsruhe, Haacke exhibited the answers to overlapping questions in the three German polls conducted in Krefeld, Kassel, and Hanover.

27. Hans Haacke, "The Constituency," first published as 'Les adhérents," in *Art actuel: Skira annuel 77*, no. 3 (Geneva, 1977); English translation, modified, in *Hans Haacke: Volume 1* (Oxford: Museum of Contemporary Art; Amsterdam: Stedelijk Van Abbemuseum, Eindhoven, 1979), 78–81.

28. "The concept 'art as an institution' . . . refers to the productive and distributive apparatus and also to ideas about art that prevail at a given time and that determine the reception of works." Peter Bürger, *Theory of the Avant-Garde*, trans. Michael Shaw (Minneapolis: University of Minnesota Press, 1984), 22.

29. Michael Fried, "Art and Objecthood," in *Minimal Art: A Critical Anthology*, ed. Gregory Battcock (New York: E. P Dutton & Co., 1968), 116–47.

30. Rosalyn Deutsche, "Breaking Ground: Barbara Kruger's Spatial Practice," in *Barbara Kruger, Thinking of You* (Los Angeles: Museum of Contemporary Art; Cambridge, MA: MIT Press, 1999), 78–79. [Reprinted in this volume.]

31. See, for instance, Benjamin Buchloh, "Hans Haacke: The Entwinement of Myth and Enlightenment," in *Hans Haacke: Obra Social*, 50.

32. Pierre Bourdieu, *Distinction: A Social Critique of the Judgement of Taste*, trans. Richard Nice (Cambridge, MA: Harvard University Press, 1984), 461; originally published as *La Distinction: Critique social du jugement* (Paris : Les Éditions de Minuit, 1979).

33. Bourdieu, *Distinction*, 460.

34. For Haacke's conclusions, see "The Constituency."

35. Howard S. Becker and John Walton, "Social Science and the Work of Hans Haacke," in *Hans Haacke: Framing and Being Framed: 7 Works 1970–75* (Halifax: Press of the Nova Scotia College of Art and Design; New York: New York University Press, 1975), 145.

36. Becker and Walton, "Social Science," 151

37. For a discussion of the real-estate pieces, see the reference in note 25.

38. Bertolt Brecht, "Writing the Truth: Five Difficulties," in *Art and Action: Tenth Anniversary Issue (1938–1948), A Book of Literature, the Arts, and Civil Liberties,* ed. Dorothy Norman (New York: Twice a Year Press, 1948), 122. Haacke cites this essay in "The Constituency," which is pervaded by Brecht's thinking. For instance, in the last line of "The Constituency," Haacke writes that the ability to turn the resources of "the consciousness industry" against the dominant ideology depends on "a cunning involvement" in the industry's contradictions. Brecht, too, stresses the contradictions that appear in every condition, and cunning is one of his remedies for overcoming difficulties in spreading the truth when it is being suppressed or concealed.

39. Brecht, "Writing the Truth," 122.

40. Brecht, "Writing the Truth," 127.

41. Foucault, "What Is Critique?" 32.

42. Michael Warner, *Publics and Counterpublics* (New York: Zone Books, 2002), 67.

43. Warner, *Publics and Counterpublics,* 87–89.

44. Warner, *Publics and Counterpublics,* 90 (emphasis added).

45. E-mail correspondence with the author, July 16, 2005.

46. Hans Haacke, "The Agent" (1977), in *Hans Haacke* (London: Phaidon, 2004), 106.

47. Emily Genauer, "Some Explanations of 'Information,'" *New York Post,* July 11, 1970.

48. Haacke, "Provisorische Bemerkungen," 65.

49. Michel Crozier, Samuel P. Huntington, and Joji Watanuki, *The Crisis of Democracy: Report on the Governability of Democracies to the Trilateral Commission* (New York: New York University Press, 1975). For an analysis of the report, see Alan Wolfe, "Capitalism Shows Its Face: Giving Up on Democracy," in *Trilateralism: The Trilateral Commission and Elite Planning for World Management,* ed. Holly Sklar (Boston: South End Press, 1980), 295–307; first published in *The Nation,* November 29, 1975.

50. Buchloh, "Hans Haacke," 55.

51. Buchloh, "Hans Haacke," 52.

52. Buchloh, "Hans Haacke," 55–56.

53. Jürgen Habermas, *The Structural Transformation of the Public Sphere: An Inquiry into a Category of Bourgeois Society,* trans. Thomas Burger (Cambridge, MA: MIT Press, 1989); originally published as *Strukturwandel der Öffentlicheit* (Darmstadt and Neuwied: Hermann Luchterhand Verlag, 1962).

54. Oskar Negt and Alexander Kluge, *Public Sphere and Experience: Toward an Analysis of the Bourgeois and Proletarian Public Sphere,* trans. Peter Labanyi, Jamie Owen Daniel, and Assenka Oksiloff (Minneapolis: University of Minnesota Press, 1993), 10; originally published as *Öffentlichheit und Erfahrung: Zur Organisationsanalyse von bürgerlicher und proletarischer Öffentlichkeit* (Frankfurt am Main: Suhrkamp Verlag, 1972).

55. Negt and Kluge, *Public Sphere and Experience*, 10.

56. Negt and Kluge, *Public Sphere and Experience*, 3.

57. Negt and Kluge, *Public Sphere and Experience*, 276.

58. Friedrich Nietzsche, *The Use and Abuse of History*, trans. Adrian Collins (1874; New York: Macmillan/Library of Liberal Arts, 1949), 14.

59. Kluge and Negt, *Public Sphere and Experience*, 276.

60. Buchloh, "Hans Haacke," 50.

61. Brecht, "Writing the Truth," 127.

62. Jacques Rancière, *Disagreement: Politics and Philosophy*, trans. Julie Rose (Minneapolis: University of Minnesota Press, 1999), 38–39.

8: Art from Guantánamo Bay

Originally published without footnotes in *Artforum*, September 2020, as "Staking Claim."

1. On the state of exception, see Giorgio Agamben, *State of Exception*, trans. Kevin Attell (Chicago: University of Chicago Press, 2005).

2. "Guantánamo Bay: 14 Years of Injustice," Amnesty International UK/Issues, January 11, 2016, https://amnesty.org.uk/guantanamo-bay-human-rights.

3. "President Obama Signs Indefinite Detention Bill into Law," American Civil Liberties Union, December 31, 2011, https://www.aclu.org/press-releases/president-obama-signs-indefinite-detention-bill-law.

4. [By July 20, 2021 the number had been reduced to thirty-nine.]

5. Mark Danner, "Guantánamo Diary" (review of *Guantánamo Diary*, by Mohamedour Ould Slahi), *New York Times*, January 20, 2015.

6. *Ode to the Sea: Art from Guantánamo Bay*, October 2, 2017–January 26, 2018, President's Gallery, John Jay College of Criminal Justice, New York.

7. Erin Thompson, "Art Censorship at Guantánamo Bay," *New York Times*, November 27, 2017, https://www.nytimes.com/2017/11/27/opinion/guantanamo-art-prisoners.html.

8. Thompson, "Art Censorship."

9. Jacey Fortin, "Who Owns Guantánamo Art? Not Prisoners, U.S. Says," *New York Times*, November 28, 2017, C7.

10. "Art from Guantánamo," https://indd.adobe.com/view/567dd3ed-81fb-43b9-83c4-869107e21d52.

11. "Interviews: Artmaking at Guantánamo," in "Art from Guantánamo," 27.

12. Paige Laino, "Art Therapy," in "Art from Guantánamo," 23.

13. Mansoor Adayfi, "In Our Prison on the Sea," in "Art from Guantánamo," 4.

14. Adayfi, "In Our Prison on the Sea," 4.

15. "Art from Guantánamo," 40.

16. "Art from Guantánamo," 40.

17. Ibraham Al-Rabaish, "Ode to the Sea," in "Art from Guantánamo," 7.

18. "Art from Guantánamo," 39.

19. Theodor W. Adorno, *Negative Dialectics* (New York: Continuum, 1999), 362; originally published as *Negative Dialektik* (Frankfurt am Main: Suhrkamp Verlag, 1966).

20. "Art from Guantánamo," 9.

21. "Art from Guantánamo," 4.

22. "Art from Guantánamo," 34.

23. "Art from Guantánamo," 24.

24. Hannah Arendt, *The Origins of Totalitarianism* (San Diego: Harcourt Brace & Company, 1948), 296–97.

25. See Claude Lefort, "The Question of Democracy" and "Human Rights and the Welfare State," in *Democracy and Political Theory* (Minneapolis: University of Minnesota Press, 1988), 9–20, 21–44.

26. Thomas Keenan, "Or are we human beings?" in *Superhumanity*, a project by e-flux Architecture at the 3rd Istanbul Design Biennial, produced in cooperation with the Istanbul Design Biennial, the National Museum of Modern and Contemporary Art, Korea, the Govett-Brewster Art Gallery, New Zealand, and the Ernst Schering Foundation. https://www.e-flux.com/architecture/superhumanity/68719/or-are-we-human-beings/.

27. Romain Gary, *The Kites*, quoted in Adam Gopnik, "The Made-Up Man," *New Yorker*, January 1, 2018. [This sentence is slightly altered from the original version of this essay.]

28. Lynn Hunt, *Inventing Human Rights: A History* (New York: W. W. Norton, 2007), 146–75.

29. Hunt, *Inventing Human Rights*, 151.

30. Morgan Jerkins, "Not Just 'Human.' Black," *New York Times*, January 28, 2018, Sunday Review, 9.

31. Jerkins, "Not Just 'Human,'" 9.

32. Bruce Robbins, *The Beneficiary* (Durham, NC: Duke University Press, 2017), 49.

33. Robbins, *Beneficiary*, 153–54.

9: Reasonable Urbanism

Originally published, without section headings, in *Giving Ground: The Politics of Propinquity*, ed. Joan Copjec and Michael Sorkin (London: Verso, 1999), 175–206. Translated and reprinted in Matthias Hasse, Marc Siegel, and Michaela Wünsch, eds., *Outside: Die Politik queerer Raume* (Berlin: b_books Verlag, 2005).

1. Neil Bartlett, *Ready to Catch Him Should He Fall* (New York: Dutton, 1990).

2. Walt Whitman, "City of Orgies" and "To a Stranger," in *The Complete Poems*, ed. Francis Murphy (London: Penguin, 1975), 158–60.

3. Guillaume Apollinaire, "Voyage à Paris," in *The Selected Writings of Guillaume Apollinaire* (New York: New Directions, 1971), 200.

4. Emmanuel Levinas, "The Rights of Man and the Rights of the Other," in *Outside the Subject*, trans. Michael B. Smith (Stanford, CA: Stanford University Press, 1994), 124.

5. Bartlett, *Ready to Catch Him*, 11 (emphasis and ellipsis in original). Subsequent references to this book appear in parentheses in the text.

6. Mikhail Bakhtin, "Epic and Novel: Toward a Methodology for the Study of the Novel," in *The Dialogic Imagination*, trans. Caryl Emerson and Michael Holquist (Austin: University of Texas Press, 1981), 22.

7. Bakhtin, "Epic and Novel," 22.

8. Bakhtin, "Epic and Novel," 28.

9. Bakhtin, "Epic and Novel," 27.

10. J. Hillis Miller, "Face to Face: Faces, Places, and Ethics in Plato," in *Topographies* (Stanford, CA: Stanford University Press, 1995), 58. Miller is discussing Plato's *Protagaras*.

11. Oscar Wilde, "The Decay of Lying" (1889), in *De Profundis and Other Writings* (London: Penguin, 1954). In this dialogue, which is filled with Wilde's characteristic paradoxes and serious wordplay, the character Vivian says, "There is such a thing as robbing a story of its reality by trying to make it too true." For Richard Ellmann, "The Decay of Lying" defines art's function as making "a raid on predictability." Ellmann, *Oscar Wilde* (New York: Random House, 1984), 304.

12. For examples of the real-unreal distinction in recent discourse about geography, see Gillian Rose, "As If the Mirrors Had Bled: Masculine Dwelling, Masculinist Theory and Feminist Masquerade," in *Bodyspace: Destabilizing Geographies of Gender and Sexuality*, ed. Nancy Duncan (London: Routledge, 1996), 56–74.

13. Ernesto Laclau and Chantal Mouffe, trans. Winston Moore and Paul Cammack (London: Verso, 1985).

14. See, for example, Doreen Massey, "Flexible Sexism," *Environment and Planning D: Society and Space* 9 (1991): 31–57; Meaghan Morris, "The Man in the Mirror: David Harvey's 'Condition of Postmodernity,'" *Theory, Culture and Society* 9 (1992): 253–79; Mark Wigley, "Theoretical Slippage: The Architecture of the Fetish," in *Fetish*, ed. Sarah Whiting et al. (New York: Princeton Architectural Press, 1992), 88–129, and "Lost and Found," in *You Are Here: Architecture and Information Flows*, ed. Laura Kurgan and Xavier Costa (Museu d'art Contemporani de Barcelona, 1995), 171–85; Gillian Rose, *Feminism and Geography: The Limits of Geographical Knowledge* (Minneapolis: University of Minnesota Press, 1993); Derek Gregory, *Geographical Imaginations* (Oxford: Blackwell, 1994); Rosalyn Deutsche, "Men in Space," "Boys Town," and Chinatown, Part Four? What Jake Forgets about Downtown," in *Evictions: Art and Spatial Politics* (Cambridge, MA: MIT Press, 1996), 195–253; and Victor Burgin, *In/Different Spaces: Place and Memory in Visual Culture* (Berkeley: University of California Press, 1996).

15. Neil Smith makes this slippage in "Contours of a Spatialized Politics: Homeless Vehicles and the Production of Geographical Scale," *Social Test* 33 (1992): 54–81. For a critique of the division between real and unreal space that sees it as an attempt to maintain a hierarchical sexual division, see Rose, "As If the Mirrors Had Bled."

16. Bakhtin, "Epic and Novel," 33.

17. Cathy Caruth, "Introduction: The Insistence of Reference," in *Critical Encounters: Reference and Responsibility in Deconstructive Writing*, ed. Caruth and Deborah Esch (New Brunswick, NJ: Rutgers University Press, 1995), 1.

18. Henri Lefebvre, *The Production of Space*, trans. Donald Nicholson-Smith (Oxford: Blackwell, 1991), 229; originally published as *La production de l'espace* (Paris: Anthropos, 1974). For a psychoanalytically informed discussion of the ways in which urban and cultural theorists have formulated the relationship between social and psychical space, see Burgin, introduction to *In/Different Spaces* (Berkeley: University of California Press, 1996) 1–36.

19. Lefebvre, *Production of Space*, 38–39. Lefebvre's social space contains another moment, which he calls "representations of space," referring to the conceptual abstractions of technocratic planners that dominate space.

20. Roland Barthes, "Rhetoric of the Image," in *Image, Music, Text*, trans Stephen Heath (New York: Hill & Wang, 1977), 44.

21. Michel de Certeau, "Spatial Stories," in *The Practice of Everyday Life*, trans. Steven Rendell (Berkeley: University of California Press, 1984), 117.

22. Bakhtin, "Epic and Novel," 30 (emphasis added).

23. Bakhtin, "Epic and Novel," 37.

24. Caruth, "Introduction," 6.

25. Miller, "Face to Face," 6.

26. Lynne Tillman, "That's How Strong His Love Is," in *The Broad Picture: Essays* (London: Serpent's Tail, 1997), 105.

27. Ellmann, introduction to *Oscar Wilde*, xv.

28. Ellmann, introduction to *Oscar Wilde*, xvi.

29. Kenneth Gross, *The Dream of the Moving Statue* (Ithaca, NY: Cornell University Press, 1992), 150.

30. Miller, "Face to Face," 74.

31. Miller, "Face to Face," 72.

32. Miller, "Face to Face," 71.

33. Miller, "Face to Face," 72.

34. Miller, "Face to Face," 75.

35. Miller, "Face to Face," 74.

36. Miller, "Face to Face," 74–75.

37. Walter Benjamin, "Theses on the Philosophy of History," in *Illuminations*, ed. Hannah Arendt, trans. Harry Zohn (New York: Schocken, 1969) 255.

38. Benjamin, "Theses on the Philosophy of History," 257.

39. Benjamin, "Theses on the Philosophy of History," 255.

40. J. Hillis Miller, *The Ethics of Reading: Kant, de Man, Eliot, Trollope, James, and Benjamin* (New York: Columbia University Press, 1987).

41. Levinas, "Rights of Man," 124.

42. Wilde, "The Critic as Artist" (1891), in *The Artist as Critic: Critical Writings of Oscar Wilde*, ed. Richard Ellmann (Chicago: University of Chicago Press, 1968), 360.

43. Claude Lefort, "The Question of Democracy," in *Democracy and Political Theory*, 19.

44. It is a very common error for critics to conclude that poststructuralist ideas about uncertainty and democracy preclude the possibility of decision-making rather than obligate us to decide.

45. Levinas, "Rights of Man," 124.

46. Levinas, "Rights of Man," 124.

47. Levinas, "Rights of Man," 125

48. Julia Kristeva, *Strangers to Ourselves*, trans. Leon S. Roudiez (New York: Columbia University Press, 1991), 103.

49. Tillman, "That's How Strong His Love Is," 105.

50. Cicero, *Tusculan Disputations*, quoted in Jacob Howland, *The Republic: The Odyssey of Philosophy*, Twayne's Masterwork Studies No. 122 (New York: Twayne Publishers, 1993), 10.

51. Simon Watney, *Policing Desire: Pornography, AIDS and the Media* (Minneapolis: University of Minnesota Press, 1987), 17.

52. Watney, *Policing Desire*, 98.

53. Mikhail Bakhtin, *Rabelais and His World*, trans. Hélène Iswolsky (Bloomington: Indiana University Press, 1984), 6; originally published as *Tvorchestvo Fransua Rable* (Moscow: Khudozhestvennia literatura, 1965).

54. Henry Urbach, "Spatial Rubbing: The Zone," *Sites* 25 (1993): 95.

55. Oscar Wilde, "The Happy Prince" (1888), in *Complete Fairy Tales of Oscar Wilde* (New York: Signet Classic, 1990), 9–22. I would like to thank Jeff Nunokawa for bringing this story to my attention.

56. Gross, *Dream of the Moving Statue*, 142.

57. Mother's play, like the novel as a whole, can be read in part as a reworking of Wilde's life, which here ends happily. For instance, The Son's love for The Lover overrides his obedience to The Father, unlike that of Lord Alfred Douglas, to whom Wilde wrote from prison, "Your hatred of your father was of such stature that it entirely outstripped, overthrew, and overshadowed your love of me." Wilde, "De Profundis," in *De Profundis and Other Writings* (London: Penguin, 1954), 126. There is another Father in *Ready to Catch Him Should He Fall*—Boy's father, one of the book's major characters. He is a fantastic character, both Boy's "real" father and, as Bartlett puts it, "the patriarchal father who forbade me to be who I am." Bartlett, quoted in Lynne Tillman, "That's How Strong His Love Is," 110. He comes to live with Boy and O, nearly destroys their relationship, and dies cradled in Boy's lap.

58. Gross, *Dream of the Moving Statue*, 147.

59. Gross, *Dream of the Moving Statue*, 142.

60. Gross, *Dream of the Moving Statue*, 198.

61. Miller, "Face to Face," 73.

62. Raymond Ledrut, "Speech and the Silence of the City," in *The City and the Sign: An Introduction to Urban Semiotics*, ed. Mt. Gottdeiner and Alexandros Ph. Lagopoulos (New York: Columbia University Press, 1986), 121.

63. Ledrut, "Speech," 122.

64. Ledrut, "Speech," 120.

65. Mary McCarthy, *The Stones of Florence* (New York: Harcourt Brace Jovanovich, 1963); quoted in Gross, *Dream of the Moving Statue*, 175.

66. Catulle Mendès, *Les 73 Journées de la Commune* (Paris: E. Lachaud, 1871), 1149–50; quoted in Kristin Ross, *The Emergence of Social Space and the Paris Commune* (Minneapolis: University of Minnesota Press, 1988), 5.

67. Certeau, "Spatial Stories," 130.

68. Certeau, "Spatial Stories," 130.

69. Sigmund Freud, "The Uncanny," in *Writings on Art and Literature* (Stanford, CA: Stanford University Press, 1997), 223.

70. Kristeva, *Strangers to Ourselves*, 182.

71. Freud, "The Uncanny," 195.

72. Kristeva writes, "It is through unraveling transference—the major dynamics of otherness, of love/hatred for the other, of the foreign component of our psyche—that, on the basis of the other, I become reconciled with my own otherness-foreignness. Psychoanalysis is then experienced as a journey into the strangeness of the other and of oneself, toward an ethic of respect for the irreconcilable." Kristeva, *Strangers to Ourselves*, 182.

73. Kristeva, *Strangers to Ourselves*, 183.

74. Freud, "The Uncanny," 227.

75. Kristeva, *Strangers to Ourselves*, 192.

76. Kristeva, *Strangers to Ourselves*, 1 (emphasis added).

77. Ellmann, *Oscar Wilde*, 444.

78. Claude Lefort, "Human Rights and the Welfare State," in *Democracy and Political Theory*, 31.

79. Gross, *Dream of the Moving Statue*, 198.

80. Alois Riegl, "The Modern Cult of Monuments: Its Character and Its Origins," *Oppositions*, no. 25 (Fall 1982), 21–51. In this 1903 essay, Riegl uses the term "unintentional monument" to designate the work of art or architecture that becomes a landmark of history only after its creation and is thus assigned a new role in new circumstances. Riegl distinguishes the unintentional monument from the "intentional monument," which is built from the start as a permanent commemoration of a historic event of person. My use of "unintentional" differs from that of Riegl, since I am suggesting that both kinds of monuments are in some sense unintentional. But this idea is also implicit in Riegl's argument, which, as Kurt Forster points out, fundamentally undermines the belief that architectural monuments possess stable meanings. Forster, "Monument/Memory and the Mortality of Architecture," *Oppositions*, no. 25 (Fall 1982), 2–19.

81. Bakhtin, *Rabelais and His World*, 39–41.

82. Bartlett, quoted in Tillman, "That's How Strong His Love Is," 111.

83. Benjamin, "Theses on the Philosophy of History," 257.

84. Benjamin, "Theses on the Philosophy of History," 257.

85. Justice Sir Alfred Wills, quoted in Ellmann, *Oscar Wilde*, 477.

86. Patricia J. Williams, *The Alchemy of Race and Rights: Diary of a Law Professor* (Cambridge, MA: Harvard University Press, 1991), 165.

87. Hannah Arendt, *The Origins of Totalitarianism* (New York: Harcourt Brace & Company, 1948), 296.

88. Lefort, "Human Rights and the Welfare State."

89. Lefort, "Human Rights and the Welfare State," 261–62.

90. Etienne Balibar, "'Rights of Man' and 'Rights of the Citizen:' The Modern Dialectic of Equality and Freedom," in *Masses, Classes, Ideas: Studies on Politics and Philosophy before and after Marx* (New York: Routledge, 1994), 49.

91. Etienne Balibar, "What Is a Politics of the Rights of Man?" in *Masses, Classes, Ideas*, 211-12.

92. Balibar, "What Is a Politics of the Rights of Man?," 211.

93. Lauren Berlant, "Live Sex Acts (Parental Advisory: Explicit Material," in *The Queen of American Goes to Washington City: Essays on Sex and Citizenship* (Durham, NC: Duke University Press, 1997), 60.

94. For accounts of contemporary debates over the meaning of the "public sphere," see Bruce Robbins, "Introduction: The Public as Phantom," in *The Phantom Public Sphere*, ed. Robbins, Social Text Series on Cultural Politics 5 (Minneapolis: University of Minnesota Press, 1993), vii–xxvi; Nancy Fraser, "Rethinking the Public Sphere: A Contribution to the Critique of Actually Existing Democracy," in *Habermas and the Public Sphere*, ed. Craig Cal

houn (Cambridge, MA: MIT Press, 1992), 109–42; Thomas Keenan, "Windows: Of Vulnerability," in Robbins, *Phantom Public Sphere*, 121–41; Rosalyn Deutsche, "Agoraphobia," in *Evictions*, 269–327.

95. Etienne Balibar draws a distinction between extensive and intensive universalism. "In the extensional, denotative sense, the universal is what addresses all people . . . in order to encompass them in a single whole and arrange them under the same law," which in this way *neutralizes* or *relativizes* their differences. . . . But more profoundly, the concept of the universal has an intensional, connotative significance: this is what *equality* (and equal freedom, equal dignity) proposes in symbolic and practical terms for all people, regardless of their differences. This intensive universality can only result from shared interests and practices." Balibar, "Critical Reflections," *Artforum* 36, no. 3 (November 1997): 101.

96. In "'Rights of Man' and 'Rights of the Citizen,'" Balibar fuses the two in his term "equaliberty," which expresses the idea that freedom and equality are one and the same.

97. Jacqueline Rose makes a similar point about the theory/social reality dichotomy in relation to ideas about psychoanalytic theory and sexual violence. She argues that writers such as Wilhelm Reich and Jeffrey Masson draw a rigid opposition between inside and outside, which corresponds to a second opposition between the psychic and the social. These writers locate violence strictly in the external world of social reality and suggest that psychoanalysis ignores this reality. For example, Masson says that Freud ignored sexual violence against women and so handed women over to that violence. Rose claims that these writers are arguing that the theory itself causes death and violence and, further, that the inside-outside, psychic-social oppositions they draw support a third opposition—between psychoanalytic theory and politics. This conceptual framework, which Rose criticizes, resembles that used by urban scholars who, as I indicate above, suggest that psychoanalytic, poststructuralist, or various other theories, which they group under the rubric "postmodernism," ignore the violence that produces and takes place in real social space. See Rose, "Where Does the Misery Come From? Psychoanalysis, Feminism, and the Event," in *Feminism and Psychoanalysis*, ed. Richard Feldstein and Judith Roof (Ithaca, NY: Cornell University Press, 1989), 25–39.

98. Henri Lefebvre, "The Right to the City," in *Writings on Cities*, ed. Eleanor Kofman and Elizabeth Lebas (London: Blackwell, 1996), 195; originally published as *Le droit à la ville* (Paris: Anthropos, 1968).

99. Lefebvre, "Right to the City," 179.

100. Lefebvre, "Right to the City," 180.

101. Lefebvre, "Right to the City," 100.

102. For a typical statement of this position, see Fred Siegel, *The Future Once Happened Here: New York, D.C., L.A., and the Fate of American's Big Cities* (New York: Free Press, 1997), especially chap. 14, "The Moral Deregulation of Public Space.

103. See, for instance, "New York Views," *New York: The City Journal* 1, no. 1 (Autumn 1990): 2–3, and *The City Journal* 2, no. 2 special issue, "The Quality of Urban Life," (Spring 1992). In conjunction with the latter issue, the Manhattan Institute sponsored a conference on the quality of life, where "Giuliani could be found seated in the audience . . . scribbling notes." Janny Scott, "Turning Intellect into Influence: Promoting Its Ideas, the Manhattan Institute Has Nudged New York Rightward," *New York Times*, May 12, 1997, B3. Note that by 1992, the journal had dropped "New York" from its title, perhaps reflecting its nationwide

influence: "Despite its focus on New York, the Manhattan Institute has had its greatest influence in other cities." Tom Redburn, "Conservative Thinkers Are Insiders," *New York Times*, December 31, 1993, B3.

104. Quoted in David Bahr, "As Piers Close, Gay Protesters See a Paradise Lost," *New York Times*, September 14, 1997, section 13, 6.

105. See Allan Bérubé, "A Century of Sex Panics," in *Sex Panic!* (brochure, 1997), 4–8.

106. Gabriel Rotello, *Sexual Ecology: AIDS and the Destiny of Gay Men* (New York: Dutton, 1997).

107. "A Declaration of Sexual Rights," statement by the National Sex Panic Summit, November 13, 1997.

108. Walt Odets, letter to the editor about *Sexual Ecology*, *New York Times Book Review*, June 22, 1997, 4.

109. Gabriel Rotello, "An Open Letter to Sex Panic," *Lesbian and Gay New York*, August 4, 1997, 4.

110. Michael Warner, "Zones of Privacy," unpublished paper (1995), 22. Warner's paper was written prior to the City Council's passage of the zoning amendment and the court challenges it has since undergone, but the questions Warner raises remain highly relevant to debates about the meaning of the urban. [The paper was later published with the title "Zoning Out Sex," in Warner, *The Trouble with Normal: Sex, Politics, and the Ethics of Queer Life* (Cambridge, MA: Harvard University Press, 1999), 149–93.]

111. Lefebvre, "Writings on Cities,"195.

112. Warner, "Zones of Privacy," 14.

113. Warner, "Zones of Privacy," 24.

114. Jane Jacobs, *The Death and Life of Great American Cities* (New York: Vintage, 1961.

115. Lewis Mumford, "Home Remedies for Urban Cancer" (1962), in *The Lewis Mumford Reader* (Athens: University of Georgia Press, 1995), 191.

116. Certeau, *Practice of Everyday Life*, 103.

117. Certeau, *Practice of Everyday Life*, 125. It is worth noting in our context that for Certeau the poetics of walking makes urbanism inseparable from eroticism. He argues that spatial practice is a way of undoing the dominant spatial order and of moving into something different. It originates in the child's differentiation from the mother's body and repeats the move toward the other initiated by this childhood experience.

118. Oscar Wilde, quoted in Ellmann, *Oscar Wilde*, 495.

10: Un-War

Originally published in *October*, no. 147 (Winter 2014), 3–19.

1. Kurt Vonnegut, *Slaughterhouse-Five, or The Children's Crusade: A Duty-Dance with Death* (1969; New York: Dial Press, 2009), 5.

2. Krzysztof Wodiczko, "Arc de Triomphe: World Institute for the Abolition of War," *Harvard Design Magazine* 33 (Fall/Winter 2010–11): 126–35.

3. Friedrich Nietzsche, *The Use and Abuse of History*, trans. Adrian Collins (1874; London: Macmillan, 1957). Walter Benjamin, "Theses on the Philosophy of History" (1940), in *Illuminations*, trans. Harry Zohn (New York: Schocken, 1969).

4. For an interpretation of all of Wodiczko's works as projections, see my "Uneven De-

velopment: Public Art in New York City," in *Evictions: Art and Spatial Politics* (Cambridge, MA: MIT Press, 1996), 346n119, and "Architecture of the Evicted," *Strategies* 3 (1990): 159–83, reprinted in *Theory in Contemporary Art since 1985*, ed. Zoya Kocur and Simon Leung (Oxford: Blackwell, 2005), 150–65.

5. For another investigation of contemporary war culture, see John W. Dower, *Cultures of War: Pearl Harbor, Hiroshima, 9-11, Iraq* (New York: W. W. Norton, 2010).

6. Krzysztof Wodiczko, *Abolition of War* (London: Black Dog, 2012), 11.

7. Virginia Woolf, *Three Guineas* (New York: Harcourt, Brace & World, 1938), 19.

8. Wodiczko, *Abolition of War*, 9.

9. Wodiczko, *Abolition of War*, 13.

10. William James, "The Moral Equivalent of War," http://www.constitution.org/wj/meow.htm (accessed January 26, 2014). This essay, first published in 1910, was based on a speech delivered at Stanford University in 1906. For more on the essay, see note 48. I am grateful to Gregg Bordowitz for a long-ago conversation in which he introduced me to James's text.

11. Wodiczko, *Abolition of War*, 13.

12. Wodiczko, *Abolition of War*, 73–83.

13. Wodiczko, *Abolition of War*, 82.

14. Gertrude Stein, *Wars I Have Seen* (1945; London: Brilliance, 1984), 9. Mignon Nixon discusses Stein's book in "War Inside/War Outside: Feminist Critiques and the Politics of Psychoanalysis," *Texte zur Kunst* 17 (December 2007): 134–38.

15. Wodiczko, *Abolition of War*, 53.

16. Jacqueline Rose, "Where Does the Misery Come From? Psychoanalysis, Feminism, and the Event," in *Feminism and Psychoanalysis*, ed. Richard Feldstein and Judith Roof (Ithaca, NY: Cornell University Press, 1989), 25–39.

17. Rose, "Where Does the Misery Come From?" 25

18. Rose, "Where Does the Misery Come From?" 29.

19. Rose, "Where Does the Misery Come From?" 30–31. Rose briefly discusses the work of Janine Chassequet-Smirgel and Bela Brunberger as an example of the psychic-reductionist approach. See Chassequet-Smirgel and Brunberger, *Freud or Reich? Psychoanalysis and Illusion*, trans. Claire Pajaczkowska (London: Free Association, 1985).

20. Rose, "Where Does the Misery Come From?" 34.

21. Sigmund Freud, trans. and ed. James Strachey, *Group Psychology and the Analysis of the Ego* (1922; New York: W. W. Norton, 1959), 2.

22. W. R. Bion, "Group Dynamics," in *Experiences in Groups and Other Papers* (New York: Routledge, 1961), 141–91.

23. Sigmund Freud, "Thoughts for the Times on War and Death," in *The Standard Edition of the Complete Psychological Works of Sigmund Freud*, ed. James Strachey (London: Hogarth Press, 1953–74), 14:285.

24. Freud, "Thoughts for the Times on War and Death," 279.

25. *Abolition of War* refers to Fornari several times and features a full-page display quote from the psychoanalyst.

26. Franco Fornari, *The Psychoanalysis of War* (1966; New York: Anchor, 1974), 248. Fornari reports that Green said this in response to Fornari's paper, delivered at the Twenty-fifth International Congress of Romance Language Psychoanalysts.

27. Fornari, *Psychoanalysis of War*, 205.

28. Fornari, *Psychoanalysis of War*, 185.

29. Fornari, *Psychoanalysis of War*, 199 (emphasis in original).

30. Fornari, *Psychoanalysis of War*, xxiii.

31. Mignon Nixon, "Sperm Bomb: Art, Feminism, and the American War in Vietnam," unpublished book manuscript. Freud makes clear that "impulses in themselves are neither good nor bad. We classify them and their expressions in that way, according to their relation to the needs and demands of the human community." Freud, "Thoughts for the Times on War and Death," 281.

32. Anthony Sampson, "Freud on the State, Violence, and War," *Diacritics* 35, no. 3 (Autumn 2005): 78–91.

33. Jacqueline Rose, "Freud and the People, or Freud Goes to Abu Ghraib," in *The Last Resistance* (New York: Verso, 2007), 166–67.

34. Wodiczko, *Abolition of War*, 82.

35. Freud, "Thoughts for the Times on War and Death," 281.

36. Hanna Segal, "Silence Is the Real Crime" (1987), in *Psychoanalysis, Literature and War: Papers 1972–1995* (Oxford: Routledge, 1997), 155.

37. Segal, "From Hiroshima to the Gulf War and After: Socio-Political Expressions of Ambivalence," in *Psychoanalysis, Literature and War*, 168.

38. Immanuel Kant, "Perpetual Peace: A Philosophical Sketch," in *Political Writings*, trans. H. B. Nosbet, ed. Hans S. Reiss (Cambridge: Cambridge University Press, 1991), 98.

39. Kant, "Perpetual Peace," 98 (emphasis in original). Kant discusses constant war as the display of evil by "the great societies we call *states*" in a footnote to "Religion within the Boundaries of Mere Reason" (1793), in *Religion within the Boundaries of Mere Reason and Other Writings*, ed. Allen Wood and George di Giovanni (Cambridge: Cambridge University Press, 1998), 57.

40. Melanie Klein, "Love, Guilt and Reparation" (1937), in *Love, Guilt and Reparation, and Other Works 1921–1945*, vol. 1 of *The Writings of Melanie Klein* (New York: Free Press, 2002), 306–43.

41. Fornari, *Psychoanalysis of War*, 207.

42. For rigorous histories and analyses of these debates, see Bruce Robbins, ed., *Cosmopolitics* (Minneapolis: University of Minnesota Press, 1998); Robbins, *Feeling Global: Internationalism in Distress* (New York: New York University Press, 1999); and Robbins, *Perpetual War: Cosmopolitanism from the Viewpoint of Violence* (Durham, NC: Duke University Press, 2012).

43. Etienne Balibar, "'Rights of Man' and 'Rights of the Citizen,'" in *Masses, Classes, Ideas: Studies on Politics and Philosophy before and after Marx*, trans. James Swenson (Oxford: Routledge, 1994), 49.

44. Joan Copjec, "Introduction: Evil in the Time of the Finite World," in *Radical Evil*, ed. Copjec (New York: Verso, 1996), xxiv.

45. Kant, "Perpetual Peace," 105.

46. Fornari, *Psychoanalysis of War*, 201.

47. Wodiczko, *Abolition of War*, 100.

48. It is interesting to contrast these proposals by courageously disillusioned peacemakers with one based on quite different, in some respects opposing, premises. In 1910,

very late in his life, William James wrote an essay titled "The Moral Equivalent of War," in which he asserts that "international solidarity should be used to resolve conflicts between nations. He begins by stating, in a manner similar to our philosophers, that warlike "pugnacity"—part of Mignon Nixon's "badness"—cannot be eliminated in modern man, who, he believes, has "inherited" it—something like original sin—from uncivilized ancestors. He also asserts that it is precisely "the horrors [of war] that make the fascination" with it. But James also agrees with "the war party" for whom the martial virtues—patriotism, "intrepidity, contempt of softness, surrender of private interest, obedience to command"—"are absolute and permanent goods." "No healthy minded person," he says, can disagree that "militarism is the great preserver of our ideals of hardihood, and human life with no use for hardihood would be contemptible. . . . Hardihoods continue the manliness to which the military mind so faithfully clings. . . . Martial virtues . . . must still remain the rock upon which states are built . . . war has been the only force that can discipline a whole community." This concession to militarism (and masculinism) leads him to conclude, following H. G. Wells, that the martial character should be bred by a force other than military conscription—the conscription of young men into a period of national service: mining, building bridges, window-washing, road-building, etc. He calls this force "the moral equivalent of war." It is not necessary to challenge James's solution or to disagree with his contention that pacifists cannot rely simply on moral argument to note that his ultimate focus on man's "nobility" and "honor"—his "manly virtues" and goodness—entails a complete turn away from the problem of what he himself has previously called man's "innate pugnacity" and fascination with horrors as causal factors of war, factors that will not be eradicated by the building of bridges. James's fetishistic disavowal of ineradicable aggressivity—simultaneously recognizing it and acting as though he hadn't—is also facilitated by his failure to question that war performs disciplinary rather than disinhibiting functions and that the state is a force for good. James, "Moral Equivalent of War," n.p.

49. Jacques Derrida, "A Dialogue with Jacques Derrida," in Giovanna Borradori, *Philosophy in a Time of Terror: Dialogues with Jürgen Habermas and Jacques Derrida* (Chicago: University of Chicago, 2004), 130. Derrida is not the only one to theorize a new cosmopolitanism. For the history of other new cosmopolitanisms of the 1990s, see Bruce Robbins's books listed in note 42.

50. Derrida reworks Kant's ideas, expressed in "Perpetual Peace," about hospitality toward the stranger in *Of Hospitality: Ann Dufourmantelle Invites Jacques Derrida to Respond* (Redwood City, CA: Stanford University Press, 2000).

51. Borradori, "Deconstructing Terrorism," in *Philosophy in a Time of Terror*, 163.

52. Mouffe, "Deliberative Democracy or Agonistic Pluralism?" Political Science Series 72 (Vienna: Institute for Advanced Studies, 2000), http:/.ihs.ac.at/publications/pol/pw_72 .pdf (accessed August 12, 2013).

53. Bruce Robbins, *Global Feeling: Internationalism in Distress* (New York: New York University Press, 1999), 19–20.

54. Robbins, *Global Feeling*, 95.

55. Robbins, *Perpetual War*, 3 (emphasis added).

56. Kant, "Perpetual Peace," 93.

57. Allen W. Wood, "Kant's Project for Perpetual Peace," in *Cosmopolitics*, 72.

11: Museum of Innocence

Originally published without footnotes in *Artforum*, September 2014, as "The Whole Truth."

1. Andrew Ross, "The Odor of Publicity," in *After the World Trade Center: Rethinking New York City*, ed. Michael Sorkin and Sharon Zukin (New York: Routledge, 2002), 130.

2. Allison Blais and Lynn Rasic, *A Place of Remembrance: Official Book of the National September 11 Memorial* (Washington, DC: National Geographic, 2011), 3.

3. David W. Dunlap, "Pataki Bars Museum from World Trade Center Memorial Site," *New York Times*, September 28, 2005; Dunlap, "Governor Bars Freedom Center at Ground Zero," *New York Times*, September 29, 2005.

4. "Governor Pataki and Mayor Bloomberg Unveil Design for the World Trade Center Cultural Center," Lower Manhattan Development Corporation, press release, May 19, 2005, http://www.renewnyc.com/displaynews.aspx?newsid=a39eccff-b8c3-43cd-972f-24 9d7cOcbfdf

5. Debra Burlingame, "The Great Ground Zero Heist," *Wall Street Journal*, June 8, 2005.

6. Douglas Feiden and Joe Mahoney, "Zero Tolerance at Ground Zero," *Daily News* (New York), June 25, 2005, 7.

7. Douglas Feiden, "Violated . . . Again," *Daily News*, June 24, 2005, 7.

8. Feiden and Mahoney, "Zero Tolerance."

9. Eric L. Santner, "History beyond the Pleasure Principle," in *Probing the Limits of Representation: Nazism and the "Final Solution,"* ed. Saul Friedlander (Cambridge, MA: Harvard University Press, 1992), 144.

10. "About the 9/11 Memorial & Museum," https://www.911memorial.org/about.

11. Mark Wigley, "Insecurity by Design," in Sorkin and Zukin, *After the World Trade Center*, 73.

12. Wigley, "Insecurity by Design," 70–71.

13. Sigmund Freud, "Analysis Terminable and Interminable" (1937), in *Therapy and Technique*, ed. Philip Rieff (New York: Macmillan, 1963), 254–56.

14. "About the 9/11 Memorial & Museum," https://www.911memorial.org/about.

12: "We don't need another hero"

Originally published in *Public Servants: Art and the Crisis of the Common Good*, ed. Johanna Burton, Shannon Jackson, and Dominic Willsdon (Cambridge, MA: MIT Press, 2016), 4–26. First presented at the Dia Art Foundation symposium "Monuments, Monumentality, Monumentalization" in May 2015. A modified version was delivered as the keynote address at the symposium "Esther Shalev-Gerz: Trust and Dialogue" at the Valand Academy, University of Gothenburg, Sweden, in June 2015.

1. Paul Ricoeur, *Memory, History, Forgetting*, trans. Kathleen Blamey and David Pellauer (Chicago: University of Chicago Press, 2004), 69.

2. Elaine Scarry, *The Body in Pain: The Making and Unmaking of the World* (New York: Oxford University Press, 1985), 62, 112.

3. Sigmund Freud, "Thoughts for the Times on War and Death," in *The Standard Edition*

of the Complete Psychological Works of Sigmund Freud, ed. James Strachey (London: Hogarth Press, 1953–74), 14:296.

4. Timothy Kudo, "How We Learned to Kill," *New York Times*, March 1, 2015, Sunday Review 1.

5. Roger Poole, "'We All Put Up with You Virginia': Irreceivable Wisdom about War," in *Virginia Woolf and War: Fiction, Reality, and Myth* (Syracuse, NY: Syracuse University Press, 1991), 99.

6. Virginia Woolf, *The Voyage Out* (New York: Harcourt, Brace & World, 1920), 69.

7. Glyn Maxwell, "The Poem Stuck in My Head: Ivor Gurney's 'To His Love,'" *Paris Review Blog*, November 11, 2013, http://www.theparisreview.org/blog/2013/11/11/glyn-maxwell-on-to-his-love.

8. Tony Judt, "What Have We Learned, If Anything?" in *When the Facts Change: Essays 1995–2010*, ed. Jennifer Homans (New York: Penguin, 2015), 273–76.

9. German chancellor Theobald von Gethmann-Hollweg, quoted in Rosa Luxemburg, *The Crisis in the German Social Democracy (The "Junius" Pamphlet)* (Brooklyn, NY: Socialist Publication Society, 1919), 23–24.

10. Walter Benjamin, "Theses on the Philosophy of History," in *Illuminations*, ed. Hannah Arendt, trans. Harry Zohn (New York: Schocken, 1968), 255 (emphasis in original).

11. Ricoeur, *Memory, History, Forgetting*, 80.

12. Friedrich Nietzsche, *The Use and Abuse of History*, trans. Adrian Collins (New York: Macmillan/Library of Liberal Arts, 1949), 12–17.

13. Leo Bersani, *Thoughts and Things* (Chicago: University of Chicago Press, 2015), xiii.

14. Jacqueline Rose, *Women in Dark Times* (London: Bloomsbury, 2014), ix.

15. Judith Barry, "The Space That Art Makes," in *A Dynamic Equilibrium: In Pursuit of Public Terrain*, ed. Sally Yard (San Diego: Installation Gallery, 2007), 47 (emphasis in original).

16. Homer, *The Iliad*, trans. Peter Green (Oakland: University of California Press, 2015), 402.

17. Fielding H. Garrison, *Notes on the History of Military Medicine*, quoted in Ana Carden-Coyne, *Reconstructing the Body: Classicism, Modernism, and the First World War* (Oxford: Oxford University Press, 2009), 70.

18. Garrison, quoted in Carden-Coyne, *Reconstructing the Body*, 70.

19. Ann Jones, *They Were Soldiers: How the Wounded Return from America's Wars—The Untold Story* (Chicago: Dispatch Books/Haymarket Books, 2013), 37, 42.

20. Carden-Coyne, *Reconstructing the Body*, 112.

21. Carden-Coyne, *Reconstructing the Body*, 126.

22. Carden-Coyne, *Reconstructing the Body*, 137

23. Marina Warner, *Monuments and Maidens: The Allegory of the Female Form* (New York: Vintage, 1985), 140.

24. For an analysis of these two works, see my "Louise Lawler's Rude Museum," in *Louise Lawler*, ed. Helen Molesworth, October Files (Cambridge, MA: MIT Press, 2013) [reprinted in this volume].

25. Nicole Loraux, *Mothers in Mourning*, trans. Corinne Pache (Ithaca, NY: Cornell University Press, 1998), 44.

26. Santner, "History beyond the Pleasure Principle," 144.

27. "A Mother's Answer to 'A Common Solider,'" *Morning Post*, August 14, 1916, https://web.viu.ca/davies/H482.WWI/poem.ALittle Mother.1916.htm.

28. Quoted in Robert Graves, *Good-Bye to All That* (1929; London: Anchor, 1958), 228–32.

29. For a discussion of various ideas about mourning in contemporary political thought, see Bonnie Honig, *Antigone, Interrupted* (Cambridge: Cambridge University Press, 2013).

30. Cindy Sheehan, *Peace Mom: A Mother's Journey through Heartache to Activism* (New York: Atria Books, 2006), 52.

31. Sheehan, *Peace Mom*, 215.

32. Douglas Crimp and Louise Lawler, "Prominence Given, Authority Taken," in *Louise Lawler: An Arrangement of Pictures* (New York: Assouline, 2000), n.p.

33. Carden-Coyne, *Reconstructing the Body*, 128.

34. Quoted in Warner, *Monuments and Maidens*, 132.

35. Rose, *Women in Dark Times*, 261.

36. Somini Sengupta, "Is the War Crimes Court Still Relevant?" *New York Times*, January 11, 2015, Sunday Review, 4.

37. Carden-Coyne, *Reconstructing the Body*, 148–49.

38. Nataša Ilić, "Sanja Iveković, *Lady Rosa of Luxembourg*," *n. paradoxa* 8 (2001): 22.

39. Luxemburg, *Crisis in the German Social Democracy*, 21.

40. Rosa Luxemburg, *The Russian Revolution* (1918), trans. Bertram Wolfe (New York: Workers Age Publishers, 1940), https://www.marxists.org/archive/luxemburg/1918/russion-revolution/ch06.htm.

41. Sanja Iveković, "Statement on the project 'Lady Rosa of Luxemburg,'" March 2001. See Benedict Anderson, *Imagined Communities* (London: Verso, 1983), 7.

42. Bojana Pejić, "*Lady Rosa of Luxembourg*, or, Is the Age of Female Allegory Really a Bygone Era?" in Simon Sheikh, *In the Place of the Public Sphere?* (Berlin: b_books, 2005), 68–99.

43. Mark Twain, *The War Prayer* (New York: HarperCollins, 1970); originally published by the Mark Twain Company, 1923. Twain wrote the parable in 1905, during the Philippine-American War, but, warned by his daughter that it would be considered sacrilegious, he decided that it should be published only after his death: "I have told the whole truth in that, and only dead men can tell the truth in this world." Albert Bigelow Paine, *Mark Twain: A Biography* (New York: Harper & Brothers, 1912); quoted in epigraph to *The War Prayer*. The HarperCollins edition of *War Prayer* is printed in the form of a poem. I have recast the passages I quote in their original prose form.

44. Robert Filliou, "Proclamation of Intent," quoted in Chris Thompson, *Felt: Fluxus, Joseph Beuys, and the Dalai Lama* (Minneapolis: University of Minnesota Press), 56.

45. *The Museum of Ante-Memorials*, curated by Eric Baudelaire, http://www.taipeibiennial.org/2012/en/participants/the_museum_of_ante_memorials/index.html.

46. Filliou, "Proclamation of Intent," 56.

47. Ricoeur, *Memory, History, Forgetting*, 87. A perfect example of abuse of the duty of memory is the National September 11 Memorial & Museum, which, erected on the footprints of the World Trade Center towers, also stands on the graves of two museums that were censored because they might have sought to understand the conditions of religious terrorism and criticized the United States. See Rosalyn Deutsche, "The Whole Truth," *Artforum*, September 2014, https://artforum.com/inprint/issue=201407&id=47864.

48. Ricoeur, *Memory, History, Forgetting*, 87.

49. Ricoeur, *Memory, History, Forgetting*, 89.

50. Ricoeur, *Memory, History, Forgetting*, 88.

13: Louise Lawler's Play Technique

Originally published in *Louise Lawler: Receptions*, ed. Roxana Marcoci (New York: Museum of Modern Art, 2017).

1. The concept of "medium specificity" as the foundation of artistic autonomy was elaborated by the American formalist critic Clement Greenberg. However, as Victor Burgin writes, Greenberg's ideas were "a particular nuancing of a more general set of assumptions" that inform Western beliefs about high art. Victor Burgin, "The Absence of Presence: Conceptualism and Postmodernisms," in *The End of Art Theory: Criticism and Postmodernity* (Atlantic Highlands, NJ: Humanities Press International, 1986), 30.

2. Douglas Crimp, "The Art of Exhibition," in *On the Museum's Ruins* (Cambridge, MA: MIT Press, 1993), 265.

3. Claude Gintz described the architectural context in his excellent feminist account of Lawler's *Projects* exhibition," *What Is the Same: Louise Lawler; The Same and the Other in the Work of Louise Lawler* (Saint-Étienne, France: Maison de la Culture et de la Communication, 1987), 31–38.

4. Gintz, *What Is the Same*, 31.

5. Andrea Fraser, "From the Critique of Institutions to an Institution of Critique" (2005), in *Institutional Critique: An Anthology of Artists' Writings*, ed. Alexander Alberro and Blake Stimson (Cambridge, MA: MIT Press, 2009), 414.

6. Sigmund Freud, "Fetishism," in *The Standard Edition of the Complete Psychological works of Sigmund Freud*, ed. James Strachey (London: Hogarth Press, 1953–74), 21:149–51.

7. The most common interpretation of "Little Jack Horner" relates the rhyme to a real estate swindle and could probably also be used to analyze Lawler's exhibition, especially as a luxury apartment building was incorporated in a 2004 renovation of the Museum of Modern Art. First published in 1725, the rhyme is thought to refer to a Thomas Horner, who lived at the time of the dissolution of the monasteries in 1536, when Henry VIII took property from the Catholic Church. Horner served the last abbot of Glastonbury, who instructed him to take a huge Christmas pie to the king. Hidden in the pie were title deeds to lesser properties as a bribe to convince Henry not to nationalize Church lands. But Horner opened the pie and extracted the deeds of the manor of Mells in Somerset, which he kept for himself. Chris Roberts, a scholar of nursery rhymes, has said that the pie was not necessarily a literal pie but a symbol of a means of concealing something. "Reason behind the Rhyme: 'Little Jack Horner," National Public Radio, http://www.npr.org/templates/story/story.php?storyId=5135080.

8. George Baker and Andrea Fraser, "Displacement and Condensation: A Conversation on the Work of Louise Lawler," in *Louise Lawler and Others*, ed. Philipp Kaiser (Basel: Kunstmuseum Basel, Museum für Geganwartskunst; Osfildern-Ruit, Germany: Hatje Cantz, 2004), 137.

9. The official exhibition brochure produced by MoMA also featured a quote from Lawler on its cover, one that also addressed the viewer: "I am showing what they are showing:

painting, sculpture, pictures, glasses and words on painted walls furnishing the same material experience; my work is to exchange the positions of exposition and voyeurism. You are standing in your own shoes."

10. Sigmund Freud, "Analysis Terminable and Interminable" (1937), in *Standard Edition*, 23:209–54

11. Here I am paraphrasing the British psychoanalyst Christopher Bollas, who has speculated that unconscious communication between analyst and analysand puts each "in touch with the other's otherness." Engaging in such communication, the analyst avoids imprisoning the analysand in the "imperial palace of conscious logic" and submitting her to the analyst's authority. Bollas's ideas about the analyst-analysand interaction could, I think, be applied as an analogy to the relationship between Lawler's art and its viewer, in which the authority of the artist is undermined in various ways, including that of encouraging the viewer's free associations. Bollas, "Violent Innocence," in *Being a Character: Psychoanalysis and Self Experience* (1992; Hove, England: Routledge, 2003), 188–90.

12. Étienne Balibar, "Althusser's Dramaturgy and the Critique of Ideology," *differences* 26, no. 3, special issue, "Dossier: Étienne Balibar on Althusser's Dramaturgy and the Critique of Ideology"(December 2015): 3.

13. Judith Butler, "Theatrical Machines," *differences* 26, no. 3 ("Dossier"; 2015), 26–27. In this passage, Butler refers specifically to melodrama.

14. Butler, "Theatrical Machines," 27.

15. By 1987, Contra forces, which had trained in Florida, were largely integrated into the "Nicaraguan Resistance" and depended on financial and military support from the United States. Congress banned such assistance, except for what it deemed "nonlethal"; the Reagan administration's covert aid to the counterinsurgency culminated in the Iran-Contra affair.

16. Crimp, "Art of Exhibition," 78–81.

17. "Arthur Young, Bell-47D1 Helicopter, 1945," Museum of Modern Art website, www .moma.org/collection/works/2234.

18. In imputing an unconscious to the museum, I do not mean to psychoanalyze—let alone make accusations against—the individuals or even the conglomeration of individuals who work at MoMA. Nor am I using psychoanalysis as an analogy. Rather, I am treating the institution as a group in W. R. Bion's sense of the term—a social entity unto itself with which the individual has a relationship. See Bion, *Experiences in Groups and Other Papers* (London: Routledge, 1961).

19. See Rosalyn Deutsche, "Lawler's Rude Museum, in *Louise Lawler*, ed. Helen Molesworth, October Files (Cambridge, MA: MIT Press, 2013), 99–118. [Reprinted in this volume.]

20. *The Letters of Virginia Woolf*, vol. 2, *1912–1922*, ed. Nigel Nicolson and Joanne Trautmann (New York: Harcourt Brace Jovanovich, 1978), 76.

21. See Molesworth, "Louise Lawler: Just the Facts," in Molesworth, *Louise Lawler*, 119–37. Mignon Nixon interprets *No Drones* within a psychoanalytic perspective in "Louise Lawler: *No Drones*," *October*, no. 147 (Winter 2014), 22–37.

22. Julia Kristeva, *Melanie Klein*, trans. Ross Guberman (New York: Columbia University Press, 2001), 147.

23. Melanie Klein, "The Psycho-analytic Play Technique: Its History and Significance"

(1955), in *The Writings of Melanie Klein*, vol. 3, *Envy and Gratitude and Other Works 1946–1963* (New York: Free Press, 1975), 137.

24. Klein, "Psycho-analytic Play Technique," 127.

25. Melanie Klein, *Narrative of a Child Analysis* (London: Hogarth Press and Institute of Psycho-Analysis, 1961).

26. Klein, *Narrative of a Child Analysis*, 263.

27. Klein, *Narrative of a Child Analysis*, 261.

28. Gertrude Stein, *Wars I Have Seen* (1945; London: Brilliance, 1984), 9; Klein, "On the Theory of Anxiety and Guilt" (1948), in *Envy and Gratitude*, 1–23.

29. Klein, "On the Theory of Anxiety and Guilt," 143. Melanie Klein, "Notes on Some Schizoid Mechanisms" (1946), in *Envy and Gratitude*, 1–23.

30. Melanie Klein, "Notes on Some Schizoid Mechanisms." Later Kleinians developed theories about the psychic dimensions of war. See Franco Fornari, *The Psychoanalysis of War* (Garden City, NY: Anchor, 1974), and Hanna Segal, "From Hiroshima to the Gulf War and After: Socio-Political Expressions of Ambivalence" (1997) and "Silence is the Real Crime" (1987), both in *Psychoanalysis, Literature and War: Papers, 1972–1995* (New York: Routledge), 157–68, 143–56.

31. Kristeva, *Melanie Klein*, 239.

32. Claude Gintz, "The Same and the Other," 32.

33. "'*Ma Jolie*,'" Museum of Modern Art website, www.moma.org/learn/moma_learning/pable-picasso-ma-jolie-paris-winter-1911-12. This work is sometimes known simply as "*Ma Jolie*": William Rubin noted that Daniel-Henry Kahnweiler, Picasso's dealer, added *Woman with a Guitar* to help viewers' "assimilation of the work." See Rubin, *Picasso in the Collection of the Museum of Modern Art* (New York: Museum of Modern Art, 1972), 206n2.

34. Gintz, "The Same and the Other," 32.

35. Lawler has said that "prominence given, authority taken," a phrase inscribed on several drinking glasses in *Enough*, "sums up my resistance." "Prominence Given, Authority Taken: An Interview with Louise Lawler by Douglas Crimp," *Grey Room*, no. 4 (Summer 2001). The interview was previously published in a slightly different form, in Johannes Meinhard, Crimp, and Lawler, *Louise Lawler: An Arrangement of Pictures* (New York: Assouline, 2000).

36. Alexander Alberro, "Institutions, Critique, and Institutional Critique," in Alberro and Stimson, *Institutional Critique*, 15.

37. Alberro, "Institutions, Critique, and Institutional Critique," 15.

38. Sonja Laveart, "Bartleby's Tragic Aporia," in *Institutional Attitudes: Instituting Art in a Flat World*, ed. Pascal Gielen, Antennae Series (Amsterdam: Valiz, 2013), 137.

39. Laveart, "Bartleby's Tragic Aporia," 137.

40. Paolo Virno, "Anthropology and Theory of Institutions," trans. Alberto Toscano, *Transversal*, May 2007, eipcp.net/transversal/0407/virno/en/print. Virno is referring to the political institution of the modern State.

41. Virno, "Anthropology and Theory of Institutions" (emphasis added).

42. Andrea Fraser, "An Artist's Statement" (1992), in Alberro and Stimson, *Institutional Critique*, 318.

14: Mary Kelly's Attunement

Published here for the first time, this essay is a substantially expanded version of a text in *Mary Kelly: The Practical Past* (New York: Mitchell-Innes & Nash, 2017). It was delivered as the Harn Eminent Scholar in Art History lecture at the University of Florida, Gainesville, in March 2018.

1. Trinh T. Minh-ha, *Lovecidal: Walking with the Disappeared* (New York: Fordham University Press, 2016), 71.

2. Mary Kelly, in Klaus Ottmann, *Mary Kelly* (1992; London: Phaidon, 1997), 143.

3. Marianne Hirsch, "Family Pictures: *Maus*, Mourning, and Post-Memory," *Discourse* 15, no. 2 (Winter 1992–93): 26.

4. Cathy Caruth, *Unclaimed Experience: Trauma, Narrative, and History* (Baltimore: Johns Hopkins University Press, 1996), 7.

5. Sigmund Freud, *Beyond the Pleasure Principle*, trans. James Strache (New York: W. W. Norton), 19.

6. Freud, *Beyond the Pleasure Principle*, 8–9.

7. Mary Kelly, "The Dialogic Imagination: An Introduction by Mary Kelly," in *Dialogue: On the Politics of Voice*, ed. Cecilia Widenheim and Mary Kelly (Stockholm: Iaspis, 2011), 110.

8. Julia Kristeva, *Black Sun: Depression and Melancholia*, trans. Leon S. Roudiez (New York: Columbia University Press, 1989), 22.

9. Juli Carson, "Mea Culpa: A Conversation with Mary Kelly," *Art Journal* 58, no. 4 (Winter 1999): 76; "The Dialogic Imagination," Mary Kelly, Sharon Hayes, Jane Jin Kaisen, Andrea Geyer, and Dont Rhine in conversation, in Widenheim and Kelly, *Dialogue: On the Politics of Voice*, 19.

10. Theodor Adorno, "Commitment" (1962), in *The Essential Frankfurt School Reader*, ed. Andrew Arato and Eike Gebhardt (New York: Continuum, 1982), 312.

11. Adorno, "Commitment," 312–13.

12. Saul Friedlander, quoted in *Representing the Holocaust: History, Theory, Trauma* (Ithaca: Cornell University Press, 1994), 213.

13. Marianne Hirsch, "Surviving Images: Holocaust Photographs and the Work of Postmemory," in *Visual Culture and the Holocaust*, ed. Barbie Zelizer (New Brunswick, NJ: Rutgers University Press, 2001), 221.

14. James Castonguay et al., "*Gloria Patri*, Gender and the Gulf War: A Conversation with Mary Kelly," *Discourse* 17, no.1 (Fall 1994): 167.

15. Carson, "Mea Culpa," 76

16. Ewa Lajer-Burcharth, "The Archaeologist of the Self: A Conversation with Mary Kelly," in *Mary Kelly: Words are Things* (Warsaw: Center for Contemporary Art, Ujazdowski Castle, 2008), 31.

17. Griselda Pollock, "Mary Kelly's *Ballad of Kastrito Rexhepi*: Virtual Trauma and Indexical Witness in the Age of Mediatic Spectacle," in *Mary Kelly*, ed. Mignon Nixon, October Files 20 (Cambridge: MIT Press, 2016), 132.

18. Virginia Woolf, *Three Guineas* (New York: Harcourt, Brace & World, 1938), 142.

19. Pollock, "Mary Kelly's *Ballad*," 140.

20. Sigmund Freud, *Group Psychology and the Analysis of the Ego* (1922), ed. and trans. James Strachey (New York: W. W. Norton, 1959), 3.

21. Dominick LaCapra, *Representing the Holocaust: History, Theory, Trauma* (Ithaca, NY: Cornell University Press, 1994).

22. LaCapra, *Representing the Holocaust*, 213.

23. Walter Benjamin, "Theses on the Philosophy of History, in *Illuminations*, ed. Hannah Arendt, trans. Harry Zohn (New York: Schocken, 1969), 253–64.

24. Paul Ricoeur, *Memory, History, Forgetting*, trans. Kathleen Blamey and David Pellauer (Chicago: University of Chicago Press, 2004), 80.

25. *Buenos Aires 1976* was not included in the 1999 exhibition at Postmasters.

26. Martin Heidegger, *Being and Time*, trans. John MacQuarrie and Edward Robinson (New York: Harper & Row, 1962), 171, 176, 237.

27. Heidegger, *Being and Time*, 139.

28. Heidegger, *Being and Time*, 140.

29. Heidegger, *Being and Time*, 172n3.

30. Jonathan Flatley, *Affective Mapping: Melancholia and the Politics of Modernism* (Cambridge, MA: MIT Press, 2008), 17, 5.

31. Matthew Ratcliffe, "Why Mood Matters," in *Cambridge Companion to Heidegger's Being and Time*, ed. Mark A. Wrathall (Cambridge: Cambridge University Press, 2013), 158.

32. Heidegger, *Being and Time*, 176.

33. Heidegger, *Being and Time*, 176–77.

34. Flatley, *Affective Mapping*, 1.

35. Sigmund Freud, "Mourning and Melancholia," *General Psychological Theory* (New York: Collier Books, 1963), 164–79.

36. Flatley, *Affective Mapping*, 81.

37. Heidegger, *Being and Time*, 175.

38. Widenheim and Kelly, *Dialogue: On the Politics of Voice*, 18.

15: Martha Rosler's Unrest

Originally published in *Martha Rosler: Irrespective* (New York: Jewish Museum; New Haven, CT: Yale University Press, 2018), 21–26.

1. Walter Annenberg Annual Lecture: Martha Rosler, New York, Whitney Museum of American Art, December 13, 2016.

2. Theodor Adorno, "Education after Auschwitz" (1966), in *Erziehung zur Mündigkeit. Vorträge und Gespräche mit Hellmut Becker 1959–1969* (Frankfurt am Main: Suhrkamp Verlag, 1993), ada.evergreen.edu/~arunc/text/frankfurt/Auschwitz/AdornoEducation.pdf. Accessed March 2, 2017.

3. Ernst Bloch, *The Principle of Hope* (Oxford: Basil Blackwell, 1986).

4. Georges Bataille, "Concerning the Accounts Given by the Residents of Hiroshima" (1947), in *Trauma: Explorations in Memory*, ed. Cathy Caruth (Baltimore: Johns Hopkins University Press, 1995), 221–35.

5. The definition of critique as a questioning relationship to power's truths is from Michel Foucault. See "What Is Critique?" in *The Politics of Truth*, ed. Sylvère Lotringer, trans. Lysa Hochroth and Catherine Porter (Los Angeles: Semiotext(e), 1997).

6. Bloch, *Principle of Hope*. Rosler's informed discontent is not, however, grounded in Bloch's biologistic and teleological views.

7. E-mail correspondence with the author, March 8, 2017.

8. Simone de Beauvoir, *The Second Sex*, trans. and ed. H. M. Parshley (New York: Alfred A. Knopf, 1952), xvi.

9. Michael J. Arlen, *Living-Room War* (Syracuse, NY: Syracuse University Press, 1997).

10. Beatriz Colomina, *Domesticity at War* (Cambridge, MA: MIT Press, 2007), 290.

11. See, in particular, Megan Katherine Ampe, "Martha Rosler's *Bringing the War Home: House Beautiful*, 1967–1972: An Interrogation of the American Dream," MA thesis, Department of Art History and the Graduate School of the University of Oregon, Eugene, 2012, 20.

12. Mark Wigley, "Untitled: The Housing of Gender," in *Sexuality and Space*, ed. Beatriz Colomina (New York: Princeton Architectural Press, 1992), 353.

13. Trinh T. Minh-ha, *Lovecidal: Walking with the Disappeared* (New York: Fordham University Press, 2016). Among other wars and acts of violence, Minh-ha's book deals with the American War in Vietnam and its legacy.

14. Sigmund Freud, *A General Introduction to Psychoanalysis*, trans. Joan Riviere (Garden City, NY: Garden City, 1943), 252.

15. Virginia Woolf, *Three Guineas* (New York: Harcourt, Brace & World, 1938), 125–26.

16. Quoted in Woolf, *Three Guineas*, 125–26.

17. Woolf, *Three Guineas*, 135.

18. I am referring to the bunch of balloons in the eponymous *Balloons*.

19. Rosler's depictions of American children contrast strikingly with the mass-media photos of dead and wounded Vietnam children that appear in several works in the series. *Balloons* includes both.

20. Jürgen Habermas, *The Structural Transformation of the Bourgeois Public Sphere: An Inquiry into a Category of Bourgeois Society* (Cambridge, MA: MIT Press, 1989), 48; originally published as *Strukturwandel der Öffentlichkeit* (Darmstadt: Hermann Luchterhand, 1962).

21. Melanie Klein, "The Psycho-Analytic Play Technique: Its History and Significance" (1955), in *The Writings of Melanie Klein*, vol. 3, *Envy and Gratitude and Other Works, 1946–1963* (New York: Free Press, 1975), and *Narrative of a Child Analysis* (London: Hogarth Press and Institute of Psycho-Analysis, 1961). Also see my account of Klein's ideas about play in "Louise Lawler's Play Technique," in *Louise Lawler: Receptions*, ed. Roxana Marcocci (New York: Museum of Modern Art, 2017), 62–69 [reprinted in this volume].

22. [Rosler also used war toys in the video *A Simple Case for Torture* (1983), moving them across a landscape of books on war. About twenty years later, she reproduced a recipe from a French magazine for something called Patriotic Jello Salad but included in the color layers a group of war toys.]

23. Woolf, *Three Guineas*, 142.

24. Woolf, *Three Guineas*, 142.

Index

Abelove, Henry, 245n31

Abolition of War (Wodiczko), 161

Abstract Expressionists, 35, 48

abstraction, 44–47, 49, 55, 95, 103; and figuration, 48; and vulnerability, 54

Acconci, Vito, 81–82

Adayfi, Mansoor, 124–26

Adorno, Theodor, 110–11, 126, 226, 232

aesthetic autonomy, 90

Afghanistan, 182, 185–86, 188–89, 193

Agamben, Giorgio, 13; state of exception, 109

AIDS/HIV, 155

Alberro, Alexander, 27–28, 31; exit strategies, 216

Alexander, Vikky, 40

Algeria, 125–26

Al Qaeda, 182

Althusser, Louis, 208–9

Aluminum Foils (Welling), 47–48

Alwi, Moath Al-, 125

American Civil Liberties Union (ACLU), 123

American Fine Arts Co., 30–31

Ameziane, Djamel, 125–27

Amnesty International, 123

anarchism, 89, 93, 97, 99–100, 103

"anarchism without adjectives" (D'Arcangelo), 100

Anderson, Benedict, 197

Ansi, Muhammed, 125

antiwar movement, 233

Apollinaire, Guillaume, 131

Arc de Triomphe, 164, 167–68; iconography of, 165; Tomb of the Unknown Soldier, 163

Arc de Triomphe: World Institute for the Abolition of War (Wodiczko), 161

Archbishops' Commission on the Ministry of Women, 235

Arendt, Hannah, 127; "right to have rights," 151

Aristotle, 91, 216

Arlen, Michael, 233

Arrangements of Pictures (Lawler), 41

art as institution, 90, 113, 115, 117; challenge to closed nature, 119; democratizing of, 92, 107; as material site, 116; politics of space, 116; as socially determined, 121; vulnerability, exploitation of, 92

Artforum (magazine), 127

Artists Space, 100; logo of, 97–98

Art Workers Coalition (AWC), 107

Asher, Michael, 24, 32, 72, 247n2

Ashes (Welling), 49–51, 54

AT&T Long Lines Building Projection (Wodiczko), 161

Auden, W. H.: on Freud, 90

Auschwitz, 111
authoritarianism, 119, 154, 235

Badiou, Alain, 243n7; ethics of truths, 243n6; fidelity to event, 2, 15–18, 21–22; "not-forgetting," 15; refusal of conservatism, 2, 15; truth process, 15–16
Baim, Richard, 40
Bakhtin, Mikhail, 133, 135–37; nonlinear time of novel, 4–5; zone of contact, 52
Balibar, Etienne, 108, 151–52, 173–74, 208; equaliberty, 268n96; extensive and intensive universalism, distinction between, 268n95
Balloons (Rosler), 281n19
Baluchi, Anmar Al-: *Vertigo at Guantánamo*, 125
Barry, Judith, 8, 72
Barthes, Roland: "having-been-there" quality of photograph, 52, 137; "rhetoric of the image," 57; structuralist activity, 40
Bartlett, Neil: *Ready to Catch Him Should He Fall*, 131–34, 136–39, 142–55, 157–58
Bataille, Georges, 232; museum, as mirror, 80
Batchen, Gregory, 50, 250n30
Baudelaire, Charles, 46
Beauvoir, Simone de, 2, 233
Becker, Howard S., 116
Belgium, 200
Bender, Gretchen, 247n4
Benjamin, Walter, 13, 49, 70, 150, 161, 187, 228; approach to photography, 43–44; political history, 22; "The Storyteller," 53–54; tradition of oppressed, 140
Berlant, Lauren, "dead citizens," 152
Bersani, Leo, 187
Bhabha, Homi, 6, 70; masculinism, 245n24, 252–53n9
Bill of Rights, 121–22
bin Laden, Osama, 182
Bion, W. R., 169, 277n18
Birdcalls (Lawler), 81–82, 84–85

black sites, 124–25
Bloch, Ernst, 232
Blood Bath (Guerrilla Art Action Group), 212
Body Beautiful: Beauty Knows No Pain (Rosler), 233
Bollas, Christopher, 277n11; generational consciousness, 4
Bourdieu, Pierre, 109, 115
Bourgeois, Louise, 79; *Fillette*, 254n31
bourgeois public sphere, 119; inner violence of, 120–21. *See also* public sphere
Brauntuch, Troy, 39
Brecht, Bertolt, 117, 122, 234, 261n38; epic theater of, 208–9; "Writing the Truth: Five Difficulties," 116
Bringing the War Home: House Beautiful (Rosler), 233
Broodthaers, Marcel, 29, 72
Brooks, Ellen, 40
Brown, Wendy, 13–14
Brunberger, Bela, 270n19
Bryson, Norman, 58–59, 95, 97
Buchloh, Benjamin, 27–30, 119, 121
Buren, Daniel, 29, 72, 101, 103; critical questioning, 102
Bürger, Peter, 73, 90, 113, 115, 260n28
Burgin, Victor, 40, 64, 72, 247n4, 248n27, 276n1
Bush, George H. W., 154
Bush, George W., 109–10, 123–24, 182, 187, 193, 255n52
Business Improvement Districts, 155
Butler, Judith, 97, 103, 109, 208–9

Cadava, Eduardo, 43–44, 49, 53–54
Calligraphie (Haacke), 121
Cambodia, 117
Camp Casey, 193
Camp Delta, 125
Canova, Antonio, 74–76
Carden-Coyne, Ana, 188–89, 193
Carey, Ellen, 40
Caruth, Cathy, 136, 224–26

Casebere, James, 40

castration, 64, 80, 193; anxiety, 78–79, 174, 206–7; Freud's account of, 63, 78; symbolic, 194

censorship, 110, 142, 185; state, 13

Central Intelligence Agency (CIA), 182; black sites, 125

Certeau, Michel de, 38, 137, 147; spatial practice, 57; and walking, 157, 269n117

Césaire, Aimé, 4, 244n14

Cesar Pelli & Associates, 203

Cezanne, Paul, 204

Charlesworth, Sarah, 40, 247n4

Chassequet-Smirgel, Janine, 270n19

Cheney, Dick, 187

Chia, Sandro, 84

Christine Burgin Gallery, 46

Cicero, 4

citizenship, rights of, 151–52

city. *See* public sphere; urbanism; urban space

City Journal (magazine), 154

Civilization and Its Discontents (Freud), 170

Cixous, Hélène, 78

classicism, 71

Clemente, Francesco, 84

Colomina, Beatriz, 233–34

colonialism, 4

coloniality, 4, 244n14

COMMEMOR (Filliou), 197, 200–201

commemoration, 201

Conceptual Art, 8, 24–26, 31, 58, 84, 117, 247n2; feminist vision, ignored, 28–29; global conceptualism, 27–28; historicity of, 27, 32, 37–38; and memory, 30, 32; multinational capitalism, 28; political economy, 28–29

concrete space, 134

Copernican revolution, 6–7

Copjec, Joan, 174

Cornella, Drucilla, 18, 22–23

cosmopolitanism, 173, 175–76. *See also* new cosmopolitanism

cosmopolitics, 175

Crimp, Douglas, 82, 84, 193, 203, 210, 254n35

Crisis in the German Social Democracy, The (Luxemburg), 196

Critical Art Ensemble, 13

critical memory, 1, 183

critical theory, 4

Cross-Disciplinary Center for Global Peace Projects (Wodiczko), 168, 174–75

Cucchi, Enzo, 84

Daguerre, Louis, 50, 250n30

D'Arcangelo, Allan, 93

D'Arcangelo, Christopher, 7; "anarchism without adjectives," 100; anarchist statements, 89, 92–93, 95, 97–100, 103; and antiwar protests, 105–6; arrest of, 93; Artists Space, 97–99; chaining himself to doors, 89; curatorial control, 105; direct-action protest, 103, 105; ellipsis, use of, 99–101; guerilla performances, 89, 105, 107; "Look Out for what you Look At," 105; museum actions, 89, 92, 97, 101; museological violence, dramatized, 95; occupations of, 95, 105; "Open Museum Proposal," 103, 105; and vulnerability, 92, 95, 97, 103, 107

D'Arcangelo Family Partnership, 92

Darwinian revolution, 6–7

Days of Rage, 233

"Decay of Lying, The" (Wilde), 133

Declaration of the Rights of Man, 108, 121–22, 129, 152; state power and the people, 141

de Cleyre, Voltairine, 100

Décor (Haacke), 121

Degradés (Welling), 47, 54–55

Deitch, Jeffrey, 93

de Man, Paul, 139

democracy, 6, 56, 57, 107–8, 140, 187, 193; aesthetic terror, 110; and authoritarianism, 119; crisis of, 119; critical speech, freedom of, 109; "democracy to come," 257n49; democratic rights, 152; demo-

democracy (*continued*)

cratic urbanism, 154, 158; Derrida's theory of, 101, 257n49; detainees as category of individuals, 109; different rights, 152; direct, 113; excess of, 119; freedom of self, 141–42; governability of, 119; Ground Zero and freedom of critical speech, 110; indeterminacy of, 141, 149; as invented, 141; and power, 149; promise of, 101; public space, 108; representative, 113; right to the city, 153; rights, claiming of, 151, 158; security, prioritization of, 109; and uncertainty, 141; universal right to politics, 151. *See also* protected democracy; radical democracy

Departure of the Volunteers. See *La Marseillaise* (Rude)

DER BEVÖLKERUNG (Haacke), 122

Der Pralinenmeister (Haacke), 121

Derrida, Jacques, 4, 57, 172, 175, 272n49, 272n50; and death, 99; democracy as radical form of society, 101; "democracy to come," 257n49; ellipsis, reflection on, 99–101, 257n45; worst cruelty, 7

de Zegher, Catherine, 110, 178

Diary of Elizabeth and James Dixon (1840–41)/ Connecticut Landscapes (Welling), 39, 50, 54; allegory of light and vision, 51; and memory, 51; uncanniness, 52

Difference: On Sexuality and Representation (exhibition), 25

direct address, 8, 41, 57, 59–60, 112, 115–16, 244n12; deictic terms, 58; exhibition space, transformation of, 58

Discursive Forum for the Abolition of War (Wodiczko), 168, 174–75

Documenta 5, 113

Documenta 7, 255n49, 255n50

Douglas, Lord Alfred, 139, 266n57

Duchamp, Marcel, 113

ellipsis, 97, 257n45; and democracy, 101; empty space, 101; lack and difference, 100; as trace of presence, 99

Ellmann, Richard, 139

El Salvador, 210

Enlarged from the Catalogue: The United States of America (Kolbowski), 34–35

Enlightenment, 129, 173–74

Enough. Projects (Lawler), 208, 213, 216–17, 278n35; airplane brochure, 209–10; Little Jack Horner, 206–7, 214, 276n7; Mother Goose photographs, 205–7

environmental racism, 157

Ess, Barbara, 40

ethical responsibility: and certainty, 60, 140; ethico-political, 60–61; and prosopopoeia, 140

ethics, 15, 60, 131, 139, 141; of failure, 25, 38; of reading, 140; and rights, 142; of truths, 243n6

ethnic cleansing, 228

European Union (EU), 163

fairy tales, and strangeness, 148

Fanon, Frantz, 4, 244n14

Fashion Moda, 255n49, 255n50

feminism, 2, 5–6, 15–17, 21, 30, 32, 34, 42; critique of modernism, 41; critiques of vision, 8; as event, 18–19; neglect of, 38; phallocentrism, 22; as political movement, 20; and politics of vision, 63–65; and postmodernism, 3; and psychoanalysis, 24–25; psychoanalytic, 1, 73; second wave, 20; subjectivity, 41; war resistance, 9

fetishism, 63, 71, 79, 207; feminist discourse about, 78; masculine subjectivity, 78; narrative, 178, 192

Fillette (Bourgeois), 254n31

Filliou, Robert, 7; *COMMEMOR*, 197, 200–201; *7 Childlike Uses of Warlike Material*, 200

Flash Art (magazine), 32–33, 35–36

Flashing Nipple Remix (Kelly), 18–19

Flatley, Jonathan, 218, 226, 230

Folkestone Memorial, 191–92

Fornari, Franco, 7, 170, 173–74, 270n26; Internal Terrifier, 171

Forster, Kurt, 267n80

Foucault, Michel, 4, 84, 108, 280n5; politics of truth, 116

Frankfurt School, 120

Fraser, Andrea, 72, 204, 207

French Revolution, 2, 15, 81

Freud, Anna, 214

Freud, Sigmund, 1, 6, 36–38, 54, 69, 80, 169, 178, 183, 185–86, 206, 208, 228, 230, 235; castration, 63, 78; *Civilization and Its Discontents*, 170; conscious mind, 225; death drive, 7; discontents, 90; dream interpretation, 73; fairy tales, 148; fetishism, 63, 71; *fort-da* game, 225–26; heroism, 185; "home" as metaphor, 234; human beings, destructiveness of, 91; interpretation of dreams, 212; masculine identity, 63; Medusa as fetish, 78; melancholia, 230; regression, 170; technique of unsettlement, 90; unconscious, 148, 171–72; unconscious violence, 91; on war, 170

Fried, Michael, 48; "Art and Objecthood," 115; bad objecthood, 42; grace, 42

Friedlander, Saul, 37

Fuchs, Rudi, 84

Gallagher, Ellen, 244n12

Galleria Apollinaire, 101

Gallery Goers' Birthplace and Residence Profile, Part 1 (Haacke), 111–12, 115, 117, 121, 260n26; art institution as material site, 116

Gary, Romain, *The Kites*, 129

Gëlle Fra (Iveković), 195; as symbol of freedom, 196–97. See also *Lady Rosa of Luxembourg* (Iveković)

generational consciousness, 5

generational objects, 4–5

genocide, 177–78, 224, 228

Germany, 110–11, 122–23, 187, 200

Geyer, Andrea, 231

Gide, André, *en abyme*, 49–50

Gintz, Claude, 204, 214, 216

Giuliani, Rudolph, 268–69n103; authoritarian policies, 154

Global Conceptualism: Points of Origin, 1950s–1980s (exhibition), 27

Gloria Patri (Glory Be to the Father) (Kelly), 226–27; masculism, 218–22; triumphalist iconography, 218

Goldstein, Ann, 9–10

Goldstein, Jack, 39

Grasskamp, Walter, 109, 111

Green, André, 170, 270n26

Greenberg, Clement, 41–42; medium specificity, 276n1

Greenwald, Alice M., 179

Grieving Mothers (Lawler), 189–90, 192–94

Gross, Kenneth, 139, 146; solid wishes, 73

Groupe de Recherche d'Art Visuel, 111

Guantánamo: art, 130; detainees, 123–27, 129

Guantánamo Diary (Slahi), 123

Guatemala, 210

Guerilla Art Action Group (GAAG), 105–6; *Blood Bath*, 212

Guernica (Picasso), 93, 107

Guernica (Spain), 107

Gulf War, 182

Gurney, Ivor, 186, 188; "To His Love," 184–85, 187

Haacke, Hans, 7, 29, 72, 258–59n4, 261n38; art and society, inseparability of, 110; *Calligraphie*, 121; "The Constituency," 113; *Décor*, 121; democracy, passion for, 108–11, 119; democratic action, performance of, 116; DER BEVÖLKERUNG, 122; *Der Pralinenmeister*, 121; direct address, 112–13, 115–16; *Gallery Goers' Birthplace and Residence Profile, Part 1*, 111–12, 115–17, 121, 259n19, 260n26; *Helmsboro Country*, 121; institutional critique, 117; *John Weber Gallery Visitors Profile 1 and 2*, 113; *Manet-PROJEKT '74*, 121; *Metro-Mobiltan*, 122; *MOMA-Poll*, 113, 117–19, 212; *News*, 113, 260n22; *On Social Grease*, 121; *Photoelectric Viewer-Controlled Coordinate System*, 112; public sphere, 109, 119–21; *Recording of Climate in Art Exhi-*

Haacke, Hans (*continued*)
  bition, 260n22; *State of the Union*, 121–22,
  260n22; *Voici Alcan*, 122; *We believe in the
  power of creative imagination*, 122
Habermas, Jürgen, 120–21; intimate
  sphere, 235–36
Hall, Stuart, 14
Handel, George Frideric, 132
Hanover (Germany), 111
Hawkinson, Laurie, 63
Heidegger, Martin: *Befundlichkeit*, 230;
  Dasein, 229–31; space, definition of, 89–
  90; *Stimmung*, 230
Helmsboro Country (Haacke), 121
Henry VIII, 276n7
Hill, Anita, 245n24
Hindenburg, Paul von, 109
Hiroshima (Japan), 180, 232
Hirsch, Marianne, 35; postmemory as
  term, 227; "retrospective witnessing by
  adoption," 227; testimonial chain, 223
Hirschhorn Museum Projection (Wodiczko),
  161
Hitler, Adolf, 109, 111, 237
Holland, 200
Holocaust, 226–27
Holzer, Jenny, 255n49, 255n50
homelessness, 154–55, 182
Homeless Projection (Wodiczko), 161
Homeless Vehicle (Wodiczko), 165, 168
Homer: *Iliad*, 188; *Odyssey*, 139
homo significans, 40–41, 55
Honduras, 210
Horner, Thomas, 276n7
House Beautiful: Bringing the War Home
  (Rosler), 233–35; *Beauty Rest*, 235–37;
  Boys' Room, 235
Howard Wise Gallery, 111–12
human rights, 127, 129
human subjectivity, 6, 233. *See also* sub-
  jectivity
Hunt, Lynn, 129
Huntington, Samuel, 119
Huntington Report, 119

iconoclasm, 149
Iliad (Homer), 188
images. *See* representation; vision, politics
  of; visual representation
"images of women," 3
Imperfect Utopia (Kruger, Hawkinson,
  Smith-Miller, Quennell), 63
inadequate history of conceptual art, an (Kolbowski), 24–28; bodily gestures, 36–37;
  hands of artist, 37; history and psychoanalysis, 36–37; individual stories, 35–
  36; and memory, 30, 35–38; soundtrack,
  32
Indochina, 212
Information (exhibition), 117–19, 212
Inkster, Dean, 99–100
institutional critique, 90–91, 92, 101, 111,
  117, 217; museum "actions," 89; museum
  as site of disciplinary power, 95; power
  in spaces, 95; spatial politics, 89; and
  vulnerability, 95
institutions, 1, 73, 91, 113, 116, 120, 207, 217,
  247n2; art, 58, 64–65, 71–72, 79–80, 89,
  90, 95, 101, 110, 113, 115, 216; critique of,
  29, 213; cultural, 70–71, 109; as dangerous, 91, 216; destructiveness of, 91; protective, 97, 216; republican, 92; social,
  29, 172–73; spatial aspects, 25
Interim (Kelly), 222
International Criminal Court (ICC), 194
International Freedom Center (IFC), 177–78
international peacekeeping, 173–74
"Interview" (Kolbowski), 32–36
Iran-Contra affair, 277n15
Iraq War, 14, 110, 182, 189, 193, 233, 255n52,
  260n22; Operation Desert Storm, 186
Island, the Waterfall, and Wreckage (Well-
  ing), 45
Italy, 170
Iveković, Sanja, 7, 194–97

Jacobs, Jane, *The Death and Life of Great
  American Cities*, 157
Jacobs, John, 233

Jameson, Frederic, 9, 33; "Postmodernism, or the Cultural Logic of Late Capitalism," 34
James, William, 271–72n48
Japan, 119
Jerkins, Morgan, 129
Jewish Museum, 113
John Jay College of Criminal Justice, 123–24
Johns, Jasper, 204
John Weber Gallery, 102, 113
John Weber Gallery Visitors Profile 1 and 2 (Haacke), 113
Joselit, David: abstraction, possibility of, 47–48; appropriation, 47
Judd, Donald, 204
Judt, Tony, 187

Kahnweiler, Daniel-Henry, 278n33
Kant, Immanuel, 175, 272n50; as idealist, 176; perpetual peace, 174; "Perpetual Peace," 172, 176; radical evil, 173
Kassel (Germany), 111
Kauffmann, Angelica, 71
Keenan, Thomas, 127
Kelly, Mary, 5, 7, 64, 72, 231, 247n4; associative process, 227–28; *Flashing Nipple Remix*, 18–19; future anterior, 22; *Gloria Patri (Glory Be to the Father)*, 218–22, 226–27; *Interim*, 222; *Love Songs*, 15–18, 21; masculinism, 218–22, 226; *Mea Culpa*, 222, 225–31; Beirut, 222, 224; Buenos Aires, 222, 224; Johannesburg, 222–23; pathological masculinity, 218; Phnom Penh, 222, 224; *Post-Partum Document*, 21, 29–30, 218, 222; restaged demonstrations, 19–20, 22–23; Sarajevo, 222–23; *Seemed Right*, 18–19, 21; *Sisterhood Is POW . . .*, 17–18; suffering, problem of, 226; and war, 227; *WLM Demo Remix*, 19, 22
Kent State, 117
Kiefer, Anselm, 84
kinship relations, 2

Kitchen Table Series (Weems), 3, 244n12
Kite, Martha, 82
Klein, Melanie, 169–70, 173, 214; *Narrative of a Child Analysis*, 212–13; play technique, 212, 237
Kline, Franz, 48
Kluge, Alexander, 120–21
Koch, Ed, 154
Koenig, Fritz, 179
Kolbowski, Silvia, 5, 7, 33, 40, 64, 72; Conceptual Art, 24–27, 31; *Enlarged from the Catalogue: The United States of America*, 34–35; feminism, engagement with, 25; *an inadequate history of conceptual art*, 24–28, 30, 32, 35–38; "Interview," 32–36; and memory, 30, 32; *Model Pleasure*, 25; vision, role of, 24–25
Korean War, 194–95
Kosuth, Joseph, 28–29
Krauss, Rosalind, 44, 51–53, 112, 244n16
Krefeld (Germany), 111
Kristeva, Julia, 16, 60, 142, 205, 214, 226; fantasy, 212; otherness, consciousness of, 148; *Strangers to Ourselves*, 148; transference, 266n72
Kruger, Barbara, 7, 9–10, 40, 47, 64, 72, 91, 186; direct address, use of, 41, 57–60; ethico-political space, 60–61, 68; morality, 60–62; *Newsweek* cover, 61–62; photomontages, 59; politics of vision, 63; public art, 251n1; social spaces, 56–57, 59; subjectivity, 62; *Untitled (It's our pleasure to disgust you)*, 60; *Untitled (Memory is your image of perfection)*, 63, 65, 67–68; *Untitled (No Radio)*, 252n19; *Untitled (Perfect)*, 63; *Untitled (You are the perfect crime)*, 63; violence, exploration of, 57–59, 62–63
Kunstverein Hannover, 113
Kurdi, Alan, 125
Kurtz, Steven, 13

Lacan, Jacques, 79–80, 254n32; future anterior, 4–5; personal history, 22

LaCapra, Dominick, 37, 228

Laclau, Ernesto, 4, 135

Lady Rosa of Luxembourg (Iveković), 195, 197. See also *Gëlle Fra* (Iveković)

Laino, Paige, 124

La Marseillaise (Rude), 81, 163, 165

L'art conceptual, une persepective (exhibition), 24, 26, 247n2

late capitalism, 9, 14

Lavaert, Sonja, 216

Lawler, Louise, 7, 39–40, 72, 253n16, 254n34, 255n49, 255n50, 277n11; *Arrangements of Pictures*, 41; Artists Space logo, 97–98; *Birdcalls*, 81–82, 84–85; *Enough. Projects*, 203, 205–10, 213–14, 216–17, 276n7, 278n35; *Grieving Mothers*, 189–90, 192–94, 255n52; humor of, 80–82; military aggression, protest against, 210–12; *A MOVIE WILL BE SHOWN WITHOUT THE PICTURE*, 84; *No Drones*, 211–12; *Pollock and Tureen*, 214; *Portrait*, 84–85; "prominence given, authority taken," 254n35; *The Rude Museum*, 80; *Statue before Painting, Perseus with the Head of Medusa, Canova*, 73–80, 84; *Untitled, 1950–51*, 203–4; *WAR IS TERROR*, 211; *Woman with Picasso, 1912*, 214, 216; *Yellow*, 206–7

Ledrut, Raymond, 146–47

Lefebvre, Henri, 91, 103, 132, 136, 158; production of space, 137; restoration, vocabulary of, 154; "right to the city," 152–54, 156–57; social space, 266n19; spatial practice, 137; traditional spatial knowledge, 134; urban space, 156

Lefort, Claude, 6, 14, 16, 101, 108, 141, 149, 151

left melancholy, 13, 16–17; feminist voice, rejection of, 14; and fidelity, 23; postmodernism, rejection of, 14

Lenin, Vladimir, 196

Leung, Simon, 27

Levinas, Emmanuel: ethics and rights, 142; non-indifference to the other, 132; reasonable being, 5, 141

Levine, Sherrie, 40, 43–44, 47, 64, 72, 247n4; *Untitled (After Alexander Rodchenko)*, 41; *Untitled (After Egon Schiele)*, 41; *Untitled (After Ernst Ludwig Kirchner)*, 41; *Untitled (After Walker Evans)*, 41

Libeskind, Daniel, 179

Life Class at the Royal Academy (Zoffany), 70, 75; sexism, 71

Light Sources (Welling), 48

Lippard, Lucy, 27

"Little Jack Horner" (fairy tale), 206, 207, 276n7

Li, Victor, 257n45

London (England), 131, 212–13, 237

Longo, Robert, 39

Los Angeles (California), 57

Los Angeles Architecture (Welling), 48

Los Angeles Museum of Contemporary Art, 26–27

Louvre, 89, 101

Love Letter (Plath), 21

Love Songs (exhibition), 15–18, 21–22

Lower Manhattan Development Corporation (LMOC), 109–10, 177–78

Luxemburg, Rosa, 187, 197; *The Crisis in the German Social Democracy*, 196

Lyotard, Jean-Françoise, 4–5

MacCannell, Juliet Flower, 36–37

Manet-PROJEKT '74 (Haacke), 121

Manhattan Institute, 154; quality of life conference, 268–69n103

Manifesta 2, 194–95

Mapplethorpe, Robert, 254n31

Marius, Gaius, 76

Marx, Karl, 173

Marxism, 34

Mary Boone Gallery, 59–60, 91, 252n19

masculine identity, 63; fixed nature of, as disavowal, 64

masculinism, 5, 16, 188, 218–22, 252–53n9; defined, 245n24; infantile roots, 237; and militarism, 186, 271–72n48; social authority, 6, 8; as term, 70; as victory-crazed, 234; vulnerability, 226; and women, 70–71

Masson, Jeffrey, 268n97

Maxwell, Glyn, 187

McCarthy, Mary, *The Stones of Venice*, 147

McCollum, Allan, 40

McKee, Yates, 110

Mea Culpa (Kelly), 225–31; Beirut, 222, 224; Buenos Aires, 222, 224; Johannesburg, 222–23; Phnom Penh, 222, 224; Sarajevo, 222–23

Medusa, 76; castration, symbol of, 78; feminist subversion, 78; as fetish, 78; and Freud, 78; iconography of, 79

Mella, Ricardo, 100

memory, 30, 35–36, 136–37; classicizing memorials, 188; duty of, 201; ethico-political, 201; exercise of, 201; and forgetfulness, 51; "good use" of, 201; and healing, 188; instrumentalized, 187, 228–29; narcissistic, 197; sites of mourning, 188; traumatic, 225; unconscious, and history, 37–38; wounded, 185

mênis, 192

Messer, Thomas, 113

metagenerational, 5

metanarratives, 4

MetroMobiltan (Haacke), 122

Metro Pictures, 39–41, 210–11, 249n1

Metropolitan Museum of Art, 79, 89–90; American Wing, 35; antiwar protests, 105–7; Great Hall Balcony, 74, 76; "Open Museum Proposal," 103, 105

Metz, Christian, 80

Michaels, Walter Benn, 42–43, 48

militarism: and masculinism, 186, 271–72n48; patriarchal, 210

Miller, J. Hillis, 133, 138–39, 144; ethics of reading, 140

Miller-Keller, Andrea, 82

Milwaukee Art Center, 113

Minh, Trinh T., 4, 218, 234

minimalism, 8, 40, 42, 58, 84, 112

Miró, Joan, 203–4

Model Pleasure (Kolbowski), 25

modernism, 58; and feminism, 41; gestural, 48; invulnerability, 48; spatial totality, 41–42

modernity, 4

MOMA-Poll (Haacke), 113, 118, 212; challenging closed nature of art institution, 119; mimicking of public opinion poll, 117

monumental classicism, 188–89

monumental history, 121, 161, 163, 187

moralism, 158, 168

moralistic urbanism, 132

Morris, Robert, 29

Moser, Mary, 71

Mouffe, Chantal, 135, 175

MOVIE WILL BE SHOWN WITHOUT THE PICTURE, A (Lawler), 84

Mulvey, Laura, 3, 78–79; "to-be-looked-at-ness," 84

Munich (Germany), 213

Museum Haus Lange, 113

Museum of Contemporary Art, 9–10

Museum of Modern Art (MoMA), 89–90, 93, 95, 105–7, 113, 117–18, 203–4, 205, 207, 212, 217, 254n31, 276n7, 276–77n9, 277n18; Bell-47D1 helicopter, 209–10; Garden Cafe, 206, 208; identification with, 208, 213–14

Mussolini, Benito, 237

My Lai massacre, 107

Mystery Photographs (Welling), 47

National Defense Authorization Act, 123

National Gallery (Oslo), 189

nationalism, 197

National September 11 Memorial & Museum, 1, 177; amnesia, 182; and censorship, 275n47; collective repressions, 178, 183; ignoring social history, 181–82; "In Memoriam," 179–80

nation-state, 174–75

Nazis, 122

Negt, Oskar, 120–21

neighborhoods, 177; control of, 156–57; threat to urban life, 157

neo-conceptualism, 26–27

Neo-expressionism, 84

neoliberal capitalism, 182

Neue Galerie, 197, 200

New Abstractions (Welling), 47; and modernism, 48

new cosmopolitanism, 272n49

New Drapes (Welling), 47–48

New Landscapes (Welling), 48

News (Haacke), 113, 260n22

New York City, 19, 25, 28, 57, 92, 97, 105, 112, 131, 182, 252n19; gay public life, 155, 157; homeless, 157; Little Syria, 181; Manhattan, 155; quality-of-life initiatives, 154–56; right to the city, 154; Times Square, 155; Zones of Privacy, 156

New York University, Fales Library, 92

Nicaragua, 209, 210, 277n15

Niepce, Nicéphore, 50

Nietzsche, Friedrich, monumental history, 121, 161

Nike (winged figure), 189–96

Nineteenth Amendment, 19

Nixon, Mignon, 69, 79, 171–72, 254n31, 271–72n48

Nixon, Richard M., 117, 212

Nochlin, Linda, 71, 244n16

No Drones (Lawler), 211–12

non-indifference, 132; ethical reading, 142

Nora, Pierre, 201

North America, 119

Norton Simon Museum, 89

not-forgetting, 2, 15, 17, 22; as term, 1

Obama, Barack, 123

October (journal), 73, 78

Ode to the Sea: Art from Guantánamo Bay (exhibition), 123–24, 126–27, 129

Odyssey (Homer), 139

Omega Institution (Fornari), 173–74, 176

Onabanjo, Oluremi Cecilia-Anne, 244n12

On Social Grease (Haacke), 121

Oslo Museum, 193

otherness, 32, 148

Owens, Craig, 3, 34, 38, 49, 58, 90

Paglen, Trevor, 124

Paris (France), 131, 153, 163

Paris Commune: right to the city, 153; Vendôme Column, 147, 163

Pataki, George, 13, 110, 178–79

Patriarchal Roll Call. See *Birdcalls* (Lawler)

Paula Cooper Gallery, 260n22

Pejić, Bojana, 197

Pellicer, Antonio, 100

Pelzer, Birgit, 73

perpetual peace, 161, 174, 176

Perseus, 76, 79, 189

Persistent Vestiges: Drawing from the American-Vietnam War (exhibition), 110

Phaedrus (Plato), 193

Philippine-American War, 275n43

Photoelectric Viewer-Controlled Coordinate System (Haacke), 112

Photograph (exhibition), 39

photography, 40, 47; absence and destruction of object, 50; abstraction in, 47; ambiguity of, 50–51; as camera, 43; and control, 50; de-constitution, 52; *en abyme*, 49–50; "having-been-there" quality of, 137; language, 48–49; as mechanical recording device, 43–44, 53; as memoir, 52–53; and memory, 51; mortality, 54; myth of photographic transparency, 39; past and present, 53; as reproduction, 42, 44; spatial immediacy and temporal interiority, 52; and technology, 43–44

Picasso, Pablo, 204; Analytical Cubism, 214; *Guernica*, 93, 107; *Ma Jolie (Woman with a Guitar)*, 214, 216, 278n33; war resistance, 93

Piper, Adrian, 72, 97, 244n12

Plath, Sylvia, 22, 246–47n19; *Love Letter*, 21

Plato, 132, 140, 142; *Phaedrus*, 193; *Protagoras*, 139; *Republic*, 133, 138–39

Pluot, Sebastien, 100

politics of memory, 178

politics of vision, 3, 4, 63

Pollock, Griselda, 29, 227–28

Pollock, Jackson, 204

Pollock and Tureen (Lawler), 214

Pompon, François, 81

Poole, Roger, 186

Pop art, 84

Portrait (Lawler), 84–85

postcolonialism, 5

Postmasters Gallery, 15, 18, 35, 229

postmemory, 227

Postminimalism, 84

postmodern feminism, 14

postmodernism, 2, 4–5, 9, 13, 34, 40–41, 45, 72, 203, 244n14; and feminism, 3; problematization of referent, 43; in visual arts, 39

"Postmodernism, or the Cultural Logic of Late Capitalism" (Jameson), 34

Post-Partum Document (Kelly), 21, 218, 222; Conceptual Art, 29–30

poststructuralism, 4; radical acceptance of vulnerability, 5

Prince, Richard, 39–40, 47

private spaces, 56

Projects (Lawler), 203

prosopopoeia, 139, 144, 146, 150–51; and ethical responsibility, 140

Protagoras (Plato), 139

protected democracy, 13–15, 122, 123; erosion of rights, 109. *See also* democracy; radical democracy

protofascism, 232

Proudhon, Pierre-Joseph, 98

psychic trauma, 225; as affective residue, 228

psychoanalysis, 4, 7, 10, 63, 169, 172–73; and feminism, 24–25; and war, 38

Psychoanalysis of War, The (Fornari), 170

Psychoanalysts against Nuclear War, 170

psychoanalytic revolution, 7

public art, 9, 251n1

public sphere, 9, 13–14, 56, 109, 121, 152, 175; and democracy, 108; elimination of, call for, 119; feminist subjectivity, 16–17; gay public life as endangered, 155; as lost democratic ideal, 120; right to the city, 153; walking in city, 157–58. *See also* bourgeois public space

quality-of-life initiatives, 154, 268–69n103; presumption of universality, 155–56

Queens Museum, 26–27

Quennell, Nicholas, 63

Rabbani, Ahmed: *Untitled (Binoculars Pointing at the Super Moon)*, 126; *Untitled (Still Life of Glassware)*, 126

racism, 4, 177–78

radical democracy, 1, 6, 10, 127. *See also* democracy; protected democracy

radical evil, 174

radical geography, 134

Rancière, Jacques, 122

Rankine, Claudine, 8

Rauschenberg, Robert, 204

Ready to Catch Him Should He Fall (Bartlett), 134, 266n57; AIDS epidemic, 142, 150; boundaries, 136; civic life, 133; contemporary urban-political issues, 142; conversational style of, 133; danger in, 132; as ekphrastic, 144; democratic urbanism, 158; fairy tale elements, 148; homophobia, 143, 150, 155; homosexuality in, 142; homosexual culture and violence, 136; London in, 131–32, 142–46; memoir, form of, 132; otherness, 142; prosopopoeia, 139, 144, 146, 150–51; public space, 152; *Republic*, spirit of, 138–39; as serio-comical memoir, 137; speaking and moving statues, 145–53, 158; theatricalization of stranger, 148–49; thunderstorm scene, 148–49; topography of London, 136, 138; unfinished quality, 138; unreal, 137; urbanism, story of, 131; walking as motif, 157; Wilde, allusion to, 139

Reagan, Ronald, 154, 209, 277n15

reasonable urbanism, 132

Reconsidering the Object of Art: 1965–1975 (exhibition), 26–27

Recording of Climate in Art Exhibition (Haacke), 260n22

Reich, Wilhelm, 168–69, 268n97

reference, 137–38; deconstruction, 136

Reiring, Janelle, 97, 249n1

representation, 6, 13, 24–26, 29, 34, 58–59, 135; of absent object, 45; critique of, 44; feminist critique of, 9; figurative, 76; and identity, 136; literary, 133; object, as comprehended, 43; patriarchal systems of, 82, 84; photographic, 42, 45; post-modern critique of, 3–4; postmodern feminist critique of, 8; referent, status of, 43; of social, 252–53n9; subjectivity in, 48, 62; topography, 138; visual, 3, 40–42, 44, 252n9

repression: discontents, 90; as spatial operation, 90

Republic, The, (Plato), 133, 138–39

Reynolds, Joshua, 71

Ribaish, Ibraham Al-, 126

Ricoeur, Paul, 1, 185, 187, 201, 228–29

Riegl, Alois, 149; unintentional monument, 267n80

Robbins, Bruce, 175; discourse of beneficiary, 129–30

Roberts, Chris, 276n7

Rockefeller, David, 118–19

Rockefeller, Nelson, 117–19, 212

Rockefeller family, 106–7, 117–18, 212

Rogers, Sarah J., 49

Rosa Esman Gallery, 105

Rose, Jacqueline, 21–22, 64, 68, 172, 187, 194, 232, 270n19; ethics of failure, 25, 38, 49; psychoanalytic theory, 268n97; sexual violence, 168–69

Rosler, Martha, 7, 281n19; art of critique, 232; *Balloons,* 281n19; *Body Beautiful: Beauty Knows No Pain,* 233; *Bringing the War Home: House Beautiful,* 233; consumerism and Vietnam War, 234; *House Beautiful: Bringing the War Home,* 233–37; and possibility, 232; *A Simple Case for Torture,* 281n22; social change and human subjectivity, 233

Ross, Andrew, 177

Rotello, Gabriel, 155

Royal Academy of Art, 70–71

Rubin, William, 278n33

Rude, François, 80; *La Marseillaise,* 81

Rude Museum, The (Lawler), 189; humor in, 80–81

Russell, Bertrand, 174

Russian Revolution, 196

Sampson, Anthony, 172

San Diego Museum of Man Projection (Wodiczko), 161

Santner, Eric L., 192; narrative fetishism, 178

Sarajevo (Bosnia and Herzegovina), 227

Saudi Arabia, 182

Scarry, Elaine, 185

Schnabel, Julian, 84

Schoenberg, Arnold, 16; twelve-tone scale, 2, 15

Schor, Naomi, 71

Scott, Joan Wallach, 26

Second Sex, The (Beauvoir), 2

Seemed Right (Kelly), 18–19, 21

Segal, Hanna, 172

Sekula, Alan, 40, 43

September 11 attacks, 121–22, 177–78, 182–83

7 Childlike Uses of Warlike Material (Filliou), 200

Sex Panic!, 155

sexual difference, 84; castration, 63–64

Sharp, Willoughby, 82

Sheehan, Casey, 193

Sheehan, Cindy, 193

Sherman, Cindy, 39–40, 42–44, 64, 97, 247n4; *Untitled Film Stills,* 41

Shields, Charles, 124

Shklar, Judith, 7

Siegelaub, Seth, 28

Simmons, Laurie, 39–40, 64, 247n4

Simple Case for Torture, A (Rosler), 281n22

Simpson, Lorna, 244n12

Sisterhood Is POW . . . (Kelly), 17–18

Situationists, 90, 91

Slahi, Mohamedou Ould, *Guantánamo Diary,* 123

Slaugterhouse-Five (Vonnegut), 161

slavery, 2, 177–78

Smith, Neil, 264n15

Smith, Valerie, 35

Smith-Miller, Henry, 63

Snøhetta, 179

Social Democratic Party, 196

social spaces, 56–57, 59, 135, 264n19; concrete location, 116; as discourses, 133–34; mental space of human subject, 137; political struggle, 134; representational space, 137; spatial practice, 137

Software (exhibition), 113, 117, 260n22

Solomon R. Guggenheim Museum, 89, 95, 97, 113

South Africa, 122, 230; apartheid, 227

space, 16, 17, 24, 49, 57, 72–73, 98, 101–2, 105, 122, 138, 157, 175, 177, 179, 188, 227, 229, 233, 257n31; aesthetic, 91, 116, 119; of art institutions, 89–90; boundaries, 67, 90; capitalist domination of, 153; closed, 55; conceptions of, 135; conceptualization of, 135; concrete, 134; conflictual nature of, 91; "criteria space," 103; critique of, 9–10; cultural, 91; definition, 89; and discourse, 135–36; display, 105; host, 156; imaginary, 148; "make a space," 8; masculinist, 9; mediatized, 168; and memory, 38; mental, 137; metahistorical, 24, 38; modernist, 58, 95; monolithic, 59; and otherness, 67; perfect, 64–65; physical, 59, 134, 137; as physically lived, 137; as political, 134–35; power of, 119; power, discourse of, 103; psychic, 90; public, 108, 152, 155, 158, 176; public art, 251n1; real/unreal dichotomy, 135, 264n15; as relational, 89; representational, 137; right to the city, 153–54, 157; ungrounded, 31; urban, 91, 133–34, 136, 143, 147, 156; "use-value" of, 153; and violence, 56, 58–59, 62, 67

Spain, 107; anarchism in, 100

spatial politics, 9–10, 135; institutional critique, 89

spatial practice, 269n17; social space, 137

Sphere, The (Koenig), 179

Spinoza, Baruch, 103

Spivak, Gayatri Chakravorty, 5; vulnerability, 42

Stalybridge War Memorial, 190–92

Staniszewski, Maryanne, 32

State of the Union (Haacke), 121–22, 260n22

state violence, 174

Statue before Painting, Perseus with the Head of Medusa, Canova (Lawler), 73–76, 79, 84, 189, 210; miscaptioning of, 78; photographic cut as figure of castration, 80; positioning of spectator, 80

Stein, Gertrude, 168

"Storyteller, The" (Benjamin), 53–54

Students for a Democratic Society (SDS), Weathermen faction, 233

subjectivity, 29, 55, 233; and feminism, 41; politics of, 153; and representation, 48

Surrealists, 212

Syria, 125, 182

Tarrida del Mármol, Fernando, 100

temporality, 4

Textron, 210

Thomas, Clarence, 245n24

Thompson, Erin L., 124

Tiepolo, Giovanni Battista, 79; *The Triumph of Marius*, 76

Tile Photographs (Welling), 47

Tillman, Lynne, 142; fiction's truth, 138

Three Guineas (Woolf), 69, 237; as antiwar polemic, 164, 186, 235

Titanic (ship), 126

Tobin, Austin, 181

traces, 17, 136–37, 178, 192, 225, 228

Tricolor Photographs (Welling), 47

Trilateral Commission, 119

Triumph of Marius, The (Tiepolo), 76

Trump, Donald, 123, 232

Turner, Tina, 186

Twain, Mark, 200; *War Prayer*, 197, 275n43

unconscious, 7–8, 173; unconscious aggression, 187; and war, 171

unconscious mind, 6; and lint, 228

United Nations (UN), 1, 174; Security Council, 194

United States, 2, 19, 92, 109–12, 117, 121–22, 129–31, 176, 182, 189, 209, 232–33, 275n47, 277n15; curtailment of civil liberties, 177–78

universalism, 173; Enlightenment, 129, 174; extensive versus intensive, 268n95

Untitled (After Alexander Rodchenko) (Levine), 41

Untitled (After Egon Schiele) (Levine), 41

Untitled (After Ernst Ludwig Kirchner) (Levine), 41

Untitled (After Walker Evans) (Levine), 41

Untitled Film Stills (Sherman), 41

Untitled (It's our pleasure to disgust you) (Kruger), 60; exploration of violence, 57–59, 62–63

Untitled (Memory is your image of perfection) (Kruger), 63; femininity of skeleton, 65; iconography of skeleton, 65, 67–68

Untitled, 1950–51 (Lawler), 203-4

Untitled (No Radio) (Kruger), 252n19

Untitled (Perfect) (Kruger), 63

Untitled (You are the perfect crime) (Kruger), 63

un-war, 168, 172–73, 175–76

Urbach, Henry, 143

urbanism, 131, 269n117; quality of life, 158

urban renewal, 157

urban space, 9, 136, 147; as host space, 156; neighborhoods, 156–57; right to walk, 157; social processes, materialization of, 134; as unreal, 133

urban studies, 133

urban theory, 131, 153

USA Patriot Act, 182

Vertigo at Guantánamo (Baluchi), 125

Vietnam War, 2, 105–6, 117, 212, 232, 234, 260n22, 281n19; as living-room war, 233

violence, 59–60, 63, 65, 68, 70–71, 93, 103, 121–22, 132, 142, 145, 153, 168, 180, 183, 187, 194–95, 197, 201, 207, 281n13; aesthetic, 110; Black female body, 3; catastrophic expressions of, 91; homophobic, 136, 155; imperialist, 210; inner, 120; internal and external, 169–70; museological, 95; psychic, 172; sexual, 237, 268n97; social, 169; and state, 171, 174; symbolic, 58

Virno, Paolo, 91–92, 97, 101, 216–17

vision, politics of, 3, 24-25, 63-64, 78

visual representation, 3

Voici Alcan (Haacke), 122

vulnerability, 5, 42, 48, 54, 80, 90, 92, 194; of collectivities, 97; danger, susceptibility to, 95, 97; democracy, as essential to, 107; interdependency, 95; masculinism, 226; and nonviolence, 97, 103; openness, 95; of spaces, 91; state of possibility, 97; and violence, 95, 97, 103

Wadsworth Atheneum, 82

Walton, John, 116

war, 2, 7, 9, 68, 70, 81–82, 106, 209, 212–14, 218–19, 226, 271-72n48; abolishing of, 168–69, 171–72, 176; atrocity of, 234; causes of, 38, 187, 228, 235; as collective madness, 164; as collective phenomenon, 168; commemoration of, 161, 187, 195; cruelty of, 170; as display of evil, 271n39; everyday life, 234; female victims of, 194; and Freud, 170; glorification of, 76; heroism in, 185; imagery of, 236; imperialist, 196, 233; as inevitable, 161; infantile barbarism, 170; infantile fixation, 235; infantilism, 186; instrumentalized memory of, 192, 228–29; liberty, struggle for, 187; as masculine fiction, 211; myths about, 235; nuclear, 171; and otherness, 70; patriarchal behavior, 186, 235; and peace, 163; perpetual war, 172, 176, 187, 231–32; and psychoanalysis, 38; psychoanalytic theory of, 170–71; responsibility for, 169, 171–72; as social institution, 10, 161, 210; state of crisis, 171; and unconscious, 171–72; war art, 163; war crimes, 222, 227–28; war crimes and lint, as affective residue, 228; war games, 163; war machine,

193; war memorials, 1, 161, 163, 168, 185, 189–90, 193–94, 197, 200–201; war museums, 163; war rape, 194–95, 237; war toys, 164, 281n22; women and prevention of, 69. *See also* un-war; war resistance

WAR IS TERROR (Lawler), 211

Warner, Marina, 189

Warner, Michael, 116–17, 269n110; neighborhood control, 156–57; right to the city, 156

"War on Terror," 109–10, 130

war resistance, 1, 6, 10, 93, 168, 187; feminism, 9

Watney, Simon, 142

We believe in the power of creative imagination (Haacke), 122

Weems, Carrie Mae, *Kitchen Table Series*, 3, 244n12

Weimar Constitution, 123

Weinberg, Adam, 232

Weiner, Cathy, 92

Weiner, Lawrence, 29, 81–82

Wellek Library Lectures, 10

Welling, James, 7–8, 40–43, 249n1; abstraction, exploration of, 45–47, 49, 54–55; abstraction, threat of, 48; *Aluminum Foils*, 47–48; and ambiguity, 48, 50–51; *Ashes*, 49–51, 54; dark tonality, 54; *Degradés*, 47, 54–55; *Diary of Elizabeth and James Dixon . . .* , 39, 50–52, 54; *Island, the Waterfall, and Wreckage*, 45; *Light Sources*, 48; *Los Angeles Architecture*, 48; materials, choice of, 44–45; and modernism, 48; modernism and invulnerability, 48; *Mystery Photographs*, 47; *New Abstractions*, 47; *New Landscapes*, 48; *New Drapes*, 47–48; *Tile Photographs*, 47; *Tricolor Photographs*, 47; vulnerability, 54; work of, as discourse, 49

Wells, H. G., 271–72n48

White, Hayden, 26

whiteness, 8

White supremacy, 2–3

Whitman, Walt, 131

Whitney Museum of Modern Art, 89–90, 92–93, 95, 97, 103, 232

Wigley, Mark, 56, 180, 234

Wilde, Oscar, 60, 101, 139, 150, 266n57; "The Decay of Lying," 133, 264n11; first trial, 149; *The Happy Prince*, 144, 146; morality and ethics, 141; as victim of moralism, 158

Williams, Patricia, 151

Wilson, Fred, 72

Wilson, Terry, 82

Winer, Helene, 97, 249n1

Winnicott, D. W., 38, 212, 214

Within and Beyond the Frame (Buren), 101–2

WLM Demo Remix (Kelly): future anterior, literalizing of, 22; restaged demonstrations, 19–20, 22–23

Wodiczko, Krzysztof, 7, 163, 169–72; *Abolition of War*, 161; *Arc de Triomphe*, 161; *AT&T Long Lines Building Projection*, 161; *Hirschhorn Museum Projection*, 161; *Homeless Projection*, 161; *Homeless Vehicle*, 165, 168; *San Diego Museum of Man Projection*, 161; "un-war," 165, 176; *World Institute for the Abolition of War*, 164–65, 168, 173–76

woman: as image, 3; as sign, 3

Woman with Picasso, 1912 (Lawler), 214, 216

Women's Liberation Movement, 2, 18–19; personal as political, 16

Wood, Allen W., 176

Woolf, Virginia, 2, 38, 71, 73, 85, 211; humor of, 69; patriarchy and infantile fixation, 235; on professional dress, 69–70; *Three Guineas*, 69, 164, 186, 235, 237; *The Voyage Out*, 186; war, causes of, 228, 235; war consciousness of, 236

World Institute for the Abolition of War (Wodiczko), 164–65, 173; cosmopolitics, 175; Cross-Disciplinary Center for Global Peace Projects, 168, 174–75; Discursive Forum for the Abolition of War, 168, 174–75; newer cosmopolitanism of, 175–76; and public sphere, 175

World Trade Center (WTC), 179–82, 275n47; Drawing Center, 13, 109–10, 177–78

World Trade Center Memorial Cultural
Complex, 177
World War I, 163, 169–70, 184–85, 187, 205,
235; advanced weaponry, 188; barbarism
of, 91; memorials, 189–90, 193–94, 197;
Nike, 189–96; propaganda, 192
World War II, 69, 194–95, 212–13, 235
Wynter, Sylvia, 244n14

Yellow (Lawler), 206–7
Young, Arthur, 210
Yugoslav Wars, 1

Žižek, Slavoj, 64
Zoffany, Johann: *Life Class at the Royal
Academy*, 70–71, 75; sexism, 71